Conceiving Sexuality

Conceiving Sexuality

Approaches to Sex Research in a Postmodern World

Edited by Richard G. Parker and John H. Gagnon

Routledge New York and London

Published in 1995 by

Routledge
29 West 35 Street
New York, NY 10001

Published in Great Britain in 1995 by

Routledge
11 New Fetter Lane
London EC4P 4EE

Library of Congress Cataloging-in-Publications Data

Conceiving Sexuality: approaches to sex research in a postmodern world /
        edited by Richard G. Parker and John H. Gagnon
            p.   cm.
        Includes bibliographical references.
        ISBN 0–415–90927–9 — ISBN 0–415–90928–7 (pbk.)
        1. Sexology—Research.   I. Parker, Richard G. (Richard Guy).   II. Gagnon, John H.
        HQ60.C66   1994
        306.7'072—dc20   94–17761
                                                                                    CIP

For
Vagner de Almeida
and
Cathy Stein Greenblat

Contents

Acknowledgments

THIS BOOK WOULD NOT HAVE BEEN POSSIBLE without the contribution of a wide range of individuals and institutions. It brings together a set of papers originally prepared for a conference on International Perspectives in Sexual Behavior Research, which was organized by the Working Group on Sexual Behavior Research of the AIDS and Reproductive Health Network and held in Rio de Janeiro in April of 1993. This meeting was made possible through the support of the John D. and Catherine T. MacArthur Foundation, the Ford Foundation, and the Rockefeller Foundation, and we would particularly like to thank Stuart Burden and Carmen Barroso at MacArthur, José Barzelatto, Margaret Hempel, and Marjorie Muecke at Ford, and Jane Hughes and Seth Berkley at Rockefeller for their commitment to work on gender and sexuality. Special thanks to Jonathan Mann of the Harvard School of Public Health, who played a key role in the conceptualization and creation of the ARHN Working Group on Sexual Behavior Research. Special thanks, also, to Pamela Gillies, Cathy Stein Greenblat, Purnima Mane, and Vera Paiva for the key contributions that they made both to the conference as well as to the Working Group over the course of its first phase of activities, and to Susana Alvino and Lilia Rossi for their assistence in preparing the manuscript.

INTRODUCTION

Conceiving Sexuality

John H. Gagnon and Richard G. Parker

INTELLECTUAL GATHERINGS THAT DEAL PRIMARILY WITH THEORIZING about sex have become increasingly frequent over the last decade. Often, theorizing is treated as a form of dilettantism by those of a more practical or empirical bent. Yet even those who pride themselves on their practicality and their lack of theory usually have many theories—one for each occasion on which they act. Theory is not a superfluous distraction, but a necessity. It is the problem-identifier and the information-interpreter in the research process. Without it there is no way to explain the facts. This is especially true during a period of paradigm shift, when there is not only a methodological crisis, but an epistemiological crisis in a field. This is such a time in the human sciences—a time of epistemological doubt, when the issues are not solely how do you know or what do you know, but whether you can know.

SEXUAL SCIENCE

In general, most researchers working on sexuality have avoided the epistemological crisis by declaring their allegiance to positivist science and to the assumptions about sexuality that have characterized what might be called the "sexological" period, dating from 1890 to 1980, in the study of sexuality throughout the European culture area. In the early decades of this period, "sexology" was the revolutionary attempt of a relatively small number of researchers and activists to bring sexuality under the control of what was then understood as "science."

Theorizing about sexuality as an enterprise conceived of and managed by members of the new secular, scientific professions gained independent force about this time. This does not mean that these new knowledge-producing disciplines or their secular ideas about sexuality had no history. In the prior one hundred and fifty years, perhaps beginning in the middle of the eighteenth century, ideas about sexuality that were not entirely based in Christian religious doctrine began to emerge in the nascent medical profession (see, for example, Foucault 1980; Weeks 1985).

The rise of the masturbation anxiety in the early decades of the eighteenth century in Western Europe, for example, was based on folk/medical theories of the loss of vital bodily fluids through ejaculation on the part of both men and women. This masturbation phobia had continuous support in medical communities until the twentieth century, though the medical theories underpinning it changed from era to era. By the end of the nineteenth century the fear of masturbation had been extended to include all sexual excitement associated with arousal and orgasm, medicine's conception moving from that of a humoral to a nervous disease. Medical professionals prescribed a variety of treatments, devices, diets and nostrums to add to self-control in the management of "lust."

In addition to the formulation of specific core beliefs about the nature of sexuality, physicians offered a wide variety of advice on matters of public policy (for example, the management of the prostitution of women and girls or the containment of sexually transmitted infections) as well as advice of a more personal sort on how to control the sexual impulse. These were the central texts of what Foucault has identified as the rising tide of "scientific" sexual discourse in the nineteenth century (Foucault 1980).

This body of discourse about sex was of course not entirely freed of the evolving religious discourses and practices that had constituted the sexual in earlier times. Indeed, the correct lifestyles suggested by medical science were identical with the lifestyles recommended by the religious programs of the new middle classes. Both Christianity and medicine viewed sex as a basic drive that needed to be thwarted through self-control and environmental purity—a drive that differed between women and men—and that in its socially correct manifestation resulted in sex between men and women in marriage for the purpose of reproduction. However, being quasi-empirical in their doctrines, the medical professions were vulnerable to greater explanatory tensions than were the dogmatic religious traditions that preceded them. Thus, medical discourses became increasingly influenced by research findings, which suggested that the various disease outcomes attributed to masturbation and sexual excess were caused by germs. (Perhaps the discovery of the bacterial origins of tuberculosis was most influential in this regard.)

It is important to point out that a more nuanced understanding is needed of the increasing volume and changing character of sexual discourse in the nineteenth century than offered by Foucault (1980). In Foucault's attempt to correct the myth that the sexual reformers of the end of that century were simply overthrowing Victorian prudery and leading an advance in human sexual liberation, he has erred in denying the importance of repression. The creation of new sexual discourses and practices as well as the repression of traditional ones coexisted in Western European culture all during the nineteenth century. The suppression of sexual information among the new middle class populations has been well documented, and some of its behavioral consequences are recorded in the twentieth century (Kinsey et al, 1948; Hall 1991). Less often recognized are the ways in which the sexual practices and beliefs of various rural populations as well as both old and new residents of urban centers were changed by contacts with representatives and institutions of the new middle classes. Doctors, social workers, school teachers, new social organizations for young and old (from the Boy Scouts to Fabians) offered new standards of respectability to the "lower orders," standards that included new definitions of sexual actors, new explanations about the "causes" of sexual behavior as well as a repertoire of proper sex conduct. In addition, increased levels of literacy offered access to new sexological literatures. These contacts suppressed certain views and practices, offered new explanations for others, and finally offered new patterns of approved sexual conduct (D'Emilio and Freedman, 1988; Weeks, 1981, 1985).

By the end of the nineteenth century, a new collection of "liberated" thinkers were let loose on the new middle classes. All over the European continent, new views of sexuality were proposed, often as modes of opposition to what was experienced as the repressive practices and doctrines of the Victorian period. Not only was sexuality an exemplary function (Freud, 1935), it was an exemplary mode of social resistance among avant-garde groups. No matter how much we now conceive these new doctrines as new forms of oppression and domination, the reformers and radicals of the times experienced them as liberating. The period was alive with men and women (more of the former than the latter) who were eager to reform sexuality. In addition, outside of the domain of sexology, Europe and to a lesser extent the United States were alive with a modernist reaction to traditional moralities which had sexual restraint at their core.

It is in this period that we find the origins of modern "sexology." Its heroic figures include Freud and his followers (though Freud looms much larger as a social theorist), Ellis, Hirschfeld, Malinowski, Stopes, Sanger, Guyon, Reich, Mead, Kinsey and his associates, and Masters and Johnson (see Robinson 1976). As a result of the catastrophes that befell all of Europe from 1914 to 1945 (and Eastern Europe to 1989), the center of sex research moved from Europe to the United States. As a consequence, with the publication of what became known as the Kinsey Reports, both sexual theory and sex research took on a cultural cast that was more in the American tradition (see Kinsey et al. 1948; Robinson 1976). Even psychoanalysis, with its roots in Europe, was unable to resist the more optimistic and individualistic cultural traditions of the United States. The sex survey quickly became the paradigmatic research method, with an emphasis on the autonomous survey respondent. Each respondent was given (in the democratic tradition) equal weight in determining the representation of the sexual life of the society.

This process of relocating the sexological tradition culturally in the United States was associated with four other interrelated transformations. The first transformation was in the identity of those privileged to explain and/or study such phenomena. The partial transition from church to medicine accomplished during the pre-sexological period remained incomplete. While an increased variety of certified experts were privileged in the period from 1890 to 1970, no one group of experts came to dominate the sexual terrain. Although a number of social science disciplines have contended for explaining rights (particularly sociology, anthropology and psychology), biologists (sometimes acting as such or in the role of socio-biologists), physicians (usually psychiatrists and psychoanalysts), religious leaders, politicians, and agents of the state (for example, police officials or social workers) have all retained important roles in the explanation of sexuality.

In the area of methods, the clinical interview and life history used to study sexuality up to the 1930s have been supplemented by the survey questionnaire and field work of the 1940s to the 1960s. Still other methods, primarily laboratory observation and experimentation, were added in the 1960s and 1970s. Ethnographic approaches become increasingly influential in the 1970s. Nearly all methods used in the social sciences were being used in sex research by the beginning of the 1980s.

In addition, the populations of interest have expanded. In the earliest days of the sexological period the focus was on those who were then considered the neurotic, the criminal and the perverted. Both who was being studied and how they were defined was transformed over the next sixty years. Even when similar groups were studied (e.g., prostitutes or bisexuals), they were thought of in different ways. Thus, while men who had sex with men and women who had sex with women were objects of inquiry from the earliest day of the sexological period, the names applied to them have changed from "sinners" and "criminals" to "members of sexual minorities" or "individuals with alternative lifestyles" (though the definition as sinner and criminal have not disappeared). In addition, the persons who Havelock Ellis described as "fairly normal people" have increasingly been added to the lists of those studied by sex researchers.

Finally, a critical change in the climate of sex research occurred in the United States after the Second World War, when the mass media became a major player in the representation of sexuality in all of its aspects. By the late 1970s, the media not only transmitted the results of sex research, it had become the major vehicle for the display and explanation of sexuality. As a result, the sex research findings of the 1980s and 1990s were foregrounded against a more sexually explicit media system. Media-originated studies of sexuality and amateur sex experts entered the research field as well. Fake research now contended with valid research in the marketplace for sexual information.

In spite of the major changes noted above which characterize the "sexological" period, a number of important commonalities in Euro-American cultural baggage could nonetheless be found during that period in virtually all thinking about sex:

1. Nearly all theorists of this period agreed, for example, that sex was a natural force that existed in opposition to civilization, culture or society. While they differed on whether sex drive or impulse was a virtuous force warped by a negative civilization (see Masters and Johnson, Kinsey, Mead, Ellis) or a negative force that required social control (see Freud and most of his followers), they agreed on the profound power of sexuality.

2. This imperious drive or instinct was embedded in the individual, and as a result it was the conduct of individuals that was central to research. Societies or cultures were primarily responsive to, rather than shaping of, the sexual impulse. In this sense the individual and the drive were prior to the social or cultural order.

3. While not universally agreeing, nearly all theorists believed that there were fundamental differences between the sexuality of women and men, differences that followed upon the natural differences between the feminine and the masculine.

4. As a corollary of these beliefs in the natural differences between women and men, theories of sexuality were normatively dominated by notions of men's sexuality and by heterosexual images and practices.

5. In this tradition, the justification for undertaking the scientific study of sexuality was to reduce sexual ignorance and to create a more balanced relation between the individual and the society. There were differences between theorists on the degree to which such a balance could be attained, with the Freudians having a more pessimistic vision. However, nearly everyone agreed that knowledge was better than ignorance and that science was capable of producing an unbiased version of sexuality, which, if generally understood and applied, would result in human betterment.

6. Finally, nearly all theorists during the period shared a belief in the privileged character of positive scientific knowledge. Such knowledge was

viewed as both trans-cultural and trans-historical. While there might be variations in cultural practices, they asserted that the underlying nature of sexuality remains the same in all times and places.

(RE)CONCEIVING SEXUALITY

By the middle of the 1960s, it was clear that the sexological paradigm was in serious trouble, particularly at the level of explanation (a paradigm is composed of an interrelated set of accepted explanations, methods and observations). The important criticisms came from social scientists within sex research and from activist groups who were attempting to reconstruct central features of the paradigm that were prejudicial to their interests.

Among sex researchers, the roots of this critical perspective (now labeled social constructionism) can be found among those who were influenced by the North American tradition of symbolic interactionism (with the emphasis on symbolic) and pragmatism, the dramatic and interpretative strategies of Kenneth Burke, and the work of Kuhn, Fleck and Mannhem in the sociology of knowledge. The crisis in sex research was part of a larger crisis in the social sciences which is reflected in the rise of local theory in anthropology, in critical studies in the humanities, and in the work of a succession of influential French philosophers and literary figures from Barthes to Baudrillard.

Within sex research, the first step was the reformulation of the general body of knowledge about sexuality within a constructionist framework that emphasized the similar character of that conduct as well as the culturally and historically specific character of the study of sexual conduct (see, for example, Gagnon and Simon 1973; Vance 1991; Weeks 1985). This challenged both the universalist conception of the sexual as well as the privileged status of scientific inquiry. Further, the constructionist view was that sexuality was not based on internal drives, but was elicited in specific historical and social circumstances. The general theory of sexual scripting emerged as a specific way of analyzing cultural, interpersonal and mental aspects of sexuality (see Gagnon 1990; Simon and Gagnon 1984).

Straddling the boundary of the academy (including sex research) and activism, the new fields of feminist studies and lesbian and gay studies have served to challenge the sexological orthodoxy in a variety of ways. The recognition that gender was a larger frame through which sexuality in Western societies should be interpreted was a critical contribution, for example, of feminist studies to sex research. This recognition took many forms: from issues of who conducted research (men did most of the research), to the models of sexual normality (the sexuality of men was the norm), to the priority of gender learning in human development (gender learning occurred prior to sexual learning), to the role of gender inequality in shaping the lives of women and men (the sexual practices of women and men were determined by inequalities in power). At the same time, though less recognized, it was clear that the relation of gender to sexuality was not fixed and that what was being observed in the Euro-American culture area was not necessarily the only relation that could exist between these two domains of action.

The development of lesbian and gay studies has paralleled the development of feminist studies, and indeed there have been important overlaps in both participants and theoretical developments. However, lesbian and gay studies have challenged different features of both social science and sexological wisdom. Because being gay or lesbian (to use the modern nomenclature) is to belong to a marked sexual category, the critiques of lesbian and gay scholars have often been construed as primarily relevant to sex research. However, these critiques, particularly the ones relevant to the relationship between identity formation, identity change and patterns of overt behavior, have more general implications for social science (see, for example, Plummer 1992).

The issue of the relationship between personal identity and behavior has always been problematic for researchers of what was once called "homosexuality." In the psychoanalytic tradition, distinctions were often made between "true" homosexuals (also called "obligatory" in some formulations) and "situational" homosexuals. Particularly troubling were persons who had incongruent patterns of fantasy, desire, identity, and behavior (often labelled bisexuals). A variety of specific solutions to this problem have been proposed (including Kinsey's decision to eliminate the identity issue), but all have foundered. More recently, it has been recognized that the relation between identity and behavior is variable and complex in most cultural and historical settings, that the categories "homosexual," "bisexual," and "heterosexual," "gay," "queer," and "clone" are all social constructs which are ambiguously tied to behavior. Clearly, this view has implications for such issues as ethnicity, religion, gender and class, in which public performances are often tied to private identities.

Another dimension of the lesbian and gay critique of sexological wisdom has been the increased importance of self-identified lesbian and gay researchers in doing research on lesbian and gay issues. In the past it was believed that "homosexuals" could not study "homosexuality" because they would be biased or engage in special pleading. It was not understood that "heterosexuals" might be equally prone to bias and special pleading—that homophobia was as dangerous as homophilia. Indeed, research by "heterosexuals" might be more biased, because heterosexuality was thought to be normal and therefore not a special form of conduct (here, heterosexuality means more than men who have sex with women or women who have sex with men). The challenge to the idea of the gay person as necessarily a special pleader was an important critique both of the positivist ideal of unbiased research and of the idea that same-gender sexual practices are abnormal.

Feminist/women's studies and lesbian and gay studies do share a number of important features. The first is that their success, while primarily based on the efforts of their proponents to define a new field of study, has been aided by the willingness of men and heterosexuals to cede the territory of gender and lesbian and gay studies. By yielding the territory these dominant groups have been able to avoid, at least in part, an analysis of men as gendered creatures as well as an analysis of the socially constructed nature of contemporary heterosexuality.

In addition, much of the most interesting work on sexuality in feminist and gay and lesbian studies has been historical in character rather than devoted to contemporary issues. This has led to significant tensions between historical studies which emphasize continuity, often framing the past in terms of current categories such as gender or gay, and the present oriented social constructionism of sociological and anthropological approaches to sexuality which treat categories such as women or gay as contemporary categories. A related issue is the degree to which theorizing sometimes reinforces contemporary realities rather than analyzing them. It is difficult to be a constructionist when engaged in social resistance since constructionism emphasizes the temporary character of both oppressors and the revolutionaries. This difficulty itself may lead to historical studies since the use of a constructionist approach to the past does not appear critical to current political challenges (e.g., it is easy to treat "sodomites" as a social construction). Yet the importance of the immediate circumstance and the need to act in a domain that is increasingly understood as a field of power, domination, and resistance, nonetheless pose a constant challenge for the development of theoretical frameworks capable of providing an effective foundation for practical action, social intervention and public policy.

This need for robust constructionist sexual theory building has become especially important over the course of the 1980s and 1990s as a direct consequence of the emerging HIV/AIDS epidemic. As the relationship between sexual conduct and HIV infection became apparent and the global dimensions of the epidemic began to emerge, a fundamental lack of understanding of sexuality and sexual conduct cross-culturally became increasingly evident—as did the direct practical and political consequences of this lack of understanding (see, for example, Daniel and Parker 1993). Even after a significant increase in funding for traditional sexological studies of behavior, attitudes and beliefs in different settings, there is, in fact, only limited understanding of the dynamics of HIV transmission. There is even more limited support for the complex task of responding to HIV infection through health promotion activities, prevention, or political activism (see Parker 1994).

On the contrary, drawing heavily on the insights of social constructionism, feminist theory, and lesbian and gay studies, by the early 1990s it had become apparent that if sex research was to make an important contribution to the fight against HIV/AIDS, it would have to focus not only on the incidence of particular attitudes and practices, but on the social and cultural contexts in which sexual activity is shaped and constituted. Research attention would have to be drawn not merely to the calculation of behavioral frequencies, but to the relations of power and social inequality within which behavior takes place, and to the cultural systems in which it becomes meaningful (see Parker 1994).

In relation to HIV/AIDS, as in relation to gender inequality and sexual oppression, an understanding of sexuality and sexual activity as socially constructed has thus refocused attention on the inter-subjective nature of sexual meanings—their shared, collective quality, not as the property of atomized or isolated individuals, but of social persons integrated within the context of distinct, and diverse, sexual cultures. This emphasis on the social organization of sexual interactions, on the contexts within which sexual practices occur, and on the complex relations between meaning and power in the constitution of sexual experience, has thus increasingly shifted attention from sexual behavior, in and of itself, to the cultural rules which organize it. Special emphasis has been given to analyzing the local or indigenous categories and systems of classification that structure and define sexual experience in different social and cultural contexts (see Parker 1991, 1994).

In a remarkably short period of time, it has become apparent that many of the key categories and classifications used in Western medicine to describe sexual life or epidemiology are, in fact, far from universal—unshared by people living in the diverse historical contexts that have been a key focus for feminist and lesbian and gay studies, or in the diverse cultural settings that have increasingly become the focus for HIV/AIDS research. On the contrary, categories as diverse as "homosexuality," "prostitution," or even "masculinity" and "femininity" may be altogether absent, or quite differently structured, in these societies and cultures—while other, local categories may be present that fail to fit neatly into the classificatory systems of Western science. By focusing more carefully on local categories and classifications, research has increasingly sought to move from what in anthropology might be described as an "outsider" perspective to an "insider" perspective—from the "experience-distant" concepts of an abstract sexual science to the "experience-near" concepts that the members of specific cultures use to understand and interpret their own sexual realities (see Geertz 1983; Parker 1991, 1994).

Sex Research in a Postmodern World

The critiques of traditional sexology and sex research by social collectivities who were often marginalized by sexology and sex research, together with the practical and political necessities that have most recently been posed by the global AIDS pandemic, have increasingly led to a new set of substantive concerns in sex research—and a new way of framing the sexual as an object of social inquiry. At the core of this re-framing is a social constructionist perspective which moves the focus of concern from the sexual actions of specific bodies to the cultural and social contexts in which sexuality occurs. And just as the sexual subject has been de-centered through this recent theoretical movement, research attention focused on the dominant patterns of contemporary Western Europe or North America has also begun to give way to a broadening concern with social contexts once ignored as little more than peripheral and cultural systems marked above all else, in relation to dominant Western patterns, by their organization of sexual difference.

These trends in contemporary sex research are, of course, themselves the function of a range of related developments in a postmodern world that is increasingly understood as fragmentary, contingent, and uncertain. Yet the de-centered subject matter of postmodern sex research should not suggest that it is impossible to to approach an understanding of the complex interaction between sexual life, in all its specificity, and more general social processes. On the contrary, a number of interrelated issues or topical areas have increasingly emerged in recent years as central to the development of research across a variety of disciplines, and have provided the framework that we have used in organizing the texts brought together in this volume.

Especially complex and difficult has been a new attempt at creating theories of desire appropriate to different cultural contexts. Traditionally, sexual desire was assumed to be natural and automatic and heterosexual and universal. The penis desired the vagina and the vagina desired the penis. Within the constraining frames of local marriage rules the male body responded to the presence of the female body, as if to a natural sign. Indeed, instead of desire, theorists wrote of lust, the drive or impulse which knew its own aims or goals.

In the deconstruction of traditional sexology and sex research, it became apparent that these concepts were based on ideology and the spirit of social coercion rather than either necessity or evidence (see, for example, the chapter by Karin Lützen in this volume). In the most recent discussions of sexual desire the focus moves from inside the individual to the external environment (see the different dimensions of this movement, for example, in the chapters by Jeffrey Weeks and Mattias Duyves). Rather than asking what internal forces create desire, the questions are, how is desire elicited, organized and interpreted as a social activity? How is desire produced and how is desire consumed? Further, sexual desire is now viewed as potentially linked to desiring in general. It is possible in some societies that sexual desire and other desires are independent practices. In advanced industrial societies, however, sexual desire is specifically linked to the desire for many commodities (in advertising for instance) and in some cases the experience of desiring things may be isomorphic with desiring sexual experiences. The shift from lust to desire is then a shift from the internal to the external, from the natural to the artificial, from the universal to the local. Desire, like the affects in general, becomes a social rather than an individual phenomenon. In this way, an entire new set of understandings begins to emerge about how desire is created, sustained and inhibited.

Recent attempts to uncover local histories of desire have been closely linked to a fundamental concern with the relationship between sexual desire and identity. The cross-cultural evidence that self-conceptions and identities are as fluid as behavior has long been regarded as important; however, studies which discuss the concrete historical and cultural contexts in which new identities emerge are quite recent (see the discussion by Gilbert Herdt and Andrew Boxer in this volume). Some of these studies show how traditional gender and sexual identities have yielded to imported ideologies and practices—for example, the emergence of the modern homosexual or the gay man in many traditional societies (see the chapters by Dennis Altman and Michael Tan)—while others examine the ways in which government regulations about gender have affected sexuality.

It is clear from all these studies that sexual identities and behaviors change at different rates and are influenced by different social factors. The question of "who am I" is not the same as "what should I do" and the relation between the two is worked out in different ways in different cultures. Indeed, for some forms of conduct in some societies the "who am I" may not be very important to "what should I do" and vice versa. However, in most modern and modernizing societies the solution to the "who am I" question has become the key to decisions about what to do.

Much of the most important work carried out on sexuality in recent years has examined the role of gender-power and inequality in creating the framework for the sexuality of women and men, regardless of the gender of their partners. While the effects of gender-power are not the same in all cultures, gender inequality is widespread and interacts with the sexual system of specific cultures to shape most aspects of sexual life.

It is both difficult and easy to document gender inequality. It is hard to recognize and attend to the way in which differences in social power affect relations within and between the genders if one takes an essentialist view of gender differences. How could the sexual worlds of women and men be any different than they are, given the natural differences between the ways in which women and men are biologically constituted? In socio-biological terms, the man has many sperm and wishes to inseminate many women; the women have few eggs and want to make sure that the fertilized egg is well taken care of; hence men have more sexual partners, like pornography more than women do, are more likely to be unfaithful in marriage than women are, etc. Current differences in conduct are easily explained by differences between the biology of the sexes. Once this theory of natural gender difference is abandoned, the evidence for social inequalities between women and men becomes striking (see the chapter by Lori Heise in this volume), and serves as one of the most important bases for understanding the difference between the sexual lives of women and men.

It becomes apparent that all questions about sex have to be interpreted in light of the differences in power between women and men (see Barbara de Zalduondo and Jean Maxius Bernard). Thus the question, "How often did you have sexual intercourse last month," must be framed by such questions as who initiated the sex, under what conditions, could one partner or the other have refused the sex, why did you have the sex then, etc. How the sex was negotiated and how the negotiation was concluded, it may then be seen, often depends on a current threat of violence or previous threat of violence into the unreflected-upon "natural order of things." Changes in patterns of negotiation often depend on distal effects—the level of education of women in the society, the rights of women to leave the home without a man's permission or the availability of contraception. At the proximate level, men's responsibility for children, whether they are employed, whether they drink in groups, and so on, have profound effects on how the sexual encounter is managed.

In order to understand the effect of gender on sexuality it is necessary to fully unpack the gender system, to locate women and men in the social space of power, and to understand that socially and culturally constituted relations of power structure not only the interactions of men and women, but of different *types* of men and *types* of women within the context of complex social, political and economic systems (see, in particular, the chapter by Roger Lancaster). Situated within these diverse contexts, the specific effects of gender power on the sexuality of women *and* men can begin to be understood in a more nuanced fashion.

Whether in relation to local histories of desire, the constitution of sexual identities, or the configuration of gender in relation to power, the focus of recent research has consistently sought to move from the isolated sexual individual to sexuality as existing not only within but between individuals. The attempt to understand sexuality through an understanding of the social networks in which people live their sexual and non-sexual lives is a way to concretize this movement. In our view, social structure is very real, though rarely static over time. To paraphrase Marx, human beings construct their sexuality, but they do not construct it as they wish. This not only means that we are born into a culture that both shapes and limits the sexuality we learn—but also that the other human beings who live in that culture continuously influence the expression of our sexuality.

The reality of social networks is larger than any single sexual actor—or any pair of actors (see the chapter by Edward Laumann, John Gagnon and Robert Michael). Stakeholders in our sexuality come in many packages, from large-scale social institutions to close friends and relatives. They seek to influence what we do when we are alone with our sexual partners, as well to influence which partners we choose.

Social structure is real in another sense. The very way in which sexual partnering is organized in the society and the investments that are made in such partners shape the opportunity to acquire or change sexual partners. In a society like the United States, where three quarters of those persons between eighteen and fifty-nine are in affectional and sexual couples (mostly married), the market for easily available partners is very limited. Depending on the social groups to which you might belong, the market for partners may be close to zero.

The study of personal or social networks as powerful influences on sexuality is a prime example of the current importance of ideas developed outside of sex research (and unthought of in traditional sexology). Many of these ideas have come from persons whose prior work was outside of the sex research tradition and who were attracted to sex research because of the opportunities offered by research in HIV/AIDS and fertility (see, for example, the chapters by Anthony Coxon and by I.O. Orubuloye on the importance of social and sexual networks in relation to HIV transmission).

Finally, as is both implicit and explicit in each of the areas discussed above, principally as a result of HIV/AIDS (though also in relation to other sexually transmitted diseases, unwanted pregnancy, sexual violence, and a host of other very real social problems linked to sexuality), what might be described as the social construction of sexual risk has become centrally important in sex research in recent years (see, in particular, the chapters by Carl Kendall and by Geeta Rao Gupta and Ellen Weiss). Indeed, the perception and response to perceived risk can perhaps best be understood in relation to a broader concern with the relationship between culture, social structure and behavioral change—a relationship that has become central to contemporary research on sexuality (see Shirley Lindenbaum's afterword to the present volume). Historically, little attention was paid to the ways in which sexuality has changed along with culture and social structure. In contacts between the colonizers and the colonized, these changes were often viewed as a good thing by dominant religious or governmental groups. In some cases, in those cultures in which sexuality was in some way considered admirable, the changes induced were viewed as a bad thing, but these were rare.

In a world increasingly concerned with the disappearance of indigenous cultures, on the one hand, and with the sexual contacts which might lead to HIV transmission, on the other, greater concern is being expressed about how to protect some cultures from change and about how to promote change in others. Such practical concerns require a better understanding of how sexuality changes—and how planned, politically responsible and culturally appropriate programs of sexual behavior change can be undertaken. The study of HIV/AIDS transmission and prevention has centered around specific issues of risky conduct, but there are clearly larger issues involved in the social engineering of sex. We must begin to address what changes are possible, at what cost, and with what consequences. Sexuality enters the world of the self-conscious policy sciences in a way that is entirely new, a way that requires new kinds of knowledge about sexuality.

As the essays that make up this volume clearly demonstrate, the road to this new kind of knowledge is rarely simple to follow. On the contrary, it is fraught with difficulties, as we attempt to understand the broader contexts and larger histories that have shaped the more specific settings that are increasingly the focus of our attention in what would seem (to use Shirley Lindenbaum's terms) an apparently disconnected world. While the conclusions that we reach are rarely simple or direct, they nonetheless offer some sense of the fundamental importance that sex research can have in seeking to understand and respond to the complexity and diversity of contemporary life.

HISTORIES OF DESIRE

Part One

La mise en discours and Silences in Research on the History of Sexuality

1

Karin Lützen

NINE O'CLOCK AT NIGHT THE TWENTY-EIGHTH OF AUGUST 1889, the forty-year old, unmarried Alfred-Hippolyte P. was arrested at a bus station in Paris. In his hand he was carrying a long pigtail, and in his pocket he had a pair of scissors. In the crowd at the bus station he had seized the occasion to cut off the pigtails from a young girl's head. Following a search of his house, sixty-five pigtails and pony tails in different nuances were found—all secretly cut off from young girls' heads. After his arrest Alfred-Hippolyte underwent a mental examination performed by three doctors who published his confession, together with their statement in a medical journal.

"For about three years," he had told them, "I have often been overwhelmed by restlessness when I was alone at night in my room. It began with anxiety and dizzyness and then I got the idea to touch women's hair. I can't say how I managed it the first time, but when I was holding the pigtail in my hand I felt such voluptuousness that I immediately got an erection and without a touch, yes, without even rubbing myself against the young girl, I got an ejaculation. I went home ashamed of what had happened, but when I thought about it the same sensations returned. Then I got the idea of possessing this hair that gave me such hitherto unknown feelings of voluptuousness. I had been to bed with women, but had never felt anything similar together with them—they repelled me more than they attracted me. But as soon as I saw loose hair I was obsessed by the idea of touching it. Soon that was not satisfying enough. I wanted to possess it and one evening I cut off a pigtail with my knife. I was holding it in my hand all the way home and at the moment I got inside my room I was overwhelmed by the same excitement as outside. I buried my hand in the hair, I let it slide over my body, I twisted it around my genitals and sensed the most lively sensations." And like that he went on cutting off sixty-six pigtails more until he was finally arrested (see Motet 1890:337).

The question now is: can these acts and the impulse provoking them be characterized as sexual? At first glance you would answer yes, because these acts included erection and ejaculation. But is that sufficient explanation? Couldn't it just as well be an expression of an uncontrolled craving for beauty—a delight in touching and admiring the long, shiny hair. Or could it be a collection mania that accidentally had pigtails as objects but equally well could have included coins or tin soldiers? Or could it be a desire for "playing hairdresser," which, without voluntary playmates, unfortunately had to result in theft?

In 1889, when Alfred-Hippolyte was examined, it was not the *sexual* aspect the doctors emphasized. They paid attention instead to his "pathological obsession" and classified it as a sign of degeneration. Thereafter they concluded that since he was insane, Alfred-Hippolyte couldn't be held responsible for his acts—therefore he should be sent to a lunatic asylum for some months and not go to prison.

Such a decision marks a growing humanization of those offenders who seem to be driven by an uncontrollable need and who previously had been sent to prison. Many such men were now presented to the scientific world, especially by French and German legal experts, and common to all of them was that they had been arrested several times because they behaved strangely and disturbingly. One of the cases was of a German who in 1871 had pursued young women, forced them into a corner and finally urinated on them (Arndt 1872). An Austrian was arrested in 1878 because he had stolen a handkerchief out of a woman's handbag. When his house was searched, fifty stolen handkerchiefs were found (Zippe 1878). A Frenchman was arrested in 1892 because he touched women's silk dresses (Garnier 1893). Two years later another Frenchman was arrested because he stabbed women's buttocks, and the year after yet another Frenchman was arrested for throwing ink and acid on women's dresses (Garnier 1990).

Within twenty years the attitude towards such acts changed completely. From having been considered sheer legal offences they were now understood as an expression of insanity, but the focus soon shifted from the pathological obsession to the fact that erection and ejaculation always were a part of the acts. Around the turn of the century these acts were isolated from other obsessions and classified as *sexual* perversions.

The Austrian psychiatrist Richard von Krafft-Ebing collected forty-five cases like these and published them under the title *Psychopathia Sexualis*. The collection was widely distributed, and in 1903 the twelfth edition was published, containing 238 cases collected from various medical journals—the above mentioned Alfred-Hippolyte, for instance, became case number one hundred. The greater the attention towards this behavior the more cases were created. Herewith, a special group of mankind was invented. Very soon it was divided into sub-groups that each got its own name and in time developed a mutual solidarity of the species. The sexual perverts had come to light—but the question is whether they actually had the sexual in common.

In 1986, Jeffrey Weeks wrote: "I am suggesting that what we define as 'sexuality' is an historical construction, which brings together a host of different biological and mental possibilities—gender identity, bodily differences, reproductive capacities, needs, desires and fantasies—which need not be linked together, and in other cultures have not been (Weeks 1986:15).

As the cases concerning Alfred-Hippolyte and company show, a range of acts and impulses can have quite a different point of departure but end up being poured into the same melting pot of definitions and coming out again as homogenous sexual perversions. The sexual scientists of the time looked at *Das Ding an sich*—at every case as an isolated phenomenon. Together with the other isolated phenomena they certainly formed a community, but in turn they were torn out of their social, historical and cultural context.

The classification zeal of medical science should be seen in connection with natural science's zeal for systematizing everything. At that time, physiology was created, since vivisection made it possible to elucidate the function of the organism. Bacteriology was developed as well, and one microbe after another was isolated and named. It seems almost as if medical science itself was stricken with an irresistable impulse to classify everything under the sun. When the science of *Psychopathia Sexualis* is viewed in connection with the development of these other classifying disciplines of the time, its appearance thus seems more understandable. The consequence of the medical classification of certain acts was that what was criminal now became humanized, what was unexplainable now was explained, and what was not quite so obviously sexual now became sexualized.

The above mentioned inclinations—the desire to cut off women's pigtails, to urinate on women, to steal women's handkerchiefs, to paw women's silk dresses, to stab women's buttocks or to throw ink or acid on women's dresses can all only take place in the anonymous crowd of the metropolis. Urbanization contributed to the creation of modernity and the city became a liberating place for all those who were looking for independence and alternatives. In the bourgeois world view, the big city had at the end of the nineteenth century a very special function. It was the embodiment of the drawbacks of industrialization, with slum areas, drunkenness and immorality. In the light of the city's dangerousness, the bourgeois home seemed all the more secure, and its function as the safe harbor of the family was reinforced. When you were leaving this home, you should be on guard because you were not only threatened by homeless children, beggars, drunkards, and streetwalkers, but also by sexual perverts. The big city was thereby further sexualized.

In addition, all these perversions were performed by men towards women. At that time, the women's movement strove to expand women's sphere of action and to create more possibilities for middle class women's employment and consequent economic independence. In moral reform movements, women argued against the bourgeois double standard and demanded instead that men learn to control themselves sexually. These women wanted a society pervaded with self-control, because it would allow women to move around in the world without fear of men's outrages. The creation of the sexual perverts acted from here as still another threat that women should pay attention to when they left home. Yet, as soon as a new danger was discovered and proclaimed, its dangerousness was weakened by the definitional encirclement. By being dissected and named and treated at a lunatic asylum, the perversions became less threatening.

When studying sexual phenomena—historical as well as present—it is therefore important to examine what has caused certain acts, desires, and life stories to be classified as sexual. A phenomenon such as the etiology of homosexuality can with advantage be studied as a cultural construction rather than as a truth of natural science. If it is examined through "indirect reading," it is possible to go behind the text and decode medical science's perception of which acts constitute a good life and which a bad life.

Homosexuality has not only been explained as having a sexual origin, but as having a negative one. It has been assumed that people become homosexual because they have been arrested in their development, have had a shocking sexual experience with the opposite sex, or have a distorted sexual hormone or gene.

If not only the etiology of homosexuality but also homosexuality itself is viewed as a cultural construction, attention may be shifted from the phenomena pulling people *away from* heterosexuality, to what pushes people *towards* homosexuality. And that could be conditions that do not have a sexual origin at all, such as the fact that the homosexual way of life allows you to transgress traditional gender roles or the fact that, by living as a homosexual, you avoid marriage, or the fact that you keep an identity as deviant—which for some people is experienced as an advantage. These suggestions are just as usable in explaining why certain people prefer to arrange their life around homosexual identity.

When studying sexual phenomena it is important, morever, to notice their cultural connection. Do they have special functions as demarcations of one culture from another, one class from another, or one gender from another? Or can these sexual phenomena be considered bugbears, stimulations, or creators of order?

To summarize: the point in mentioning Alfred-Hippolyte and the creation of the category "sexual perversion" is, quite simply, that in research on sexuality and sexual behavior it is important to throw light upon the origin of the characterization of a phenomenon as sexual.

My next point concerns discourse and silence, as it is viewed by ethnologists and historians of mentality. Michel Foucault introduced the concept *La mise en discours*, suggesting that sexuality at the end of the nineteenth century was put into discourse through the classifications of sexual science and through the debates of the moral reform movements. Inspired by this viewpoint, many discourse analyses of exactly these historical texts have been made which, together, elucidate explicit attitudes towards sexuality.

But sexuality is—just like death—one of the phenomena in cultural history that, separated from the public discourse, is wrapped in silence. It is very interesting to see what historical personages said about sexuality, but it is at least as interesting to look at what they *didn't* say. Silence must in certain instances be interpreted as exactly silence. With silence as a track, one must reconstruct the attitude causing the refusal to talk (see Florén and Persson 1985).

The French historians of mentality have emphasized silence in writing about the study of death. Michel Vovelle has recommended that iconographic and archeological sources get just as important a place as written ones. The aim should be to find out what was expressed but not said about a certain topic (Vovelle 1982).

Still another method to apply in analysing the unsaid is what the Swedish ethnologist Orvar Löfgren calls "symbolic inversion" (Löfgren 1987:111). He points out that cultural identity is built up through contrasts. The nineteenth century's middle-class, for example, created its own class's culture in contrast to the culture of both the aristocracy and the proletariat. According to Löfgren, symbolic inversion is an important technique in performing cultural analysis. It means that you map out the culture pattern of a certain group by studying its stereotypes and conceptions about "the others"—the culturally different.

This method implies, for example, that middle-class conceptions of the proletariat aren't a reliable source of knowledge about the living conditions of this class. Instead, such material can offer excellent knowledge of middle-class self-knowledge. Changes in bourgeois self-knowledge can therefore be studied in the bourgeoisie's changing images of working class culture.

These methods I will apply here in analyses of Magdalene Home—a rescue home for fallen women founded in Copenhagen in 1877 by Indre Mission—a large Christian fundamentalist organization. Magdalene Home was a place where women who voluntarily wanted to leave their occupation as prostitutes could seek shelter. Here they would be re-educated, that is, learn new virtues and discard old sins. Since this was a home that centered around sexual behavior, it is interesting to notice how sexuality was talked about—or how it was silenced. For this purpose I want to look specificaly at how sexual relationships between women were viewed.

In her pathbreaking article from 1975, "The Female World of Love and Ritual," Carroll Smith-Rosenberg showed that devoted and passionate love relationships between middle-class women were an important part of women's culture in the nineteenth century (Smith-Rosenberg 1975). As far as is known, these relationships did not include sexual desire, but if the strength of their feelings is therefore belittled, a foolish anachronism is committed.

In women's studies there has been a long international debate concerning the riddle: "Did they or didn't they?" In other words, did these romantic, middle-class friends have sex or didn't they? This truly is a riddle, since sexual relationships between two women do not result in pregnancy—a silent proof, in itself, of sex between a woman and a man. Two women together don't beget such telling evidence, and their sexual practice is therefore almost impossible to detect. Though it is an anachronism to *judge* the strength and depth of love relationships between these women from the occurrence of sex, it is an interesting source of silence. Middle-class spinsters praised desirelesssness in their public discourse, but privately they might have experienced passion and desire. Though they are silent about their own practice, they perhaps knew and talked about sex between women from another social class—women they met in their philanthropic rescue work.

In nineteenth century philanthropy, asylums and other institutions of former times were replaced by rescue homes established with the bourgeois home as an ideal. Most of the rescue homes couldn't afford to provide single rooms and had to let the residents sleep in dormitories. But in Magdalene Home, where the residents should be rescued from an *immoral* life, it is noteworthy that they were separated at night. By applying discourse analysis to the public arguments for establishing these single rooms and by using silence as a track, it might be possible to say something about sexual experiences between women.

The arguments are varied. Pastor Blume stated in 1902 that Magdalene Home made it possible for the women to feel what it was like to live in a real home (see Blume 1902). They had without doubt previously lived with their families crammed into a one-room apartment and now they got a chance to experience one of the privileges of the middle-class, that is, privacy. The residents should not only learn what a good bourgeois home implied—they themselves should also practice the upkeep of a home.

For this purpose single rooms were—so to speak—preliminary drafts, which the Principal, Miss Thora Esche, explained in her memoirs in 1920: "It is impossible to give you an ample idea of what a blessing each little girl's cozy room with bed, table, chair, washstand, mirror and picture on the wall—yes, and then the two flowers in a flower pot that always were my first gifts to her—has been to my dear wards. The two flowers that had to be tended to were usually followed by more. These small rooms were the sanctuaries that contributed to making the Home into a home for each of its residents" (Esche 1920).

Since Magdalene Home was run by Indre Mission it meant that the rescue work was two-sided. On the one hand, the women should both be saved from their immoral existence and be guided into a decent way of life, but at the same time they should be "saved for the Lord"—that is, become good Christians. Single rooms were therefore presented as a kind of religious closet, a fact which Pastor Blume also mentioned: "The little room is of enormous importance for the rehabilitation and salvation of the young girl; here she can, should she want to, without being mocked, go down on her knees and seek help where help is to be found; here she can fight her fights, and should she want to do harm, here she can injure only herself" (Blume 1902:18).

Miss Thora Esche had herself been thinking about something of the sort when she in 1877 negotiated with the Board of Governors concerning the arrangement of the rooms. The Board of Governors maintained they only could afford a dormitory like in other homes. But, as Thora Esche later wrote, she had to stress "how the large dormitories would mean that everything that had been built up during the day would be broken down at night and that if a young girl really felt the need to bend her knees and pray she would lack the courage to do so from fear of being mocked by the other girls" (Esche 1920:79).

The question now is: is this a silence we can hear? What is it that would be broken down at night in a dormitory? Respectability, devotion—or morality? Let's suppose it was morality she feared was broken down. Did she then imagine that the women at the dormitory would provoke each other by telling stories from their former life in sin? Or could they perhaps be tempted to seek an intimacy with each other that also included physical closeness?

Thora Esche herself was silent, and the jubilee publications were silent. Is this silence then an expression of the refusal to talk or of the fact that neither Esche nor Blume actually had anything to say? Is it completely mistaken to try to find an answer to the content of their worry, and is this effort just an example of the predilection of the present for seeing something sexual in everything?

And will it be possible to break the silence by searching in other sources? Both Blume and Esche were speaking the language of the moral reformers colored by Christian rhetoric and concealment. Their view of life marked their discourse. According to their Christian view of life, it was a disgrace that the State would allow young women to degrade themselves and sell what they ought to share exclusively with a beloved husband. The discourse of the philanthropists went therefore simply like this: "How can we save women out of the muddy puddle of sin?"

Other people who dealt with prostitution had another view of life and, therefore also another discourse. Rudolph Bergh, the chief physician at the hospital where the prostituted women were examined, used the language of natural science and his discourse went instead like this: "How can the spreading of venereal diseases be prevented?" Though this was what he described in his annual report he actually also touched on sexual relationships between women and his matter-of-fact accounts can perhaps be presumed to serve as the "other source" to lift the veil of silence.

Bergh, too, had formed a conception of what would happen if several prostituted women spent the night in the same room. In 1888 he referred to a French study by Parent-Duchâtelet, who, concerning Parisian conditions, wrote that "such an inclination is often acquired when in custody the girls are kept together; detention conditions in Copenhagen have hitherto frequently necessitated the keeping of two to four young girls together around the clock, probably with the same consequent depravation" (Bergh 1888).

He thus was not completely certain that such a way of spending the night would lead to sex between the women. But he did not doubt that some of the women working as prostitutes had mutual sexual relationships. They only came to his acquaintance, though, when they had become violent, and one of the women was taken to the hospital due to bruises from a fight with her lover. But the fact that he as a medical doctor knew about these relationships does not mean that Miss Thora Esche also knew about them. His talking is therefore not necessarily an answer to her silence after all.

Then we have the iconographic and archaeological material recommended by Michel Vovelle, the French historian of mentality. Rudolph Bergh can also supply us with an iconographic source, namely tattoos, since in 1902 he published a study of the occurence of tattooed, prostituted women. The previous year he had examined nearly seven hundred prostituted women at the hospital and about two hundred of these women had been tattooed. The most common motifs had been burning hearts, a pair of folded hands or a rose, but many of the women had names tattooed as well and, of these, thirteen had a woman's name. One of the women had five different women's names tattooed, whereas another, as he wrote: "on three different parts of the body with six engravings commemorated the same mistress" (Bergh 1902:951).

Tattoos seem to us to be such a conspicuous source of information about sexuality that Miss Esche hardly could have overlooked them. But maybe she never noticed them because she only saw the residents fully dressed. Or perhaps precisely the tattooed women would not even dream about asking Magdalene Home to please rescue them. Or perhaps Miss Esche didn't have a context that made tattooed women's names understandable. In her perception, sexuality was something men forced on women and that women themselves were completely devoid of. Even if she had seen the woman with the five different women's names, she could have understood it as a memorial to five sweet cousins, without the slightest secondary meaning.

The conclusion must therefore be that either Thora Esche obviously didn't know that women could have sexual relationships with each other, or she knew everything and her silence illustrates perfectly the concealment with which such relationships were met.

I have now mentioned two things researchers ought to keep in mind when dealing with the study of sexuality. One is the question of whether a phenomenon now viewed as sexual also was seen as sexual in the past, and of what the motives are for now viewing it as sexual. To illustrate this point, I used as an example the story about Alfred-Hippolyte, the hair despoiler, and the creation of the idea of the sexual pervert.

The other thing a researcher ought to keep in mind is that the study of sexuality is not only a study of *La mise en discours*—but also of silence. In some instances silence must be interpreted as silence, and with this silence as a track one must reconstruct the attitude causing the refusal to talk about and touch on certain areas. To illustrate this point, I used as an example the silence of a spinster-reformer concerning sexual relationships between prostituted women.

As a third point, I will state some instances where silence concerning sexual relationships between two spinster-philanthropists is broken by the discourse of the authorities. Where, in the previous example, I put emphasis on class, I will now look at gender, and for this occasion I will introduce the phenomenon I choose to call "the heterofication of homosociality."

The separate spheres of the middle class caused unmarried women to create their own female world. The spinster role had wide limits, however, and in service of the good cause some philanthropist-spinsters juggled elegantly with two gender roles. At the inauguration of Magdalene Home in 1877 the pastor of the Home said to Miss Esche: "Now remember, Thora, here you are both Father and Mother—don't ever forget it" (Esche 1920:85). She didn't forget, though she prefered to accentuate her mother role—while she assigned the daugther role to the residents. As soon as she retired as matron, it was the father role that prevailed. In 1909 her successor wrote, after a year on her post, that "although she was no longer Mother to the children, Miss Esche has been, as she herself says, like a father to our large family. A father one could safely approach when needing advice and guidance about the many serious and difficult incidents and experiences with which one is confronted" (Smaatræk fra det dadlige Liv 1903:3).

Since Thora Esche continued to be the absolute leader of the Home, she had to take on the two gender roles successively. Other women who ran homes found a partner who could take on one of the roles, as did Miss Caroline Mathisen. From 1887, she ran a home for deaf-and-dumb children with Miss Anna Thorup, and when they retired in 1899 the journal of the deaf-and-dumb noted that: "'Foster mother' and 'Aunt Anna' knew how to make a true home for the children. Seldom have two women each in her way, possessed such rich potential to be 'Father and Mother' for deaf-and-dumb children as these two, but it is also seldom that two women in complete understanding and agreement used their talents as they did." Those who had visited the home over the years would be able to remember "when 'Foster mother' as 'father' of the house presided over the dinner table with all the little chicks sitting along both sides of the long table, whilst 'Aunt Anna' made sure that everyone was fed" (Smaablade for Døvstumme 1899:947).

The separate gender spheres of the middle class home were introduced to philanthropic institutions, and in a homosocial universe the residents were educated in the ways of the heterosexual nuclear family. It was an accepted fact that precisely unmarried women were well-qualified to work at rescue homes. Numerous cases illustrate that it was equally welcome for a spinster couple to run a home together. But since the residents should have an object lesson in how the role distribution took place in a heterosexual couple, what I call the "heterofication of homosociality" took place. As shown, it implied that a spinster alternated between the mother and father role or that a spinster couple divided the roles between them.

This was all very well, and these spinster parents were praised to the skies in the official discourse. It was quite unthinkable to imagine that sexual acts took place between two spinsters, just as nobody suspected the symbolic gender shift to be literal or that the spinster "father" really wanted to be a man.

One day in 1893, such an idyll in Copenhagen was hit by a terrible shock. Miss Vilhelmine Møller, the matron of the children's home, Kana, was arrested on a charge of having murdered Volmer, one of the boys in the home. She confessed and explained that she had killed him because she was afraid he would disclose that they had had sex together. A month after her arrest she told the judge that there was something abnormal about her. A subsequent medical examination confirmed that her genitals should be characterized rather as male than as female. She was now declared to be a man, and half-a-year later "she" was allowed to take a new identity as a man and to call "himself" Vilhelmi.

A year after the crime was committed, Vilhelmi was taken to court, accused of indecency towards two children in his charge, and of having killed one of them. He was committed to prison for life. The indictment was published in the Journal of the Supreme Court (Højesteretstidende 1894:292–304) and there was certainly no silence about the character of the sexual relationship Vilhelmi had had with the two boys.

Miss Vilhelmine Møller had been a very respected person in the world of children's homes, and after her arrest some male principals of children's homes publicly expressed their horror. They just couldn't understand how such a devout and clever woman could kill a child, and they asked everybody to plead for her. About her motive for the crime they were, on the other hand, completely silent—or ignorant.

Two years after the murder, a medical doctor who had had access to the documents published his analysis of the case in a medical journal (Stilhoff 1895). He now wrote that Miss Møller, the mother of the home, also had had a sexual relationship with the aunt of the home—a young widow. This woman had told the police court that Miss Møller had done with her like men do when they have intercourse with women. Moreover, it appeared that the children at the home had been well aware both of the relationship between mother and aunt as well as the relationship between mother and the murdered boy. They had even already given the name of Oskar to the child they expected to be the outcome of that connection. Not even when the whole country was in a commotion would the philanthropists break the silence about sexuality, and once again it is other sources that talk—in this case, law and medicine.

The murder at Kana is an interesting case since it shows that sexual relationships could occur between spinster philanthropists. The question then is whether it was of frequent occurence and only was exposed when a crime was committed. It is also noteworthy that a spinster's transgressing her gender role—by not only "playing" father but by also being it sexually—turned out to be caused by her actually *being* a man.

Fourteen years later, hermaphroditism was once again linked to sexual relationships between women, but in the meantime the newly discovered sexual deviation called "Homosexuality" had become well-known. The scandal began when a Social Democratic member of the Parliament, Peter

Sabroe, brought the conditions at the Danish reformatories into focus. He called attention to cruelty, punishment and neglect of the children and contrived to have several commissions of inquiry set up.

In 1907, he concentrated on Hebron, a reformatory exclusively for girls, governed by Edle Bransholm from Indre Mission. Just like other accused leaders of reformatories, she was supposed to have cruelly ill-treated her girls. But what was really special about Edle was that she—as Sabroe said—united whips and kisses. In the Social Democratic newspaper he wrote about how she once had whipped twelve girls on their naked buttocks, had become tired and in a sweat, but how that "did not prevent her from taking one of the prettiest of the whipped girls to her own room at night where she kissed and caressed the child in the name of Jesus" (Sabroe 1907). Sabroe also had found out that Edle Bransholm had several female friends whom she had kissed and spent the night with.

A commission of inquiry was set up to investigate the accusation of cruelty at the home. The witnesses were also asked about Edle Bransholm's friendships, and both women and men said they had seen her kiss her girl friends but nobody had thought anything about it. In their opinion, kisses and caresses were common among members of Indre Mission. She herself had nothing to deny and explained that the reason her girl friend was sleeping in the same bed as herself was that she simply had only one bed. The mutual caresses were solely a manifestation of their friendly feelings: "Sensuality and eroticism were not a part of it" (Forhøret angaaende Forholdene paa Pigehjemmet "Hebron" 1908:135).

All this is a matter of culture clash. In the Danish countryside, kisses and caresses between women including Christian philanthropists, were quite common and even as late as 1907 they were not at all suspicious. For a big city socialist like Sabroe, on the other hand, these kisses were comparable to "Homosexuality." He also hinted that Edle Bransholm wasn't a real woman and he dwelt on her "big, mannish, grey-white face with the not that small tendency to a moustache" (Forhøret 1908:7). His persistent denigration of her sex caused her to submit to a medical examination, but the doctor couldn't find anything suspicious and he declared that "she doesn't show the slightest sign of hermaphrodism" (Forhøret 1908:185).

In the nineteenth century, the middle class had presented the working class as carrier of all such despisable characteristics as lack of self-control, immorality and laziness. In Denmark, in the beginning of the new century, it was now a socialist who presented the middle class religious philanthropists as carriers of characteristics the socialists wanted to combat, such as perversion, suggestiveness, abuse of power, and religious hypocrisy. By using "symbolic inversion" on the texts of Sabroe it is possible to say something about which characteristics the later Danish Social Democrats valued and which they wanted to exterminate.

Sabroe was an advocate of the removal of childcare from private religious philanthropy, and instead wanted it taken over by the cool-minded state apparatus. The niche obtained by the bourgeois spinsters, with their gender role changes and romantic friendships, was floodlit and made suspicious by Sabroe's socialist gaze. The new century ushered in a new epoch with a transition from private care to public welfare and from homosociality to a culture divided into sexual dichotomies.

Finally, I will summarize how I imagine this essay can be used by others doing research in sexuality and sexual behavior. All the examples I have used have indeed been historical because I have more experience in doing historical research. Nevertheless, I am convinced that the theoretical and methodological questions I have raised can be applied also in research on conditions of the present.

When starting such research I find it important to not just take for granted that a phenomenon now designated as sexual also was seen as sexual in the past. Maybe it has quite different functions as well, which are important to explain.

Secondly, it can't be stated too often that the existing gender, class and regional differences in any society naturally also penetrate the sexual area and therefore always must be accounted for in sex research. Methodologically, it is interesting to look at not just how sexual behavior takes place, but also what is *said* about sexual behavior within the context of the differences mentioned above. For that purpose, silence can be analyzed as well as discourse.

History, Desire, and Identities   2

Jeffrey Weeks

CURRENT PREOCCUPATIONS WITH QUESTIONS OF DESIRE have a certain logic of development. Recent research about sexuality, including my own, has been shaped by a rejection of essentialist arguments, and an attempt to elaborate what has generally, though inadequately, been called "social constructionism." The basic assumption of this research has been that it is deeply problematic to think of sexuality as a purely natural phenomenon, outside the boundaries of society and culture, that we have all too readily believed that sexuality is the most natural thing about us, our drives fixed and inherent, our identities dictated by that nature and those drives, and a history of sexuality therefore no more than an account of reactions to those basic biological givens.

Over the past twenty years most of these older assumptions have been profoundly challenged, following a century of challenges to essentialist modes of thought in general. Through anthropology and social analysis we have strengthened our awareness of the relativity of sexual norms. From Freud we can derive (though sadly most interpretors have not) insights into the complexities of desire, and the tentative and always provisional nature of gender and sexual identities. From the new social history we have become aware of the multiple narratives of sexual life. After feminism, lesbian and gay politics and the theoretical challenges of Michel Foucault, we are increasingly sensitive to the subtle forms of power which invest the body, and which make us simultaneously subjected to and subjects of sex. All these influences in turn feed into the deconstructionist project, which questions the fixities and certainties of post-Enlightenment humanism, rationalism and progressivism (see Weeks 1985, 1991).

At the core of this position has been the argument that we can only understand sexuality through understanding the cultural meanings which construct it. This does not mean that biology is irrelevant. Nor does it mean that individuals are blank pieces of paper on which society writes its preferred meanings. Take, for example, homosexuality. To say that lesbian and gay identities have a history, have not always existed and may not always exist, does not mean that they are not important. Nor should it necessarily be taken to imply that homosexual feelings are not deeply rooted. I personally have no special knowledge on that question, and I suspend judgement on it (though I remain sceptical, I have to confess, about recent "discoveries" of a "gay brain" or the "gay gene"). It is in any case irrelevant to the argument. The real problem does not lie in whether homosexuality is inborn or learned. It lies instead in the question: what are the meanings this particular culture gives to homosexual behavior, however it may be caused, and what are the effects of those meanings on the ways in which individuals organize their sexual lives. That is a historical question. It is also a question which is highly political: it forces us to analyze the power relations which determine why one set of meanings, rather than another, are hegemonic; and it poses the further question of how those meanings can be changed, and changed to what.

The crucial factor is not the truth or mythic nature of identities, but identities' effectiveness and political relevance. And that puts squarely on the agenda the question of values. What the historical approach has achieved is to make us more aware of the complexity of forces that shape the social, and to sensitize us to the power relations which organize the meanings we live by. Ideology works precisely by making us believe that what is socially created, and therefore subject to change, is really natural, and therefore immutable. But why should we believe that of all social phenomena, sexuality is the least changeable? On the contrary, it is probably the most sensitive to social influence, a conductor of the subtlest of changes in social *mores* and power relations. If that is the case, then we need to be clearer than ever before of the values that motivate us. Sexuality, as Foucault put it, is not a fatality. It is a possibility for creative life (Foucault 1984). And in creating that life, we need above all to be able to affirm and validate our values.

But this brings us to another set of issues and debates, around what, for want of a better term, we still call "postmodernity." There are striking parallels between recent debates on sexuality and the wider debates about the nature of the postmodern. Postmodernity is clearly a relational term defined by something that came before (or, at least, is now passing) "modernity." The term carries with it that sense of an ending which has been a crucial element in recent sexual writings.

However we characterize the present age, there can be no doubt of its sense of radical change and uncertainty. And most relevant to the present discussion is one of the most discussed elements of the postmodernity debates: the challenge to the "grand narratives" that characterized high modernity. The "Enlightenment project" of the triumph of reason, progress and humanity, the sense that science and history were leading us inexorably to a more glorious future, has been subjected to searching deconstruction, and its roots have been shown to be murky. Reason has been reduced to a rationalization of power, progress has been seen as the tool of white, Western expansionism, and humanity as the cloak for a male-dominated culture which treats women as Other. Inevitably, this deconstruction has had its echoes in the discourses of sexual progressivism. A number of feminists have seen the science of sex as little more than a tattered cover for the reaffirmation of male power, imposing a male-oriented "sexual liberation" on women. Foucault has famously challenged our illusions concerning the very notion of sexual "liberation," and by many others sexual liberalism has been denounced as little more than a new garb for the incessant process of sexual regulation and control.

With such challenges this has gone the original bases for the enlightened hopes of the pioneers of sexual reform at the end of the nineteenth century. In his Presidential address to the 1929 Congress of the World League for Sexual Reform, the pioneering sexologist Magnus Hirschfeld declared that: "A sexual impulse based on science is the only sound system of ethics." He proclaimed on the portals of his Institute for Sexual Science the words, "Through Science to Justice" (see Weeks 1986:111). Part of that hope died as the Institute burned under the Nazi torch. Much of the rest faded in the succeeding decades as the sexual scientists squabbled over their inheritance, and disagreed over everything from the nature of sexual difference to female sexual needs, homosexuality and the social consequences of disease.

Behind this challenge to sexual reform was the more subtle undermining of the sexual tradition which had been defined in the nineteenth century, in sexology, medico-moral practice, legal enactments and personal life. A single narrative was challenged, to be replaced by a number of new narratives, many by those hitherto disqualified by the would-be science of sex. If the hall-mark of the nineteenth century pioneers of sex reform and science was a belief in the efficacy of science and the revelation of the laws of nature, the characteristic note of modern sexual activists is self-activity, self-making, the questioning of received truths, the contestation of laws which elevate some and exclude others. Scientific sexology has been challenged by a grass-roots sexology; reform from above by community organization from below; and a single narrative of sexual enlightenment by a host of separate histories, from women, lesbians and gays, racial minorities and others. So where does that leave the relationship between desire and identity? Locked into, I suggest, a series of paradoxes.

THE PARADOXES OF IDENTITIES

Identities are troubling because they embody so many paradoxes: about what we have in common, and what separates us, about our sense of self and our recognition of others, about conflicting belongings in a changing history and a complex modern world, and about the possibility of social action in and through our identities. And few identities are so paradoxical as sexual identities. Sexual identities have a special place in the discourse of identity. They are like relay points for a number of interconnected differences, conflicts and opportunities. For the past few centuries, at least, sex has been central to the fixing of the individual's place in the culture, offering, in Foucault's famous phrase, the "truth of our being."

But it has not only been a categorization and placing for a *sexual* identity (as normal or pervert, heterosexual or homosexual, or whatever), but for a whole set of social positionings. Concepts of national identity have been intricately bound up with notions of appropriate gendered or sexualized behavior. The injunctions of imperial propagandists to the young innocent to "be a man" and eschew masturbation, homosexuality or nameless other secret sins; or to embody motherhood and purity for the sake of the race: such ascribed identities brought together race, gender and sexuality into a potent brew which locked normality and sexuality into a fixed hierarchy that few could escape, even if not so many lived up to it. The settling of class identities in the first wave of industrialization in the nineteenth century also froze the fluidity of gender differences and sexual behavior. "Respectability" betokened more than a middle-class modesty and discretion; it became a way of life where sexual desire and gendered activity was regulated by approved and approvable behavior. Alfred Kinsey in the 1940s was not the first, nor the last, to notice the distinct class accents to human sexual behaviour. And the generation of a "Western identity," with its distinct sexual classifications and typologies, in turn depended upon the identification of the colonized of the world as distinctly "other," more primitive, more priapic or blatant, and certainly less "civilized," which in turn served to confirm "our" superiority, and the truth of "our" sexualities.

Sexuality is woven into the web of all our identities, which is why the emergence over the past two hundred years, and in a rush since the 1960s, of alternative or oppositional sexualized identities, lesbian and gay, "queer," bisexual, transvestite and transsexual, sadomasochistic—an exotic parade from the catalogues of sexology, dancing into history with a potentially infinite series of scripts and choreographies—is so unsettling to sexual conservatives of all political colors: such identities breach boundaries, disrupt order, and call into question the fixity of inherited identities of all kinds, not just the sexual. Which is also why, no doubt, identities are also so problematic for those

committed to sexual change: if we assert them too firmly are we fixing identifications and values that are really necessarily always in flux; and if we deny
their validity too completely, are we disempowering ourselves from the best
means of mobilizing for radical change?

Let's look a little more closely at some of the paradoxes embodied in
identity.

*Paradox 1: Sexual identity assumes fixity and uniformity while confirming the
reality of unfixity, diversity and difference.*
We like to say who we are by telling of our sex: "I am gay/straight"; "I am
male/female." It places us securely in recognized discourses, embodying
assumptions, beliefs, practices and codes of behavior. Yet the truth is rather
more complex. "Possibility and many-sidedness," Rosenblum has argued,
"are built into the very idea of identity formation" (Rosenblum 1987:149).
This is especially true of sexual identities. Academically, theoretically, we
increasingly recognize both the diverse desires, needs and passions of individuals and the diversity of (often conflicting) social obligations and belonging,
pulling us in a variety of directions. Yet we fear the uncertainty, the abyss,
the unknown, the threat of dissolution that not having a fixed identity
entails. So we try to fix identities, by asserting what we are now is what we
have really, truly always been, if only we had known.

But consider the realities. We all know life-long heterosexuals who
suddenly come out as lesbian or gay. We know self-identified gays who
equally suddenly opt for a heterosexual lifestyle. Which is more true to the
essential person? In her book on cross-dressing, *Vested Interests*, Marjorie
Garber tells us of the spokesperson for the International Foundation for
Gender Education, one Yvonne Cook. Yvonne is a biological male who
cross-dresses, and identifies as a woman, as a lesbian. She dates a biological
woman who cross-dresses as a man (see Garber 1992). Which label corresponds to the real her—or him? Here sexual identities seem endlessly fluid,
taken up and used rather than realized, a glittering performance or complicated game rather than a truth claim, unless we allow the argument that all
truth claims are simply games about truth.

Since the nineteenth century, the placing of individuals into clearly
demarcated sexual categories, and hence identities, has gone hand in hand
with the presentation of plentiful evidence detailing the fluidity and uncertainty of desire. The binary divisions we take for granted, between men and
women, heterosexual and homosexual, normal and perverse, provide barriers against, in the words of Epstein and Straub, "the uncontrollable elasticity
and terrifying lack of boundaries within or between bodies" (see Epstein
and Straub 1992). They simplify the complexity of desires, they order the

potential multiplicity of our identifications. But those barriers are fragile, inadequate blocks to the flux of contemporary life. The repressed always returns, sometimes in distorted and damaging ways (such as the homophobia of the "repressed homosexual"), sometimes, and hopefully these days more often than in the past, in liberating and creative ways, in the elective communities where oppositional sexual identities, at least, are forged and confirmed. Then identities can become genuinely enabling. Yet, I would argue, they are still only ever provisional. We can put on a good performance with them. But we should never believe they are final, or embody some unique truth about ourselves. "Unfixity," write Laclau and Mouffe, "has become the condition of every social identity"—and especially, I would add, of every sexual identity (see Laclau and Mouffe 1985:85).

Paradox 2: Identities are deeply personal but tell us about multiple social belongings
All cultures seem to depend on their members having a secure sense of self, and a placing in the order of things. But there is no reason to think that the modern individual is a reflex product of his or her "instincts." "The unity of a human life," suggests Alasdair MacIntyre, "is the unity of a narrative quest" (MacIntyre 1985:219). Self-identity, at the heart of which is sexual identity, is not something that is given as a result of the continuities of an individual's life or of the fixity and force of his or her desires. It is something that has to be worked on, invented and reinvented in accord with the changing rhythms, demands, opportunities and closures of a complex world. The modern self, as Giddens argues, is a reflexive project, made and remade by the person in terms of his or her biographical experiences (see Giddens 1991:52–3). It is not an all or nothing phenomenon; the real question we need to ask is: am I more or less the same person today as I was ten years ago? (see MacIntyre 1984:139). The answer cannot be given *a priori*; it depends on the effectiveness of the biographical narratives we construct for ourselves in a turbulent world; on our ability to keep a particular narrative going.

We apparently need a sense of the essential self to provide a grounding for our actions, to ward off existential fear and anxiety and to provide a spring-board for action. So we write into our personal narratives the elements which confirm what we say we are. And here our bodily feelings and presence become central. In a world of apparently constant flux, where the fixed points keep moving or dissolving, we hold onto what seems most tangible, the truth of our bodily needs and desires, or, in the age of AIDS, our vulner-abilities. It is not surprising that the making and re-making of the body then becomes so basic to our assertion of identities. We worry about its health and the forces that can undermine it (smoking in relative private becomes more tabooed than having sex in public; our cholesterol levels more important than our protein intake); we run and work-out to ward off its infirmity and temporality (even as we collapse from exhaustion, sore feet, or painful muscles); we adorn it in clothes that affirm our sense of individuality (but which also provide a badge of our belonging to one sub-group or another; or our enslavement to the whims of the market place); we assert the imperatives of its desires and potentiality for pleasure (though they as often wrack us with their contradictory messages as confirm a single bodily truth.) For the body is seen as the final court of judgement on what we are or can become. Why else are we so worried if sexual desires, whether homosexual or heterosexual, are inborn or acquired? For what other reason are we so concerned whether gendered behavior corresponds with physical attributes? Only because everything else is so uncertain do we need the judgement that our bodies apparently dictate.

Of course, the fact of different bodies matters; on the physiological differences of biological men and women have been built an empire of division. But the body is a fickle master or mistress: its needs change; it falls prey to want or plenty, to sickness and physical decay; its sources of pleasures can be transformed, whether through chance, training, physical alteration, mental control—or, increasingly, the demands of a new regime of "safer-sex." Even the apparently most decisive of differences between biological men and women, reproductive capacity, is now subject to major medical intervention and potential manipulation. The body is no more immune to the power of culture, and its transforming possibilities, than our mental attitudes or social identifications. The body, as Giddens suggests, "in late modernity becomes increasingly socialised and drawn into the reflexive organization of social life" (Giddens 1991:198). So we use the body as the focus of our sense of biographical continuity, whilst implicitly acknowledging our social belongings and cultural baggage.

The sexual persona, like the whole personality, is, in Connell's phrase, a social practice when seen from the perspective of the life history (see Connell 1987:220), but the sources of that personal history are inevitably cultural. The socio-sexual identities we adopt, inhabit and adapt work insofar as they order and give meaning to individual needs and desires, but they are not emanations of those needs and desires. Indeed, they have no necessary connection at all to the contingencies of the body. The sources of the narratives that keep us going, that make sense of our individual peculiarities, are deeply historical, dependent on social bonds that provide the map for personal meaning and cultural identification. And those bonds are multiple: we come from different nations, classes, statuses, religions, racial and ethnic groupings, different genders and generations and geographical areas, each of which contains a sliver of experience, a residue of a personal history, which we try to integrate into our personal biographies, in order to shape our individual identity. Sexual identity involves a perpetual invention and reinvention, but on ground fought over by many histories.

Paradox 3: Sexual identities are simultaneously historical and contingent.
There is now plentiful historical evidence to sustain the statement that whilst heterosexual and homosexual (and many other sexual) practices may always have existed, clearly demarcated categories and identities of "the heterosexual" or "the homosexual" are of very recent provenance.

The idea that sexual identities are not simple expressions of bodily truth but are historical phenomena—and therefore constantly changing—is itself a relatively recent one, pioneered largely by feminist and lesbian and gay scholars. Its orgins were, then, largely political, demonstrating the historicity and potential ephemerality of the categories we take for granted as natural and inevitable, even as their power was acknowledged. Behind this position is a clear assumption that, as Laclau puts it, "the constitution of a social identity is an act of power and that identity as such is power" (Laclau 1990:30). Sexual identities embody power relations, rooted in many histories.

We still know more about the constitution of Western homosexual identities over the past few hundred years than about any other form of sexual identity, particularly the overarching categorization of heterosexuality and heterosexual identities. Nor is this surprising, for the dominant or hegemonic form of any social position becomes the given, the taken for granted, part of the air we breathe, from which everything else becomes a deviation at best or a perversion at worst. As such everything else tends to escape thorough investigation—though this is now changing. We are increasingly accustomed to seeing sexuality as a spectrum along which lie many potential sexual desires and many different identities. But that easy pluralism obscures the fact that historically, sexual identities have been organized into violent hierachies, where some positions are marked as superior (more natural, healthier, more true to the body than others.) The shaping of a distinctive categorization of "the homosexual" over the past century or so has been an act of power, whose effect, intended or not, has been to reinforce the normality of heterosexuality. As Eve Sedgwick has put it:

> The importance—an importance—of the category "homosexual". . .comes not necessarily from its regulatory relation to a nascent or already constituted minority of homosexual people or desires, but from its potential for giving whoever wields it a structuring definitional leverage. . .(Sedgwick 1985:86)

The emergence since the eighteenth century, she subsequently argues, of an institutionalized homophobia and homosexual panic, brutally separates men from men, but, more crucially, serves to confirm and consolidate male (heterosexual) power not only over other men but over women, for:

> the domination offered by the strategy is not only over a minority popula-tion, but over the bonds that structure all social form. (Sedgwick 1985:87)

In other words, the apparently neutral description of men as either homosexual or heterosexual since the nineteenth century conceals the intri-cate play of power, of domination and subordination, which minoritizes the homosexual experience, and consolidates male power in a new, effective pattern. In the same fashion, it has been argued, the categorization, in psychology, sexology and a variety of other social practices, of some women as homosexual and others as very definitely not, breaks the continuum of all women, and hence serves further to consolidate the sexual power of men.

The fact that such arguments are still not only controversial in themselves but contested even as a starting point for debate is a testimony to the power of the categories that have become sedimented in our consciousness over the past century, and to our cultural preference for neat divisions of people and identities: you are either this or that. But the process of trying to divide people into heterosexual or homosexual groups has been a complex one, and one that is, in Eve Sedgwick's phrase, still "radically incomplete" (Sedgwick 1990:159). There are two related points that must be made here.

The first is that the discursive construction of categories of sexual subjects is a constant process, and involves a struggle over definitions on a sexual–polit-ical terrain that is ever-shifting. The agents of sexual regulation, whether states, churches or other institutions such as those of medicine or psycholgy, are involved in an effort of definition that is never-ending, and the reason for this is quite simply because sexual identities, including, perhaps especially, heterosexual ones, are profoundly unstable. Take two recent sexual–political events in, respectively, Britain and the United States. The notorious "Clause 28" of the British Local Government Act passed in 1988 banned the "promotion of homosexuality as a pretended family relationship" by local authorities. Whatever the political context in which it took place, its only rationale could have been an assumption that without such an act, the influ-ence of an activist lesbian and gay movement could radically overflow the boundaries between heterosexual and homosexual, to the detriment of the former (Weeks 1991). In the *Bowers v. Hardwick* decision by the USA Supreme Court in 1986, which denied the right to privacy to homosexuals, the court:

> not only set the Constitution's imprimatur on punishment of "homosexual sodomy" but equated that act with "homosexuality" and indeed with "homosexuals"—a group now not only defined but known by its sodomiti-cal essence. (Halley 1992:356)

Here, the legal decision went in a different direction from the British case, taking a radical step towards taking for granted an immutable homosexual essence, defined by particular sexual practices. But in both cases, despite the contrary arguments, the clear aim and intention was to delimit the rights and claims of the lesbian and gay minority—in the interests of sustaining a heterosexual value system that was seen as simultaneously natural and inevitable, and fragile and undermined by the homosexual experience.

The second point is that these categorizations and imposed defintions cannot and do not exhaust the actual lived experience of sexuality or the proliferation of oppositional identities. In the case of homosexuality, there is plentiful evidence that cultures of opposition, pleasure and self-identification were emerging prior to, and then against, the opprobrious categorizations that emerged in the law, medicine, sexology and so forth in the course of the nineteenth century. It is a characteristic of what Dollimore has called the "perverse dynamic" (Dollimore 1991:160) that a political and sexual ordering is always internally disordered by the very perversities it produces, and sets up against itself. The power to define may have set the limits on what could be said, done or spoken, but those apparently fixed by the definitions nevertheless produced their own resistances and identities. More recently, the emergence of a distinctive identity-politics around sexuality has articulated a growing recognition that the power to define oneself combines a multiplicity of powers and hierarchies, not only around gender and sexuality, but also around race and ethnicity, class and status, which in turn has produced new frontiers in sexual politics, and new forms of resistance. Sexual identities are enmeshed in relations of domination and subordination, where many histories intertwine.

Yet if histories (rather than History) and various forms of power relations (rather than a single Power) provide the context for sexual identities, our assumption of them is not determined by the past but by the contingencies, chances and opportunities of the historic present. As I have already suggested, there is no necessary relationship between a particular organization of desire and a social identity. Many people who practice various forms of homosexual activity fail to recognize themselves in labels such as homosexual, lesbian and gay, queer, or whatever the available identity is at any particular time, even in the West, where such descriptions and self-descriptions are hegemonic. In other parts of the world, homosexual practices, where they are not banned totally, are integrated into various patterns of relations, without giving rise to Western-style identities, though other forms of identity do, of course, exist. This has become particularly crucial in the age of AIDS.

It has sometimes been said that HIV and AIDS, in their spread across the world, tell the truth about identity, revealing in infection what is concealed in social life. But it is more accurate to say that HIV reveals the truth about often-concealed sexual activities. The assumption that evidence of certain practices reveals the prevalence of identities is not only a fallacy, but a dangerous one, when it comes to health and safer-sex education, because it assumes that people will recognize themselves in social identities that are peculiar to very specific parts of the world. (The development in AIDS work of a well-intentioned label of "men who have sex with men," is an attempt to recognize that existing labels do not exhaust homosexual activity, but compounds the problem by offering a social position that no one recognizes themselves in. Most men who have sex with other men, who refuse a gay self-description, probably see themselves as heterosexual.)

Available identities are taken up for a variety of reasons: because they make sense of individual experiences, because they give access to communities of meaning and support, because they are politically chosen. These identities can, however, equally be refused, precisely because they do not make sense to an individual, or because they have no cultural purchase.

Paradox 4: Sexual identities are fictions—but necessary fictions.
Sexual identities are historical inventions, which change in complex histories. They are imagined in contingent circumstances. They can be taken up and abandoned. To put it polemically, they are fictions. This is not, of course, how they are seen or experienced, or what we wish to believe. Worse, in the age of uncertainty which we are currently struggling through, to say this often seems a betrayal of what we need most desperately to hold on to; through an arid intellectualism which leaves minorities without hope, and the vulnerable defenseless. As HIV disease visibly and remorselessly spread in the male gay communities of the West from the early 1980s, it was the existence of strong lesbian and gay identities and communities which provided the essential context for combatting the virus, in providing social networks for support and campaigning, in developing a grammar for safer sex, in developing a language of resistence and survival. The homophobia which AIDS encouraged and, to some, justified, demanded, and in fact greatly strenghtened, lesbian and gay identities; without them, it often seemed in the embattled 1980s, there was nothing.

But to say that something is a historical fiction is not to denigrate it. On the contrary, it is simply to recognize that we cannot escape our histories, and that we need means to challenge their apparently iron laws and inexorabilities by imagining alternatives. Oppositional sexual identities, in particular, provide such means and alternatives, fictions that provide sources of comfort and support, a sense of belonging, a focus for opposition, a strategy for

survival and cultural and political challenge. A fictional view of identity does
two things. First of all it offers a critical view of all identities, demonstrating
their historicity and arbitrariness. It denaturalizes them, revealing the coils of
power that entangle them. It returns identities to the world of human beings,
revealing their openness and contingency.

Secondly, because of this, it makes human agency not only possible, but
also essential. For if sexual identities are made in history, and in relations of
power, they can also be re-made. Identities then can be seen as sites of
contestation. They multiply points of resistance and challenge, and expand
the potentialities for change. Identities, particularly those identities which
challenge the imposing ediface of Nature, History, Truth are a resource for
realizing human diversity. They provide means of realizing a progressive
individualism, our "potential for individualization" (Melucci 1989:48) and a
respect for difference. Myths, Frank Kermode has argued, are the agents of
stability, "fictions are the agents of change" (Kermode 1967:39).

From this perspective, the dominant (hetero)sexual identities in our
culture have some of the qualities of myths: they speak for an assumed natu-
ralness, eternity and truth which belie their historical and contingent nature.
The radical, oppositional identities which have arisen in and against the
hegemonic ones can be seen as fictions: they offer an imagined alternative
which provide the motivation and inspiration for change. In that sense, they
are not only fictions—they are necessary fictions. Without them we would
have no basis to explain our individual needs and desires, nor a sense of
collective belonging that provides the agency and means for change.

The danger is that these historical inventions, these fictional unities
become closed, the exclusive home of those who identify with them: "neo-
tribes" in Maffesoli's phrase. As such they can become barriers to change
themselves. But if their historicity, openness, flexibility—fictional qualities—
are acknowledged fully, they provide the opportunity for thinking not only
about who you are, but also about who you want to become. By making
power visible, they reveal the power relations that inhibit change. And once
we accept that sexuality takes its form from historically specific power relations, then it becomes possible to imagine new forms of desire which are not
blocked by a sense of powerlessness and inevitability. Oppositional sexual
identities provide vistas for a yet unimagined future. By interrogating and
challenging the normalizing and imposed forms of identity, it becomes
possible to explore the limits of subjectivity, to invent oneself in new ways.

Identities in this sense are less about expressing an essential truth about
our sexual being; they are more about mapping out different values: the
values of relationships, of belonging, of difference and diversity. They
provide continuous possibilities for invention and re-invention, open

processes through which change can happen. As Foucault put it, specifically referring to gay identities, but with a wider echo:

> There ought to be an inventiveness special to a situation like ours. . .We must think that what exists is far from filling all possible spaces. To make a truly unavoidable challenge to the question: what can we make work, what new game can we invent? (see Lotringer 1989:209)

That, of course, means that sexual identities are more than troubling on a personal level; they also cause trouble on a social level. I agree with Judith Butler's summing up of the paradox of identity:

> I'm permanently troubled by identity categories, consider them to be invariable stumble-blocks, and understand them, even promote them, as sites of necessary trouble. (see Butler 1991:14)

I want now to look at some of the trouble that sexual identities must necessarily cause, and the possible inventions that can take us into unchartered territory.

AUTONOMY AND SEXUAL CITIZENSHIP

"What to do? How to act? Who to be?": such questions, Giddens suggests, are focal for everyone living in circumstances of late modernity, and they presuppose choice where the possibilities are varied and diverse (Giddens 1991:70). "Choice" is a term that comes naturally to the postmodern person. And choice of lifestyles is central to radical sexual politics; choice to realize our sexual desire, choice in the pattern of sexual relationships, choice in our general ways of life. Increasingly the sexual world is made up of different ways of life, some cohabiting more or less equably, others in often violent conflict, a kaleidoscope of many colored forms of living, each expressing and sustaining different personal and cultural identities. Diversity appears to be the only truth about postmodern sexuality.

Sexual diversity provides the space for what John Stuart Mill in the last century called "experiments in living," and with such experiments come the possibility of expanding further the range of choice and the potentialities of different ways of living (Mill 1975:79). For a radical sexual ethos those practices can only be, in Foucault's term, "practices of freedom" (Foucault 1988:3). But what do such practices involve? Freedom for what?

To construct the self as a creative self, to allow the individual to become the artist of his or her life, in sexual as in other aspects of social existence: these provide the goals of a radical sexual politics. Such a position does not take for granted that these possibilities already exist. Instead it suggests the values by which we can critique the normative and restrictive systems that do exist, and the potentialities that can be realized if the barriers were to be removed. Sexual autonomy is not a description of what exists; it is an aspiration which we can progressively move towards, if never fully achieve.

Autonomy in this sense is a private and personal goal. It demands an impartiality and fairness in the acceptance of individual choices. It assumes a right for the individual to make certain personal choices. And it offers a goal for personal development. For Rorty, that privatization of goals is not only necessary but sufficient: "The vocabulary of self-creation is necessarily private, unshared, unsuited to argument" (Rorty 1989:xiv). The enhancement and protection of privacy, especially with regard to sexual matters, is indeed a desirable aim, but to see that as enough is inadequate. It ignores the social context in which the private and the self is always constructed, and the cultural and political consequences of arguing for individual autonomy and choice in a world still enshrouded in moralistic endeavors (Shusterman 1988:333).

The goal of autonomy and choice therefore presupposes a more public project. Individual life, as Rorty (1989:43) acknowledges, is a constant reweaving of a web of relations, which are deeply social, and it is only in and through social involvements that autonomy can be realized.

The social movements concerned with sexuality that have emerged since the 1960s, the feminist and lesbian and gay movements especially, assume that it is though social involvment and collective action that individualty can be realized. The new movements can be interpreted as a revolt against the forms of subjectification that the contemporary world has given rise to, a challenge to the technologies of power which, by defining individuals in particular ways, pin them to particular, subordinated identities and locations in society. Such movements reveal the complexity of modern social relations, and the intractability of the contradictions and tensions these give rise to.

These movements are clearly not expressing a pre-existing essence of social being. Identities and belongings are being constructed in the very process of organization itself. But the political language that has developed, the language of community, is one resonant with history and meaning.

By definition, communities are not fixed once and for all. They change as the arguments over time continue, and as other communities exercise their gravitational pull. But, at the same time, the social relations of a community are repositories of meaning for its members, not sets of mechanical linkages between isolated individuals (Cohen 1986:98). A community offers a "vocabulary of values" through which individuals construct their understanding of the social world, and of their sense of identity and belonging (Cohen 1986:114). Communities provide embeddedness in a world which seems constantly on the verge of fragmentation.

But if community is constitutive, it is also imagined. The idea of community has different meanings for its members, depending on their own outlooks, experiences, and allegiances. It is the idea of the community itself, whether a village, an ethnic group, a religious affiliation, a sexual minority, that is the true integrative element.

A sexual community, then, has the potential to go beyond the limits of what is; it provides an agenda for other ways of being. Community stands for some notion of solidarity, a solidarity which empowers and enables, and makes individual and social action possible. The sexual movements of recent years have both encouraged and built on a sense of community, a space where hitherto execrated sexual activity and identities have been affirmed and sustained. Such a validation of community has been at the center of the response to HIV and AIDS by the group most affected in the west, gay men. It has made possible a social and cultural response whose aim, in Richard Goldstein's words, is "to promote survival, demand attention, and defeat stigma" (Goldstein 1991:37). As Watney has argued, it is also a sense of belonging to some kind of community "that will always determine the development of a resilient sense of self-esteem which is demonstrably the sine qua non of safer sex education" (Watney 1991:13). The absence of a sense of community around sexual issues amongst other groups affected by the epidemic has been a critical factor in limiting the development of a culture of safer sex and personal responsibility. (And it worth noting that it is only in the wake of the AIDS crisis that the term "heterosexual community" has come into use; a term defined more by its absence of meaning than by its resonant social presence.)

"Sexual dissidence," to use Jonathan Dollimore's phrase, is ultimately dependent upon the growth of that sense of common purpose and solidarity represented by the term community. With the development of a sexual movement with a sense of its own history and social role, the idea of community becomes a critical norm through which alternatives are opened up.

It makes possible, in the first place, acts of transgressive subversion. Transgression, the breaching of boundaries, the pushing of experience to the limits, the challenge to the Law, whatever it is, is a crucial moment in any radical sexual project. As an individual act it speaks of a self obscured by an ignoble sexual order. For many, this act of defiance is the expression of a buried truth. It would be difficult, argues Dollimore, "to overestimate the importance in modern Western culture of transgression in the name of an essential sense which is the origin and arbiter of the 'true,' the real (and/or natural). . ." (Dollimore 1991:39). But even when the social origins of identities and the complexities of desire are recognized, the living out of individual acts of defiance can challenge the status quo. As Garber says, one of the most important aspects of cross-dressing "is the way in which it offers a challenge to easy notions of binarity, putting into question the categories of 'female' and 'male'. . ." (Garber 1992:10). In the same way, the appearance of self-affirming groups of militant lesbians or gay men in the 1970s disrupted expectations of the natural order of heterosexuality.

The difficulty with transgression, however, is that the limits are always flexible and changing. At one time, it seemed transgressive to be open about one's homosexuality. Today, in many circles, people are more shocked to hear that a self-declared lesbian or gay man is having a heterosexual affair. In an age when Madonna's recycling of well-worn sado-masochistic iconography sells millions of copies through mainstream publishers, it is difficult to believe that any individual act in itself will shock. What matters more are the critical elements and the alternatives spelled out in the transgressive transactions, the new niches of possibility that appear, and these depend on the changing social geography of sexuality.

As Teresa de Lauretis argues, homosexuality today:

> is no longer to be seen simply as marginal with regard to a dominant, stable form of sexuality. . .it is no longer to be seen as merely transgressive or deviant vis à vis a proper natural sexuality. . .according to the older pathological model, or as just another optional "lifestyle," according to the model of North American pluralism. Instead, male and female homosexualities. . .may be reconceptualized as sexual and cultural forms in their own right, albeit emergent ones and thus still fuzzily defined, undercoded, or discursively dependent on more established forms. (de Lauretis 1991:iii)

But though the alternative sexual and cultural forms may be notoriously fuzzy, and highly contested within and without, the perverse and transgressive dynamic is still at play, though now not simply as an individual act of subversion but as a collective activity. Witness as evidence of this the appearence in the early 1990s within the lesbian and gay communities of North America and elsewhere of the idea of a new "queer politics":

> A new generation of activists is here. They have come out into communities devastated by the HIV epidemic and into political consciousness through the struggle around AIDS. But AIDS is not their main focus. . .The new generation calls itself queer, not lesbian, gay and bisexual—awkward, narrow and perhaps compromised words. Queer is meant to be confrontational—opposed to gay assimilationists and straight oppressors while inclusive of people who have been marginalized by anyone in power. . .(Berube and Escoffier 1991:12)

Just as the widespread adoption of the term "gay" in the late 1960s betokened a rejection of the cautious, adaptive and what appeared to the new activists as the apologetic style of the old homophile movement, so the new queer politics signals a break with the minoritizing and integrationist strategies of the lesbian and gay politics of the 1970s and 1980s—ironically at the very moment when that politics was successfully breaking into the mainstream:

> The queers are constructing a new culture by combining elements that usually don't go together. They may be the first wave of activists to embrace the retrofuture/classic contemporary styles of postmodernism. They are building their own identity from old and new elements— borrowing styles and tactics from popular culture, communities of color, hippies, AIDS activists, the antinuclear movement, MTV, feminists and early gay liberationists. Their new culture is slick, quick, anarchic, transgressive, ironic. They are deadly serious but they wanna have fun. (Berube and Escoffier 1991:14)

Like their forebearers in the radical sexual politics of the 1970s, there is a dual movement at work: the construction of a new identity, with all the characteristic paradox of asserting similarity and difference, and a challenge to rigid categorizations, by embracing all who would identify with the new politics, whatever their previous sexual identities, preferences, or activities.

Queer politics has all the defects of a contestatory style: although it seeks to deconstruct old rigidities, it creates new boundaries; although it is deliberately transgressive, it enacts its dissidence through the adoption of a descriptive label which many lesbian and gays find offensive, often seeking enemies within as much as enemies without. Despite this, it is an important phenomenon not only because of what it says or does, but because it is a reminder of the perpetual inventiveness of a collective sexual politics which stretches towards alternative ways of being. Whatever one thinks of it, it illustrates the continuing construction of identities and a sense of community which transcends old certainties and divisions, whilst challenging the epistemology of sexuality itself:

> Queer culture and politics herald a lesbian and gay sexuality that is SEXUAL, SEXY and SUBVERSIVE—not only of heterosexist notions of being, but of former lesbian and gay orthodoxies. . .Queer promises a refusal to assimilate into invisibility. It provides a way of asserting desires that shatter gender identities and sexualities. . .(Smyth 1992:59-60)

This is a mode of politics that is simultaneously deconstructive (contesting what is as arbitrary and restrictive), and reconstructive (asserting the validity of desires and ways of being that have been ignored or denied). But as we know only too well, different ways of life frequently come into conflict with one another. How can we live with difference, with choice, without threatening to obliterate the pluralism on which difference and choice are based?

This is the key question of sexual politics (as indeed of other forms of politics) today. The establishment of a norm (as opposed to a reluctant acceptance) of pluralism and diversity demands further normative guidelines or principles. This requires that respect for "otherness" is brought within the bounds of validity, and becomes a norm itself. Desire is multi-faceted, contradictory, subversive: its inevitable social organization requires that we are engaged in a continuous conversation about both its possibilities and limits.

Framing Preferences, Framing Differences

3

Inventing Amsterdam as a Gay Capital

Mattias Duyves

> Sexual conduct of all kinds, no matter how studied, has to be understood as
> local phenomena (Gagnon 1990)

APPARENTLY MY MOTHER'S GRAND THEORY OF HOMOSEXUAL DESIRE
was that dirty men and innocent boys meet at twilight time in twilight
zones. She wanted me to stay away at night from the park that was "melting
in the dark" behind our building, ignorant of men's meetings under a starry
ceiling of spot-lights in the toilets of a prestigious department-store. A
gentleman welcomed me to this unpromised land of pleasures with his
personal theory "that there you get to see first what you get to see last in
other circumstances." Lately on the gay radio, in a program on week-
ending, I happened to hear him theorizing that "desire makes everything
else circumstancial."

Everything but space maybe. Urban space facilitates the civic culture of
desire among men more than any other environment known in Western
culture. The urbanization of desire is a crucial element in the formation of
gay life. In this paper I will focus on the role of urban space in gay culture.
In the first section, I will develop a social theory of the use of space for the
expression and regulation of desire. In the second part, I will describe the
image and meaning of Amsterdam as a gay capital.

I

The mysteries and mechanisms of sexual desire have constantly been
sources for social theories which, in turn, serve as sources for the formation
and transformation of desire in society. The multiplication and fragmentation of theories is considerable. In early modern Europe (1450–1850) the
basic elements of sexual theories was kept within the dotted lines of two
partly incongruent value-systems, Christianity and Enlightenment.
Abundant evidence delineates a flow of deterministic and restrictive views
against the unnatural differentiation of desire. Its leading versions cut down

desire to sound passions, identities, objectives and manifestations (see Leibbrand and Wettley 1972; Hekma 1987). How sweeping the imaginations and the consequences, the old and the new, in thinking passion was basically straight, and closely intertwined with each other.

Viewed in retrospect, early modern life was exposed to a *shortage* of theories capable of encompassing the emerging diversity of desire. The relatively small sample has stretched, by development, accumulation, differentiation and specialization, into a wider range of theories. A general condition of post-modernity is that too *many* of them are circulating at once to be able to grab desire's diversities. A flood of differing, open-ended, loose ideas on the modernity and identity of desire can be as confusing as a lack of flexible concepts and perceptions. The social worlds of the flesh have almost induced a richer variety of doctrines than of desires—possibly, for the comfort of our senses, with the mythical exception of passionate Brazil (see Parker 1991; Rabinow 1992).

Public and private ignorance of the variety of sensual preferences has decreased drastically, while confusion on the diversity of theories and concepts has increased. The early-modern type of innocence (perforce not knowing what you don't know) has turned into its modern and postmodern versions (just knowing by choice what you know and just knowing what you don't know). Social scientists have tried to overcome the epistemological tensions between biodynamic and sociodynamic designs of desire in a growing debate on essentialism and constructionism. The dispute has factorized the ideological dominance of sexual nature over social nurture. In addition it has generated a range of social constructionisms probing into the sources and spectacles of sexual desire (see, for example, Aldrich 1992; Duyves 1986; Gagnon and Simon 1973; Gagnon 1990; Greenberg 1988; Stein 1990; Vance 1991, 1991; Weeks 1991).

At present, constructionist studies cover a wide range of social and cultural responses concerning sexual differences and preferences. Yet it is striking that in the vast majority of constructionist theory, spatial scenarios of desire have hardly been inserted. The making of desire in the cockpit of the mind, in the shell of time, and in the hull of nature have been faced more succesfully than the framing of desire in space. Neither the use of space due to sexual preferences nor the manifestations of such preferences due to space figure frequently in sex research. The sexology of spaces and geographies of desire limp far behind philosophical, anthropological, historical, psychological and sociological outgrowths in scripting theory and constructionism. Spatial theory and sexual scripting theory have barely touched each other, although the social organization of sexual culture and the use of space frequently overlap.

Spatial scenarios and place-scripts based on sexual imagination—in other words, spatial situations that call for sexual responses—are central in a spatial theory designed by the British–Canadian sociologist Rob Shields (1991). He introduces the concept of *social spatialization* in order "to designate the ongoing social construction of the spatial (which is a formation of both discursive and non-discursive elements, practices, and processes) at the level of the social imaginary (collective mythologies, presuppositions) as well as interventions in the landscape (for example, the built environment)" (Shields 1991:7).

To a degree, Shields' conceptualization of space seems to fit in with Gagnon's scripting perspective or Foucault's discursive approach. However, Shields critizes the French cartography of power as culturally determinist, namely spatially behavioristic, because it lacks a theory on the individual constitution of spatial preferences and decisions. Shields' discussion of the spatial scripting of conduct analyzes the construction of *place-images* which convert places into "places for" (Shields 1991). Place-images can script any place anywhere into a "place for"; once place-images overwhelm the impression of a place, they give life to a *place-myth*. A place with many conflicting place-myths makes up a spatial mythology or cosmology which, together with *local routines* (sleeping, working, listening, negotiating or anything else) and *spatial divisions,* induces a *sense of place.* A collective sense of place awakens an emotional topography of invented spaces and imagined communities and even incites a *regime of space.*

Examples of the coercive construction of *imaginary geographies* (see Shields 1991) range from microspatial conduct in elevators to spatial affinities in bohemia or suburbia and macrospatial relations at the level of the nation-state. Spatial worlds can become social worlds because of social spatialization, or the other way around, social worlds can become spatial worlds with the help of imaginary geographies.[1] Social spatialization results in the (dis)appearance of places for imagined communities based on the use of physical and/or imaginary space. Shields then designates *how* spatial scenarios script order and action in places and spaces by means of simplification, stereotyping and labelling (respective reduction of a place to just one place-image: the Dark continent, the Far East; enlargement of its place-image to a place-myth: Lotus Land, Shangri-la, Waterloo, the Promised Land, the Evil Empire; and earmarking of its imaginary geography: the Iron Curtain, the Equator).

Shields' spatial constructionism, which he calls a cultural geography, based on the scenario of social spatialization, prepares a wide understanding of the relationship between spatial culture and cultural spaces for desire. His concept of spatialization, unlike other concepts in spatial thinking (habitus, superstructure, objective social forces), points to all spatial relations that arise around a social phenomenon: the imaginary, emotional and intimate sides of spatial experiences as well as their objective, historic and public sides. It pushes the imaginary aspects of spatial culture and the material aspects of spatial control together in a way that allows differences between these features, but also smoothes them over.

Shields's cultural geography makes research into the spatialization of sexual culture as promising as attention to its social, historical, political and ethical scripts has already turned out to be. Sexual order and action make a societal phenomenon which is mind- and time- but also place- and space-related. In the theory of the social spatialization of sexual culture, in particular, of the urbanization of sexual preferences, is a tentative collection of concepts which on the one hand refers to use of space as source of sexual culture and, on the other hand, to sexual culture as source of spatial culture. The idea places the relationship between spatial culture and sexual preferences at the center of attention.

Up until now sexual preference has been, in the first place, an intimate individual characteristic to which rarely any notice is given in spatial studies. This blind spot coincides with the chaotic situation in which "the contemporary study of homosexuality, bisexuality and heterosexuality, or more generally sexual orientation or sexual preference is in a muddled state" (Gagnon 1990). It is a variable about which hardly any notion existed a century ago. The modern notion of sexual preferences has emerged bit by bit only since its very first indication in 1869 as a side-issue of the Germans' political unification of the moral law (see Herzer 1985). But the position of this idea is, at this moment, also far from complete. Sexual preference has principally been scripted as a source of erotic experience and intimacy in private.

The great privatization of sexual preference has not made the confusion about its public content and context disappear. Sexual preferences are certainly not only a source of sexual choices and activities but also of social impressions, relations, divisions, and pursuits. Cultivation of one's own and others' sexual preferences is a downright individual attribute, but also a throughly sociocultural phenomenon. Far outside the scope of personal life, it can be a source of public happenings, societal adventures and spatial relations. It is a basis of both sexuality and of a sociality that shows itself in public in the shape of a social world of preference—a spatial world according to the one's and others' sexual preferences.[2]

Only in the past few decades has the source of gay life and gay worlds been sought in the social construction of sexual preferences. The spatialization of preferences forms a combined frame of reference for the spatial location of gay life and heterosexual life in the local environment. In his own study of a seaside town and of a tourist resort, Shields has shown how social spatialization of heterosexual preferences runs through their history and their geography like an artery. As Brighton became England's national center of adultery with malice aforethought, Niagara Falls in North-America went from a destination for newly-weds to a destination for misconduct, and ended up being a premarital holiday resort (see Shields 1991).

The spatialization of sex also leaves its mark on the local impetuousness of Amsterdam; in the cultural geography of Amsterdam's public heterosexual life, the "Wallen" area stands out at once because most spatial relations in this Red Light District address straight preferences (see Ashworth, White, and Winchester 1988). The spatial relations that have been established around homosexual preference in Amsterdam have led to an imaginary geography of the city as "gay capital of Europe," an imaginary accepted in both local and international gay life. The urbanization of gay life has produced its own array of meanings which contribute to the image and meaning of Amsterdam. A cultural geography, framed by the relation between space and desire, provides the groundwork for a review of the role of urban space in the formation and transformation of desire among men.

II

Self-perception and self-expression of gay life in Amsterdan has produced slogans such as "The why-not city," "Amsterdam has it!," "Amsterdam gay capital of Europe" and "the world of your preference in the city of your preference." But do these spatial images really coincide with local circumstances? Is this spatial representation founded on the local reality of Amsterdam gay life or only on the abundant imagination of brokers in tourist traffic? In 1992 the city's tourism industry suddenly started extolling Amsterdam abroad as "gay capital of Europe" (Duyves 1992). Not because the desired response was not forthcoming, but because there was some commotion in their own ranks about the reputation of the city, the sponsors, the Amsterdam Tourist Information Office and the Dutch Bureau for Tourism, have since put the promotion on the back burner (Verkerk 1993; De Jong 1993). The management feared counterreactions—a premature phantom, considering the scale of realization of the project. There is also another reason why the campaign has been less successful. Amsterdam's position as gay center in Europe is still as shadowy as ever. This next section would like to change that.

The volume, density and heterogeneity of gay life in Amsterdam are higher than elsewhere in the Netherlands. Oppression and discrimination in rural areas are often recognized as an absolute frame of reference for the unequal spatial dispersal of Dutch gay life. Due to such pressure, only metropolitan life, with it's bustle, variegation and easygoing atmosphere, would leave room for the cultivation of latent and manifest gay life. This functionalistic view considers the emergence of a local gay world as spatial counterpoint or resistance to the surrounding oppression. This relationship between gay life and urban life echoes through spatial metaphors like "gay ghetto Amsterdam," "gay underground" and "the pink lining of obscure Amsterdam" (Hekma et al. 1992). The underlying thought is that without discrimination there would be no need for such a protected environment.

The wane of discrimination against gays in the Netherlands since the 1960s has, however, created room for new manifestations and ramifications of urban gay life. Amsterdam has gained a more emancipated gay life, which is well integrated and highly specialized. This transformation teaches that oppression and discrimination are not the fundamental basis of gay life, but at most the sources of the shadowy manner in which it has announced itself for centuries. Also not a fundamental source, the recent emancipation is rather a circumstance in which gay life in the whole country can take different courses. Gay discrimination and emancipation are not so much the basic causative sources of urban gay life, as conditions in the spatialization of sexual preferences.

The various manifestations of Amsterdam gay life differ thoroughly in character and development. They are at first sight a hotch-potch of formal, informal, latent, manifest, material, imaginary and other dissimilar functions. Together they form an urban system in which gay life benefits from the city as much as the city benefits from gay life. The image of a gay capital is a compelling metaphor for its spatial formation. Its imaginary contours are evoked due to the interplay of living urban relations found by gay preferences. It contains five major components: street culture; clientele culture; community cultures; event culture; and promotion culture. Each of these components I will sketch out briefly.

The oldest form of Amsterdam gay life is *streetlife*. In 1689 the names of four men were taken who were blackmailing cruising men in the neighbourhood of the Dam and the Old Bridge. So the very first name we have of a man involved in cruising in Amsterdam, Jacob Brouwer, belongs to a waylayer, instead of a lover, of men. This is the earliest lead to homosexual streetculture that has been found in Amsterdam (Meer 1988). In other words: gay life was born in the streets. That aspect has never been lost completely. Amsterdam's public spaces still know such meeting-places and erotic rendezvous as street benches, quays, public gardens, parks and recreational areas.

It is the case though, that the use of public space for gay purposes has in some ways changed strongly during the last three centuries. The range of

gay streetlife has not remained limited to the old inner-city. The spatial
hierarchy of gay streetlife acknowledges centers and a periphery. The
centers are situated in the inner-city. They are scattered at the edge of four
areas of night-time economy where the bright lights and the dark lanterns
burn (Oude Kerksplein, Rembrandtsplein, Leidseplein and
Reguliersdwarsstraat). Here gay streetlife does not focus on secret, open-air
sex anymore, but on hanging about boisterously on the pavement or the
terraces of gay pubs.

The use of public space has changed considerably since the 1960s.
Clandestine gay streetlife has made way for social and ceremonial use of
center space. Gay life is no longer only hiding but also striking; and it
nowadays addresses mutual contact within the gay population as well as
social contact with other sections of the population. Of the over fifty covert
meeting-places known from streetlife in the 1950s, there were only two left
in 1991. After gay protests against the removal of a third one, the city council replaced it in full glory in 1990, but men are not reported to have found
their way to it again (see Duyves 1992, 1993; Arnoldussen 1993). ("Where
have all the sissies gone?," one wonders.) As for the city center, the devotees
of gay streetlife have moved their erotic outdoor pursuits to meeting-places
indoors, to city parks outside the center and to remnant areas and recreational areas on the edge of town (see Maatman and Meijer 1993). The
transformation of the traditional use pattern of public space for sexual
purposes results from a decrease of street opportunity in the inner city and
the increase of bars with dark rooms, private homes (no more landladies
anymore) and private cars (allowing a decentralization and deconcentration
of mating-grounds.)

The gay use of the city center received totally new emphasis from about
1970. After the general introduction of happenings, extra-parliamentary
campaigns and street theater in the 1960s (a metamorphosis of Dutch public
life in which Amsterdam led the way), there followed an activistic use of
space by local gay movements in the seventies. After some gay dance-ins in
the streets at the end of the 1960s, the first gay demonstration took place on
Dam Square at the National Commemoration of the Dead on May 4th in
1970 and led to a two-day street riot (see Tielman 1982; Koenders 1987).
The erection of the national Gay Monument on the Westermarkt in 1987,
the official naming of certain streets after certain gay heroes, yearly street
events such as the "Pink Wester Festival" on the Queen's birthday and a
recurrent street gala in September mark recent folkloristic street relations
between gay and urban life. Use, care and dress-up of public space on behalf
of gay life are a modest contribution to a local identity reflecting social space,
erotic meaning and life diversity (Young 1990).

A second spatial impact of Amsterdam's gay life on the city's urban system stems from the level of *gay amenities* there. The supply of services consists of a mixed economy of commercial, non-commercial and political agencies: enterprises, foundations, associations and links with authorities. Gay commercial activity is concentrated in a leisure oriented retail and service trade (male underwear, hairdressers, postcard-shops) and the hotel and catering industry. The most visible institution is the pub or bar. (The oldest known gay pubs, dating from eighteenth century Amsterdam, no longer exist.)

The still-open pub called "De Huyschkamer" (The Living-room) was a beerhouse frequented by sodomites at the end of the nineteenth century just like it is now, but this was not the case for most of the twentieth century (Hekma 1982). Café "'t Mandje" (Little Basket) existed from 1927 until 1983. This was the first address with a regular gay clientele in twentieth century Amsterdam; presumably no pub in or outside Europe has been able to sustain this role as long as the Little Basket. At present, Café Monico, opened in 1941 in the Red Light District, is Amsterdam's oldest gay pub with the longest uninterrupted record. Even its founder, blond Sarah, has not left her post after all these years (Hekma 1992). Since 1927, Amsterdam has known over 350 different gay-oriented establishments (bars, small hotels, some restaurants). At the end of 1992, the municipal count was 120 gay-oriented addresses, of which more than one hundred were located in the city center.

The oldest non-commercial gay service institution is the COC, dating from 1948 with roots that go back to before the first world war. A new, separate law against sexual contact between men of age and those under age was the foundation for an early gay movement in 1911. As a result, by the end of the fifties, for the first time, a somewhat open club-and-foundation-life developed in Amsterdam's local gay landscape. It satisfied needs on a limited scale through individual aid (counselling), communal cultural pursuits (publishing, theatre, poetry, sociability) and the first gay social lobbying in the surrounding world (negotiating with religious, educational, medical and legal institutions). This last effort resulted in a philosophy of integration at the beginning of the seventies directed at social and political adjustment of discrimination. Now Amsterdam counts over sixty non-profit affiliations that contribute with various services to public gay life.

The supply of services has been supplemented in the eighties by the development of local links with institutions from outside gay life. Growing collaboration with local partners in politics and government carried the integration of gay life a step further. In 1982, the municipality of Amsterdam took the first steps in the direction of a coherent gay-emancipation policy—and the last ten years have been directed principally at removing oppositions and arrears through anti-discrimination policy. Recently, a broadening emphasis can be detected, in which the benefits of a healthy gay community for all residents of Amsterdam are promoted.[3] This tentative emphasis on local revitalization by empowering gay urban life can be found again in views on the promotion of gay tourism and on the prevention of HIV/AIDS in the gay community.

Distinct from at-least-three-centuries-old gay streetlife is the contemporary combination of for-profit, non-profit and political gay services generated in less than thirty years. This network of services is spatially concentrated in the city center around the previously mentioned quartet of commercial centers, clubbing areas such as the Warmoesstraat, the Rembrandtsplein, the Reguliersdwarsstraat and the Kerkstraat, each cluster having its own joys and sorrows.[4] The volume, density and heterogeneity of service-addresses produce a concentration of urban gay life that is more professional, extensive and varied than in other Dutch cities. Within the Amsterdam gay scene people can meet each other as intimates as well as in the role of customer, professional, client, manager, member, volunteer, visitor, citizen, civil servant or politician. Its local concentration in a spatial network with features of an economic market, a social movement and a political organization makes the gay community a source of improved urban life in Amsterdam, inspiring the self-identity and urban revitalization of the inner city (Musterd and De Pater 1992).

Urban life in Amsterdam recognizes a few more manifestations of gay life. Like the two already mentioned, streetlife and business/service amenities, they are of particular importance for the imaginary picture of Amsterdam as a gay urban system. A third is the presence of a regular *gay public*, though the size of this public is difficult to figure out in a reliable way. Demographic statistics overlook sexual preferences, so the precise number of gay men in Amsterdam shall probably always be an unsolved mystery. This is not of prime importance, however, as the social spatialization of an urban gay public does not depend only on the exact number of men with homosexual preferences.

The gay public that I am speaking of does not exclusively consist of homosexual men and certainly not of all men in the city population of 21,500 homosexual and bisexual men.[5] On the one hand not all gay Amsterdamers take part in local gay life; on the other hand there are men and women with other sexual preferences who do take part. Also, men from all over the globe are attracted by the gay life of Amsterdam. Strictly speaking, the urban gay public is constructed out of everyone who, in one way or another, participates in local gay life, regardless of sexual preference. Its social structure is directly dependent on its participants—its composition determined by not only their sexual preference but, more importantly, their social and spatial participation in gay life in the city center.

The Amsterdam gay public is built up out of inhabitants and vistors to the city. Only a fraction of the gay public residing in Amsterdam was born there. The natural growth of participants raised in Amsterdam is being checked by the relatively small size of the population in the capital. The natural growth of the city can hardly keep up with the selective migration from the Netherlands and other countries.

There are many people in Amsterdam who have moved their bed and fled from elsewhere to the city. Some of them only wanted to flee from where they came and simply ended up in Amsterdam, while others moved to Amsterdam for a reason. Some participants in the gay scene settled in the city partly because of gay life, others especially for the gay scene and one or two exclusively because of it. Illustrative is the welcoming by Mayor Van Thijn to the seven hundred thousandth Amsterdamer who came to register in 1991. The new fellow-townsman appeared to be a foreigner who came to make a living in Amsterdam because of good experiences with local gay life. Despite the growing integration of homosexuality in the country outside Amsterdam, the pull towards the city continues.

Some visitors stay for only a weekend, others return again and again, try to stretch their stay, or are able to settle down for a longer period of time. The international interest of gay tourists in Amsterdam's gay life is intense but limited and directed at satisfying their needs immediately. They are in the mood and have the opportunity to see and "do" local gay life quickly. The international gay public creates the basis for the gay amenities of Amsterdam, but this means that the community boasts more companies and stores than foundations and societies.[6]

A local gay *calendar of events* makes up a fourth aspect of Amsterdam's relationship between gay and urban life. Without going deeper into time management in urban space, suffice it to point out the role of "the weekend" and "nighttime" in gay life. These intervals are at the same time sources, illustrations and answers related to the urbanization of the night and the festivalization of city life (see Schlörr 1991). Other public moments, such as pink festivals on April 30th, the remembrance of gay resistance-fighters on May 4th, a permanent AIDS memorial day, and so on, recur on fixed dates: dates derived from the external Dutch calendar. Events in store for Amsterdam include a pink Europride festival in 1994 and the Gay Games in 1998.

Public events give a stucture and a rhythm to the relationship between gay and urban life. Events are no longer clandestine, but are broadcast by various gay and strait media. No one is able to make all points in gay life his own anymore. The comparative abundance is a counterpoint to the average scarcity outside the urban environment. Overt access for larger groups to social activities and relations on the basis of homosexual preference is relatively new.

What once was at most "eccentric," a clandestine or conspicuous part of high or low urban culture (cf. dandyism and bohemianism), required local participation in a narrow social elite or a social underground, instead of today's wide range of choices for "coming out" and proliferation of "lifestyles." (see Duyves 1989). The composition of a local gay calendar is a network response to coming out's consequences, paradoxically resulting in a "second coming-out": some men convert into devotees of gay sports activities, others identify in specialized sexual networks, others start gay careers in professional settings. Amsterdam's gay calendar tends both to proliferate, differentiate and separate the lifestyle-activities in the local gay world and to bring them together in a culture of gay events.

The fifth and last building block of urban gay life in Amsterdam is the promotion of the city as a center of national and international gay tourism. The promotion around the theme "Amsterdam, gay capital of Europe" only marked a new moment in an image-creation which had been initiated long before. Transitory eruptions such as "the sixties" and especially the "sexual revolution" have not remained limited to the private domains of personality, intimacy, and one's own household. They are mega-manifestations which have also left their mark on social relations on an urban, national and international scale.[7]

Under the influence of these forces, Amsterdam's image has gone through clear changes. In a few decades, leisure industries such as youth-tourism, drugs tourism (see Jansen 1989) and sex tourism have grown to massive proportions in the city center. The gay world in Amsterdam has also gone through a scaling-up in this short time. Even if an underground network of national and international importance has existed uninterrupted in the capital since the middle of the eighteenth century (see, for exemple, Römer 1906; Hirschfeld 1914; Barnhoorn et al. 1941; Meer 1984; Noordam 1984; Duyves 1989), Amsterdam only received the reputation of "gay capital of Europe" in gay circles in the last three decades. In international gay life the canal-delta between the Amstel and the Schinkel is seen as Europe's most attractive urban gay plaza and a must destination (Groot and Veen 1985; Kinnich 1992; True 1992).

The creation of an image of Amsterdam as a lilac prima donna is intensive and is effected by rhetorical components that reinforce each other, derived from *journalism, photography, literature* and *gayspeak*. For approximately twenty years, yearly renewable travel brochures for gay target groups have been published. In 1970, for the first time, the French, German and English edition of the *Spartacus International Gay Guide* was published, with all sorts of practical tourist information and addresses of gay amenities all over the world. Amsterdam is summarized in the following sentences:

> Amsterdam has long been famous as a world mecca of gay life, and whilst it
> is not as wild as it once was, gay tourists arrive in daily droves, and even out
> of season there is plenty of life. As always, everyone makes for the big city
> and forgets that there are other places beyond. Whilst it is great fun to visit
> the vast saunas and clubs in Amsterdam, we say "why buy a whole loaf when
> you only want one sandwich?" (Sparticus Gay Guide 1973:201)

Using a fancy five-star rating-system in order to compare the gay acco-
modations in different capitals, the message of the guide is clear: Amsterdam,
not the biggest, simply the best. Gay magazines at home and abroad still
contain letters, cover stories, fiction, pictures, news items, travel advice and
addresses in which the city plays an important part. The largest British
monthly, *Gay Times*, also has a permanent Amsterdam page. Visitors can
purchase address books totally devoted to gay Amsterdam, such as *The Man
to Man Guide* and *The Best Guide*, whilst under the title *Amsterdam in your
Backpocket* a gay city guide was brought onto the market in 1984 with background details about local life in the capital:

> The gay city Amsterdam exercises great attraction on gays from at home and
> abroad for a few decades, like Berlin was the Mecca in the Golden Twenties.
> As contrasted with other cities in the States, Amsterdam does not know a
> gay district, which you can make for immediately as a tourist. The city is, as
> a whole, swarming with homosexual life. We would, however, do the city
> and the reader wrong by merely listing the addresses. There is more going
> on, especially because of the variety of homosexual ways of life and their
> influence on the city. (Marcus and Verstraeten 1984)

From research done by the French weekly *Gai Pied* into gay emancipation and preventention of AIDS in the twelve countries of the EEC, it
appears that the Netherlands and especially Amsterdam are ahead of the rest
of Europe. The Netherlands offer relatively the greatest legal protection, the
most tolerance, the best AIDS-prevention programs and subsidies, the most
gay amenities, the most varied gay culture and the most reliable political
support, according to the publication. Amsterdam is the only European city
that scores very well on the degree of development of the gay movement,
the gay media, the pub and club scene, sex-accomodations, AIDS-prevention and supportive social life (Lacombe 1989).

The image of a gay capital for men is reinforced by press photography,
literature and gayspeak. There are plenty of postcards for sale which give an
impression of the relations between gay and urban life. (The anti-erotic
picture postcards with touristic take-offs of fat ladies and henpecked
husbands at the seaside have more or less vanished from the streets. This
coarse humor has had to make way for postcards with hyper-erotic suggestions. The more artistic gay eroticism on the postcards comes from artists

that were lured to Amsterdam by the city's atmosphere; selective migrants such as Erwin Olaf, Hans Abbing, Michaël Eisenblätter and Jan Carel Warffemius.) In pornography, prose, poetry, cabaret and theatre, local Amsterdam appears more than once in gay shape in the background, or even plays opposite the dramatic story-line (see Venema 1972; Heijer 1989).

A final important element in the promotion of Amsterdam as gay capital is "gayspeak," the particular sound and subjects of chit-chat in gay circles (see Chesebro 1981). Population-groups, including population-sections with a different sexual habitus like adults and children, men and women, heterosexuals and homosexuals, faggots and dykes, all create their own topics. Whilst sport-, work- and car-related subjects have a permanent place in conversation among straight men, home, school, clothes, children and relations are safe topics among women. Among the gay public, erotic dialogues about sex, cities and traveling light up communication.

During the past thirty years the reputation of Amsterdam as a gay El Dorado has increased gradually in national and international gay circles, but has not penetrated beyond them. The process of image-creation was carried out completely (and controlled almost exclusively) by the gay public and it occurred fairly arbitrarily. With modest efforts by the Amsterdam Tourist Office and the Dutch Bureau for Tourism, for the first time general institutions have tried to benefit from the gay image of Amsterdam. The future shall tell if this approach was simply an experiment.

CONCLUSION

Thus far I have tried to analyze the image of an imaginary city. An imagined city, but not a meaningless city. I have pointed out its social spatialization as a gay capital according to five spatial manifestations of urban gay life: the use of public space or street culture, the level of amenities or clientele culture, the gay public or community culture, the local gay calendar or event culture, and the gay image of the city or promotion culture. These manifestations have created, through their mix, the social and spatial foundation for the image of a make-believe gay capital in its current phases. The spatialization of sexual preferences has led to a gay urban system for which the spatial metaphor of a gay capital is enlightening.

The meaning of Amsterdam as a gay hub is, however, not only dependent on the self-perception and self-expression of the local gay community, but equally on responses of the whole city—the municipality. In view of Amsterdam's gay qualities, these responses are half-hearted and unbalanced. Since 1970, gay emancipation in the city has not only promoted equality of rights, legal security, and citizenship in the city, but it also offered a stimulus to the local service-economy. Nevertheless the potential of Amsterdam as a center of international gay life is not fully comprehended in the city hall and by the Chamber of Commerce. Tourism and AIDS-prevention are two areas in which the gay community and local officials could cooperate more closely to the benefit of both.

The city hall has a tiny sub-division, called Gay Affairs, with an annual budget of ƒ300,000 guilders (US $170,000), but a low status in the ranks of the bureaucracy. At the Chamber of Commerce, baptised lovingly by its own employees as the Bedchamber of Commerce, it indeed seems as if everyone has fallen asleep. There is a vague notion of tolerance, but no notion of how integration between gay life and urban life can be utilized. Officials show themselves to be tolerant but scarcely innovative and hardly creative. The friendly Tourist Information Office campaign hit the captains of commerce like a clenched fist.

Although the gay scene is a tourist attraction in Amsterdam, it has not been taken into account during the decision-making process. The institutions I mentioned would rather pass it by completely. Only fleeting emergency contacts in exceptional cases of conflict, rather than supportive links, have been created between local government or the Chamber of Commerce and the over one hundred gay commercial venues in the city. Communication within the gay world has a ring of superficiality, but contacts among urban officials and the gay business sector is even more volatile. The nostalgic image of Amsterdam as workshop of Rembrandt, treasure chamber of Van Gogh, capital of the Golden Age, hiding-place of Anne Frank and branch of Madame Tussaud's is preferred. The touristic promotion of the city threatens continually to mimic a city lying in state.

Amsterdam could use its place as European center of gay cultural expressions more fruitfully (Advisory Report 1992). During the reconstruction of the local economy, the fate of its inner-city is closely linked to the growth-market around tourism, culture and urban recreation. Amsterdam's cultural offerings do not only consist of its historic center and arts, but also of a concentration of ways of living. The city is not only visited for her ancient façades, but also for her new lifestyles, living-communities and leisure networks. Indeed, there are visitors that come exclusively to meet other visitors. Nonetheless the relationship between gay life and urban life is not yet seriously considered in the redevelopment of the inner city.

If policy remains unaltered, Amsterdam, which is presented internationally as a city living in the past, will miss out on a specific innovation of the urban recreational and touristic climate. The average inhabitant of Amsterdam is not a supporter of an urban open-air museum, since revitalization will not gain by it. On the contrary, joint efforts are needed to cherish the inner city as an open-air club for inhabitants with different ways of living and for visitors from different leisure-communities.

The image of Amsterdam as an imaginary gay capital rests on spatial relations that are real, though the responses offered by the city are not yet real enough. Gay life penetrates and absorbs urban life to a certain point, but this does not happen as completely the other way around. Therefore let us ask ourselves, finally, what gay life has that the rest of Amsterdam does not. The easiest answer is probably that it gives access to sexual intercourse between men. It is certainly interesting to see how it is constructed using spatial solutions such as "cruising areas" and "dark rooms." But far from the whole gay scene is involved in this.

A more intriguing aspect of gay life is the area of tension, or the new balance, it creates between real and imaginary urban life. Public gay life, just like the straight life in the city, creates a world founded on the imagined dividing line between sexual preferences. This dividing line does not cause tensions between homosexuality and heterosexuality (it rather causes a feigned harmony), but creates, in contrast to the repeating intelligence that rules everyday life, its own symbolic area of tension between the local and the sublime. Urban gay life offers, through its spatial concentration of manifestations, a protected environment for a safe shifting of boundaries from the local in the direction of the sublime.

Seen in the light of a transgression between the local and the sublime by means of the use of space, gay life seems to be a type of foreplay with urban life. It is a spatial and social game that promotes urban life to a leading actor in the spatialization of sexual preferences. A recurring gay motif in the works of writers such as Kavafy, Warhol, Bartlett and the Dutch writers Reve and Moonen is the local eroticism of anonymous encounters in the streets, in shops, trams and among the public. The penetrating gaze of gay life cast on the city lifts it to a societal and spatial object of desire, instead of degrading it.

The sensual cultivation of the city founded on the spatialization of sexual preferences is not only literary or imaginary. It is a precondition for a multicultural urban world. It will not dawn upon the city by itself, but it needs to be built up.

Urban planning only knows a very limited spatial organization of the senses. But declarations and expressions of love do know a spatial organization. Within this spatial framework, urban life is a top-location to make the gay world rotate, as gay life might be a top-location to discover urban life.

NOTES

1. The term "social world" refers to the construction and organization of interactional and communicative spaces which have as common sociological characteristic a lack of completely and accurately delineable boundaries; these include crowds, scenes, informal networks, local subcultures, situational communities, lifestyle and trend categories.

Social worlds based on voluntary lifestyles operate through self-reduction (sorting out), self-expression (specialization) and self-management of experience, these include the cultivation of high culture, low culture, dandyism, camp, vogueing, being a *parisiene* or a clone.

2. Social spatialization of sexual preferences is, in other words, an analytical concept intended to question all the cultural ways in which social world, spatial world and sexual world possibly intersect.

3. Respective reports concerning gay and lesbian affairs in the municipality of Amsterdam on behalf of the City Council and the College of Mayor and Aldermen: 1982, "Nota van het reaadslid Van Schijndel inzake homo-emancipatie; 1983 "Preadvies op de nota van het raadslid Van Schijndel"; 1987, "Voortgangsnota inzake homo-emancipatie"; 1989, "Notitie stand van zaken homoemancipatiebeleid"; 1992 "Aktiepolan homo-emancipatie 1992–1994."

4. See, for example, the "Pink Map of Amsterdam," *Holland Boys International/Gay Amsterdam News*, 1993, and the "Gay Map of Amsterdam," *Trash in the Streets*, Amsterdam's free gay newspaper, 7 April 1993.

5. A representative survey of the Amsterdam male population between eighteen and fifty-five years classifies 21,500 men (10%) as homo or bisexual, according to their preference and sexual behavior. An HIV-seroprevalence of 16-17% (3400-3600 men) among this section was estimated for January 1990.

6. Due to the incoming gay tourism, gay clubbing areas have emerged in Amsterdam. In spite of its own regular gay population, Amsterdam lacks the gay residential concentrations known in some American cities with significant gay populations. The low gay residential concentration stems in particular from the strong intervention of social housing distribution (about 90%) on the local housing market. Sexual preference is not a registered criterion for social housing policies. One could say that the asexual housing democracy steers the local housing distribution market more than is common in the United States.

7. In 1989 Amsterdam was the only Dutch city in which single households had become the largest section in all age groups over eighteen years old. See Molenaar en Floor 1989 in: Musterd and de Pater, op. cit. 1992:65. See also Hekma 1990.

GENDER, SEXUALITY, AND IDENTITY

Part Two

Bisexuality   4

Toward a Comparative Theory of Identities and Culture

Gilbert Herdt and Andrew Boxer

THE UNDERSTANDING OF HUMAN SEXUAL BEHAVIOR AND IDENTITY has been troubled by the confound of some unusual problems in conceptualizing and representing the relationship between erotic potential and expression, on the one hand, versus developmental identity and social surrounding, on the other; and nowhere are these problems more confusing, condensed, and worth pondering than in that perpetual quagmire of sexual theory, "bisexuality."

From the mid-nineteenth century to the present, sexology, followed by psychoanalysis, and later survey sociology and international health epidemiology, have consistently endeavored (without great success) to map out and represent the relationship between the erotic identities, behaviors, and cultures that surround the "black box" of bisexuality (CDC 1989; Gagnon 1989; Herdt 1990; Klein and Wolf 1985; Parker, Herdt and Caballo 1991; Tielman et al. 1991). This chapter attempts a preliminary analysis of the interactive processes involved in one aspect of the problem: developmental relations between sexual/gendered identities and the cultures of persons either classified as bisexuals by investigators or self-identified as such.

FOUR NOTIONS OF BISEXUALITY

Bisexuality is uniquely suited to serve as a paradigm of both theorizing and empirical work because it represents the locus of several quite distinctive and divergent domains of study. Research scholars in the area of human sexuality have argued repeatedly, particularly with the onset of the AIDS epidemic, that bisexual behavior is a central element of the research, education, and prevention effort needed to break the chain of HIV transmission across populations, and within subcultures or generations of the same population (see Gagnon 1989; Herdt and Lindenbaum 1992; Turner et al. 1989).

Anthropologists, historians, and symbolic sociologists have labored to deconstruct the category "bisexuality," seeing within it the particular formations of local cultures and historical periods (Weeks 1985; Herdt 1991a, 1991b). By contrast, sexologists and medically oriented gender theorists have tended to reproduce earlier cultural representations, most of which derive from the nineteenth century (reviewed in Weeks 1985).

We may speak of four dimensions of "bisexuality" in attempting to capture these conceptual valences and divergent perspectives. "Bisexuality" will now be placed in quotation marks to indicate the attempt to distinguish these levels and to untangle their meanings (and behavioral consequences) across the course of life in particular cultures. Thus, the following levels of analysis have been documented in the research literature as "core" areas of "bisexuality":

1. Biological Bisexuality	Sexual attraction to both sexes as innate drives.
2. Psychological Bisexuality	Relations with both sexes as self-function.
3. Behavioral Bisexuality	Relations with both sexes as interpersonal behavior.
4. Cultural Bisexuality	Relations with both sexes as cultural idea.

Furthermore, there is a historical series or sequence in these levels: the biological level derives earliest, in the nineteenth century, followed by the other levels in historical time. The earliest literature of the last century, especially concerned with biological factors of bisexuality and inversion, is typical of the first level of study described above (reviewed in Stoller 1975; see also Freud 1905; Money 1987). By contrast, the research literature suggests that most contemporary investigations have been concerned with the second and third levels of bisexuality, as instanced in the significant volume edited by Klein and Wolf (1985). (Many publications in this area, however, often confuse or conflate the first two levels, sometimes lumping with them factors or variables deriving from the first and fourth levels.) Kinsey and his colleagues, for instance, were primarily interested in level three, though Kinsey's notion of "sex drive" obviously borrowed from Freudian and zoological principles to highlight an individual's typical threshold of sexual arousal and behavior potential (Kinsey et al. 1948; reviewed in Herdt 1990). The fourth level is newer and more difficult to map. The reasons for this have to do with the conceptualization of "identity" as a later twentieth century socio-political concept that articulated social diversity and sexual heterogeneity in complex societies, such as the United States, in a time when scholars such as Erikson (1963, 1982) were attempting to refine gender development in society during the intense social controls following the onset of the Cold War (D'Emilio and Freedman 1988; Herdt and Boxer 1993).

Now let us contrast these levels further. In the first level, the idea of biological bisexuality is strongly associated with medical sexology, with Lamarkian and Darwinian thought in the effort to describe natural selection in human phylogeny.

In the second level, psychological bisexuality has sometimes been conceptualized to mean areas of self-function and regulation, at any of several distinctive levels of biological and psychological development. Freud's (1905) "folk" notion of libidinal bisexuality is an effort to position sexual attraction potential for both sexes as part of a generalized "hard wired" image of human nature. Current work by John Money (1987) continues this line of thinking, with aspects of psychobiological development conceptualized as being part of the deep structure of human nature.

The emergence of the idea of psychological bisexuality is strongly associated with psychoanalytic and psychological discourse on sexuality, and this has tended to pathologize the relevant phenomena. In Freud's work, the emphasis was upon drives and their expressions, which sometimes meant (as it did in the writings upon homosexuality by psychoanalysts) the fixations of arrested development. Academic psychology largely avoided work in this area, though sexologists, most notably John Money (1987) and colleagues, studied the topic. In the work of the psychoanalyst Heinz Kohut (1971), by contrast, the emphasis shifted to the more positive study of self-psychology, so that one could speak of a different line of thinking about psychological bisexuality. Here, work would center on the regulation of self-esteem in the individual's effort to achieve satisfaction from having intimate relations with one or both sexes. The need to derive self-esteem from sexual and intimate relations with both genders in this paradigm must be distinguished from the "pathological" forms of "bisexuality" commonly identified with the clinical experience of a few individual patients. Typically, in these latter cases, individuals with diffuse and weak boundaries of self and fluid self-representations may wax and wane in their sexual desires according to tension states which are associated with sexual intimacy with both genders. (Frequently this is identified clinically with the so-called "borderline" personality, a form of psychopathology that should not be confused with other developmental expressions of sexual contact with both genders.)

In the third level, bisexuality has increasingly indicated interpersonal sexual relations with both sexes. This category is itself confounded by the problem that sexual intercourse typically does not occur with both sexes at the same moment in time. The same individual may, on occasion, be involved with only one sex, and not the other, which may perdure for a significant phase of the development life-course, only to be followed by a "crossing over" to erotic relations with the other sex again. This individual history of sexual interactions is often not aggregated within research for the same individual (as indeed Kinsey et al. 1948 did not do), with the effect that bisexuality emerges as a situational or functional outcome, rather than as a product of the life-history of the individual.

In the fourth and most recent level, bisexuality may refer to cultural ideas about sexual relations, or to ideals regarding what a proper, moral person should or should not do, with both sexes. This ideal type of "cultural bisexuality" obviously intersects with conscious desires of the second level, and behavioral interactions of the third level. Yet the cultural level remains autonomous of these and distinct. Indeed, in the history of the study of bisexuality, study of cultural context and historical setting were typically omitted until the advent of "social constructionism" in the past several decades. In the accounts of social psychologists, for instance, they often strip away the meanings of the sociological and cultural "scripts" of the actors (Gagnon and Simon 1973). In short, what the newer fourth level has done is to problematize "bisexuality" as a matter of collective, rather than purely individual, meanings, agency, and conduct.

SEXUAL IDENTITY AND BISEXUALITY

In our multi-dimensional perspective on bisexuality we are positioning identity theoretically as a primary mediator of sexual development and cultural identity.[1] However, we are not claiming that this is the "core" or "determinant" of sexual interaction. Bisexual identity is here linked to a general model of sexual identity development and of the expression of desires. *Sexual identity* is represented as including modes of sexual being, which encompass such matters as erotic desire, sexual orientation, sexual object choice, and sexual drive; and *sexual action*, which includes such phenomena as erotic practices and tastes, sexual sequences of behavior, and sexual lifestyles. Where the former impinges upon the inner world of sexuality, the latter evokes much of what is important in the social construction of sexuality. Desires, according to recent work, are associated with three kinds of symbolic action in the person: at the level of fantasy, such as thinking about pleasures and "rehearsing" them in the person, in the manner of what John Gagnon and William Simon (1973, 1990) call "scripts"; at the level of the formation of object images and representations, such as the persons (real or fictitious) who the individual daydreams about; and at the level of participation in cultural activity, when individual desires are inserted into social relations.

Such a schema may be seen in historical perspective, for example, in generational age cohorts (Elder 1980) influenced by the changing meanings of sexuality, objects, and cultural practices in their real-life worlds. In Chicago, for instance, we have found that a major difference distinguishing older from younger persons who desire the same sex is that the older cohort consistently hides its desires from biological parents; whereas the younger cohort typically reveals these desires to parents or expects to do so within the near future (Herdt and Boxer 1993).

Desires and identity are thus much more a part of the social production of life course development and its vicissitudes in culture, a view we have developed in our work (Herdt and Boxer 1993). Physical transformations of sexual being associated with the onset of puberty have long provided a paradigm for this area of modelling. Puberty involves a rather dramatic set of changes in which a child's body gradually comes to approximate that of an adult. Physical maturation presages other changes; for example, one of the outcomes of puberty is the attainment of mature reproductive potential. The adolescent's self-image is affected, as well as assumptions and expectations regarding sexual behavior and social interactions. The new physical status of the postpubertal adolescent (physical size, body shape, etc.) is accompanied by a variety of social and psychological expectations. Significant others, such as friends, teachers, and family members, may begin to react differently to a young adolescent, effecting a shift in the socially shared definitions of the self (reviewed in Boxer et al. 1993).

The concept of identity, as used by Freud and his daughter Anna Freud, Erikson, and later developmentalists such as Robert Stoller, is generally conceived of as an intrinsic process, necessary for full formation of the person. It is not seen as culturally constitutive. Our approach, by contrast, straddles halfway between ideas of culturally constructed identity and ideas of internal self. With regard to sexual identity, we are concerned with the significant process of transforming desires into sexual being and doing; but what we mean by sexual identity is not the same as gender identity or sexual orientation, as used by many others (e.g., Kinsey, Stoller, Erikson). Sexual identity is thus more holistic than it was often characterized, at least until the onset of the AIDS epidemic led to significant new areas of research and education, which have in turn opened up new questions about the conceptual position of the identity in context. In short, significant attention is needed to further clarify the cultural dimension of bisexuality in these studies.

IDENTITY SYSTEMS IN CULTURE

Let us continue the discussion of bisexual identity with the insight that virtually all studies of bisexual conduct or sexual interaction have neglected significant study of the cultural context in which this occurs. Bisexual identity has conventionally signified, that is, individual acts or individual meanings—the psychological level—rather than sexual acts in cultural context, which would include individual acts and meanings as two parts of a whole. Another way of arguing this view is to suggest that bisexuality is an identity system that must be described as including both historical-cultural context and individual actions (see Herdt 1984).

Thus, our problem is to conceptualize the actor or agent in cultural context as a total unit of analysis. For this purpose, we may rethink bisexuality not as a lone child in "nature," but rather as one of a series of categories of identity (heterosexual/homosexual; gay/straight, as argued by Herdt 1992), conceptualized as a cultural system. Such a system links features and components of individual persons' experiences with their conduct in social settings and networks.

PARADIGM ONE: THE SAMBIA OF PAPUA NEW GUINEA

Over a period of approximately fifteen years, one of us, Gilbert Herdt, has described aspects of the ritual traditions and sexual and gendered lives of the Sambia of Papua New Guinea, especially of male development.[2] The overall theme of this work has been to show the relation between cultural context and social practices, and the unfolding of sexual desire and behavior. Same-sex relations in particular have been the subject of study because of the widespread practice, universal among Sambia males in earlier development, of relations between older and younger unmarried males (Herdt 1981). Originally, these practices were termed "ritualized homosexuality," and "ritual homosexual behavior" (Herdt 1984). It turns out that approximately fifty different cultures in the South Seas area of Melanesia practice a variant of this age-structured same-sex relation. Conceptual discussions of the phenomena have been provided by Barry Adam (1986) and David Greenberg (1988), among others (reviewed in Herdt 1993). Greenberg in particular has pointed out the failure of anthropologists to provide descriptions of the erotic component of theses activities, which Herdt and Stoller (1990) have also criticized. Greenberg has also rightly critiqued the tendency of anthropologists to abstract the practices and treat them as social matters, rather than as activities having to do with "sexual behavior."

These studies in Melanesia represent a watershed that broke through a critical impasse (Read 1980). The structural trend in Western epistemology has been to collate, consolidate, and wrest from a comparison of Western sexuality with these other sexualities the supposedly shared common denominators of human sexual nature, suggesting that, ultimately, a rose is a rose no matter what its color.[3] "Homosexuality" has been especially problematic for anthropologists because we have remained divided over whether this is a universal or local condition of culture and "human nature" (Herdt

1991a, 1991b). It remains as controversial today as it was a decade ago, in part because the AIDS epidemic has thrust itself into the cultural representation of same-sex relations.[4]

It is now clear from study of the Sambia and other cases that we must place the term "homosexuality" in quotation marks because its folk theory merges the distinction between kinds of cultural identity and types of sexual practice. What we once thought of as a unitary entity—homosexuality—is in fact not one but several "species" of same-sex relations. They differ not only in symbolic form, but also in their deeper nature. Thus, the received category "homosexuality" known in Western culture must now be represented as one of several different sociocultural types known around the world. It is now argued by many experts that such "traditional" forms of culturally conventionalized same-sex erotic practices as appear among the Sambia occur in clusters and culture areas of the world (Adam 1986; Greenberg 1988).

Indeed, four ideal types of same-sex practice can be contrasted: age-structured, gender-structured, role- or class-structured, and gay or egalitarian-structured homosexualities.[5] In the Austro-Melanesian area, "age" is the key to "cultural homosexuality," and is the defining factor in the same-sex relation between the boy and his sexual inseminator, just as in Ancient Greece and Tokugawa Japan (see Herdt 1984). To refer to this practice as "homosexuality" seems now inelegant and unreflective (see Herdt 1993); it is better to represent this symbolic type of same-sex practice as boy-inseminating rites (Herdt 1991b). Here is why.

The Sambia are a hunting and gathering tribe of the Papua New Guinea highlands, marked by an emphasis upon war and sexual antagonism. Their kinship system traces descent through the male line. All marriages are politically arranged with neighboring groups, who may be classified as hostile or even enemy villages. The division of labor is entirely gender coded, with men hunting and warring, and women gardening and tending children. The villages, often no larger than one hundred persons in number, are sex segregated, with men's clubhouses off-limits to women and children, and women's menstrual huts forbidden to men and older children. As in other New Guinea societies, this complex of warfare, marriage, and ritual practices creates an extraordinary context for individual development and social elaboration, which presents a curious mixture of ideas that emphasize both pleasure and reproduction, with the difference that "reproduction" is symbolically defined to include the insemination of boys.

Boy-inseminating rituals implemented in a series of male initiations have made the Sambia notable for their acceptance of men's pleasures with both sexes. Like the Ancient Greeks, the Sambia recognize a range of sexual practices having different functions and eventual outcomes. The following ideas are reviewed extensively in Herdt (1981, 1984). On one level the practice of placing semen in the bodies of boys is a necessity due to the local belief system. Sambia believe that the male body is inherently incapable of the manufacture of semen. Since semen is not only the main stimulant to male growth and the masculinization of the body (including the attainment of puberty and the growth of secondary sex characteristics, such as facial hair and muscles) but also an elixir of life—the greatest power for human growth and vitality—the need to artificially introduce semen into boys is enormous. Beginning at ages seven or eight, and continuing until their mid-teens, boys are placed in the role of being orally inseminated by older bachelor males, in a sequence of secret initiations. During this time they completely avoid women and children, on pain of death. They experience six initiations in all, leading from childhood to manhood in their early twenties. During middle adolescence the boys undergo a third-stage initiation which results in their "switching" roles to become the active inseminators of a new crop of younger boys. They also learn ritual techniques, such as nose-bleeding rites, to rid themselves of the pollution of women's menstrual blood, as well as semen-replenishing techniques, such as the drinking of white tree sap milk (believed to be functionally like semen), in order to maintain their vitality.

Sexual intercourse has three functions for the Sambia. First is to reproduce, to create boys who will be heirs and warriors, and girls who will be traded in the marriage exchange system. Second is to grow masculine boys. And third is to have pleasure: first with boys (orally) and later with women (orally and genitally). In fact, a hierarchy of functions of semen transactions suggests that Sambia do not privilege sexual procreation any more than they do other sexual transactions. Why is this so? Primarily it is because the creation of a new cohort of young warriors to protect village and tribe is always pivotal in the minds of Sambia, men and women alike. They know that the village may be attacked at any time; and they believe that boys will not "naturally" achieve adult competence without the interventions of ritual. As Herdt and other ethnographers have demonstrated in describing these practices, the arousal of youth and men is strong and they experience the inseminating of boys as highly pleasurable. We must not think that their sexual practices are merely a product of sexual seclusion from women or sexual exploitation of boys and women by men. Rather, parallel lines of sexual pleasure develop in Sambia culture, supporting the idea that there are multiple functions of sexual practice, with sexual pleasure being a significant but not overriding function. Women and boys are sexual objects and in some ways are treated by men as a sexual commodity. Yet these women and boys also experience their own pleasures and necessities, including masculine growth (boys) and sexual pleasure and reproduction (women) (reviewed in Herdt and Stoller 1990).

The insemination of boys ideally ends when a man has married and fathered a child. In fact, the vast majority of males do terminate their relations with boys. Perhaps 90% or better of men do so, in part because of taboos, and in part because they have "matured" to a new level of having exclusive sexual access to one or more wives, with genital sexual pleasure being conceived of as more exciting than intercourse with boys. Nonetheless, a small number of individual men continue inseminating boys, some of them boys exclusively, in defiance of custom. One such man, Kalutwo, has been studied in depth, and his sexual and social history reveals a pattern of broken, childless marriages, with an exclusive attraction to boys. Another, larger, category of men are best designated as "bisexual" after marriage in the sense that they enjoy pleasure and reproduction with their wives, but they continue to enjoy oral sex with boys on the sly. These men seem unable to give up the pleasures of intercourse with both sexes, and they do not appear to experience any loss of self-esteem or social approval as a result. They most nearly match the "polymorphous perverse" image of having a multifaceted sexuality, though always in the dominant position of being the active inseminator (see Herdt 1981, 1993).

PARADIGM TWO: URBAN ADOLESCENTS IN CHICAGO, USA

Between 1987 and 1990, we conducted a cultural and developmental study of 202 gay and lesbian identified adolescents (aged 14–20) and their families in Chicago. We also conducted an historical and cultural study of the setting within which the project took place: Horizons Social Services, a large gay and lesbian community center. We used a modified "Kinsey" type identity scale. Our work in Chicago suggests the existence of three historically specific processes of culturally constituted sexual development in youth (Herdt and Boxer 1993). We follow the sexual identity model referred to above to denote three distinct levels. The first process is largely concerned with the emergence of aesthetic tastes, preferences and appetites from birth to puberty. The second process is focussed upon the experience of the erotic as this begins in childhood and continues through puberty. The third process focussed upon postpubertal experience and the social desires and adjustments which match social selves to real-life worlds. The first and second processes, we believe, are more strongly influenced by intrinsic desires and feelings, signified by the concept of "sexual orientation." However, they are also heavily controlled by performative factors in culture. The third process is more sociocentric, but must still invoke the inner world of awareness and desire.

The Horizons Center was founded in the early 1970s by gay activists in

Chicago who, in turn, created the first coming out support group for youth. Approximately 700 adolescents attended the informal drop-in meetings on Saturday afternoons which we observed. These are extremely diverse youth, most of whom live at home and attend school. We drew a sample of ethnically diverse youth from a variety of backgrounds, of both genders, to implement our interview study. Interviews with individuals were in-depth, narrative one-to-one and paper and pencil format. Most youth reported that this was a positive experience, the first time they had told their "whole story" of being gay, lesbian, or bisexual.

In the youth settings of Chicago, bisexuality has a specific meaning, which historical and ethnographic study has shown to be dramatically changing at the present time. In the Horizons youth group, as in American society in general, bisexuality is a contentious state of identity. The bisexual is "betwixt and between" sexualities; and at Horizons it follows that for many, though by no means all, youth, bisexuality is a social phase and certain developmental step, into the formation of gay or lesbian identified social selves and relationships.

The meaning system of self-identifying as bisexual at Horizons depends upon the social surrounding and the particular individual. Before the existence of Queer Nation, this was "gay turf," to use Richard Herrell's (1992) term; youth found it perplexing to desire both sexes erotically. Hardly anyone desires the opposite sex as much as the same sex, at any rate (see Herdt and Boxer 1993). Rare is the youth who desires both sexes equally at the same point in development. No wonder many youth poke fun with a favorite saying—to quote one young informant on this point, "Bisexuality is what you say until you are OUT." Cultural factors that govern the general process of coming out play a part in the reliance upon bisexuality. Adolescents of color and the working class have a harder time emerging from secrecy, because of the traditional standards of their ethnic communities, with the effect that there is a somewhat greater tendency for younger Black men and women refer to themselves as "bisexual" (see also Peterson 1992). Young Anglo women experience difficulties because of the gender role pressures that make them conform to heterosexual standards enforced by boyfriends and families. Social oppression and internal repression thus combine, leading to an alienation from the desires of the self.

The puzzles of development and bisexuality are embodied in "Straight Sam," a member of the youth group. The group gave him this nickname in part to poke fun at him, and in part to mock his often repeated saying, "I'm straight." Sam was an intelligent but awkward nineteen year old white youth. He was the original "nerd" in the group—acne, rumpled clothes, horn-rimmed glasses, and a big mop of uncombed brown hair, a stark contrast to the other, usually carefully coiffured youths. In both his formal interview (done with the rest of the group) and in two additional, informal interviews conducted alone with Herdt, Sam consistently maintained that he was heterosexual.[6] In his sexual identity scores, he rated a strong heterosexual interest in almost all domains, except in his social life, where he preferred to interact with gays. Sam had doubts about his sexuality; but upon questioning, he said that he had never been involved with the opposite or same sex intimately. He "had not had sex." He came to the group on Saturdays, he said, to "get rid" of his homophobia, which he "inherited" from his lower middle-class parents in the suburbs. In fact, Sam enjoyed being around gay and lesbian teens; that was clear. He suggested at one point that he liked his "gay friends better than his straight friends." We discovered that Sam was actually the target of harassment at high school—the "school fag," as it turns out. The youth at Horizons sometimes tried to discover his sexuality, as when one of the boys suggested that Sam might like to come to a party, insinuating something sexual. Sam turned him down. Sam's interest was not sexual, and he would not get closer to the other youth. Sam desired a gay symbolic space but had the cultural identity of being bisexual—a refugee from suburban life who was transforming along the way.

Same-sex contact between heterosexually active adolescent males is typically not defined as "homosexuality" and does not necessarily lead to the sexual identity "gay" or "homosexual" (Gagnon and Simon 1973). Conversely, at Horizons the youth's descriptions of their participation in opposite-sex activity revealed the normative socialization of the larger society toward participation in heterosexual activity. Many youth engage in such behavior, but only transiently, since it is discrepant with their erotic desires and feelings. The participation in heterosexual experience suggests that these youth were testing their own homoerotic desires, simultaneously engaging in expected behavioral outcomes of heterosexuality, and that these experiences served as a benchmark of comparison. As the cultural identity of "bisexuality" has emerged, this has afforded an alternative pathway of development.

From our quantitative analysis, we have begun to build a model of sexual and identity pathways that help us to understand bisexuality. The youths' accounts of their feelings about the same and opposite-sex experiences highlighted the comparisons that they made. Many youth who tried heterosexual intercourse commented on the lack of feeling and passion they encountered; often, this was magnified if it was preceded by a satisfying homosexual experience with which to compare it. We found that most youth in our sample of 202 teens reported a sequence that began with an awareness of their same-sex desires, proceeded to sexual fantasies, and progressed to some type of same-sex experience. On average, this began between the ages of nine and a half to ten years of age for both males and females. The one significant gender difference occurred with regard to age at first same-sex activity, with males reporting an average age (13.1) significantly younger than did females (15.2) (t = 3.64, p <.001).

Experiences with the opposite sex are illuminating. A significant number (fifty-five percent) of our gay and lesbian identified youth (thirty-seven females and seventy-four males) reported having had some type of opposite sex experience. Such heterosexual experimentation may be parallel to the same-sex encounters described by heterosexual youth (Kinsey et al. 1948). Sixty-seven percent of all females and fifty percent of all males reported these experiences. For males this occurred at 13.7 years on average, very close to the average age of 13.6 years for females. Both males and females reported mixed reactions to opposite-sex relationships. Kevin, a white (twenty year old) male described his first heterosexual experience at age thirteen this way:

> It was just kissing, she felt me out, I didn't put my hands in her pants or any of that. I was a little turned on by it, but it wasn't great for me really.

Gay and lesbian youth appear to diverge from psychological bisexuals in their cultural pathways to the sexual. The difference between boys and girls is one way of seeing this. The divergence of average ages for first same-sex but not first opposite-sex experiences indicates that, for males, first homoerotic sex typically preceded first heteroerotic sex. For girls, however, the average age of same-sex experience is later than the average age of first sex with a male, thus confirming the existence of divergent developmental pathways into sexual identity formation.

In classifying youth according to which of a series of three sequences occurred in their initial sexual encounters, we begin to perceive this. Thirty-five percent of the youth were categorized in the "first homo then-hetero" sequence; twenty-eight percent were in the first "hetero then homoerotic" sequence; and thirty-seven percent in the "homoerotic" experience only sequence. Larger proportions of male teenagers were found in the homoerotic/heteroerotic, and homoerotic-only groups, while the percentage of females was higher in the first hetero-then/homoerotic group. Thus females were significantly more likely to have had a heterosexual experience before a homosexual one. Previous analyses of these data have confirmed that gender is significantly related to the youth's sequencing of first same-sex and opposite-sex experiences, regardless of the influence of other factors, such as the youths' minority status, employment status, or age at the time of the interview (Boxer 1990). Only twenty-seven (13%) of the teens did not fit into any of these sequences, for reasons such as having had no sexual experiences (neither heterosexual nor homosexual) at the

time of the interview (N=6); having had heterosexual experiences exclusively (N=11); having had their first heteroerotic and homoerotic
experiences at the same age (N=9), or because of missing information
regarding sexual sequencing (N=1). The youths' descriptions of their feelings and experiences regarding same-sex and opposite-sex initiations
suggest that their comparisons of these experiences were used to help clarify their feelings about their sexual identities.

For teenagers ambivalent or less positive about their first same-sex relationship, their comparing of this to opposite-sex experiences helped clarify
feelings otherwise difficult to admit or accept. A boy in the "first homoerotic then/heteroerotic" category, for example, described his first same-sex
experience as one in which "we enjoyed the act but didn't enjoy thinking
about it." In these narratives, differing sexual identity pathways serve as
developmental milestones through which the self compares erotic experiences. One's basis for comparison may affect how positively or negatively
same-sex and bisexual relations, especially intimate ones, are experienced
(Herdt 1984). How the youth regarded their first sexual experience may
have thus been influenced by these comparisons. Likewise, these initial
sexual encounters may also have been formative of how Horizons youth
constructed their gay and lesbian identities in contrast to others who self-
identify as bisexual.

These youth describe first heteroerotic experiences as "sex without feelings." Regardless of whether it was preceded by a same-sex experience or
not, a feeling of "unnaturalness" and lack of affective intensity in their first
heterosexual sex was mentioned repeatedly. This theme was present in the
accounts of both males and females—although females tended to describe
heterosexual experiences as something that they simply expected to
happen, whereas males often sought out these experiences.

What if the teens' first homoerotic experience was initiated at a later age,
but still prior to their opportunity to experience opposite-sex relations? To
examine this possibility, we compared the mean ratings of feelings about
first same-sex and opposite-sex activity for "ambivalent" youth in each of
the three pathways. These self-ratings ranged from 1 through 5 (1=very
bad, 2=bad, 3=OK,/mixed positive and negative, 4=good, and 5=very
good). Respondents in all three groups rated their initial homosexual experiences fairly positively, in the 3.5 to 3.7 range (between okay and good).
They are also similar in the uniformly lower ratings they give to their first
heterosexual activity. There is nearly a one-point drop in the mean rating
from homoerotic to heteroerotic activity for both the "homosexual/hetero-
sexual" and "heterosexual/homosexual" groups (from 3.6 to 2.8 among the
heterosexual/homosexual youth, and from 3.7 to 2.8 among the homosex-

ual/heterosexual youth.) The sequencing of the youths' first sexual experiences does not therefore appear related to the ages at which same and opposite-sex activity first occurred, nor to the youths' feelings regarding these first experiences. It is, rather, gender that plays the key role in the sequencing of first same-sex and opposite-sex relations, independent of other factors.

Boys revealed that they often sought heterosexual experiences, while girls often described heterosexual sex as something that had only happened to them at an earlier age. It is possible that the greater likelihood of sexual pressure and coercion experienced by females from heterosexual males predisposes them to the heterosexual/homosexual sequence, as a consequence of growing up in a society where females encounter such experiences much more commonly than males. Sexual socialization of young females, in public schools for example, typically prepares them to experience their sexuality in passive, non-agentic ways (Fine 1988). Girl's initial (and relatively less pleasurable) heteroerotic activity may serve as a basis of comparison that facilitates the translation to lesbian identities. For the first time, they may express what they want to desire as agents of their own desires. While both males and females are the object of heterosexual assumptions from family, peers and significant others in their milieu, males may experience greater cultural and familial expectations for heterosexual behavior, impelling them to engage or experiment with it regardless of their desires. Similar to the subject of reports on gay and lesbian adults (Weinberg and Williams 1974; Bell, Weinberg and Hammersmith 1981), some teens have told us that their wish was that, by engaging in opposite-sex behaviors, they would make the same sex desires go away.

The youths struggle beyond the feeling of hiding and remorse, facing for the first time how to relate their experiences to existing practices and structures in the culture. The fear that they are "really bisexual" and not gay or lesbian is important for two fundamental reasons. Historically, as we have seen, bisexual represents the nineteenth century mediation between "homosexual" and "heterosexual" in the conventional American cultural system. But as a new twentieth-century species, the liberated hedonist, the "bisexual" mediates "gay" and "straight" in the emergent cultural system of sexuality in the United States. Here, the new emphasis is upon an ideology of hedonism. There is, however, another factor: the sense in which to "come out," youth must confront whether he or she is not bisexual, rather than gay or lesbian, in terms of cultural roles and desires. Here, it is in this sense that contemporary "bisexuality" represents states of becoming and being that are transitional: the essence of liminal passage both for individuals and for cultures.

CONCLUSION

This paper compares the assumptions about bisexuality present in the research literature, with the greatly differing cultural realities of New Guinea and gay and lesbian-identified youth in Chicago. We have suggested that four views of bisexuality can be contrasted. With the exception of the first biological level, the other three are critical in social and behavioral research on sexuality and recent study of health and sexually transmitted diseases. We have suggested that the concepts of desire and identity have been conflated in sexual theory until recently, and sexual identity has had a floating meaning that undermines the nature of empirical data related to observed development, at least in Western urban populations. Culture has often been left out of the description of these phenomena. This has caused the investigation of "bisexuality" to leave the study of cultural action and historical context out of its total system of analysis. We claim that this was a critical error in the scientific modelling and research of past generations. New efforts should be devoted to investigating the cultural and historical contexts of bisexual identities, sexual interaction, and sexual cultures in Western and non-Western settings, in order to further understand the significance of bisexual conduct for the human species as a whole.

NOTES

Acknowlegments: Some of the data presented in this paper were collected under the auspices of the Project, "Sexual Orientation and Cultural Competence: A Chicago Study," G. Herdt, principal investigator, and we should like to thank the Spencer Foundation for their support. The arguments and supporting material from the two case studies of this paper are drawn in modified form from material discussed in two sources: see G. Herdt, "Introduction to the Paperback: Ten Years After *Ritualized Homosexuality in Melanesia*," in Herdt, Ritualized Homosexuality in Melanesia, 2nd ed. (Berkeley: University of California Press, 1993); and Gilbert Herdt and Andrew Boxer, *Children of Horizons* (Boston: Beacon Press, 1993). The writing of this chapter was made possible by Gilbert Herdt's sabbatical from the University of Chicago. Special thanks to Provost Edward O. Laumann for his support of this leave. For comments on the paper, we are especially indebted to Jeffrey Weiss and Richard Parker.

1. The material in this section is adopted in modified form from Herdt and Boxer 1993.

2. The material in this section is adopted in modified form from Herdt 1993.

3. Further, we may perhaps trace this desire for a common form (that is like the Western form) to our long-standing Western preoccupation with shared "psychic unity" and human nature (Herdt 1991a, 1991b; Spiro 1987).

4. See, especially, Herdt and Lindenbaum (1992) on AIDS and gays.

5. See, for a history of these typologies, the works of B. Adam, S. Murray, and more recently D. Greenberg, reviewed in Herdt (1990, 1991a).

6. Herdt interviewed Sam in part because our graduate student interviewers were reluctant to take him on. They felt that he was a fake, and they could not understand his self-image; another manifestation of the issues related to transference and counter-transference in a project of this kind. In fact, Herdt found him tentative and confused, but interesting and benign.

From *Bakla* to Gay

5

Shifting Gender Identities and Sexual
Behaviors in the Philippines

Michael L. Tan

THE FIRST REPORT OF HIV INFECTION IN THE PHILIPPINES dates back to 1984. Since then, the cumulative number of reported cases has reached 382 HIV positives and eighty-six AIDS cases as of the end of 1992. Health department officials acknowledge that the small number is due to underreporting and that the numbers of HIV infection may range from 5,000 to 35,000.

Among the cumulative reported cases, self-identified homosexual and bisexual men constitute seven percent of total HIV positives and forty-four percent of total AIDS cases. It is impossible to estimate what the real figures are for the general population or for men who have sex with men (MSMs), but the available statistics do suggest that HIV disease can become a significant problem among MSMs in the Philippines.

HIV prevention programs for MSMs in the Philippines need to be guided by sound research to explore the sexual networks within this population.[1] Unfortunately, other than research on contraceptive prevalence, the Philippines has never conducted comprehensive surveys on sex and sexuality. The emergence of HIV/AIDS created justification for such surveys, which have been mostly Metro-Manila based. One important survey, commissioned by the U.S. AIDSCOM project (and which I was later asked to analyze [Tan 1990]), was conducted in Metro Manila in 1989 by a marketing research firm among "sentinel populations." One of the surveyed populations consisted of a random sample of 150 young adult males (aged eighteen to twenty-four years), where fifteen percent of respondents said they had had same-sex sexual encounters. The figure here comes significantly close to the reported statistic of seventeen percent with another sentinel population: a convenience sample of young male overseas contract workers.

The statistics suggest that there are significant numbers of Filipino MSMs. However, this population is far from being homogeneous, and consists of many sub-cultures defined by variables such as socio-economic status, age, ethnicity, rural/urban origins, and religious affiliation.

In this paper, my main reference group will be participants in a series of workshops sponsored by The Library Foundation (TLF), a Metro–Manila based group of self-identified gay men. Since 1991, TLF has conducted twelve weekend workshops for about 300 men who have sex with men, addressing HIV prevention in the context of the psychosocial needs of the population. I will cite some information derived from self-administered workshop question-naires,[2] as well as from interviews and group discussions with the participants both during and after the workshops.

I choose the TLF workshop participants as a reference group because they represent a subculture that is emerging in many developing countries, one whose members self-identify as "gay," and who are beginning to identify with an emerging "gay" community. Passing references to similar groups are found for the *homos* in Indonesia (Oetomo 1991) and the *entendidos* in Brazil (Parker 1985). Such groups remain a minority within the larger population of MSMs but may prove to be crucial as organized responses to the HIV/AIDS epidemic, not just within the MSM population but also in AIDS service organizations in general, where gay men and lesbians have become increasingly active.

THEORETICAL AND METHODOLOGICAL PREMISES

The TLF program to reach MSMs in the Philippines works on the premise that this population's risk for HIV emerges from the stigmatization of homo-sexuality. It is this stigmatization that forces MSMs to circulate within "shadow" sexual networks where sexual encounters are necessarily anony-mous and casual. Over the last year and a half, as the program developed, it became clear that this explanation of "anonymous and casual sex" was inade-quate. Even among MSMs who had "come out" and self-identify as "gay," comfortably socializing in the few gay establishments in Metro Manila, there are still problems with social networking, sexual negotiations, and HIV risk-reduction.

One important issue that emerged during the workshops was the partici-pants' own observation that risk-reduction in sexual behavior is, to a large extent, dependent on specific social settings, particularly "who you are having sex with." In this paper, I will show how these different forms of social interac-tions relate to sexual identity and how this identity is in turn related to dominant sexual ideologies, including homophobia.

As Dollimore (1991:28–29) points out, the problem of homophobia is that it is not, as the term phobic suggests, an essentially personal problem. Rather, homophobia, especially in relation to HIV/AIDS, intersects with misogyny, xenophobia, racism and, I would add, discrimination based on class and other socioeconomic status variables. In this paper, I will cite several examples of these intersections not just from outside the MSM population but, more importantly, from within.

AN OVERVIEW

There are a number of Filipino MSM sub-cultures that are fairly visible to the public. The visible sub-cultures are all urban-based and consist mainly of people aged below thirty.

1. *Call Boys.* These are male sex workers, whose clientele includes MSMs from different subcultures, as well as middle-aged women (*matronas*). Most call boys self-identify as "straight" and many have wives and children. Many come from urban and rural poor families. The sex workers rarely have fixed incomes except for those who do "macho dancing" or work as waiters. Most call boys are "on call" with various bars and massage parlors, receiving payment only when they have clients. There is also a large number of free-lance call boys who cruise the many shopping malls scattered throughout the metropolis.

    Call boys are an important segment of the MSM population. In cities outside Metro Manila, there are no gay bars but there are many free-lance male sex workers. In Metro Manila itself, there were as of February 1993 at least sixteen gay bars and massage parlors offering male sex workers, as against three exclusively "gay" and six "gay-friendly" establishments that do not actively promote male sex workers. Even in these "non-commercial" establishments, there will be a few free-lance sex workers, including in some instances waiters of the establishments, offering sex for pay.

2 *Parloristas.* This is a generic term for low-income MSMs, many of whom work in beauty parlors although there are also those working as domestic servants, small market vendors, and as waiters. For the average Filipino, the *parloristas,* who are found throughout the country, represent the entire "homosexual" population, defined as *bakla,* a gender label which I will explain later in this paper. The *parloristas* rarely patronize "gay" establishments and tend to organize their own activities, usually drag beauty pageants, through neighborhood associations.

3. *Gays.* This group has become visible only in the last two decades in Metro Manila. Many self-identify as "gay," "homosexual" or "bisexual," and in contradistinction to the lower-class *bakla/parlorista.* The group is far from being homogeneous, and can basically be divided into those with middle-class origins[3] and those from high-income groups. It is the middle-class group that has been actively organizing the country's gay men's organizations. This gay population remains partly in the shadows, socializing in gay establishments in Metro Manila but keeping its sexual orientation discreet at

home and in their workplace. The middle-income groups, far more
vulnerable to economic dislocation, tend to remain in the closet even as
they become active in gay groups. High-income gay men are more willing
to come out, but are essentially apolitical and limit their activities to socializing. These three visible populations have varying linkages with the larger,
shadow MSM population consisting of individuals who may self-identify as
homosexual but are not "out," as well as others who self-identify as bisexual
or heterosexual. Sexual encounters between the "overt" and "covert"
sectors of the MSM population are limited to such places as bathhouses,
moviehouses, shopping malls, or establishments with male sex workers.

SOCIAL CONTEXT: FROM THE OUTSIDE LOOKING IN

The Filipino term most widely used as a gloss for "homosexual" is *bakla*, a
contraction of the words *babae* (female) and *lalake* (male). As an adjective, *bakla*
means uncertainty, indecisiveness. Other, less often used terms carry similar
connotations: *binabae* (like a woman) and *syoki* (evolved from the Southern
Chinese Hokkien words *syo k'i*, meaning weak-spirited).

As in many other societies, there are no Filipino terms for the different
categories of sexual orientation, i.e., "homosexual," "bisexual," or "heterosexual." *Bakla* refers specifically to men who are effeminate, with cross-dressing as
a major index feature. It is the concept of effeminacy, of a man with a woman's
heart (*pusong babae*), that dominates public discourse, lumping together homosexuals, transvestites, transsexuals, and hermaphrodites. The English term
"effeminate" is frequently used, and is defined in Webster's as recently as 1979:
"having the qualities generally attributed to women, as weakness, gentleness,
delicacy, etc.; unmanly."

The term "homosexual," of recent vintage even in the West, remains
ambiguous in the Philippines. It is most often interchanged with *bakla*, with an
emphasis on effeminacy and cross-dressing. The "sexual" in "homosexual"
seems to have introduced a new element of recognizing sexual activity as possibly, but not necessarily, present among the *bakla*.

The public perception of bisexuality is even more enigmatic, mainly
because of the difficulty with dissociating effeminacy and homosexuality.
Some Filipinos, including many self-identified homosexuals, will declare that
bisexuals are "really" homosexuals in the closet. A hybrid term, "macho gay,"
is sometimes used to refer to bisexuals.

Curiously, the term "gay" has also become widely used, mainly as a
synonym for homosexual. I should emphasize that "gay" is used like the term
"homosexual," which still centers on the *bakla*, the effeminate male or the male
with a woman's heart, expanded to include, rather hazily, a sexual persona.

The medicalization and pathologization of homosexuality in the West has been incorporated into Filipino popular perceptions of the *bakla*. Freudian theories that attribute male homosexuality to a dominant mother and absent or weak father continue to be widely invoked, perhaps because they offer a "logical" explanation for the consequences of a subversion of machismo norms. Male sex workers fret about eventually turning *bakla*. Parents explain their sons being *bakla* as resulting from going around with other *bakla*. *Bakla* is *nakakahawa*, contagious, an interesting conflation of concepts of danger and contagion.

Recent U.S. research into the genetic origins of male homosexuality has had great impact on popular myths. The "gay brain" theory has been especially popular and has been repackaged by the lay public into what I call a "smaller brain" theory.[4]

The reduced or deficient gay brain image fits into other popular myths, such as homosexuality being equated with effeminacy, which is in turn explained as being due to hormonal deficiency and a small brain. The emergence of HIV/AIDS has contributed toward remedicalizing and repathologizing homosexuality, with the discourse centering on the "perversion" of sodomy.

This discussion of the "outsider" perspective is important in contextualizing gender identities among MSMs. We will see how the definition of a *bakla* as a feminized male is ideologically dominant, shaping MSMs' own constructions of gender identity and behavior.

SELF-IDENTIFICATION: GAY OR BAKLA?

I will now discuss native or ethnic perspectives starting with the participants in TLF's workshops. The workshop participants were demographically homogeneous: most were aged under thirty (eighty-eight percent), raised in Metro Manila (seventy-eight percent), college-educated or current college students (ninety-four percent), and Roman Catholic (eighty-three percent).

About seventy percent of the workshop participants self-identified as homosexual, twenty-five percent as bisexual; two percent as heterosexual and the remaining four percent having no response or not being sure. The differences in self-ascribed sexual orientation, particularly for "homosexuals" and "bisexuals," are important.

Most TLF participants seem to prefer the label "gay," rather than *bakla*, which is identified with the low-income *parlorista*. Among middle- and high-income MSMs, the social construction of the *bakla* as an effeminate cross-dresser generates an extraordinary amount of cognitive dissonance which in turn affects the process of self-identification. One TLF workshop participant could not have summarized it better than when he described his alarm that he might be "abnormal," the abnormality being defined as a contradiction between his being attracted to other men, and yet never having the desire to cross-dress.

Among the few participants who have come out to their family, some describe how their parents accept the disclosure with one request: that they do not cross-dress like a *bakla* (read *parlorista*). The emphasis seems to shift toward status-defined norms and even desexualization. There may, in fact, be underlying messages that "as long as my son does not cross-dress like my hairdresser, he probably will not be having sex with other men."

I must emphasize that many "feminine" behavioral traits and cross-dressing have been adopted by the TLF workshop participants. However, they do distinguish their "feminized" behavior from that of the *parlorista*. Most of the TLF workshop participants consider as unacceptable "routine" daily cross-dressing as the *parloristas* would do. Moreover, "feminization" follows class distinctions between the *colegiala* (product of convent schools) and the *palengkera* (a woman market vendor.) A person who does not behave like an *Assumptionista* (a graduate of the Assumption, an elite girls' school) is labelled as a graduate of Madam Kollerman's, a vocational school that trains beauticians and dressmakers. Being gay seems to be different from being *bakla*.

There is recognition of types within the population, corresponding loosely to the Americans' differentiation of "butch" and "fem" types. Those tending toward masculinity are called *"pa-om"* while *"pa-girl"* is used for the more feminine types. *"Om"* is a phonetic rendition of the abbreviated *hombre*, Spanish for male. The prefix *"pa"* describes mimicry, loosely translated as "to be like." The linguistic choice here reifies perceptions of a liminal status: neither male nor female, only like-male and like-female. A "real" male remains an *om* (or *hombre*) and a "real" female remains a girl.

COMING OUT: *PAGLADLAD NG KAPA*

Coming out is described in Filipino gay jargon as *pagladlad ng kapa* or an unfurling of one's cape. The process is long and difficult. Someone calling himself "Spartan Warrior" (1993) wrote to a clinical psychologist/newspaper columnist expressing his conflicts as he discovers he is attracted to other men. The feelings, he says, are "strange" because "you see, I am cursed with an athletic body. . ." Spartan Warrior says that he intends to remain in the closet: "I cannot do what the *ladlad na bakla* would do externally—act effeminately, dress effeminately, etc." The letter is excruciatingly self-absorbed as Spartan Warrior alternates between expressions of contentment and depression over his situation. Yet, Spartan Warrior probably is typical of Filipino MSMs. It is not surprising that in a gay play produced in 1992 about the problems of "coming out" in the Philippines, the lead character is portrayed by a "butch" type while his alter ego is a drag queen impersonating Diana Ross. This

dialectical angst seems to permeate the discourse among MSMs, and is dangerous in the way it becomes a device for self-marginalization: me against the
world, including the queens.

Given that effeminacy is the gold standard for coming out as *bakla* or as "a
gay" (Filipinos use gay more often as a noun, rather than as an adjective), it
should not be surprising that people opt to remain in the closet, or, to tenta-
tively move into self-identification as bisexual. During TLF workshop sessions
discussing "gay issues," the issue of bisexuality often emerged with many
participants, almost always the more fem types, expressing their view that there
was no such thing as a bisexual, i.e., that bisexuals were simply "gays who have
not come out."

While it is tempting to dismiss such observations as facetious, we can look
back at the statistics for the TLF participants. While twenty-five percent self-
identified as bisexual, only nine percent of all the participants reported having
sex with both men and women in the past year. Note, too, that this figure of
nine percent included a number of participants who self-identified as homosexual.

Self-identification as a bisexual, at least among the TLF workshop participants, may represent an "in process" mode as individuals come to terms with
their sexuality. One of TLF's male-to-male helpline counsellors told me, "I get
all these calls from men who claim they are bisexual simply because they had
sex with a woman eight years ago." Margarita Go-singco Holmes, a clinical
psychologist who writes the newspaper advice column I referred to earlier,
says she gets many letters similar to the calls received at TLF's helpline from
people asking if they are "gay," always prefaced by a reference to a girlfriend, or
to sexual experiences with women a few years back.

The term "defense bisexuality" has been suggested to refer to sexual behavior in societies that stigmatize homosexual roles (Ross 1991:23). In the same
way that many textbooks describe "homosexuality" as a passing stage, I suggest
here that self-ascribed bisexuality may in fact represent a transient "heterosexuality" for Filipino MSMs still unravelling their sexuality. It is significant that
among the TLF participants, the average age of self-identified bisexuals was
significantly lower than that of self-identified homosexuals.

I find it significant that self-ascribed bisexuality would emerge within the
TLF group. For self-ascribed bisexuals, if we understand this to be a code for
"sexuality-in-process," attending a three-day live-in workshop publicized as
being for MSMs can be daunting, representing a major step in a public unfurling of the cape.

I am not suggesting that "bisexuals," as defined in Western societies along
the criterion of sex object choice, do not exist in the Philippines. Neither am I
suggesting that the "bisexuals" in the TLF workshops exist only as semantic,

self-ascribed categories. The TLF workshop surveys in fact showed very important differences in the sexual behavior of homosexuals and bisexuals. Yet, it is significant that when I cited the survey statistics showing that twenty-five percent of the participants self-identified as bisexual, most of the TLF members I talked with expressed surprise, and could not identify who the "bisexuals" were. "Bisexual," in the context of the TLF workshop participants, defies existing definitions of homosexual and bisexual, *pa-om* and *pa-girl*, gay and macho gay. These gray areas affect the processes of coming out and acceptance into the emerging gay community.

CHOICE OF SEXUAL PARTNERS: AVOIDING THE CLASH OF CYMBALS

It is interesting that many Filipino self-identified gay men will shift from statements such as "There is no such thing as a bisexual—they're all closet gays" to an observation like "Most Filipino males are bisexual," in reference to the perception that many "straight" males will have sex with another male.

This takes us into a discussion of sexual object choice. Among *parloristas*, sex between two *bakla*, or two self-identified gay men, is labelled "lesbianism" and is described as a clash of cymbals (*pompyangan*). A *bakla* can have sex only with a "straight man." This "rule" finds support in the Metro-Manila survey I mentioned earlier in this paper. One sample of that survey included 200 "overt" gay males, with fifty-seven percent expressing a preference for "straight males" as sex partners, while only eight percent said they prefer "co-homosexuals." All this fits into the social construction of the *bakla* as feminine.

It is interesting how the *bakla*-as-feminine image emerges in the sex object choice of MSMs who self-identify as "straight." With this subculture of "straight MSMs," the preference is for someone who is "*pa-girl*." There is logical consistency here because a self-identified straight male going to bed with an equally masculine (by his standards) male would forfeit his claims to being straight. "Girl" is again relative. One male sex worker explains: "I cannot do it with someone with a penis larger than mine. *Hindi bagay sa bakla*. It (a larger penis) does not fit a *bakla*."

It is instructive to look into the following account from a physician who conducted interviews in a bathhouse whose clients are MSMs mainly self-identifying as "straight" or "bisexual."

> I had this guy who said he doesn't use condoms. When I asked him why, he answered: *"Straight ako. Hindi naman ako gumagalaw; ako ang ginagalaw. Ako ang sumusubo."* (I am straight. I do not move; I am moved. I am the one who feeds.)

Two keywords are worth analyzing here. One is the verb *galaw*, to move, which is used in conversational Filipino to refer to sexual intercourse. Usually, it is the man who "moves" a woman, meaning to have sex with a woman. In fact, all the Filipino verbs used to allude to having sex put the male in an active role: *trabaho* (to work); *banat* (to hit); *tira* (to hit); *gamit* (to use). All these terms reflect the male's role as penetrator. Yet, in the context of a self-identified straight man who has sex with other men, validation of his sexual identity is grafted on to the concept that it is a *bakla* who initiates sex. The "straight" man is now the one "moved."

The other key word is *subo*, to feed. The straight man's sexual passivity is qualified by his active role in oral sex—he feeds, the *bakla* eats.[5] Perhaps more important for HIV/AIDS programs is that all this discourse, despite its play on the active and passive roles, continues to place the "straight" man having sex with other men in a penetrator role while the *bakla*, consistent with his constructed feminine role, is defined as the one being penetrated whether in oral or anal sex.

It is not clear how much of stereotype corresponds to reality. I have strong doubts about the hegemony of this penetrator/penetrated dichotomy even in sexual activities between a self-identified straight male and a *bakla*. Nevertheless, the rhetoric is important in that a straight male is defined as a "natural" sex object choice for the *bakla* and that this straight male takes a dominant role which includes being the one chased, courted, moved, worked on, fed on, by a *bakla*.

Let us look now at the TLF workshop participants. In contrast to the stereotype, preferences for bisexuals and gay men dominated. At the same time, there were significant numbers indicating preference for "straight" men, either as a sole choice or in combination with "bisexual."

Preferred Male Sex Partners of TLF Workshop Participants

	Homosexuals (n=147)	Bisexuals (n=52)	Total
1) Bisexuals only	28	34	62
2) Gay only	57	3	60
3) Straight only	28	4	32
4) Gay and bisexuals	8	5	13
5) Straight and bisexual	8	5	13
6) Gay, bisexual or straight	12	1	13
7) Straight and gay	6	0	6

Put briefly, the TLF workshop participants represent an incipient subculture that retains elements of a dominant sexual ideology, particularly the preference for a straight male. At the same time, there are shifts in these preferences, such as a willingness to have gay or bisexual partners sometimes with a provision that they "look straight." It would be useful to remember that a "bisexual" is often perceived as a "straight-looking gay male."

In a focus group discussion where I presented the statistics on preferred choices for sexual partners, the consensus that emerged was that "choices" were made at different levels. A "straight" man may be preferred for a casual sexual encounter, but a "gay" or "bisexual" male, preferably "straight-looking," would be preferred for a lover.

The willingness to go into a "lesbian" relationship is apparently class-bound. For a middle-class self-identified "gay" person, homosexual or bisexual, a relationship with a *parlorista* would be unthinkable. Here, the rhetoric of the clashing of cymbals would be invoked: a *parlorista* is too "fem" to be a sex partner or even a date. Class definitions of "decency" (*pagkadesente*) are clearly present, intersecting with a fear of being "outed" (*mabuking*, always used in the passive voice) by being seen with a *parlorista*.

The distinction between casual sex partners and lovers is important. This differentiation sets boundaries for a network of dating and steady relationships with people from the same class background even as the boundaries can, and are, easily crossed for casual sex, as they would be with low-income male sex workers or other pick-ups.

Rules extend into roles in oral and anal sex. In the focus group discussion, participants agreed that, with oral sex, alternating of roles (insertor and insertee) occurs more frequently than it does with anal sex. Apparently, the masculine/feminine imagery in anal intercourse is much more powerful, especially as it translates into roles of penetrator and penetrated. Discussions about anal intercourse tend to be protracted, evoking images of male and female roles. It is also interesting how some TLF workshop participants view anal intercourse as representing a relationship of domination and submission.

The implied power relationships in sexual activities are crucial. Rules are recognized as being flexible, depending on who the sexual partner is. One participant explained: "You can't just tell your lover, 'Bend over'," implying that this is possible in other situations, such as with a sex worker. Curiously, during the focus group discussion there was no consensus on when such transgressions are permitted. Some said there are fewer prohibitions in casual sex while others said such "don'ts" were more important in a relationship with a lover.

The growing HIV/AIDS threat may provide new rhetoric that will affect gender identity and sexuality, even as such rhetoric draws on existing sexual ideologies. It is here where we find sharp intersections with misogyny, xenophobia, and class discrimination. For example, the popular perception of HIV and sexually-transmitted diseases (STDs) in the Philippines is still that of *sakit ng babae*, or women's disease. It is not surprising, then, to hear Filipino MSMs talking of HIV risk-reduction in terms of avoiding men who have women, especially women sex workers, as partners.

This concept of STDs as women's diseases interfaces with the perception of the *bakla*. As early as 1985, patrons in a bar patronized by high-income gay men complained to me about how the establishment had been invaded by "cheap *parlorista* queens who probably have AIDS." The rationale here was that the *parloristas* (actually, transvestite sex workers) were the only ones willing to have sex with tourists, who by that time were shunned as being potential "AIDS carriers."

In a kind of time warp, it was not until this decade that I began to hear comments from male sex workers expressing their reluctance to have sex with wealthy Filipino clients because such clients had lived in the U.S. and Europe where their "*Kano*" (a generic term for Caucasians) partners were presumed infected with HIV. Such comments conflict with other sex workers' views that it is safer to pick a client who looks *decente* (decent) because such clients are *malinis* (clean).

SYNTHESIS: FROM EPIDEMIOLOGY TO EPISTEMOLOGY

Social scientists working on HIV/AIDS often reduce their research to an epidemiological framework of asking, as a recent editorial in *The Lancet* did: "How often, and in what ways, and with whom people have sex." Vance (1991:880) describes this as "the tendency to count acts rather than explore meaning." The biomedical framework drops off four other important questions that need to be asked: "Where, when, why and why not?"

In this paper, I have tried to show how the expanded framework is important in understanding the social context for HIV transmission in relation to the MSM population in the Philippines. This is, in a sense, an attempt to reconstruct, as cultural history, "a chronicle of intentions, contigencies, and relationships: among people, in a culture, over time" (Fox 1991:95).

I have given examples to show how the socially-constructed definition of *bakla*, a man with a woman's heart, dominates discourse on male homosexuality and bisexuality. Further complicating sexual ideology are other dominant values such as misogyny, xenophobia, and class discrimination.

I have discussed the impact of this rhetoric on gender and sexuality among a small group of MSMs in the Philippines, one that challenges tradition even as it remains bound to it. The shifts in gender definitions are important, especially in terms of how one comes out of the closet, how one chooses sexual partners, and how one enters (and exits) relationships, whether casual or long-term.

Despite the rhetoric of a community whose members can openly relate to each other, and to the "straight" public as gay men, there are still many problems in social and sexual negotiations. While many Filipino gay men are aware of gender asymmetry in a relationship between a gay man and a straight man, there tends to be less sensitivity to similar problems between or among self-identified gay men. Among TLF workshop participants, about half of those presently having a lover said they did not know or were unsure if their current lover was having sex with other partners. The problems are inevitable: in an incipient subculture, traditional social and sexual scripts may be insufficient. In the process of transcending gender stereotypes, the emerging "gay" community has to create and ratify a new intersubjectivity.

This intersubjectivity will be an important consideration in HIV prevention programs. The self-esteem and individual change of values that comes with affirmation of one's sexuality may not be enough. In fact, given the middle-class definitions of "being a gay" in the Philippines, this group could easily lapse into creating a moral *cordon sanitaire,* thinking of themselves as "safe," in contradistinction to "the others," whether they be foreigners, women sex workers or the *parlorista/bakla.*

Such dangers may even be amplified among those in a relationship with a lover. At the same time, there may be a danger in over-emphasizing the risks of "anonymous, casual encounters," since high-risk activities may happen more often in the search for a longer lasting relationship, i.e., when one party thinks he has to "prove" his commitment by consenting to unprotected anal intercourse.

Considering that Philippine society continues to be heavily dominated by strong patron-client relationships, it is easy for high-income and middle-class gay men to attempt to reproduce their "values" and sexual ideological framework as they begin to reach out to low-income men who have sex with men, including the *parlorista.* The shifts in gender identity, and in sexual behavior, will continue. Undoubtedly, HIV/AIDS will be a major force in the reshaping of boundaries. The problem is identifying the boundaries as they exist both for the visible populations and for the shadow populations—for example, older MSMs; MSMs married to women; MSMs in areas outside Metro Manila. More importantly, we need to better understand the social dynamics involved in the shaping of these boundaries, both as they draw from and resist dominant ideologies.

Notes

1. Despite its biomedical and behaviorist emphasis, I will use the term MSM because it is internationally accepted among groups working on HIV/AIDS.
2. Data cited in this paper comes from only 210 questionnaires since The Library Foundation revised its forms several times, resulting in difficulties in comparing information.
3. "Middle-class" here refers to the petty-bourgeoisie including students, white-collar workers and professionals on fixed wage income. The monthly incomes range from US $200 to US $1500 in a country where the average monthly household income in 1991 was US $210 (National Statistics Office 1992).
4. An example comes from a woman writing in a community newspaper, where she urges parents not to beat up their *bakla* sons because (citing "Le Vay, neurobiologist from the Salk Institute") being *bakla* is physiological. The writer's interpretation of Le Vay: "when growing up they got less neutrons in their hypothalamus" (Austria 1993).
5. This is a reversal of the terms described by Fry (1985) and Parker (1991) for Brazil, where the *homem,* by playing the penetrator role, eats, while the *bicha,* the insertee, gives.

Political Sexualities   6

Meanings and Identities in the Time of AIDS

Dennis Altman

FEW AREAS OF HUMAN LIFE ARE AS SOCIALLY SHAPED AS SEXUALITY, although few are as often discussed as if they were biologically determined. Popular discourse is full of comments which assume certain forms of "natural" sexuality: men are assumed to be "naturally" promiscuous, women to be "naturally" monogamous; sexual attraction is attributed to "body chemistry"; homosexuality is condemned by traditional moralists as "unnatural" or justified by reference to the fact that it can be found in many animal species. Even though one can find evidence of almost any possible pattern of sexual behavior in some animal species, the temptation to anthropomorphism remains strong, and otherwise sensible people who would not, presumably, dismiss clothing or French cuisine on the ground that "animals don't do it" nonetheless use such arguments when it comes to sexuality.

At the other extreme is what one might call a postmodern constructionism, one which defines sexuality as totally a product of culture without any reference to its biological basis. One of the most frustrating aspects of postmodern discourse is its striking ignorance of the social sciences, and the belief that the human construction of sexuality and, indeed, of "human nature" itself, was only understood since a handful of writers in the inner arrondissements of Paris developed theories of discourse, otherness and the relativity of power. The fact is that such ideas grow out of long-standing debates built on readings of both Freud and Marx, and have been powerful counter-forces to empiricism and positivism throughout most of this century. As Juliet Mitchell wrote (in 1971): "Freud discovered the crucial importance of the social construction of the human animal; that this biosexual interpretation of the anatomical-biological made the person a person, constructed the mind, the conscious and the unconscious" (Mitchell 1971).

This view is parallelled by writings which grew out of a Marxist view of human nature. Those Marxists, such as Wilhelm Reich or Herbert Marcuse, who tried to marry a social analysis with the insights of psychoanalysis are now largely ignored, although such is the rapidity of academic fads that their re-discovery is surely imminent. Those of us in the early days of the gay and women's movement who were influenced by such ideas—as well as Mitchell and myself, I think of Shulamith Firestone, Mario Mieli, Guy Hocquenghem—are almost entirely unread by a new generation of literary critics who seem to believe that social constructionism, if not the discovery of "difference," began with Foucault and has ended with Queer Nation (see, for exemple, Altman 1972; Firestone 1971; Hocquenghem 1978; Mieli 1980).

The point of this aside is to stress that we are dealing with the intersection of the biological and the social: sexual behaviors, identities, meanings, fears, and desires are all products of the vast diversity and ingenuity with which humans make sense of their bodies and its potentials. For all sorts of historical and socio-political reasons these potentials become transformed into cate-gories, and then into identities, so that we speak of "pedophiles" and "sado-masochists" rather than of the much more complex—and threaten-ing—possibility that these are potential desires and practices within all human beings. This construction of sexual categories is very marked in the response to the HIV/AIDS epidemic: most notably, of course, in the case of the male homosexual—now transformed into the Man Who Has Sex With Men—but also apparent in the descriptions of others in the cast: "the commercial sex worker"; "the promiscuous woman"; etc. (Connell and Dowsett 1992).

This paper discusses several major areas where HIV/AIDS has shaped both discourses and behavior around sexuality, and where the political nature of how we understand sexuality is sharply apparent. In so doing I am very conscious of the relatively privileged position from which I write, as a gay man living in an affluent and relatively progressive society where consider-able resources have been made available both for HIV prevention and treatment programs. My contribution is necessarily a partial one, and I shall try to explore the limits of that partiality at the end of this paper.

THE POLITICAL CONTEXT OF CURRENT DEBATES ON SEXUALITY

Three points should be made about AIDS in this context: where it was first identified, amongst which groups, and at what point in history.

While the HIV virus has undoubtedly been around in some form for much longer than we have spoken of it, and may well have been infecting humans for many decades, a syndrome of acquired immune deficiency was first iden-tified among American homosexual men in the early 1980s. Thus AIDS—and remember that for a short time it was actually referred to as "Gay Related Immune Deficiency"—was defined as both homosexual and American, identifications which have continued to shape responses to the epidemic. For many years the response to AIDS in a number of countries was to flirt with ideas of quarantining those perceived as "risk groups"—which quickly came to include I.V. drug users, Africans and Haitians—or at least to submit such groups to increased surveillance (see Altman 1986). Even today such attitudes persist—though only Cuba has made quarantine a central part of its AIDS control program—and, as all those branded as "risk groups" well know, have contributed considerably to growing prejudice and discrimination.

But even if we are now aware that HIV is restricted by neither geography nor sexual/behavioral categories, the ways in which we understand the epidemic is very much marked by the legacy of the 1980s. This is clearest in terms of bio-medical knowledge; without the advances made in the previous decade in virology there would have been no possibility of identifying HIV, and of making even the limited advances towards arresting its ravages which have been achieved. But in social and political terms as well, the history of the epidemic bears the mark of the contemporary world: routes of transmission, spread of knowledge about HIV, political responses (or lack of them), availability of resources to combat the epidemic are all very much contingent on the larger political environment. This has, of course, been extensively documented in the case of the limited efforts in the United States to prevent transmission, as the needs of effective AIDS prevention collided with other agendas, mainly moralistic ones born of the Republican Party's courting of the religious right. Equally significant, pressure from such groups and the economic rationalism which became the dominant ethos of the decade has restricted many international donor agencies and helped slow-down any concerted global response to the epidemic. The growth of the epidemic over the past few years has been accompanied by a general slow down in development assistance, in turn a product of both economic recession in the rich world and of the collapse of Cold War tensions. (Ironically, the collapse of Communism in Eastern Europe and the former Soviet Union, has greatly increased vulnerability to HIV in that zone, with marked increases in population movements, prostitution and drug use, and the full or partial collapse of many medical services.)

More specifically, in terms of our concerns here, AIDS came along in an historical epoch which had seen the development of gender and sexuality as the basis for political mobilization, and many of the more effective responses to the new epidemic were framed by the discourses and experiences of certain social movements. Most important for the argument I shall proceed to make in the next section, one might argue both that the spread of HIV *and* some of the most effective programs against it were facilitated by the emergence of gay affirmation and politics.

In those developed countries where community organizations first developed to meet the challenges of the new epidemic, they almost always built on the already existing networks and personnel of the lesbian/gay movement. Whether through the building of new organizations, such as Gay Men's Health Crisis in New York (probably the first community-based response to the new disease), or through already existing structures, which was the pattern in much of northern Europe, the gay community often provided the first non-government responses to the epidemic, providing information, counselling, and support services to clients drawn from across society. As the epidemiology of the disease changed, this has produced considerable strain on the original gay-based agencies, which is a point worth discussion (see Padgug and Oppenheimer 1992).

Less often remarked is the role of gay communities—sometimes lesbian and gay communities, as in Nicaragua and Peru—in developing countries. To take the part of the developing world I know best, namely Southeast Asia, what is striking is the role played by gay men in establishing AIDS organizations in a number of countries. The most impressive example probably comes from Malaysia, an officially Islamic country, in which the group Pink Triangle—and the name is as resonant of a gay consciousness as was G.M.H.C. some years earlier in New York—has led the major community iniative in developing a response to AIDS, not only among homosexual men but also within the larger society. Similar comments could be made of Singapore, Indonesia, Thailand, and the Philippines, and in the latter two countries gay groups have worked closely with groups of commercial sex workers to develop community-based programs designed to prevent the transmission of the virus.

One of the consequences of the role of gay-based organizations was to increase considerably the recognition of a gay community as a legitimate player in pluralist politics (and thus, as its detractors like to say in Australia, the emergence of "a gay lobby.") How far the state has been prepared to officially recognize the gay community as deserving recognition, participation in policy making, and state funding has varied enormously, from situations such as those in Australia, San Francisco, and Denmark, where radicals within the community deplore the co-option of "their" institutions into the bureaucratic establishment, to situations such as exist in Japan, most of southern Europe, and many parts of the United States, where gay participation is possible only through the back door.

Sexuality was already politicized before AIDS, whether in rich countries—where arguments around abortion, pornography, homosexuality, etc., seemed to have inherited the passion formerly reserved for class disputes, or in developing ones, where basic questions around women's sexuality and reproduction were often the base for unstated conflict around the basic rights of women and human rights in general. AIDS has made it harder to deny the enormously political significance of what is often defined as belonging to the personal sphere, and hence regarded as the preserve of religion or tradition. With HIV it is no longer possible to believe that Papal pronouncements against birth control, or Hindu and Islamic prohibitions of homosexuality, are "merely" questions of personal values or traditional beliefs; people will live or die depending on how far traditional prejudices and superstitions are allowed to survive.

Above all, AIDS has given an added urgency to issues of gender inequality, as women find themselves doubly affected by the epidemic, both because of their vulnerability to infection and because social expectations make them most responsible for care of the sick and the surviving. Just as we must acknowledge the work of gay communities in a number of countries, so it is important to acknowledge the absolutely central role played by women and women's organizations in much of Africa and South Asia, in the Caribbean and the Pacific. Here we find a reversal of the unconscious assumption that the western world becomes the model for the developing one: while this is largely true of gay men, in the case of women the first initiatives came from groups such as TASO in Uganda or those organizations working with sex-workers such as Kabalikat (Philippines) or EMPOWER (Thailand), and awareness of their efforts has had some impact on women working on development and health issues in Western countries.

THE STRENGTHENING OF SEXUAL IDENTITIES

To revert for a moment to the example of Pink Triangle: as it has developed, and also as other non-government organizations such as the Malaysian Council of Women have come to place greater priority on AIDS, there has been something of a debate on how far Pink Triangle should emphasize its gayness. The space opened up by the epidemic has allowed for a new openness about not just homosexuality but also about the growth of self-conscious homosexual *identities* in much of Asia; at last year's AIDS in Asia and the Pacific Conference held in Delhi, one of the most active caucuses was the lesbian/gay one, which included groups from a number of Asian countries. (The caucus was forced to meet in a park across the road from the official conference venue where no rooms for it could be found—and that contrast illuminates many of the problems facing emergent gay groups in the developing world.) Homosexual organizations across the world, in the Philippines, Poland, and Peru, as much as in Norway and New Zealand, face the dilemma of having to simultaneously stress that there is nothing inherent about homosexuality which links it to HIV, while also stressing the enormous impact the epidemic has had and is having on their communities. As Steve Epstein put it:

> This dehomosexualizing of AIDS, supported by gay activists in the hope that it would destigmatize the disease, seems instead to be resulting in the increasing marginalization of gays and lesbians within anti-AIDS efforts. Now that AIDS has become a "national" (or heterosexual) concern, the voice of the gay community is being muzzled by the mainstream experts, the media and the politicians. (Epstein 1988)

Thus while gay groups can fully support the analyses which link HIV to gender inequality and socio-economic structures, there is also an uneasy sense in which they see these absolutely correct analyses being used in practice to deny the special risks and consequences of the epidemic to themselves. This combination of a sense of vulnerability and of denial of their very existence has been a powerful factor in strengthening the centrality of homosexuality to many people and in the emergence of gay identities and communities in a number of countries which had not known them prior to the epidemic. In particular, it has led to an assertion of gay identity which combines some of the political analyses drawn from the Western homosexual world with a growing interest in the often buried homosexual traditions of non-Western cultures and societies.

A particular issue which arises here is the complex relationship between lesbians and gay men. On the face of it AIDS could be expected to increase the gap between the two communities, and indeed some lesbians have been very bitter about what they perceive as the enormous resources and attention the epidemic has won for gay men. When I argued this a few years ago at a conference in Amsterdam I was strongly contradicted by some women, particularly from the United States, where lesbians had played a significant role in AIDS organizations from the outset. Cross-national generalizations are almost impossible, but certainly AIDS has been a central issue in coalition politics, even as there has tended to be greater co-operation between lesbians and gay men in most Western countries with which I am familiar over the past few years. In several Asian countries, the new gay assertion born of the HIV epidemic has led to attempts to reach out to women who are constructing lesbian identities and communities for themselves.

Just as the AIDS epidemic has contributed to the strengthening of gay identity, so too it has helped construct "the sex worker" as a discrete identity/category, partly born of the sociological gaze, partly out of agitation by sex-workers themselves. The term is very different in its connotations from the more common "prostitute." Most significant, for this argument, it implies a particular definition, about which it is assumed there is little room for confusion: if one engages in sex primarily to make money one is, ipso

facto, a sex worker. "Prostitute" is a far more ambivalent term, recognized in
its common usage to describe those who engage in all sorts of non-sexual
activities; journalists, politicans, and lawyers are often accused of "prostitut-
ing themselves," even when there is no suggestion of the transaction
involving actual sex.

In all but the most rigid of societies the relationship between money and
sex is complex and fluid, and the demarcation of prostitution correspond-
ingly vague. While many societies tend to divide women into "whores and
madonnas" or "good and bad girls," this binary divide is no more than a
male fantasy, and there will always be women (and men as well) who fall into
the terrain between, whether it be Joan Collins's toy boys in *Dynasty* or
village women trying to make ends meet by accepting presents from passing
truck drivers for sexual favors. The creation of the idea of the sex-worker, a
very common theme in HIV prevention literature, denies this ambivalence,
and because it creates an identity it poses real problems for the wo/man who
might occasionally "sell" sex, but who does not read this act as defining
her/his identity. (Indeed the role of money in sexual transactions varies
considerably from culture to culture; perhaps the one generalization that
rings true is that there is usually considerable hypocrisy surrounding it.) This
of course is hardly a new phenomenom; the creation of the category of "sex
worker," often for the purpose of HIV surveillance, has remarkable echoes of
late-nineteenth century creations of "the prostitute," in part to control the
spread of venereal disease (Walkowitz 1980). There are also echoes of nineteenth century feminist attempts to "save" girls from prostitution by
redirecting them to "useful trades" in many of the arguments heard today in
developing countries.

One should mention a third concept of identity linked to the epidemic,
and that is the identity of the "HIV-positive person," or "Person (Living)
With AIDS." The development of this concept, and the assertion of the
central role of HIV-positive people in the management of the epidemic, has
been one of the most radical political aspects of the HIV story. In the Western
construction of history, the concept of a PWA identity was first articulated by
HIV-positive gay men on the two coasts of the United States, and clearly
grew out of already existing gay discourses of "coming out," which in turn
depend upon a particular individualistic view of identity. The concept of a
PWA identity has become internationalized, and the Global Network of
People Living with HIV/AIDS now has representation from all continents. It
is not always an identity which is easily adopted, either at an individual or a
social level. For many who are positive, asserting their positivity as a marker
of public identity can be seen as restricting them to an identity which is both
stigmatized and implies "illness," even though they may not yet feel anything

but well; for those living in societies where communal and family bonds are strong, the identity has been criticized as unnecessarily divisive.

In other parts of the world, some people with the virus developed somewhat different strategies for self-help, making use of different models of identity, which drew little on the American PWA model. Whereas there are many African self-help groups built around HIV-positive people and their families—and the Ugandan group, TASO, was founded by people who are themselves positive—they strike me as very different in their ethos and perceptions. Speaking as "a positive person" in Africa does not imply the same sharp differentiation from family which it does in the more individualistic West, where many gay men feel totally abandoned by their biological families, nor has it been accompanied by the militant stance which has come to be associated with a Western PWA identity, typified by responses such as ACT UP demonstrations or Gregg Araki's film, "The Living End." Reading the very powerful words of the Brazilian writer, Herbert Daniel (who spoke for a number of years before his death of the experience of living with AIDS in a country whose epidemic has characteristics of both the "developed" and the "developing" world), reminds us that, as he puts it:

> The epidemic will develop among us according to our specific cultural characteristics—our sexual culture, our material and symbolic resources for dealing with health and disease, and our prejudices and capacity to exercise solidarity. AIDS inscribes itself upon each culture in a different way. Each culture constructs its own particular kind of AIDS—as well as its own answers to the disease. (Daniel 1993)

The balance between the particular and the universal in the creation of a PWA identity should remind us of the deep political, economic, and cultural constraints within which we are living the epidemic.

THE FUTURE OF SEXUAL LIBERATION

Early in the epidemic—I am speaking now of a decade ago—I remember speaking with a group of undergraduate lesbian and gay students at a small American college. Some feared that the very possibility of a gay identity would be swept away in a tide of repression unleashed by AIDS, others that even if this did not happen a rigid sexual moralism would reappear and destroy what gains had been made by the lesbian/gay movement in the previous decade. Many of us who wrote about the epidemic in its early years saw the disappearance of what were felt to be the hard won gains of the 1970s, above all the recognition of sexual diversity and the right to sexual pleasure. In the old balance between sexual pleasure and danger—the title of one important U.S. anthology—danger once again seemed triumphant, and AIDS seemed set to unleash what Jeffrey Weeks, drawing on the work of Stan Cohen, referred to as "moral panic" (Weeks 1985).

This has not happened, even as, in Barry Adam's words, "AIDS has ushered in a further development of sexual speech which cannot but partake of the larger twentieth century 'obsession' with sexuality and its colonization by the professions, the media and the state" (Adam 1992). In the Western world, at least, it is striking that, while there has been considerable reassessment of the sexual liberation ethos of the late 1960s/early 1970s, this reassessment has led to an assertion that for all its excesses and undoubted sexism, much of the era's gains are worth preserving. The period of AIDS has seen a flourishing of sexual celebration, whether in the form of Hollywood movies and rock videos—often distinguishable from soft-core pornography only by the quality of their better cinematography and the size of the salaries paid to their actors—or in the growth of events such as Gay and Lesbian Mardi Gras in Sydney, which this year attracted half a million spectators. While some have read the message of AIDS as requiring a new chastity or at least monogamy, it seems that the dominant message has been about safer, not less, or less varied, sex.

Indeed, there is some evidence that, despite AIDS, "sexual liberation"—for all the ambivalence of that phrase—has continued to increase. The last decade has seen a proliferation of sex-oriented publications for women, an increase in sex-on-premises venues largely, but not entirely, for homosexual men, and a marked increase in interest in sexual adventure and unorthodox practices in most lesbian communities. While city governments closed homosexual bathhouses in much of the United States and Sweden, new ones have opened in Paris, Brisbane, Montreal, and Bangkok. The globalization of world culture, with new messages carried across national boundaries by television and radio, has meant an expansion of what in the 1970s seemed a particularly American form of sexual consumerism. Before we denounce such developments as irresponsible, it is important to note that they have been accompanied by large scale promotion of "safe sex": the condom, as much as the sex club or the videos of Madonna, has become an emblem of sexuality in the modern world.

Nonetheless, it is largely true that this form of sexual liberation depends upon the affluence of Western capitalism and the comparative freedom of Western liberalism. Sexuality cannot be divorced from power relationships, and it is meaningless to speak of "sexual liberation" to the great majority of teenage girls in Bangladesh or Chad. A modern reading of Freud's *Civilization and its Discontents* might suggest that the discontents of sexuality are as dependent upon socio-economic structures as upon psychological dynamics. Thus, whereas the assertion of sexual adventure and pleasure seems to me essential in devising HIV prevention programs for gay men—

and by extension for adolescents and others in Western societies—it is less clear that this will be appropriate in more traditional societies. (Kippax et al. [1990] have pointed out that it has limited relevance for young women even in Western societies.) In countries where women are defined as the vehicles for male pleasure, and denied the right to any form of autonomous sexuality, the ideologies of "sexual liberation" can be misused to merely justify the perpetuation of these inequalities. It is the failure to understand this that has led some American AIDS activists to badly misread the calls in non-Western countries for people to reduce the number of sexual partners and remain monogamous, so that a slogan like the one used in Zambia—"One man, one woman for life"—is read as if it is indistinguishable from the moralism of Jesse Helms and the C.D.C. (see, for example, Talbot 1990). A similar sort of romanticism can sometimes surround the Western view of sex-work, where declarations of the right of women to choose how they use their bodies blinds us to an understanding of the economic imperatives which make the term "choice" a meaningless and cruel concept.

For those of us who come from Western, affluent, and liberal societies, the new concept of "queer," carrying with it a stress on sexual fluidity, ambiguity, adventure and experimentation, has seemed to symbolize the possibility of preserving the gains of the sexual liberation movements in the context of the HIV epidemic. In many developing countries AIDS activism has been a heroic model to groups, usually based in homosexual communities, which are struggling to define themselves and to assert power in social and political spaces far less hospitable to them than is true in most of the West. But sexual liberation, if it is to have any real meaning, must be based upon a larger project of strengthening civil society and rectifying the imbalances of gender and of economic resources. What is now required is a very honest dialogue about the limits of Western-derived discourses of sexuality, and their relevance to the lives of millions of poor women, children, and even some men in parts of the world where HIV has reinforced the real and the perceived dangers of sexuality. For this to happen we need to recognize that the possibilities of sexuality are both shaped and limited by larger questions of political economy: far from being irrelevant to postmodern or identity politics, a Marxist anaysis of the state and the economy remains fundamental to making sense of the ways in which humans construct, understand, and even deconstruct their sexuality in any given period or social setting.

GENDER
POWER

Part
Three

Violence, Sexuality, and Women's Lives 7

Lori L. Heise

MY FEMINIST PROJECT OVER THE LAST THREE YEARS HAS BEEN to inter-
ject the reality of violence against women into the dominant discourse on
AIDS, women's health, and international family planning. My overall aim
has been two-fold: to improve public health policy by making it more reflec-
tive of the reality of women's lives, and to marshal some of the resources and
technical know-how of the international health community to assist
women's organizations fighting gender violence in the developing world.[1]

To date, the failure of the global health community to recognize gender-
based abuse has put both important public health objectives and individual
women at risk. By ignoring the pervasiveness of violence within relationships, for example, the current global AIDS strategy (which is based heavily
on condom promotion) dooms itself to failure. The research shows that
many women are afraid to even broach the subject of condom use for fear of
male reprisal (Elias and Heise 1993; Gupta and Weiss, in this volume). As
Anke Ehrhardt, co-director of the HIV Center for Clinical and Behavioral
Studies, observes, "We have not only ignored the fact that women do not
control condom use, but we have rushed headlong into prevention efforts
aimed at getting women to insist on condom use without taking into
account that they may risk severe repercussions, such as violence and other
serious threats to their economic and social support" (Ehrhardt 1991).

This is but one example of the potential costs of failing to explore the
intersection of violence, sexuality, gender, and public health. In this chapter,
I lay out what is known about violence and sexuality, especially with respect
to its implications for women's sexual and reproductive lives. More importantly, I discuss several risks I see present in the feminist project of
introducing ideas about violence and sexuality into the professional world of
public health. Focusing the "bio-medical gaze" on violence risks reinforcing

negative images of woman as "victim," an impression that can undermine women's own sense of self-efficacy and can justify continued inattention to women's needs. (For example, when faced with women's initial difficulty in "negotiating" condom use, some AIDS experts recommended shifting the entire focus of condom promotion and training to men, instead of exploring ways to strengthen women's ability to protect themselves.) Increased attention to the pervasiveness of violence, especially sexual violence, also risks fueling popular notions of sexuality as biologically driven and of male sexuality as "inherently predatory"—both notions experiencing a resurgence in popular culture. As I will show, however, the cross cultural record does not support a vision of male sexuality as inherently aggressive. To the extent that male sexual behavior is aggressive in certain cultures, it is because sexuality expresses power relations based on gender.

A MULTIPLICITY OF DISCOURSES

Sexuality and gender have become the subjects of sociological and bio-medical inquiry only within the last century or so. Within this short history, several distinct discourses have laid claim to the domain of human sexual experience. The first, "sexology," emerged as a discipline in the late nineteenth century. Typified by Havelock Ellis, Alfred Kinsey, and Masters and Johnson, sexology has been most concerned with sexual function, dysfunction, and the physiology of the sexual response. To its credit, sexology views women as agents of their own sexual lives, and takes as given women's right to sexual pleasure (see Table One).

Many feminists have criticized sexology, however, for neglecting the "dangerous" side of sex for women: abuse, unwanted pregnancy, STDs, humiliation, rape. As feminist Lenore Tiefer points out, "Sexology's nomenclature of sexual disorders does not describe what makes women unhappy about sex in the real world, but narrows and limits the vision of sexual problems to failures of genital performance" (Tiefer 1992). According to Tiefer, sexology looks at sexuality from the position of male privilege, where the sexual narrative has to do with erotics: intercourse, arousal, pleasure, erection, orgasm. "All well and good," she notes, "but hardly the stuff at the center of many women's sexual experience" (Tiefer 1992:4).

Feminists also fault sexology for failing to confront and work against gender-based power differentials. Significantly, none of the breakthrough studies that first documented the pervasiveness of nonconsensual sex, illegal abortion, and STDs in women came from mainstream sex research. Sexology has resisted challenging male power over female sexuality—in the form of coercive sex, male-defined religious doctrine, or lack of contraceptive research—because it fears "politicizing" what it sees as a basically neutral, "scientific" subject. According to feminists, however, sexologists—like all professionals—can either *support* institutional norms which ignore women's reality, or they can *subvert* those norms. As Tiefer maintains: "Any attempt to be neutral, to be 'objective' is to support the status quo" (Tiefer 1992:5).

A second more recent discourse on sexuality emerges from the "population control" and international health establishment. International health's interest in sex focuses almost exclusively on behaviors that have implications for demographics and/or for disease. A review of over 2,100 articles from five of the top family planning and health journals, for example, reveals that between 1980 and 1992, sexuality and male-female power dynamics are mentioned only within three narrow contexts: how women's attitudes about sexuality influence contraception use and effectiveness (forty-one articles); how adolescent sexual activity and contraception use are related to teen pregnancy (twenty-four articles); and how "high risk" sexual behaviors are related to the spread of sexually transmitted diseases, including AIDS (eleven articles) (Dixon-Mueller 1992). The preoccupation in public health has been with sexual danger and with counting disembodied acts (e.g., the number of instances of unprotected penetrative intercourse in the last month) not with meaning, context, or pleasure. In this discourse, women are frequently seen as means to an end—as "targets" for demographic initiatives or as reproductive vessels—rather than as individuals with independent needs and a right to sexual self-determination and pleasure (Dixon-Mueller 1993).

A third prominent discourse, which I shall call "anti-pornography feminism," is best represented by women such as Andrea Dworkin, Catherine MacKinnon, Kathleen Barry, and Evelina Giobbe. These women have dominated one side of what has come to be known in feminist circles as the "sex wars"—basically an internal debate over the "appropriate" boundaries (from a feminist perspective) of human sexual behavior. At issue are such themes as pornography, sadomasochism, prostitution, and how society should respond to these phenomena (Valverde 1987; Cole 1989). The anti-pornography feminists argue for intervention and insist that women will never achieve equality as long as their sexuality is commercialized, and as long as domination and economic exploitation are conflated with sexual pleasure. The "sex radical" critique on the other hand, sees long term danger in any effort to censor sexual behavior between consenting adults, arguing that such efforts can too easily be used against sexual minorities and women (Vance 1984).

While my work shares a common motivation with the anti-pornography feminists, there are strains in their thought that I find troubling. I commend this paradigm for its focus on gender-based power inequities and for its activist stance, but it tends to be profoundly pessimistic, and easily degenerates into portraying women solely as victims. In their zeal to highlight the dangers

Table One: Sex Research Paradigms

Sexology	Population Control/ Public Health	Anti-Violence Feminism	Integrated Feminist Approach
Acknowledges PLEASURE but focuses on genital performance	Focuses on DANGER (STDs; un-wanted preg-nancy; "high risk sex")	Focuses on DANGER (Rape, child sexual abuse; pornogaphy)	Acknowledges DANGER but Claims Women's Right to Sexual PLEA-SURE
Ignores Gender Power Imbalances	Attempts to Override Imbalances through Technology	Fights Against Gender-Based Power Inequities	Fights Against Gender-based Power Inequities
Focuses on Behavior and Physiology	Focuses on Behavior and Technology	Focuses on Context and Meaning (although tends toward negative)	Focuses on Context and Meaning but recognizes prag-matic realities
Women Seen as Agents	Women Seen as a Means to an End (e.g. to achieve demo-graphic targets)	Women Seen as Victims (or potential victims)	Women Seen as Agents Operat-ing within Restricted Options
Adherents See themselves as Scientists	Adherents See themselves as Practitioners	Adherents See themselves as Activists	Adherents See themselves as Activists and Practitioners
Risks Trivilizing Women's Reali-ty by Ignoring "Danger" part of Sex for Women	Ignores Gender-based Power Relations to the Detriment of Program Success	Fuels Essentialist Notions of Male Sexuality as Inherently "Predatory." Reinforces Im-age of Women as Victims.	Seeks Strategies that Empower Women and Promote Long Term Social Change while Meeting Wom-en's Immediate Needs.

of sex, anti-pornography feminists have also tended to overlook sex's plea-sures. In a radically "sex negative" culture, overcompensation—even in the face of a culture largely indifferent to women's victimization—carries certain dangers. It also contributes to the popular "demonization" of men and of male sexuality. It is the importation of these pitfalls that I fear in my effort to introduce the reality of violence into the family planning and international health field. To the uninitiated, the very pervasiveness of violence can be so overwhelming as to justify dismissing the situation as impossible to change.

Understandably, such concerns have been used to question efforts to integrate violence into the public health mainstream. Rather than tolerate naivete and gender-blindness in the health and development field, however, I think anti-violence activism must seek to transform public health discourse and research, encouraging a greater emphasis on social context, meaning, power differentials, and gender. It is with this vision that I offer a new paradigm for sex research and practice within public health, combining the strengths of the three other models. Table One includes a brief summary of the existing sex paradigms as well as a suggested model for a new approach. This new option—which I call the "integrated feminist approach"—is most closely approximated today by the feminist women's health movement (e.g., groups such as the Boston Women's Health Book Collective, authors of *Our Bodies, Ourselves*, and the Colectivo Feminista Sexualidade e Saúde in São Paulo Brazil).

While this chart admittedly oversimplifies three complex and pluralistic fields of inquiry, it nonetheless allows a quick (and I hope useful) comparison of some of the existing stakeholders in women's sexuality. It also summarizes the integrated approach to sexuality that I strive for in my own work. The following section explores what we currently know about violence and coercion as it relates to women's sexual and reproductive health. In the last section of this chapter, I offer an interpretation of this data and explore my concerns about the anti-pornography discourse in greater detail.

THE IMPACT OF VIOLENCE ON WOMEN'S SEXUAL AND REPRODUCTIVE LIVES

Regrettably, we know very little in social science about how violence or fear of violence operates in women's lives. Only recently have researchers begun to document the pervasiveness of gender-based abuse and virtually no attempt has been made to investigate how violence affects women's sexuality. There are important questions in need of exploration: What is the role of coercion in sexual initiation? How do force and fear affect women's experience of sexual pleasure? How does violence affect women's reproductive health? The following section summarizes the information available on each of these questions. Of necessity, much of the analysis remains speculative.

The Prevalence of Violence Against Women.

The most endemic form of violence against women is wife abuse, or more accurately, abuse of women by intimate male partners. Table Two summarizes twenty studies from a wide variety of countries that document that *one-quarter to over half* of women in many countries of the world report having been physically abused by a present or former partner. Although some of these studies

Table Two: Prevalence of Wife Abuse, Selected Countries

Country	Sample Size	Sample Type	Findings	Comments
Barbados (Handwerker 1991)	264 women and 243 men aged 20–45	Island-wide national probability sample	30% of women battered as adults	Women and men report 50% of their mothers beaten
Antigua (Handwerker 1993)	97 women aged 20–45	Random subset of national probability sample	30% of women battered as adults	Women and men report that 50% of mothers beaten
Kenya (Raikes 1990)	733 women from Kissi District	District wide cluster sample	42% "beaten regularly"	Taken from contraceptive prevalence survey
Papua, New Guinea (Toft 1987)	*Rural* 736 men; 715 women *Urban Low Income* 368 men; 298 women *Urban Elite* 178 men; 99 women	Rural survey in 19 villages in all regions and provinces Urban survey with oversample of elites	67% rural women beaten. 56% urban low income women beaten. 62% urban elite women beaten	Almost perfect agreement between percent of women who claim to have been beaten and percent of men who admit to abuse
Sri Lanka (Sonali 1990)	200 mixed ethnic, low income women from Colombo	Convenience sample from low income neighborhood	60% have been beaten	51% said husbands used weapons
India (Mahajan 1990)	109 men and 109 women from village in Jullundur District, Punjab	50% sample of all scheduled (lower) caste households and 50% of non-scheduled (higher) caste houses	75% of lower caste men admit to beating their wives; 22% of higher caste men admit to beatings	75% of scheduled caste wives report being beaten "frequently"
Malaysia (WAO 1993)	713 women and 508 males over 15 years old	National random probability sample of Peninsular Malaysia	39% of women have been "physically beaten" by a partner in the last year	Note: This is an annual figure. 15% of adults consider wife beating acceptable (22% of Malays)
Colombia (Profamilia 1992)	3,272 urban women 2,118 rural women	National probability sample	20% physically abused; 33% psychlogically abused; 10% raped by husband	Part of Colombia's DHS survey

Country	Sample Size	Sample Type	Findings	Comments
Costa Rica (Chacon et al. 1990)	1,388 women	Convenience sample of women attending child welfare clinic	50% report being physically abused	Sponsored by UNICEF/PAHO
Costa Rica (1990)	1,312 women aged 15 to 49 years	Random probability sample of urban women	51% report being beaten up to several times per year; 35% report being hit regularly"	
Mexico (Jalisco) (Ramirez and Vazquez 1993)	1,163 rural women; 427 urban women in the state of Jalisco	Random household survey of women on DIF register	56.7% of urban women and 44.2% of rural women	Experienced some form of "interpersonal violence"
Mexico (Valdez Santiago and Cox 1990)	342 women from Nezahualcoyotl	Random probability sample of women from city adjacent to Mexico City	33% had lived in a "violent relationship"	
Ecuador (CEPLAES 1992)	200 low income women	Convenience sample of Quito barrio	60% had been "beaten" by a partner	Of those beaten, 37% were assaulted with a frequency between once a month and every day
Chile (Larrain 1993)	1,000 women in Santiago ages 22 to 55 years involved in a relationship of 2 years or more	Stratified random probability sample with a maximum sampling error of 3%	60% abused by a male intimate; 26.2% physically abused (more severe than pushes, slaps, or having an object thrown at you)	70% of those abused are abused more than once a year
Norway (Schei and Bakketeig 1989)	150 women aged 20 to 49 years in Trondheim	Random sample selected from census data	25% had been physically or sexually abused by a male partner	Definition does not include less severe forms of violence like pushing, slapping, or shoving

Country	Sample Size	Sample Type	Findings	Comments
New Zealand (Mullen et al. 1988)	2,000 women sent question-naire; stratified random sample of 349 women selected for interview	Random probability sample selected from electoral rolls of five contiguous parliamentary constituencies	20.1% report being "hit and physically abused" by a male partner; 58% of these women (>10% of sample) were battered more than 3 times	
United States (Straus and Gelles 1986)	2,143 married or co-habitat-ing couples	National ran-dom probabil-ity sample	28% report at least one episode of physical vio-lence	
United States (Grant, Preda & Martin 1991)	6,000 women state-wide from Texas	State-wide random prob-ability sample	39% have been abused by male part-ner after age 18; 31% have been physical-ly abused	>12% have been sexually abused by male partner after age 18
United States (Teske and Parker 1983)	3,000 rural women in Texas	Random probability sample of communities with 50,000 people or less	40.2% have been abused after age 18; 31% have been physical-ly abused	22% abused within the last 12 months

are based on convenience samples, the majority are based on probability samples with a large number of respondents (e.g., Mexico, United States, Colombia, Kenya).[2]

Statistics around the world also suggest that rape is a common reality in the lives of women and girls. Six population-based surveys from the United States, for example, suggest that between one in five and one in seven U.S. women will be the victim of a completed rape in her lifetime (Kilpatrick, Edmund and Seymor 1992).[3] Moreover, there are well-designed studies of rape among college-aged women from New Zealand (Gavey 1991), Canada (Dekeseredy and Kelly, 1992), the United States (Koss, Gidycz and Wisniewski 1987), and the United Kingdom (Beattie 1992) that reveal remarkably similar rates of completed rape across countries, when using similar survey instruments (based on Koss and Oros 1982).[4] A study among adult women (many of them college students) in Seoul, Korea, yielded slightly lower rates of completed rape, but an equally high rate of attempts (Shim 1992) (see Table Three).

Table Three: Prevalence of Rape Among College-Aged Women

Country	Authors	Sample	Definition of Rape[a]	Completed Rape	Completed & Attempts
Canada	DeKeseredy and Kelly 1993	National probability sample of 1,835 women at 95 colleges and universities	Anal, oral or, vaginal intercourse by force or threat of force SES # 9,10	8.1% (by dating partners since high school)	23.3% (rape or sexual assault by anyone ever)
New Zealand	Gavey 1991	347 women psychology students	Anal, vaginal intercourse by force or threat; or because a man gave alcohol or drugs SES # 8,9,10	14.1%	25.3%
United Kingdom	Beattie 1992	1,574 women at six universities	Vaginal intercourse by force or because a man gave alcohol or drugs SES # 8,9	11.3%	19.3%
United States	Koss et al. 1987	3,187 women at 32 colleges & universities	SES # 8,9,10	15.4%	27.5%
United States	Moore, Nord and Peterson 1989	Nationally representative sample of 18 to 22 years old	Forced to have sex against your will, or were raped?	12.7% of whites; 8% of blacks (before age 21)	
Seoul Korea	Shim 1992	2,270 adult women (quota sample)	SES # 9,10	7.7%	21.8%

a) Estimates of rape and attempted rape are based on the legal definition of rape in the country concerned and are derived from different combinations of the following questions taken from the Sexual Experiences Survey (Koss and Oros, 1984):

   4) Has a man attempted sexual intercourse (getting on top or you, attempting to insert his penis) when you didn't want to by threatening or using some degree of physical force (twisting your arm, holding you down, etc.) but intercourse did not occur?

   8) Have you had sexual intercourse when you didn't want to because a man gave you alcohol or drugs?

   9) Have you had sexual intercourse when you didn't want to because a man threatened or used some degree of physical force (twisting your arm, holding you down, etc) to make you?

   10) Have you engaged in sex acts (anal or oral intercourse or penetration by objects other than a penis) when you didn't want to because a man threatened or used some degree of physical force (twisting your arm, holding you down, etc.) to make you?

Not surprisingly, given the extremely sensitive nature of the subject, reliable data on child sexual abuse are even more scarce. Nonetheless, the few studies that do exist—along with ample indirect evidence—suggest that sexual abuse of children and adolescents is a widespread phenomenon. In the United States, for example, population-based studies indicate that twenty-seven to sixty-two percent of women recall at least one incident of sexual abuse before the age of eighteen (Peters, Wyatt and Finkelhor 1986).[5] An anonymous, island-wide, probability survey of Barbados revealed that one woman in three and one to two men per one hundred reported behavior constituting childhood or adolescent sexual abuse (Handwerker 1991). And in Canada, a government commission estimated that one in four female children and one in ten male children are sexually assaulted prior to the age of seventeen years (Canadian Government 1984).

Elsewhere, indirect evidence suggests cause for concern. Two studies from Nigeria, for example, document that a large percentage of female patients at STD clinics are young children. A 1988 study in Zaria, Nigeria found that sixteen percent of female patients seeking treatment for STDs were children under the age of five and another six percent were children between the ages of six and fifteen (Kisekka and Otesanya 1988). An older study in Ibadan found that twenty-two percent of female patients attending one STD clinic were children under the age of ten (Sogbetun et al. 1977). Likewise, a study conducted in the Maternity Hospital of Lima, Peru revealed that ninety percent of the young mothers aged twelve to sixteen had been raped by their father, stepfather or another close relative.[6]

A final indication of the prevalence of sexual abuse comes from the observations of children themselves. In 1991, when the Nicaraguan NGO, CISAS held a national conference for the children involved in their "Child to Child" program (a project that trains youngsters aged eight to fifteen to be better child care providers for their siblings), participants identified "sexual abuse" as the number one health priority facing young people in their country.

Experience of Sexual Pleasure
When coercion enters the sexual arena, it invariably affects women's experience of sex. While we know something about the impact of rape or sexual abuse on women's sexual functioning, little is known about how subtle or overt coercion within consensual unions affects women's sexual lives. Research indicates that from fifty to sixty percent of women who are raped experience severe sexual problems, including fear of sex, problems with arousal, and decreased sexual functioning (Burnam 1988; Becker et al. 1982). But what of forced sex within relationships, or of the role of coercion in women's sexual initiation? Both are topics deserving much greater exploration.

Little information is available, for example, on the degree to which young women feel coerced into their first sexual experience. In one study, forty percent of girls aged eleven to fifteen in Jamaica reported the reason for their first intercourse as "forced" (Allen 1982). A qualitative study of sexual initiation among adolescent girls in the United States—aptly entitled "Putting a Big Thing into a Little Hole"—indicates that many girls recall their first intercourse negatively (Thompson 1990).[7] Many girls mention pain, fear, disappointment, and a sense of not being in control of the situation. While most do not frame their experience as "coercive," few in this group were prepared for or actively wanted the sex to happen. As author Sharon Thompson observes: "Often they did not agree to sex. They gave in, they gave up, they gave out" (Thompson 1990:358).

Also at issue is how young girls experience first intercourse when forced into arranged marriages at a very young age. While the rate of child marriage is declining, a significant portion of girls are still married off at a very young age, often to unknown men many years their senior (see Table Four). Evidence from a qualitative study of sexual initiation among child brides in Iran confirms that early intercourse, even when culturally supported, can be very traumatic for young girls. Anthropologist Mary Hegland interviewed exiled Iranian women living in the United States about sexual initiation in Iran (Hegland n.d.). Many gave graphic details of forced defloration of young girls, most whom were totally ignorant of sex (often a young girl was held down by relatives while the man forced himself on her). While the women said the term "rape" would never be applied to this experience in Iran, they freely used terms like "rape" and "torture" to describe the experience, after being exposed to this language in the United States. This new language merely gave voice to feelings they already had.

Table Four: Percentage of Women Aged 20 to 24 Today Who Were Married Before the Age of Fifteen, Selected Countries

Country	Percent	Year of Report
Uganda	17.8	1989/90
Nigeria	26.7	1990
Mali	26.7	1987
Cameroon	21.3	1991
Liberia	16.6	1986
Guatemala	12.6	1987
Dominican Republic	9.0	1991
Mexico	6.2	1987
Trinidad/Tobago	6.0	1987
Egypt★	15.0	1988
Indonesia	10.0	1991
Pakistan	11.4	1990/91

★ Before the age of 16
SOURCE: Selected Demographic and Health Surveys.

Given the prevalence of violence in women's lives, there is a remarkable lack of information on how it effects women's sexuality. Only one study, published recently in the *Journal of Family Violence*, explicitly looks at the effects of violence on women's experience of sex (Apt and Hurlbert 1993). Compared to nonabused women in distressed marriages, women living in violent relationships had significantly lower (i.e., more negative) responses on nine scales designed to measure sexual satisfaction, intimacy, arousal, and attitudes toward sex. Nonetheless, they had significantly more intercourse.

This high rate of intercourse is not surprising given the frequency of coerced sex within physically abusive relationships. Whereas fourteen percent of all U.S. wives report being physically forced to have sex against their will, the prevalence of coercive intercourse among battered women is at least forty percent (Campbell and Alford 1989). In Bolivia and Puerto Rico, fifty-eight percent of battered wives report being sexually assaulted by their partner, and in Colombia, the reported rate is forty-six percent (Isis International 1988; Profamilia 1992). Given the percentage of women around the world who live with physically abusive partners, it is likely that sexual coercion within consensual unions is quite common.

There is also a remarkable gap in our knowledge about the meaning and experience of sex among women who live in non-violent relationships. Even here, the experience of sex for women is often humiliating and degrading—one they tolerate rather than enjoy. Commenting on how their husband's treated them sexually, the Iranian women interviewed above used such phrases as "I'm not a toilet," "I'm not just a hole," "It's like swallowing nasty medicine" (Hegland n.d.). In focus group discussions with Mexican women about men, sex, and marriage, many women likewise expressed deep resentment about how men treated them in sexual relationships (Folch-Lyon, Macorra, and Schearer 1981). Women in particular mentioned:

- Physical abuse by husbands to coerce the wife's sexual compliance;
- Widespread male infidelity;
- Men's authoritarian attitude toward their wives;
- Threats of abandonment if wives failed to meet their husband's sexual demands or his demand for more children; and
- An abiding sense of depersonalization, humiliation, and physical dissatisfaction during sex.

Perhaps more than anything, the Spanish phrase women commonly use for sex captures their sentiment: *"el me usa"* (he uses me). Such comments raise the question of the nature of "consent" within the patriarchal institution of marriage. Would women consent to such treatment if they had the economic resources to survive independently and the social permission to seek sexual gratification elsewhere?

Ability to Control Fertility

The family planning literature documents that, for many women, fear of male reprisal greatly limits their ability to use contraception (Dixon-Mueller 1992). Men in many cultures react negatively to birth control because they think it signals a woman's intentions to be unfaithful. (Their logic is that protection against pregnancy allows a woman to be promiscuous). Where children are a sign of male virility, a woman's attempt to use birth control may also be interpreted as an affront to her partner's masculinity. While male approval is not always the deciding factor, studies from countries as diverse as Mexico, South Africa, and Bangladesh have found that partner approval is the single greatest predictor of women's contraceptive use.[8] When partners disapprove, women either forgo contraception or they resort to family planning methods they can use without their partner's knowledge.

The unspoken reality behind this subterfuge is that women can be beaten or otherwise abused if they do not comply with men's sexual and childbearing demands. In a recent interview, Hope Mwesigye of FIDA-Uganda, a non-profit legal aid organization for women in Kampala, recounted the story of a young married mother who was running from a husband who regularly beat her. Despite earning a decent wage, the woman's husband refused to maintain her and their two children. To avoid bringing more children into the world whom she could not feed, the woman began using birth control without her husband's consent. The beatings began when she failed to bring forth more children; they became more brutal when he learned of her contraceptive use (Banwell 1990).

In other countries, legal provisions requiring spousal permission before dispensing birth control can actually put women at increased risk of violence. According to Pamela Onyango of Family Planning International Assistance, women in Kenya have been known to forge their partner's signature rather than open themselves to violence or abandonment by requesting permission to use family planning services (Banwell 1990). Nor are Kenyan women alone in their fear of such consequences. Researchers conducting focus groups on sexuality in Mexico and Peru found that women held similar concerns—fear of violence, desertion, or accusations of infidelity—if they brought up birth control (Folch-Lyon, Macorra, and Schearer 1981; Fort 1989). Not surprisingly, when family planning clinics in Ethiopia removed their requirement for spousal consent, clinic use rose twenty-six percent in just a few months (Cook and Maine 1987).

Not all women who fear violence in this context are necessarily at risk of actual abuse. In fact, some recent studies suggest that many men may be more open to family planning than most women suspect (Gallen 1986). Communication in marriage can be so limited, however, that spouses often do not know their partner's views on family planning. Women thus assume that their husband's attitude will mirror the cultural norm, which frequently says that men want large families and distrust women who use birth control. The discrepancy between women's perceptions and reality also speaks to the ability of violence to induce fear by example.

Risk of Acquiring STDs

Not surprisingly, male violence also impedes women's ability to protect themselves from HIV and other STDs. Violence can increase a woman's risk either through nonconsensual sex or by limiting her willingness and/or ability to enforce condom use. In many cultures, suggesting condom use is even more threatening than raising birth control in general, because condoms are widely associated with promiscuity, prostitution, and disease. By bringing up condom use, women either insinuate their own infidelity or implicitly challenge a male partner's right to conduct outside relationships. Either way, a request for condoms may trigger a violent response (Elias and Heise 1993; Worth 1991).

Indeed, an AIDS prevention strategy based solely on "negotiating" condom use assumes an equity of power between men and women that simply does not exist in many relationships. Even within consensual unions, women often lack control over the dynamics of their sexual lives. A study of home-based industrial workers in Mexico, for example, found that wives' bargaining power in marriage was lowest with regard to decisions about if and when to have sexual intercourse (Beneria and Roldan 1987). Studies of natural family planning in the Philippines, Peru, and Sri Lanka (Liskin 1981) and sexual attitudes among women in Guatemala (DataPro and Asociación Guatemalteco para la Prevención y Control de SIDA 1991) also mention forced sex in marriage, especially when the men arrive home drunk.

Childhood sexual abuse also appears to generate responses that put individuals at increased risk of STDs, including AIDS. Several studies, for example, link a history of sexual abuse with a high risk of entering prostitution (Finkelhor 1987; James and Meyerding 1977). Researchers from Brown University found that men and women who had been raped or forced to have sex in either childhood or adolescence were four times more likely than non-abused individuals to have worked in prostitution (Zierler 1991). They were also twice as likely to have multiple partners in any single year and to engage in casual sex with partners they did not know. Women survivors of childhood sexual assault were twice as likely to be heavy consumers of alcohol and nearly three times more likely to become pregnant before the age of eighteen. These behaviors did not translate directly into higher rates of HIV among women, but men who experienced childhood sexual abuse were twice as likely to be HIV positive as men who did not.

Impacts of sexual abuse on sexual risk-taking have also been documented in a developing country—on the island of Barbados. Based on a probability survey of 407 men and women, anthropologist Penn Handwerker has shown that sexual abuse is the single most important determinant of high risk sexual activity during adolescence for both Barbadian men and women (Handwerker 1991). After controlling for a wide-range of socio-economic and home-environment variables (e.g., absent father), sexual abuse remains strongly linked to both the number of partners adolescents have and to their age at first intercourse. Further analysis shows that direct effects of childhood sexual abuse on partner change remain significant into the respondent's mid-thirties. For men, physical, emotional and/or sexual abuse in childhood is also highly correlated with lack of condom use in adulthood, after controlling for many other variables.[9]

Pregnancy Complication and Birth Outcomes

While pregnancy should be a time when the health and well-being of women is especially protected, surveys suggest that pregnant women are prime targets for abuse. Results from a large, prospective study of battery during pregnancy among low income women in Houston and Baltimore in the United States, for example, indicate that one out of *every six* pregnant women was battered during her present pregnancy (McFarlane 1992). The study, sponsored by the Centers for Disease Control, followed a stratified cohort of 691 White, African-American and Hispanic women for three years in Houston and Baltimore. Sixty percent of the abused women in this study reported two or more episodes of violence, and they were three times as likely as non-abused women to begin prenatal care in the third trimester. Other studies indicate that women battered during pregnancy run twice the risk of miscarriage and four times the risk of having a low birth weight baby compared with women who are not beaten (Stark et al. 1981; Bullock and McFarlane 1989). Birth weight is a powerful predictor of a child's survival prospects in the first year of life.

Battering during pregnancy is likely to have an even greater impact on Third World mothers who are already malnourished and overworked. A survey of 342 randomly-sampled women in Mexico City revealed that twenty percent of those battered reported blows to the stomach during pregnancy (Valdez Santiago and Shrader Cox 1992). In another study of eighty battered women who sought judicial intervention against their partner in San Jose, Costa Rica, forty-nine percent report being beaten during pregnancy. Of these, 7.5 percent reported miscarriages due to the abuse (Ugalde 1988).

A prospective study of 161 women living in Santiago, Chile, likewise revealed that those women living in areas of high social and political violence had a significantly increased risk of pregnancy complications compared to women living in lower violence neighborhoods. After adjusting for potential confounders (income, education, marital status, underweight, cigarette smoking, dissatisfaction with neighborhood, life events, alienation, uncertainty and depression), researchers found that high levels of sociopolitical violence were associated with an approximately fivefold increase in risk of pregnancy complications (such as pre-eclampsia, premature labor, threat of miscarriage, gestational hypertension, etc.) (Zapata et al. 1992). If the stress and trauma of living in a violent neighborhood can induce complications, it is reasonable to assume that living in the private hell of an abusive relationship could as well.

SOME THOUGHTS ON THE IMPLICATIONS OF THESE FINDINGS

After reading the above review, it is hard not to share the profound pessimism about men and about male sexuality that runs throughout much of the anti-pornography literature. It is important to consider, however, the appropriate message to be taken from these data. Unfortunately, the conclusion some have drawn is that women are essentially powerless and that men must be aggressive by nature. Generally there is indignation at male abuse, but it is often accompanied by a sense that the problem runs too deep to be addressed. Whether justified by biological arguments (evolution has endowed men with an aggressive sexual nature) or socio-cultural determinism (patriarchy is everywhere and not easily changed), these beliefs can rationalize inaction.

Ironically, the very research and ideas that can be used to justify inaction often come from individuals who probably would not support the use of their data in this way. I, for example, oppose the view that male sexuality is inherently aggressive or that women are essentially victims. Most of my anti-violence colleagues would likely agree, although few have made a point of arguing against the interpretation of their work in this way. Given the appeal of "essentialist" notions of sex and gender in popular culture (and the political implications of such arguments), it is my belief, however, that anyone who promotes new ideas in mainstream discourse has a responsibility not only for what they meant to say, but for how their words can be construed and used. It is out of this sense of responsibility that I offer the following interpretation of the data on sexuality and violence that I present above.

First, despite the powerful ability of violence to exact obedience and exert control, women are not totally powerless. In fact, women have proven incredibly capable of exerting agency even within the most constrained social conditions. Extremely poor women in India, for example, have been known to exert control over their sexual lives by declaring extended religious fasts, a socially sanctioned activity (imbued with taboos against sexual relations) that even violent men are reluctant to violate (Savara, personal communication). Likewise, research has shown that far from being passive, battered women often adopt complex coping and management strategies that serve to lessen the impact of the violence on themselves and their children (Browne 1987; Bowker 1983; Okun 1986). Even some prostitutes interpret their decision to turn tricks as an empowered choice—a way to make money for sexual services exacted from other women through marriage (Delacoste and Alexander 1987). This is not to say that women do not deserve broader choices than these examples imply. Such acts do represent, however, a creativity and resourcefulness in the face of powerful social forces that is important to acknowledge and affirm at all times. Failure to recognize the possibility of agency within patriarchal structures fuels fatalism and can undermine women's sense of self, with disempowering results.

In her speech "Does Sexuality Have a History?," for example, feminist attorney, Catherine MacKinnon advances a very deterministic and fatalistic picture of women and sexuality. Taking issue with the prevailing view of academic historians that sexuality is basically socially constructed and highly plastic, MacKinnon (1991) writes:

> I would hypothesize that while ideologies about sex and sexuality may ebb and flow. . .the actual practices of sex may look relatively flat. . . . Underneath all of these hills and valleys, these ebbs and flows, there is this bedrock, this tide that has not changed much, namely male supremacy and the subordination of women. . . . For this feminists have been called ahistorical. Oh, dear. We have disrespected the profundity and fascination of all the different ways in which men fuck us in order to emphasize that however they do it, they do it. And they do it to us. (MacKinnon 1991:6)

In a later edition of the *Michigan Quarterly*, the same journal which reprinted the original speech, author Suzanne Rhodenbaugh (1991) accuses MacKinnon of committing a "new violence" by denying women the agency to define their own sexuality. In her reply essay, "MacKinnon, May I Speak?" Rodenbaugh writes:

> MacKinnon, with probably good intention to empower women, seems to me in her essay another voice reducing us, one saying we are creatures mainly acted upon. This feels greatly over-simplified, and finally untrue. It feels further, like new injustice. For if my "history of sexuality" includes such facts as my having been raped, having been beaten by a husband, having gone through a pregnancy against my will, and all else that has happened to my body and my sexual attention that I did not seek but was subjected to. . . then presumably as a sexual creature I'm little more than victim, and am predominantly passive. (Rhodenbaugh 1991:442)

MacKinnon likewise implies that male sexual behavior is hegemonically abusive (. . . however they do it, they do it. And they do it to us). But Rhoednbaugh refuses to cede her agency, saying: "I'm just one individual woman, but I'm not of a mind to exchange the name 'invisible' for the name 'victim.' Neither name will hold me" (Rhodenbaugh 1991:422).

Indeed, Rhodenbaugh's comments captures the essence of the dilemma faced by anti-violence activists: in exposing the reality of violence, we risk gaining visibility at the price of promoting the image of woman as victim and the notion of sex as all danger and no pleasure. One way to avoid this pitfall is to always counterbalance the pessimism engendered by the tenacity of patriarchy with examples of women's creative attempts at resistance within existing constraints. Another is to constantly imbue the antiviolence discourse with reminders of why feminists fight sexual violence in the first place. As author Naomi Wolf points out, "Feminists agitate against rape not just because it is a form of violence—but because it is a form of violence that uniquely steals from the survivor her sexual spontaneity and delight. . . . The right to say no must exist for the right to say yes to have any meaning" (Wolf 1992). Regrettably, this recognition is all too often lost in feminist discussions of sexual violence.

A second pitfall of anti-violence work is the danger of fueling popular notions of sexual essentialism by drawing attention to the pervasiveness of gender violence. Essentialist explanations for social phenomenon are generally dangerous because they provide a powerful justification for the status quo. If what exists is biologically based, then it is "natural" and by extension, "good" (or at least not open to change). Essentialist interpretations have a long history, beginning with scientists such as Freud and Konrad Lorenz who saw aggression and sexuality as "drives" or "instincts" that needed periodic release or they were likely to "discharge" in destructive ways. This "hydraulic" image of sexuality is one that still holds much popular appeal. Indeed, the notion that men "need" frequent sex with many partners is a myth used in many cultures (including my own) to justify and condone sexual behavior by men that can be exploitive and hurtful to women.

While most psychologists now reject the drive theory, it still captures the imagination of many in the general public. The meteoric rise of author/academic Camille Paglia attests to the enduring appeal that such essentialist notions command. Although Paglia, a latter-day Freudian, would likely object to being characterized as a biological determinist, her writings and public statements smack of determinism and her analysis of sexual violence draws exclusively from biology, psychology and ethics rather than from an analysis of power or gender role socialization. In *Sex, Art and American Culture*, for example, Paglia writes:

> Aggression and eroticism are deeply intertwined. Hunt, pursuit, and capture are biologically programmed into male sexuality. . . . I see in the simple, swaggering masculinity of the jock and in the noisy posturing of the heavy-metal guitarist certain fundamental, unchangeable truths about sex. . . . We must remedy social injustice wherever we can. But there are some things we cannot change. There are sexual differences based in biology. Academic feminism is lost in a fog of social constructionism. (Paglia 1992:50-53)

A careful reading of Paglia's text reveals that she does believe that the male "tendency toward brutishness" can be overridden through socialization (in some cases, at least), but it is easy to see how her purposefully provocative statements about male sexuality could be construed to support popular notions that "boys will be boys." Given the potential of such rationalizations to promote behavior harmful to women, Paglia has a responsibility not only for her beliefs but for how her words are likely to be heard. Once she steps out of academia and onto the TV talk-show circuit, Paglia has an increased duty to guard against the misuse of her ideas by paying careful attention to language and by countering likely misinterpretations of her ideas.

Likewise, feminists who uncover the pervasiveness of violence should not leave the impression that aggression is an immutable part of male sexuality. With understandable frustration, some in the health and development field have reacted to the violence data with the question: What is it about male sexuality that makes men that way? I think, however, that this is the wrong question. Rather we should be asking: What is it about the construction of masculinity in different cultures that promotes aggressive sexual behavior by men? And, what is it about the construction of femininity and the structure of economic and social power relations in societies that permits this behavior to continue?

The reason that it is wrong to frame the question in terms of "maleness" (which is normally interpreted to have biological roots), is because the cross-cultural record does not support the view that male violence against women is universal. Three separate cross-cultural studies confirm that there are at least a handful of societies where rape and/or wife abuse does not exist (or did not exist in the recent past). In her study of 156 tribal societies, for example, feminist anthropologist Peggy Reeves Sanday classified forty-seven percent of the cultures she studied as essentially "rape free" (i.e., rape was totally absent or extremely rare) (Sanday 1981). Even if one cedes that some of the societies designated "rape free" probably represent inadequacies in the ethnographic record rather than truly non-violent societies, the number of examples cited (and the descriptions of life in these societies) suggests that there are (or have been) at least some cultures not plagued by gender-based abuse.

Likewise, two other studies of wife abuse cross-culturally (Levinson 1989; Counts, Brown and Campbell 1992) unearth additional examples of cultures where gender-based violence is absent or exceedingly rare. In his ethno-graphic review of ninety peasant and small scale societies, Levinson (1989) identified sixteen that could be described as "essentially free or untroubled by family violence." Among the Central Thai, for example, domestic violence was extremely rare according to detailed ethnographies collected in the 1960s. Central Thai families were remarkable for the absence of any meaningful division of labor by sex: men were as likely as women to carry out household duties including childcare, and women as likely as men to plow or manage the family business. Divorce was common, people prefer-ring to separate rather than live with discord. Community norms disdained aggression; other non-violent means of conflict resolution were plentiful and preferred (Phillips 1966).

The existence of such cultures—even if few in number—stands as proof that violence against women is not an inevitable outgrowth of male biology, male sexuality, or male hormones. It is "male conditioning," not the "condi-tion of being male," that appears to be the problem. Although what it means to be "male" varies among different cultures and within different segments of the same culture, the importance of the masculine mystique appears to be a common element in many, but not all, societies. In his book *Manhood in the Making: Cultural Concepts of Masculinity*, anthropologist David Gilmore notes that across many cultures "there is a constantly recurring notion that real manhood is different from simple anatomical maleness, that it is not a neutral condition that comes about spontaneously through biological maturation but rather is a precarious or artificial state that boys must win against power-ful odds" (Gilmore 1990:11). Gilmore observes that this notion exists among both peasants and sophisticated urban peoples, and among both warrior peoples and those who have never killed in anger. He argues further that "manhood" represents an "achieved status" different from parallel notions of womanhood. "As a social icon," he writes, "femininity. . . usually involves questions of body ornament or sexual allure, or other essentially cosmetic behaviors that enhance, rather than create, an inherent quality of character. An authentic femininity rarely involves tests or proofs of action. . . ." (Gilmore 1990:11).

Although I would disagree with Gilmore's last statement (in many cultures a woman must bear a child before she is considered fully human, much less a mature, adult woman), his observations about the elusive quality of manhood are nonetheless important for our analysis of sexually aggressive behavior in men. It is my belief, shared by other theorists (such as Lancaster 1992; Stoltenberg 1989; and Olsson 1984) that it is partly men's insecurity about their masculinity that promotes abusive behavior toward women. The fear that accompanies this insecurity derives in part from a gendered system that assigns power and status to that which is male and denigrates or subordinates that which is female. Men in many cultures wage daily battle to prove to themselves and others that they qualify for inclusion in the esteemed category "male." To be "not male," is to be reduced to the status of woman, or worse, to be "queer" (see below).

Since gender is socially constructed, it must be actualized through action and sensation—by doing things that repeatedly affirm that one is really male or really female while avoiding things that leave room for doubt. As social theorist John Stoltenberg observes:

> Most people born with a penis between their legs grow up aspiring to feel and act unambiguously male, longing to belong to the sex that is male and daring not to belong to the sex that is not, and feeling this urgency for a visceral and constant verification of their male sexual [read: gender] identity—for a fleshy connection to manhood—as the driving force of their life. The drive does not originate in the anatomy. The sensations derive from the idea. The ideas gives the feelings social meaning; the idea determines which sensations shall be sought. (Stoltenberg 1989:31)

Many societies have evolved elaborate rituals and rites of passage to help induct young men into manhood. Some involve brutal hazings and tests of courage while others require endurance, aptitude and skill. They all share the underlying premise that real men are made, not born. This feeds into men's gender insecurity.

One way to feel unambiguously male in many cultures is to dominate women, to behave aggressively, and to take risks. A "real man" in the Balkans, for example, is one who drinks heavily, fights bravely, and shows "indomitable virility" by fathering many children (Denich 1974:250). In eastern Morocco, "true men" are distinguished based on their physical prowess and heroic acts of both feuding and sexual potency (Marcus 1987:50). On the South Pacific island of Truk, fighting, drinking, defying the sea, and sexually conquering women are the true measures of manhood (Caughey 1970; Marshall 1979; Gilmore 1990).

Significantly, sexual conquest and potency appear as repeated themes in many cultural definitions of manhood, placing women at increased risk of coercive sex. This is as true in the United States as it is elsewhere. Recently, nine teenage boys from an upper-working class suburb of Long Beach were arrested for allegedly molesting and raping a number of girls, some as young as ten. The boys, members of a group called the Spur Posse, acknowledge having sex with scores, or underage girls, as part of a sexual competition. In tabulating their sexual exploits, the boys make reference to the uniform number of the sports stars who are their heros—"I'm 44 now—Reggie Jackson. I'm 50—David Robinson." Tellingly, some of the boys' fathers appear boastful of their son's conquests. In a recent *New York Times* article, one father praised his son as "all man" and insisted that the girls his son had had sex with were "giving it away" (Gross 1993).

The salience of sex to some versions of masculine identity is likewise recognized in a Swedish Government report on prostitution, published in 1981:

> The male confirms and proves his maleness, his virility, through his sexuality. It becomes the core, the very essence around which he consciously and unconsciously forms his idea about himself as a man. The female sexual identity has not been formed in relationship to sexuality, but in the need to be chosen by a man. . . . By being chosen the woman receives the necessary proof of her value as a woman—both in her own eyes and in others. (Olsson 1984:73)

Indeed, some theorists go so far as to assert that notions of masculinity help construct the experience of sex itself. Speaking from an Anglo-American perspective, John Stoltenberg argues that "so much of most men's sexuality is tied up with gender-actualizing—with feeling like a real man—that they can scarcely recall an erotic sensation that had no gender-specific cultural meaning. As most men age, they learn to cancel out and deny erotic sensations that are not specifically linked to what they think a real man is supposed to feel" (Stoltenberg 1989:33).

To the extent that masculine ideals are associated with violence, virility, and power, it is easy to see how male sexual behavior might emerge as predatory and aggressive. Indeed, the more I work on violence against women, the more I become convinced that the real way forward is to redefine what it means to be male. When masculinity is associated with aggression and sexual conquest, domineering sexual behavior and violence become not only a means of structuring power relations between men and women, but a way of establishing power relations among men. As Roger Lancaster observes in his ethnographic study of gender relations in Nicaragua, within many gendered systems sexual exploits are part of a system of posturing among men where women are merely the mediums of competition (see Lancaster 1992; see also Chapter Eight in this volume).

Since men have a collective interest in the perpetuation of gender hierarchies, individual male behavior is closely monitored by the male community (and sometimes by mothers acting on behalf of their sons). When the behavior of men or boys does not live up to the masculine ideal, they are frequently rebuked by invoking another gendered symbol: the male homosexual, however culturally defined. "Real men" are almost always defined in opposition to the queer, the *hueco*, the *cochón*, the sissy. Homosexual stigma is invoked to enforce the masculine ideal; it becomes part of the glue that holds male dominance together.

As Lancaster points out in his Nicaraguan example, homosexual stigma helps structure and perpetuate male sexual and gender norms. Lancaster maintains that by adolescence, boys are in open competition for the status of manhood. "The signs of masculinity," he argues, "are actively struggled for, and can only be won by wresting them *away from* other boys around them" (Lancaster 1992; Chapter Eight in this volume).

Fortunately, the ethnographic record provides us with examples to prove that the world need not be constructed this way. After exhaustively reviewing existing information on masculinity cross-culturally, Gilmore notes that while "ideas and anxieties about masculinity as a special-status category of achievement are widespread in societies around the world, being expressed to varying degrees. . . they do not seem to be absolutely universal" (Gilmore 1990). He cites several exceptions: cultures where manhood is of minimal interest to men and where there is little or no social pressure to act "manly."

Among Gilmore's examples are the Semai people of Malaysia and inhabitants of Tahiti. In Tahiti, for example, there are no strict gender roles, no concept of male honor to defend, and no social expectation to "get even." Men share a cultural value of "timidity" which forbids retaliation, and even when provoked, men rarely become violent. According to Gilmore, the concept of "manliness" as separate from femininity is simply foreign to them (Gilmore 1990). An extensive ethnographic record reveals that a similar description would be appropriate for the Semai of Malaysia as well (Dentan 1979).

What is intriguing about these two examples is that they conform well to the picture of other societies known to have low or non-existent levels of violence against women. Indeed, both Peggy Sanday's cross-cultural study of rape and the anthology, *Sanctions and Sanctuary*, a cross-cultural look at wife beating, found that one of the strongest predictors/correlates of societies with high violence against women was the presence of a masculine ideal that emphasized dominance, toughness, or male honor (Counts, Brown, and Campbell 1992).[10] While these types of studies cannot prove causality, they do begin to suggest which factors appear especially predictive of high rates of violence against women versus those that predict low rates of gender violence. Table Five presents a simplified account of the major findings of the Levinson, Sanday, and *Sanctions and Sanctuary* studies.

Interestingly, the findings strongly support the feminist contention that hierarchial gender relations—perpetuated through gender socialization and the socioeconomic inequalities of society—are integrally related to violence against women. Male decisionmaking in the home and economic inequality between men and women are strongly correlated with high rates of violence

Table Five:
Correlates of Gender Violence Based on Cross-Cultural Studies

Predicitive of High Violence	Predicitive of Low Violence
1. Violent interpersonal conflict resolution (1)(3)	1. Female power outside of the home (1)(2)(3)
2. Economic inequality between men and women (3)	2. Active community interference in violence (2)(3)
3. Masculine ideal of male dominance/toughness/honor (1)(2)	3. Presence of exclusively female groups (work or solidarity) (2)(3)
4. Male economic and decision-making authority in the family (3)	4. Sanctuary(shelters/friends/family) (2)

(1) = Sanday, P. 1981. "The Socio-cultural Context of Rape: A Cross Cultural Study." Journal of Social Issues 37(4):5-27.
(2) = Counts, Dorothy Ayers, Brown, Judith and Jacquelyn Campbell (eds.). (1992) Sanctions and Sanctuary. Boulder, Co.: Westview Press.
(3) = Levinson, David. (1989) Violence in Cross-Cultural Perspective. Newbury Park: Sage Publishers.

against women, while women having power outside of the home (either political, economic, or magical) seems to offer some protection against abuse. Another particularly strong factor seems to be the social acceptance of violence as a way to resolve conflict: where interpersonal violence is tolerated in the society at large, women are at higher risk. Given that much behavior is learned by children through modeling, this finding is hardly surprising.

This generic picture conforms well to actual ethnographic descriptions of societies with little or no violence against women. Sanday uses the Mbuti Pygmie, a forest dwelling people, to illustrate her point. Violence between the sexes, or between anybody, is virtually absent among the Mbuti Pygmie when they are in their forest environment. There is little division of labor by sex. A man is not ashamed to pick mushrooms and nuts if he finds them, or to wash and clean a baby. Decision-making is by common consent; men and women have equal say because hunting and gathering are both important to the economy (Turnbull 1965). This description sounds remarkably similar to that offered for the Central Thai, the Semai of Malaysia, and the Tahitians, described earlier.

The factors that emerge as predictive of low violence are also enlightening. In addition to female power, the presence of all female coalitions or work groups appears to be significant. Whether this operates by increasing women's economic power or through female solidarity and consciousness-raising, remains unclear. Especially significant appears to be the presence of strong sanctions against violence and access to sanctuary (hence the name of the anthology, *Sanctions and Sanctuary*). Sanctions can take the form of swift legal response, or they can involve informal community sanctions, like public humiliation. Likewise, "sanctuary" can be formal shelters or merely the cultural understanding that neighbors and/or family members will take in a woman whose partner is threatening her. Violence appears especially common in cultures where women leave their natal village to get married; not only are family members not present to intervene in disputes, but it is more difficult for the woman to seek refuge when relatives are distant (Counts, Brown, and Campbell 1992). In fact, active community or family interference in violent events emerged as an important predictor of low violence in both of the wife beating studies.

CONCLUSION

These cross-cultural tidbits suggest that the possiblity of a world without violence against women is not a hopeless fantasy. Societies have existed, and may still exist, that are essentially free of gender-based abuse. But social movements must have both vision and a sense of responsibility to those who must live within today's reality. The overwhelming presence of violence in many women's lives demands that we work on two fronts: to challenge the gender-based inequities and beliefs that perpetuate male violence and to provide services and support to those attempting to survive, despite the social forces allied against them. A range of professions—public health, family planning, sexuality research—have important roles to play. They can marshall their resources to help untangle the complex web of social forces that encourage violent behavior; they can design programs to empower women and enlighten men; and they can identify and refer women to helpful services. Given the health and social consequences of abuse, this is not only their prerogative, but their obligation.

NOTES

1. As it stands, most international development funders see violence as outside of their area of responsibility. International funding tends to be very sectoral, with aid streams targeted specifically to education, agriculture, population control, or health. Since anti-violence initiatives, such as crisis centers, law reform efforts, and public education do not fall easily within any of these categories, they frequently cannot get outside funding or support. The *Violence, Health and Development* project helps articulate the links between violence and women's health with an eye toward recruiting more health dollars for violence related programming.

2. Although individually valid, these studies are not directly comparable because each

uses a different set of questions to probe for abuse. The vast majority of studies ask the respondents whether they have been "abused," "beaten," or "involved in a violent relationship." A subset (e.g., the studies from Barbados and United States) make this determination based on a list of "acts" that a woman may or may not have been subjected to during her lifetime (e.g., hitting with fist, biting, being hit with an object, etc). Clinical and research experience suggests that allowing women to self-define abuse, if anything, underestimates the level of physical and psychological violence in intimate relationships. In many cultures, women are socialized to accept physical and emotional chastisement as part of a husband's marital prerogative, thereby limiting the range of behavior women consider "abuse." Moreover, women are sometimes reluctant to report abuse out of shame or fear of incriminating other family members. Both factors suggest that the prevalence rates in Table Two are likely to be underestimates of actual abuse.

3. All of the studies use legally-grounded definitions of rape; thus, forms of penetration other than penile-vaginal are included and women were not instructed to exclude rape by husbands. Questions were typically framed to define explicitly the behaviors that should be included in the definition. For example: "Has a man made you have sex by using force or threatening to harm you? When we use the word 'sex' we mean a man putting his penis in your vagina even if he didn't ejaculate (come)?" This is followed by: "If he did not try to put his penis in your vagina, has a man made you do other sexual things like oral sex, anal sex, or put fingers or objects inside you by using force or threatening to harm you?"

4. The estimates in Table Three are based on existing legal definitions of rape in the United States which recognize penetration of any orifice by physical force or threat of force, or because a woman is incapacitated due to drugs or alcohol.

5. In evaluating the sources of variability in prevalence of sexual abuse, Peters, Wyatt, and Finkelhor (1986) suggest that differences in definitions and the various methods used in these studies probably account for most of the variations reported.

6. This figure is quoted in "Rape: Can I have this Child?" a photonovela produced by Movimiento Manuela Ramos, Lima, Peru, as part of their campaign to decriminalize abortion in cases of rape.

7. Another significant subset reported positive initiations. While recalling some lack of pleasure due to inexperience, these girls actively agreed to intercourse and considered it part of an on-going process of sexual discovery that began earlier in life with sex play, petting, and masturbation.

8. By no means is male approval always the greatest determinant of contraceptive use. For examples of cases where it is, see Gallen (1986) and Kincaid (1992).

9. Variables controlled for include: years in legal or common law union during previous five years; raised in lower class home; education of mother; education of father; raised in stable nuclear family; raised solely by mother; raised with a step father; degree of affection mother's partner showed her; degree of physical and emotional abuse to mother; degree of affection mother showed son; degree of affection mother's partner showed son; degree to which mother's partner physically and emotionally abused son; man's educational status; man's occupational status.

10. There are examples of peaceful societies that do have a notion of "achieved manhood," but generally this manhood is not linked to dominance, male honor, or aggression but to skill, often in the realm of hunting. In these societies—such as the Mbuti Pygmies and the !Kung Bushmen—hunting is not an "outlet for agression," but is seen as "a contribution to society of both indispensable economic and spiritual value. . .truly a kind of indirect nourishing or nurturing" (Gilmore 1990:116).

"That We Should All Turn Queer?" 8

Homosexual Stigma in the Making of Manhood and the Breaking of a Revolution in Nicaragua

Roger N. Lancaster

IN A BROAD SENSE, THE SANDINISTA REVOLUTION WAS UNDERMINED by an all-round war of aggression. On the military front, the U.S.-sponsored contra war had left thirty thousand people dead in a country of some three million. Contra attacks targeted schools, clinics, electrical facilities, bridges, and farms, traumatizing the country's economic infrastructure and disrupting social services. On the economic front, the U.S. economic embargo deprived Nicaragua of its historical market for agricultural products and, more importantly, of direct access to spare parts for its U.S.-manufactured machinery. And on the international front, U.S. vetos deprived Nicaragua of any relief it might have received from lending agencies.

As a result of this three-pronged attack, Nicaragua's per capita gross domestic product fell to roughly half its pre-war level. By the late 1980s, defense was consuming over sixty percent of government expenditures, and in 1988 the annual rate of inflation soared to thirty-five thousand percent. The cumulative effects of war and embargo totalled up to $17 billion in direct and indirect damages—in a country whose gross domestic product never much exceeded three billion, even in good years. The result was social, economic, and personal discombobulation.[1]

In a narrower sense, though, Nicaraguan families, structured by a "culture of machismo" and rent by unresolved gender conflicts, proved the most effective medium of an intimate, low-intensity conflict that ate away at the revolution's base of popular support. Nicaraguan family life has long been characterized by widespread patterns of male abandonment. At the time of the revolution, some thirty-four percent of Nicaraguan families were headed by women, and the figure was closer to fifty percent in the cities. Brittle conjugal relations, in the context of a patriarchial economic structure, necessarily put women and children in a structurally disadvantageous social position.[2]

Such patterns of oppression had provided the context for the dramatic and unprecedented mobilization of women and youth in the Sandinista revolution. By the 1979 revolution, women constituted some thirty percent of the FSLN guerrilla combatants (Molyneux 1985:227). Women and young people were active in the ensuing revolutionary process of the 1980s. In many civic projects—literacy campaigns, grass roots health care initiatives—women's participation far exceeded men's (Collinson 1990:97, 124). And from the beginning, the Sandinista revolution included a strong current devoted to women's, even to feminist, issues. AMNLAE (Asociación de Mujeres Nicaragüenses "Luisa Amanda Espinoza"), the Nicaraguan women's organization, politicized a broad array of gender questions and family issues. AMNLAE-sponsored legal reforms and political mobilizations attempted to change what AMNLAE and the Sandinistas called "the culture of machismo."

Under the Sandinistas, new legislation attempted to redress the obvious gender inequalities. A diverse package of laws, collectively known as the "new family laws," aimed (1) to enhance the legal, social, and political position of women and children; (2) to secure the protection and well-being of children; and (3) to stabilize the Nicaraguan family, seen by many as being "in crisis." The reforms of this period have been criticized for not going far enough. But on paper, and by comparison with past precedent, they appear radical and far-reaching indeed. New laws outlawed sex discrimination, declared legal equality for women, treated domestic violence as a serious criminal offense, established equal social and economic rights for illegitimate children, and specified procedures for establishing paternity in cases of abandonment.[3] Family life was a site of multiple personal conflicts, vigorous political contestations, and frequently ambiguous power plays.

The results of these legal reforms were mixed. More women went to school, entered the labor force, and became involved in politics. However, women enjoyed increased educational and job opportunities in a context where real wages declined precipitously. Women and children benefitted early on from consumer subsidies, but those subsidies largely disappeared as the war and crisis dragged on. Despite greater legal remedies at their disposal, women and children bore the brunt of the economic crisis. And despite legal reforms and good faith efforts, families were in no sense "stabilized"—and it is difficult to see how they might have been. Traditional patterns of male abandonment were probably exacerbated under conditions of war and hardship. Only now, men left home not to live in another Nicaraguan town or province, but to take up residency in Miami, or New York, or Los Angeles, where they were both far from traditional pressures to provide some assistance to abandoned families, and beyond the scope of new child support laws.

In the context of the extended social, political, and personal crises of the

1980s, it would be difficult to overstate the effects of gender politics on the national-level politics of the state. In a political strategy that duplicated the appeal of the New Right in the United States, conservative elites in Nicaragua attacked AMNLAE/Sandinista reform efforts as "communistic attacks on the sanctity of the family." Such diatribes targeted logical audiences: more traditional elements of society, whose values were being contested, and especially men, whose powers and prerogatives were being legally restricted. At the same time, however, in the popular classes, poor, middle-aged housewives and mothers emerged as a bulwark of opposition to Sandinismo (see IHCA 1988). The reason for this development is not mysterious. As war and crisis dragged on, single mothers plainly bore the brunt of economic hardships. And mothers in general, in their role as care-providers, were most acutely confronted with soaring food prices, diminishing resources, and attendant difficulties in provisioning for families. Moreover, mothers became the main source of overt opposition to the unpopular military draft. What few anti-draft demonstrations that occured were organized by mothers, not by teenagers. The combination of open yet unresolved gender conflicts and a declining real standard of living encouraged some people—men and women, old and young—to entertain a nostalgic, conservative, Catholic traditionalism on gender issues.[4]

Such political openings were well understood by the internal opposition, and by the U.S. State Department. Violeta Chamorro—mother, grandmother, widow—was an effective symbol from many angles. Her 1990 presidential campaign simultaneously rallied culturally conservative opposition to the Sandinistas, mobilized poor and working class frustration with economic conditions, and articulated maternal opposition to the draft (Lancaster 1992:290–293). In short, Chamorro's campaign actively trafficked in the traditional cult of motherhood: in its appeal to and through Nicaraguan women as domestic peacemakers, and in its promise to restore the "true dignity of womanhood."

My ethnography, *Life is Hard: Machismo, Danger, and the Intimacy of Power* (1992), traces the fissures and fault lines that existed within Nicaraguan families before the revolution and gradually widened in postrevolutionary society—the divides of gender, generation, and sexuality. My use of the term "culture of machismo" not only quotes my informants, but deliberately echoes Oscar Lewis's phrase, "culture of poverty." Lewis (1966:8) argued that what he called "the culture of poverty" would not simply go away with a transformation of the economic conditions that create poverty. He argued that "any movement—be it religious, pacifist, or revolutionary—that organizes and gives hope to the poor. . . must effectively destroy the psychological and social core of the culture of poverty."

I would argue that many of the characteristics Lewis attributed to a "culture of poverty" belong not to some special culture of poor people in Latin America, but to an overarching gendered world that might more accurately be called the "culture of machismo." Whether one even grants the existence of a culture of poverty, and despite the troubled and troubling legacy of this concept, Lewis's basic argument provides a reasonable analogy with the case I make concerning Nicaragua.[5] No one should slight the importance of certain structural factors (U.S. aggression, Nicaragua's dependency on agro-exports, a long-term agricultural recession in the international marketplace) in shaping the outcome of the revolution. But surely, the culture of machismo was itself one such factor. A pre-existing pattern of gender and sexuality did not simply "wither away" after the revolution; it proved more resilient than the revolutionaries. Many of the conflicts and frustrations that eroded the revolutionary project belong most logically and most directly to the culture of machismo. And changing it would have required a revolution within the revolution.

LITERAL READINGS AND EVERDAY OCCURRENCES

What this chapter addresses in detail is a dimension of gender studies that remains to be fully addressed in the ethnographic literature: not the role of male-female interaction in generating gender norms, but the role of male-male interaction; specifically, not the role of heterosexual norms in establishing homosexual stigma and a minority status, but the role of homosexual stigma in structuring male sexual and gender norms; and finally, not simply the role of homosexual stigma in thus producing and consolidating masculinity, but also its role as a crucial requirement in the reproduction of gender relations at large.

Nicaraguans themselves sometimes comment on such connections. I was interviewing Jaime, then a teenager, on the conception of masculinity within the culture of machismo. Jaime constrasted the current, changing situation with the past, and illustrated his argument as follows: "A man helping his wife out around the house was unthinkable before the revolution. No man would be caught dead washing dishes or cooking or ironing. If his wife asked him to give her a hand, he would just say, '*Yo no soy cochón*' (I'm not queer) and that would be the end of it. . . ."

What happens to our analysis of gender relations if we take this statement literally? Whence come the distinctions that, from men's perspective, define gender differences and reinforce appropriate masculinity? In an age of increasingly subtle reading strategies, it might be interesting to try the novel approach of listening straightforwardly to such remarks.

Or, consider an event I observed during a visit between neighbors. Guto, a teenage boy, was holding Esperanza's and Pedro's daughter, Auxiliadora. Guto's sister Aida was holding her son, Ervin. Guto decided to have the children, both of them two, "fight" a mock battle. He manipulated the smaller girl's hands into lightly hitting Ervin. The boy began to cry. "*Veni, cochón!*" ("Come on, *cochón* [queer]!"), Guto cajoled, mimicking the voice of a small girl, "Come on, *cochón!*" The baby in his arms seemed confused by the goings-on around her. Embarrassed by such antics, but responding nonetheless, Aida pushed her son Ervin forward and began manipulating his hands in mock battle. The four of them played this way for a few seconds until Ervin began to cry again. "*Cochón, cochón!*" Guto chastised, while Aida soothed her son.

Only a couple of days before, in the rowdy and drunken atmosphere of Santo Domingo, there had been what could only be described as a collective outbreak of domestic violence in the neighborhood. Several couples fought; several women were beaten by their husbands. Indeed, Esperanza and her *compañero* (companion) had exchanged blows after Pedro had punched her in the face. With events of the other day still no doubt very much on her mind, Esperanza said to me: "Now just look at that. They're teaching him how to beat women." And so they were.

Again, what happens to our analysis of gender if we give such an event the literal reading it was given by Esperanza? Esperanza was commenting narrowly on the lesson Guto was teaching Aida's son; more generally and most tellingly, she might have been commenting on a whole structure of child socialization. The lesson for Ervin—an inescapable one, reinforced at every juncture of a boy's experience—is: show aggressiveness, dominate women, or be deprived of your masculinity. Despite the best intentions and reform efforts, even in politically conscious households (like the one described above: Esperanza and Pedro were labor unionists and activists; Aida was a member of AMNLAE), the overall regimen of child-rearing remains highly-gendered, and is very much designed to instill the core values of machismo in successive generations:

1. Boys are typically teased, taunted and provoked by their older siblings until they display an appropriate rage; once solicited, these rages are tolerated, and are punished only when they exceed broadly-defined limits. Girls receive no such training, and their signs of rage are neither indulged nor tolerated.

2. When young male children are learning to speak, and pick up profane language from the adults and older children around them, their outbursts are greeted with amused tolerance, even encouragement; punishment ensues only when they direct their invective against adults. Female children receive no such indulgence, and even mild vulgarities from them receive swift punishment.

3. Boys who are still toddling and scarcely able to talk might be sent on various short errands or allowed to play without adult supervision at some distance from the house. Girls are not pushed toward personal autonomy at such an early age; when they wander from the house, they are more quickly retrieved, and are frequently punished for doing so.

4. Past adolescence, teenage boys are allowed to roam the neighborhood in the evening and to socialize with their friends in a relatively unsupervised manner; teenage girls absolutely are *not* allowed to do so.

5. Indeed, boys are given great leeway in ignoring or flouting their mothers' orders; girls are issued many fewer warnings before being whipped.

6. Corporal punishment diminishes and ceases for a boy at a much younger age than it does for a girl.

7. And when a teenage boy comes home in the evening smelling of alcohol, his mother is unlikely to make too many inquiries; if a teenage girl comes home smelling of alcohol, her mother is almost certain to beat her with a belt.

By many means over many years, a boy's training actively solicits the hallmark traits of machismo: an ideal of masculinity defined by assertiveness, aggression, and competition; relatively privileged access to space and mobility; disproportionate control over resources; and a willingness to take risks. . . . But how is such a routine concretely maintained? Not simply by a system of rewards—for most males at any age, the rewards are minimal, and the costs (in injury, humiliation, exertion, and fiscal expenses) can be quite high. What sanctions, then, are invoked? What disciplinary measures *force* compliance with machismo's gender norms for males? The answer is clear: Boys are constantly disciplined by their elders—by parents and siblings alike—with the humiliating phrase, "*No sea cochón!*" ("Don't be a queer!") when their demeanor falls short of the assertive, aggressive, masculine ideal. Any show of sensitivity, weakness, reticence—or whatever else is judged to be a feminine characteristic—is swiftly identified and ridiculed. By adolescence, boys enter a competitive arena, where the signs of masculinity are actively struggled for, and can only be won by wresting them *away from* other boys around them (see Lancaster 1992:245–47).

Justifiably, the regimen of this socialization might be called "brutal"; its whole purpose is to induce a certain insensitivity—and its effect is to produce an irresponsibility—in men. That conjugal pairings are so often volatile, violent, and brief is a logical consequence of this form of masculine socialization. That the fate of so many Nicaraguan men is alcoholism, broken health, loneliness, and early death is also a direct consequence of this atomizing and isolating socialization.

This routine, its disciplinary forces, the values it incubates, all set in motion cultural devices from which even women find it difficult to extract themselves, despite their obvious victimization in the culture of machismo. For example, women do indeed speak ill of men—for excessive drinking, for womanizing, for beating women—but when men gather, it is usually the women who send for liquor and prepare the chasers, and they usually do so without being asked. By and large, men who are considered too mild-mannered or too passive in their personal interactions are not considered good prospects for husbands—even if they are demonstrably industrious and hard-working. Although women frequently mitigate the discipline of harsh fathers, it is nonetheless to some extent women—mothers—who solicit independent, aggressive, even violent behavior in their sons, while keeping their daughters on a far shorter leash: they want their sons to be strong and independent, not soft, and they want their daughters to behave like acquiescent young ladies.

Yet a final literal reading of the situation: Even while the Sandinistas devoted themselves to combatting machismo in some arenas, the logic of this sexual construct, and its disciplinary force in creating and consolidating a genre of masculinity, was ultimately reinforced by conditions of war. In 1986, I asked Charlie what he was going to do in another year or so, when he would reach the age of mandatory military service. What he said, and how he said it, were both indicative. "When it's my time, I'm not going to run. I'd rather stay in school and study, but when I have to, I'll go into the service, and do my time. Only the *cochones* run." Charlie (reluctantly) struck the machista pose: only a queer would run. Charlie's sentiments were almost stereotypical of my conversations with young men. It is clear that most young men would have preferred not to serve. Most said as much. The Sandinistas were aware of this. So in addition to the usual appeals to patriotism and revolutionary ardor, the government and the Sandinista mass organizations occasionally manipulated prevailing conceptions of masculinity as an additional measure to discourage draft evasion. The following graffiti, splashed on a prominent wall in Granada, is typical of its genre and carries this force: "*Sólo las maricas son evasores*" ("Only sissies are evaders").

GENDER, SEXUALITY AND THE BODY: THEORETICAL APPROACHES AND IMPASSES

Most previous theoretical approaches to the production of masculinity have generally failed to explore the dimension that I have been sketching.

The classical research on patterns of machismo in Central America (and similarly situated geographies) views it, effectively, as a cultural and ideological superstructure, resting atop an economic base.[6] The historical thrust of this paradigm can be readily summarized: the rise of large-scale, capital-intensive agriculture in the nineteenth century deprived peasants and small farmers of land, thus creating a popular class of landless, mobile, male laborers. Women and children became the "fixed" pieces of family structure, men the detachable parts, and an ideology arose to justify the resulting flexible patterns of householding. This explanation has the advantage of a certain materiality, but the disadvantage of reducing gender relations to an ideological gloss on economic relations. It never makes inquiries into the materiality of the body in the production of gender, sexuality, and other cultural values. It also takes gender inequality almost as a given, and proposes only to understand the brittle nature of conjugal pairs and the prevalance of informal unions.

Beyond Latin American studies, most existing efforts at theorizing gender have viewed gender relations through the lens of relations between men and women. Moreover, since gender studies emerged first and primarily from feminism, the literature has tended to concentrate on the female side of the question. Women's studies has offered important theoretical contributions and practical correctives to androcentric bias. But gender is not simply feminine. Contemporary gender studies should seriously theorize masculinity, as well, and it needs to theorize both masculinity and femininity beyond the simple dyadic models that have repeatedly devolved into essentialist and biologically-grounded arguments.

An exception to the usual pattern of research is Gilmore's (1990) cross-cultural study of masculinity. Yet whatever its merits might be in other settings, Gilmore's hypothetically typical construction of masculinity seems not at all applicable to machismo in Nicaragua. Gilmore's notion of manhood, like Chodorow's (1974, 1978), emphasizes its achieved and competitive orientation; but Gilmore also attributes to it a protective, nurturing effect: as women are to children, so men are to women and children. None of my female informants invoke such qualities when describing traditional patterns of masculinity in Nicaragua. Nor, for that matter, do men. Both speak of "the macho" in terms of risk-taking, gambling, self-assertion, and violence. The underlying theme is irresponsibility, not nurture.

Those approaches that have attempted to consider both gender and sexuality as part of a single cultural system have produced mixed results, owing in part to the simplicity of the models proposed. Especially in the work of Dworkin (1987, 1989) and MacKinnon (1987, 1989), crucial distinctions are lost, not simply between gender and sexuality, but also between innumerable oppositions: between the system as a whole and individual experience; between the existing system of sexuality and the sex act for any two people; between the hegemony of the sexual code and sexual reinscription and subversion. . . . In a paradoxical move that would seem to enhance the existential responsibility of theory, such analyses have actually unhinged theory altogether from the responsibility of human reciprocity. In this iron cage of analysis, every sex act becomes indistinguishable from rape and terrorism. So extreme have been the abuses of this model that even Gayle Rubin, who first popularized the gender/sexuality model (1975), has expressly urged their more rigorous separation into distinct analytical domains (Rubin 1984). And there is a real danger here, if distinctions are not maintained—if every sex act without exception is taken as nothing other than the simple and direct expression of a pre-existing system. A theory incapable of differentiations is inadequate to any task of cultural criticism. Haraway (1990:200–01) has described such work as a virtual parody of feminism; others have remarked on its affinities with Puritanism. Its fundamental and recurring structure duplicates the logic of Stalinism, in the sense described by Sartre (1963): everything specific, individual, and particular must be made to defer to the general, the systemic, the totality. And what will not readily defer to theory is dissolved "in a bath of sulfuric acid."

Gay theory has since its inception theorized sexuality, especially male-male sexuality. It has frequently done so in connection with the prevailing system of gender norms, and without the indulgences of an anti-sex Puritanism. Gay and lesbian theory provides a good starting point for the kind of analysis I have been pointing toward. But gay theory, especially its essentialist and universalist varieties, too often begins and ends with the experiences of a sexual minority. At its most sophisticated—that is, in social constructionism—it marks the historical limits and describes the social conditions of homosexual identity and resistance.[7] But in either case, as long as it is motivated primarily by the politics of identity, it retains both a minority and *minoritizing* perspective.

Poststructural theory and postmodern experimentation afford analytical mobility, a turn from the facile temptations of "depth models," a romp of differentiations, and a rigorous challenge to the politics of identity. Foucault's *History of Sexuality* (1980) provides a rough draft of what a genuine political economy of the sexual body might be. I have drawn freely on his "productive" view of sexuality—not sexuality as productive in the sense of producing something else (wealth, class, commodities), but as itself, in itself, directly, productive. Productive, indeed, of identities and statuses and values which are themselves arbitrary, contrived, relational, conventional, and ephemeral.

However, much of postmodern academic discourse duplicates the process of abstraction, reification, and fetishization inherent in the commodification process (Marx 1967:71–83; Lukács 1971). Fredric Jameson (1991) thus describes postmodernism as "the cultural logic of late capitalism." For cultural criticism, we need a theory of fetishes, not theoretical fetishism. Even Foucault's work, which properly treats power as a relational realm, also has the effect of virtually severing power relations from the real human beings who produce, maintain, and transform them. In such theory, human agency and social practice have been disengaged from our understanding of the world. Little wonder that the system appears all-powerful in the post-modern politics of disengagement.

To unfashionably invoke a return of the repressed, we might today consider the example a currently eclipsed approach. Critical Marxism, especially the work of Marcuse (1966) and Brown (1990), attempted to articulate Freud's "economy of desire" with Marx's critique of political economy. Marcuse maintained a conception of "really existing sexuality" as systematically distorted, but he never viewed pleasure—sexual or otherwise—as inherently exploitative. Rather, he tried to theorize the conditions under which pleasure was either repressed or made to serve the ends of exploitation. Unfortunately, the limitations of Marcuse's analysis are coterminous with Freud's view of human nature, based on a theory of innate drives. The ballast for Marcuse's critical mission was always a conception of Nature, against which was pitted the Un-Natural excrescences of capitalism: commodities, exploitation, sublimation. But at its broadest, and read at a novel angle, Marcuse's work wrestled with fundamental questions that need to be re-asked: Not simply, "What are the productive applications of repression?" But also, and more enduringly: "Can one distinguish, rigorously and a priori, between eros and economics, desire and consumption, love and political economy? And how might we integrate these elements into a comprehensive yet subtle critical theory?"

The approaches described above, taken individually, are not "wrong," but even taken collectively they are not quite adequate, either. They are not quite adequate for understanding the gendered body as a locus of cultural meanings, historical practices, and physical sensations—as simultaneously ambiguous, yet concrete; as socially constructed, but at the same time constituent of social structures. Previous approaches have not provided the conceptual tools for diagramming the multiple links between everyday life and the system of gender/sexuality in various social formations. And up until very recently, existing approaches have scarcely attempted to theorize how male-male transactions structure masculinity, what homosexuality has to do with homosociality, or how these affect gender and (hetero)sexual relations. But increasingly, such topics define the horizon of research in many disciplines.

All theory arises from a context, addresses questions of immediate concern, and carries traces of its own birth, omens of its own death. The coming body of critical theory emerges against a political and cultural back-drop: the maturing and diversification of second-wave feminism; the simultaneous globalization and decentering of the gay and lesbian political movements; responses to the worldwide AIDS epidemic by those most affected; the new technologies of body discipline, and new tactics of body rebellion; the development of a "late marxism" amid these conditions of late capitalism; the fragmentation of modern, totalizing political projects, including Marxism, in a "postcolonial" world that nonetheless remains colonial because it remains capitalist.

These decentered conditions pose new questions, whose answers might be sought by innovating recombinant, practical variations of pre-existing theory. We need a theoretical approach faithful to the humane spirit of critical Marxism, steeped in the lessons of gender studies and gay studies, observant of the real contributions of poststructural and postmodern theory—yet without all the latter's distracting bells and whistles. We need a model with the theoretical mobility and sophistication of modern cultural studies, but ethnographically attentive to the mundane conditions of everyday life—an epistemologically "grounded" critical method (Scheper-Hughes 1992:4, 24) that dares to engage in issues that are of real interest to real people while always remaining concretely connected to their fundamental life experiences. To follow the circuitries of power in culture, we need an approach that can demonstrate concrete links between gender and sexuality, where those links exist, but without collapsing distinctions between the two or naturalizing their interrelationships. That is, we need "a political economy of the body" that neither confuses itself with the more standard political economy of an economic mode of production, nor attempts to duplicate its every move, and is unwilling to say—before the fact—where the one ends and the other begins, or even whether there is a logical demarcation at all between the two.

There is indeed a growing literature that engages the body in the same spirit that Marx engaged political economy—which is to say, as a critique of existing political economy. Not all of this literature belongs to gay/lesbian studies, but it all entails a certain "denaturalization" of the body, its care, meanings and habits. These works allow us to view the body itself as an ensemble of social practices. Jean Comaroff (1985) puts a modified conception of Bourdieu's (1977) habitus at the center of anthropological concerns with the social process of embodiment (see also Comaroff and Comaroff 1991:19–39.). Much of Thomas Lacqueur's (1990, 1992) emphasis is to historicize the body in a political-economic sense. M. Elaine Combs-Schilling (1989) diagrams a multi-leveled political economy of gender and sexuality in Morocco, and Richard Parker (1991) surveys the physical and social terrain of Brazilian sexual culture as enacted through carnival. The works of the Bakhtin school have provided a most productive site for recent attempts at theorizing the body, discourse, and culture (Bakhtin 1981, 1984; Vološinov 1993), while Donna Haraway's (1989, 1991) original work explores postmodernity's pliable borders, where nature and artifice, biology and technology, increasingly blur. Much of Nancy Scheper-Hughes's (1979, 1992; Scheper-Hughes and Lock 1987) work, collectively, points toward a critical political economy of the body, its practices, and regimes of family life.

Closer to the topic at hand, Gilbert Herdt's (1981, 1982) research in Papua New Guinea clearly establishes links between sexuality and the production of appropriate gender, but the configuration is very different from that which obtains in either Nicaragua or in the countries of the North. Dennis Altman (1971, 1982) was an early practicioner of this radical political economy of the body, and Jeffrey Weeks (1977, 1981, 1985) has long labored on this overall project. Judith Butler's *Gender Trouble* (1990) represents an attempt at theorizing the relationship between the system of asymmetrical gender relations and compulsory heterosexuality. Eve Sedgwick's *Between Men* (1985) and *Epistemology of the Closet* (1990) are direct attempts at theorizing the articulation of the homosocial, the homosexual, and the heterosexual in Western society, although these books' emphasis on elite literary texts leaves them with few points of access to forms of everyday life.[8]

It might be objected that this angle is an improbable one; that it stretches metaphors to speak of a "political economy of the body." Clearly, the literal mechanics of appropriation, exploitation, and production *are* different in the two domains connected by this metaphor.[9] What "political economy" usually designates is material production and consumption, along with the attendant political regime that both supports and is supported by a given mode of production. The "political economy of the body" alludes to that ensemble of representations and relations configured around the human body; to all the social, cultural, and economic values produced out of the raw material of the physical body; to the sum of gender transactions and sexual exchanges that collectively constitute the social body; and to all those power relations supported by and which support a given body regime.

I would argue that the "mechanics" are roughly comparable in either case. Any mode of production works over some raw material—whether it be physical material, or the matter of the physiology—to produce products of some value. Those products—whether they embody the value of commodities or the values of men and women—are circulated and exchanged according to certain implicit rules. All exploitative and inegalitarian modes of production and exchange produce certain conflicts over the allocation of goods, rewards, and powers. In any given political economy, these relations and conflicts give rise to an ensemble of political, representational, and juridical relationships. Acting as transactors and following the logic of the system they inhabit, humans are produced—or, rather, they produce themselves, and their consciousness, in the process of their overall activity.

To speak of a political economy of the body, or to conceive the body as a field of productive relations, is not to draw rigorous, one-to-one analogies with material production but to reiterate that what is produced in any case is not a "good" but a "value." What "economy" means in all cases is a system where value is assigned based not on any "intrinsic" worth of an object but rather on the object's position in the system of production and exchange. Thus, the value of a commodity is calculated in relation to other commodities and by the comparative social labor that produced it. Classes, too, are defined relationally: by their relations to each other in the social production process. In the political economy of "colorism" (Lancaster 1991), one's value as a person is determined within a system of material and symbolic exchanges, in terms of relations between the lexical clusters around *blanco* (white) and *negro* (black).

All theory is metaphorical, but to keep closely to Marx's arguments, it is no less metaphorical, no less concrete, to speak of a "political economics of the body" than to speak of a "political economy of material production." Such an emphasis returns Marxism to its original reflections on the production of the human condition (Marx and Engels 1964): it is a given form of humanity that is ultimately produced by any given mode of production.[10]

The culmination of these theoretical developments and mediations should result not simply in some well-demarcated "queer theory," but in *the queering of theory* as we all know and use it. Without forgetting the limits and conditions of homosexual identity, such an approach would consider the circulation of stigma in, through, and around sexuality—not simply how a minority identity is constructed, but how the stigmatization process affects everyone. Such theory begins but does not end with the simple affirmation of identities; it understands its subjects in the context of a general political economy of sexuality. It is capable of discovering concrete links beyond the realm of sexuality proper. As is implicit in the term "political economy," this model links sexuality to systems of gender, to modes of economic production and distribution, and to the corpus of bureaucratic and military coercions that constitute the state. A practical theory so conceived might allow us to develop a different kind of politics: a politics of solidarity, not identity, whose purpose is to change systems of practice and meaning rather than to simply carve out new minority rights within a preexisting system.

TOWARD A POLITICAL ECONOMY OF MACHISMO

To return, then, to the line of questions that prompted this essay: What, concretely, is machismo? What does it mean to be a man in the culture of machismo? And why do Nicaraguan men behave as they so often do (and as Nicaraguan women so vigorously complain): beating their wives, simultaneously fathering multiple households of children, abandoning *compañeras* and children, gambling away hard-earned money, and drinking to excess? And why did a decade of efforts to roll back the culture of machismo achieve so few tangible results?

An easy answer to the final question would be that the strain on Nicaragua's economic resources has made social restructuring impossible for the time being. That is indeed a partial answer. For those men already engaged in the culture of machismo, what AMNLAE and the Sandinistas call "responsibility" would prove costly, even under the best of circumstances. Under the current economy of scarcity, it would perhaps be prohibitively costly. Perhaps under a recovered economy, men might be more likely to support the children they father, and perhaps under better circumstances, sex education and contraception might make alternatives to the status quo available. Amidst the dislocations of war and hyper-inflation, however, and among all the personal turmoils thus engendered, it is difficult to imagine any systematic restructuring of the personal life and of personal relations.

But there is more to the matter than that, for the arrangement of inter-personal relationships is dependent on far more than the immediate state of the economy. The question of machismo cannot be addressed adequately if it is viewed as an *ideology* in the classical sense of the term. Machismo is not merely a set of erroneous ideas that somehow got lodged in people's heads. Rather, it is an organization of social relations that generates ideas. Machismo, therefore, is more than an "effect" produced by other material causes. It has its own materiality, its own power to produce effects. The resilience of machismo has nothing to do with the tendency of ideology to "lag" behind changes in the system of economic production, for machismo itself is a real political economy of the body. In the political economy of machismo—that is, within the horizon of the masculinized, male body—one's standing as a man is gauged by the execution of certain transactions (drinking, gambling, womanizing) in relation to other men.

As a field of power relations, machismo entails every bit as much force as economic production, and no less influences economic production than it is influenced by it—otherwise, why would poverty have a feminine face in Nicaragua? Why would women and children be specially disadvantaged? Why else would weakness, failure, and fear be conceived within the logic of the *cochón*? And why would local understandings of wealth, success, and effective politics revolve around a blurred constellation of male dreams of omnipotence: *el hombre grande*, it goes without saying, is *un gran macho*, who is, naturally, also a *caudillo*. . . Although we might acknowledge the difficulty in domesticating masculinity under conditions of acute crisis, there is no particular reason to believe that men could be brought into the fold of the family more readily under conditions of surplus than under conditions of scarcity, for machismo produces its own surpluses and scarcities. And we cannot even begin to prejudge which activities characterize the political economy of the body and which ones characterize the economic relations of production; where machismo leaves off as a system, and where this distinct region of peripheral neocolonial capitalism begins.

Nor can the question of machismo be fully addressed as a matter of relations between men and women. It is that, but it is also more. Machismo (no less than North American concepts of masculinity and appropriate sexuality) is not exclusively or even primarily a means of structuring power relations between men and women. Indeed, men are never in a situation of direct competition with women for male honor. The rules of the game effectively exclude women from this male domain; by definition, it is only with other men that a man directly competes. Machismo, then—and the conception of masculinity it implies—is a means of structuring power between and among *men*. Like drinking, gambling, risk-taking, asserting one's opinion, and fighting, the conquest of women is a feat performed with two audiences in mind: first, other men, to whom one must constantly prove one's masculinity and virility; and second, one's self, to whom one must also show all the signs of masculinity.[11]

Machismo, then, is a matter of constantly asserting one's masculinity by way of practices which show the self to be "active," not "passive" (as defined in a given milieu). Every gesture, every posture, every stance, every way of acting in the world, is immediately seen as "masculine" or "feminine," depending on whether it connotes activity or passivity. Every action is governed by a relational system—a code—which produces its meanings out of the subject matter of the body, its form, its engagement with other bodies. Every act is, effectively, part of an ongoing exchange-system between men (in which women very often figure as intermediaries, but never directly as transactors). To maintain one's masculinity, one must successfully come out on top of these exchanges. To lose in this ongoing exchange system entails a loss of face, which is to say a loss of status, and a loss of masculinity. The threat, and the fear, is a total loss of status, whereby one descends to the zero point of the game, and either literally or effectively becomes a *cochón*.

The *cochón*, itself a product of machismo, thus grounds the system of machismo, holds it in its place, and vice versa.

EMBODYING POWER: HOMOSEXUALITY AS MEDIUM OF EXCHANGE

An earlier essay of mine diagrams the construction of homosexual stigma in Nicaragua (Lancaster 1988). There, as in much of Latin America, the stigmatized identity is configured not simply around homosexual intercourse, but in terms of the receptive, especially anal, "passive" role in sexual intercourse.[12] Whatever else a *cochón* might or might not do, he is tacitly understood as one who assumes the receptive role in anal intercourse. His partner, defined as "active" in the terms of their engagement, is not stigmatized, nor does he necessarily acquire a special identity of any sort.

This implies a very different demarcation for the *cochón* than that which circumscribes the North American homosexual. In the United States, outside of a few well-defined contexts, homosexual intercourse—indeed, homosexual desire—of any sort in any position marks one as a homosexual. But it is not simply a minority status which is differentially produced. What is also produced, in either case, is a majority, "normative" status. It is heterosexual honor in the United States to never, under any circumstances, feel or express homosexual desire. Masculinity here is constructed atop the repression of homosexuality.

In Nicaragua, however, homosexual activity—both figuratively and literally—is the very medium of a masculinity defined most bluntly in terms of use-values (not the value of repression.) This is not to say that there are not other media; there are. What is unique about the homosexual medium is that it signifies most directly and without intermediaries the male-male nature of machismo. Figuratively, the *cochón* is held to represent the degredation of a fallen man. At every turn, and in innumerable discourses, the honor of "*los machos*" is measured against his shame. This gauging is never simply a passive comparison. Masculinity is relational: not simply as a "vis à vis", but as a practice of imposition and domination; it must therefore be actively demonstrated, enacted, and maintained. Literally, in terms of male-male sexual relations, when one "uses" a *cochón*, one acquires masculinity; when one is "used" as a *cochón*, one expends it. The same act, then, makes one man an *hombre-hombre*, a manly man, and the other a *cochón*.

The *machista's* "honor" and the *cochón's* "shame" are opposite sides of the same coin, alternate angles of the same transaction. A value is produced, circulated, and reproduced in sexual transactions between men, and so is a stigma. Indeed, this value can only be measured against stigma. (Put in political-economic terms: in systems of exploitation, every "surplus" value is produced by an act of appropriation, and thus implies the creation of a "deficit" somewhere else.) Each act of intercourse "produces" moreover a system of masculinity—a system that explicitly regulates relations between men, but which no less conditions relations between men and women. Whatever the private sentiments of those involved—and relations between *machistas* and *cochones* are sometimes quite tender—these terms unambiguously denote winners and losers in the public game of masculinity: a game which structures male actions and interactions.

To open up the question of homosexual stigma to its farthest parameters: What is at stake is not simply a question of the construction of minority sexual identity through stigma, but moreover the elaboration of a majority status and a prevailing culture through the circulation of stigma. The definition of masculinity rides piggy-back, as it were, on the stigma of the *cochón*.[13]

THE CIRCULATION OF STIGMA

That being said, of course, sex is never so precise, and the real circulation of stigma is never so categorical. The stigma of the *cochón* applies, in its strictest and most limited sense, to a relatively small minority of men: those who are the "passive" participants in anal intercourse. In its broadest sense, however, the stigma threatens, even taints, all men.

The circulation of stigma implies a complex economy, an ambiguous discourse, and incessant power-struggles. In the words of Erving Goffman, stigma requires of us a carefully-staged "presentation of self in everyday life" (1959); it entails multiple levels of public, private, and intermediate transactions. To extend the dramaturgic metaphor, it brings into play many stages, many backstages, and many choruses. Or, to employ a game analogy: everyone wishes to pass the stigma along; no one wishes to be left holding it. As cunning and artful as are those who dodge it, by that very token must the invocation of stigma be coarse, generalized, and to some degree nondiscriminating. While the system of stigma produces certain distinct categories, then, its operation is never entirely categorical, for stigma is necessarily "sticky."

In the culture of machismo, the *cochón* is narrowly defined as anal-passive, but the concept of anal passivity serves more loosely as a sort of extreme case of "passivity." The term "*cochón*" thus may be invoked in both a strict and a loose sense. Which aspect of the concept is emphasized—anality or passivity—will determine whether it encompasses a small minority or a potentially large majority of men. Therein lies the peculiar power of stigma to regulate conduct and generate effects: it ultimately threatens all men who fail to maintain a proper public face. In machismo, the ambiguity of discourse is a highly productive feature of the system.

Thus, the *hombre-hombre*'s exemption from stigma is never entirely secure. He might find his honor tainted under certain circumstances. If an *hombre-hombre*'s sexual engagement with a *cochón* comes to light, for example, and if the nature of that relationship is seen as compromising the former's strength and power—in other words, if he is seen as being emotionally vulnerable to another man—his own masculinity would be undermined, regardless of his physical role in intercourse, and he might well be enveloped within the *cochón*'s stigma. Or if the *activo*'s attraction to men is perceived as being so great as to define a clear preference for men, and if this preference is understood to mitigate his social and sexual dominion over women, he would be seen as eschewing his masculine prerogatives and would undoubtedly be stigmatized. However, the Nicaraguan *hombre-hombre* retains the tools and strategies to ward off such stigma, both within and even *through* his sexual relationships with other men, and his arsenal is not much less than that which is available to other men who are not sleeping with *cochones*.

This is a crucial point. These kinds of circumstances are not perhaps exceptions at all, but simply applications of the rules in their most general sense. Such rules apply not only to those men who engage in sexual intercourse with other men; they apply equally to men who have sex only with women. The noise of stigma is the clatter of a malicious gossip that targets others' vulnerabilities. Thus, if a man fails to maintain the upper hand in his relations with women, his demeanor might well be judged "passive," and he would be stigmatized, by degrees, as a *cabrón* (cuckold), *maricón* (effeminate man), and *cochón*. Whoever fails to maintain an aggressively masculine front will be teased, ridiculed, and, ultimately, stigmatized. In this regard, accusations that one is a *cochón* are bandied about in an almost random manner: as a jest between friends, as an incitement between rivals, as a violent insult between enemies. Cats that fail to catch mice, dogs that fail to bark, boys who fail to fight, and men who fail in their pursuit of a woman: all are reproached with the term. And sometimes, against all this background noise, the charge is leveled as an earnest accusation.

That is the peculiar and extravagant power of the stigmatizing category: like a "prison-house of language," it indeed confines those to whom it is most strictly applied; but ambiguously used, it conjures a terror that rules all men, all actions, all relationships.

CONCLUSION: THE *COCHÓN*, MACHISMO, AND THE POLITICS OF GENDER

A rule is best preserved in its infractions. And a structure, a system of practices, is most readily defined, not by what is central to it, but by what is apparently marginal to it. The *cochón*, by violating the standards of appropriate male behavior, defines the conception of appropriate masculinity in Nicaragua. His passivity, as the opposite of activity, defines the latter (even as it is defined by the former). His status constitutes the ultimate sanction within a political economy of the body, its practices, its instrumentalities.

The *cochón* occupies the space and defines the nexus of all that is denigrated in men and among men. His presence allows the construction of another nexus, where the symbolic capital of masculinity is accumulated. In the cultural code of machismo, a series of couplings deploy themselves and define reality: masculinity/femininity, activity/passivity, violence/abuse, domination/subordination. Decoupling such a chain of associations would have to entail a political program far more radical than anything AMNLAE proposed or the Sandinistas actually tried.

Very much to the point: when I interviewed Nicaraguan men on the New Family Laws (with their stipulation that paternity entails economic responsibility, both inside and outside marriage) and their intention (to minimize irresponsible sex, irresponsible parenting, and familial dislocation), my informants very frequently took recourse to the same standard constructs. First, the interrogative: "What do the Sandinistas want from us? That we should all become *cochones*?" And then, the tautological: "A man has to be a man". That is, a man is defined by what he is not (a *cochón*).

From one angle, the distinction between men and women might seem enough to keep machismo's dynamics in play. Not so. For men do not "fall" to the status of *women* when they fail to maintain their pre-defined masculinity; they become something else: not quite men, not quite women. It could be said, then, that they fall both further and less far than women's station. *Less far*, because for some purposes and in some contexts, despite his stigma, a *cochón* can usually maintain some masculine prerogatives. *Farther*, because a woman is not stigmatized for being a woman, per se, not even for being a strong woman whose demeanor violates certain gender norms. One is, however, stigmatized for being less than a man.

It might moreover seem tempting to understand the sexual stigma of the *cochón* as a direct extension of the logic of gender onto the realm of sexuality: as man is to woman, so the *hombre-hombre* is to the *cochón*. This equation partly holds, but is not quite adequate. While it is clear that the *cochón*'s denigration is cast in strongly gendered terms, it is also cast in excess of those terms: as failure, inadequacy, weakness, and defeat.[14] Such meanings can scarcely be directly attributed to Nicaragua's traditional conceptions of womanhood, which celebrates a cult of elevated motherhood. This "excess" marks all that is ingredient in the production of manhood. Not simply the opposite of femininity, masculinity proper is itself the locus of important distinctions.

The arguments I have been developing here attempt to demonstrate the connections between gender and sexuality without theoretically collapsing the two. This model also represents an attempt to understand the concrete connections between micropolitics and macropolitics, between sexuality and the state.

Did the Sandinista revolution fail because it failed to emancipate *cochones*? Not per se, and that is not the argument that I would like to make. Did the revolution decline because it deferred a revolution in gender roles? Again, to put it that way would be an exaggeration. In the aftermath of the 1990 electoral defeat, some have argued in effect that the revolution failed because it was not radical enough (see Gonzalez 1990; Randall 1992). Such arguments are not convincing. An agenda of legal and social reforms were already underway. More militancy on such issues, under the circumstances, probably would have been more divisive. More divisions, in the context of war and crisis, would probably have shortened the life of the revolution. While the results of legal and social reforms were ambiguous at best, a decade is scarcely long enough to break family habits, change the meaning of gender, and overhaul the sexual economy.

The argument that I would construct goes more like this: the war, the embargo, and the crisis were all felt most intimately in Nicaraguan family life, through increasing gender conflicts, accelerated rates of male abandonment, the surplus impoverishment of women and children. . . . And how could one speak meaningfully of "working class solidarity" while its families remained divided by an oppressive culture of machismo, and were at war within themselves? The fabric of personal life, already tattered and patched together at best, unravelled. And with it, a revolution.

It is in this context that the stigma of the *cochón* and the practices of homosexuality were relevant to the larger course of history. For the structure of family life and the nature of gender cannot be understood—or altered—without reference to homosexuality. Homosexual intercourse and homosexual stigma play a clear and major role in the construction of appropriate gender for men. Their force on the male body is both differentiating and disciplinary. And machismo's ultimate reinforcement is the sanction: that one might be seen as, or become stigmatized as, or become, a *cochón*, if one fails to maintain one's proper masculinity as defined by machismo. If the New Family Laws, the project of the New Man, and attempts at rolling back the culture of *machismo* have largely failed, this is because such attempts at cultural reconstruction left undeconstructed the grounding oppositions of the system, and thus left *machismo*'s driving engine largely untouched.

However, I do not wish to conclude by making that system appear all-powerful. The role of theory should never be to bolt every window and bar every escape hatch from such a prison-house. No less than any other system of arbitrary power, privilege, and exploitation, machismo's routine operation generates innumerable resistances, evasions, and conflicts (Certeau 1984). Among men, these have not yet been as systematically mobilized as they have been among women, though the slow emergence after 1990 of an open gay liberation movement in Managua would seem to mark an important turning point in Nicaragua's political culture.

But even in a public world defined by power and cruelty, there are private worlds that turn on love. I have already said that in their personal relations, some couples—even couples that define themselves as consisting of an *hombre-hombre* and a *cochón*—conduct their affairs in a humane and tender way. These relationships violate the rules of the system, subvert its operation, play with its meanings, and elaborate new possibilities, even to the point of rendering null the opposition between "*hombre-hombre*" and "*cochón.*" In private transactions, then, the political economy of machismo is routinely subverted. Should such private arrangements ever be aired in open discussion, they would constitute a radical challenge to the stablity of the system.

On the public occasion of *carnaval*, and in other carnivalesque festivities, the official body is travestied and a rebellious libidinal body is liberated. The political economy of machismo is transgressed, and its values are rudely reversed.[15] Queers are not the only ones who enjoy the antics of *carnaval*; everyone becomes a bit queer. It might be countered that carnival time comes but once a year, or that it affords only a momentary reprieve from the strictures of everyday life, and that is true. And carnival is, after all, only play. But play is not a trivial matter. Carnival play is very different from those serious games that make boys into men. It models new perceptions, alternative bodies, utopian realities. This spirit of play has been growing and developing inside *carnaval* for the better part of five centuries. And when that spirit of play escapes *carnaval,* it will remake the world.

NOTES

Acknowledgments: Some sections of this essay are drawn from my book, *Life is Hard: Machismo, Danger and the Intimacy of Power in Nicaragua* (University of California Press, 1992). This essay developed over the course of time from talks given in several places: Modern Times Bookstore in San Francisco; the Evergreen State College in Olympia, Washington; the departments of anthropology at the University of California, Columbia University, and Yale University. It was formally presented as part of the "Gender Power" panel at the 1993 conference on International Perspectives in Sex Research held in Rio de Janeiro. I am grateful to all of the above audiences for their helpful criticisms. Specific thanks are in order to Samual Colón, Elaine Combs-Schilling, John Gagnon, Paul Kutsche, Rachel Moore, Stephen O. Murray, Richard Parker, Jim Quesada, Nancy Scheper-Hughes, and Michael Taussig. It is too late to thank the ardent Nicaraguanist and tireless gay activist, Tede Matthews, who died of AIDS in 1993. His work, networking, and sense of humor were all invaluable resources for several political communities. We miss him, and I dedicate this essay to his memory.

1. For a thorough overview of the economic consequences of war and embargo, see Conroy 1990. See also Walker 1987.

2. See Dirección de Orientación y Protección Familiar 1983; IHCA 1984; Molyneux 1985; Collinson 1990.

3. Dirección de Orientación y Protección Familiar 1983; IHCA 1984; Borge 1985; Molyneux 1985; Dirección Nacional, FSLN 1987.

4. See Lancaster 1992:283–293. Cf. Stacey's (1990) and Ginsburg's (1984, 1989) parallels regarding evangelicals, women, and the religious right in the United States.

5. Critiques include Leacock 1971; Valentine 1968; and Rigdon 1988. For a more recent discussion of the resurgence of "culture of poverty" theory implicit in many discussions of the "black underclass," see Reed 1991.

6. See Adams 1956:892; Adams 1957:189–95, 457–58; Anderson, 1971:13; Brown 1975.

7. Boswell's (1992) position is nuanced; he prefers the term "realist" to "essentialist," and avoids speculating on the "causes" of sexual preference. However, Ruse's (1988) gay-friendly sociobiology proposes a genetic anchor with hormonal wiring for the essential sexual orientations. The flurry of recent brain studies and twin studies attests to the popularity of such vulgar essentialist groundings. The media have sagely announced with each study "compelling new evidence" that homosexuality is genetically-fixed or biologically-shaped (Burr 1993), although the research methods employed in these studies were poorly conceived, and their findings have been ambiguous at best (see Rist 1992; Fausto-Sterling 1992:245–256). For sophisticated developments of the so-called "constructionist" position, see Halperin 1990; see also Weeks 1977, 1981, 1985; and Ponse 1978.

8. See also Steward 1984; Hennessy 1993.

9. Yet it must be remembered that all theory is metaphorical. The work of theory, like that of metaphor, is to construct models. Models, by design, work by analogy: they draw out connections between two (or more) different things, based on resemblances (of elements, characteristics, activities, or effects) held in common between them.

10. I am touching here on arguments that I have offered elsewhere. For a fuller review, see Lancaster 1992:19–21, 223–24, 280–82, 319n3–4.

11. Male power, it would seem, is a largely homosocial phenomenon. If we take homosociality—of secret societies, male cults, men's clubs, the military, sports—as homosexual desire *sublimated*, then the role of the homosocial in structuring both the heterosexual and male power deserves a distinctly *queer* reading. Levi-Strauss's (1969) classical analysis of kinship argues that men structure political alliances between themselves through the exchange of women; in this version, political society emerged as a bonded male-male relationship mediated by women. Rubin (1975) took this account of kinship as the point of departure for a critical understanding of male power and female powerlessness. Sedgwick (1985, 1990), too, understands the patriarchy as a social inheritance passed from one generation of men to the next through the cultivation of male homosocial power, structured by the sublimation of overt homosexual desire (see also Castiglia 1988). And Sanday (1990:12–14) understands gang rape as both an instrument of male dominance and a method of male bonding, conducted precisely through a homoerotic medium where homosexual desire is simultaneously expressed and repressed.

12. See also Adam 1989; Almaguer 1991; Carrier 1976a; Carrier 1976b; and Parker 1985.

13. A pun, but an appropriate one. The term *cochón* apparently derives from the Spanish term for "pig." Plainly, the term is meant to dehumanize; it most likely emerged by analogy with the prone-receptive position in intercourse. At the micro level (in a sexual relationship), one man maintains his masculinity by assuming the insertive role in intercourse; at the macro level (in society at large), the circulation of stigma and its assignment to a well-demarcated minority of men creates the "surplus" value of masculinity, which is distributed to the unlabelled men.

14. See Loizons and Papataxiarchis's (1991:227–228) similar argument regarding the stigma attached to the receptive partner in homosexual intercourse in contemporary Greece.

15. See Bakhtin 1984; Davis 1978; Lancaster 1988:38–54; Lancaster 1992:233, 251–252; Parker 1991.

Meanings and Consequences of Sexual-Economic Exchange

9

Gender, Poverty, and Sexual Risk Behavior
in Urban Haiti

Barbara de Zalduondo and Jean Maxius Bernard

SINCE THE OUTSET OF THE HIV/AIDS PANDEMIC, behavioral scientists have stressed that sexual behavior including HIV/STD risk behavior must be studied in its sociocultural context. Though our material objective may be to change behavior in the interest of health promotion, we can accomplish this only indirectly—by influencing people's *internal* psychological states and resources (e.g., feelings, knowledge and skills) or through identifying and changing features in the *environment* and/or context to which people with their states and actions respond. At the theoretical level, we know that the substance and meanings of sexual knowledge, perceptions and behaviors *all* are culturally constructed and socially reproduced (see e.g., Caplan 1987; Gagnon and Simon 1973; Herdt and Lindenbaum 1992; Ortner and Whitehead 1981; Parker 1991; Weeks 1981). That is, they are learned, in a particular context, through experience with people and institutions which pressure, express and enforce a particular system of ideas and values. Since learned cultural beliefs and meanings are both individually held and collectively shared by members of the same cultural groups, sexual culture affects behavior, both as an *"internal"* (intra-individual) and as and *"environmental"* determinant of sexual feelings, expectations and behaviors.

An additional dimension of the "environment" that is of recognized significance for sexual behavior is the economic context in which people live. As gender, sex, and (more recently) AIDS researchers have emphasized, sex is a resource with both symbolic and material value. As a source of sensual and emotional pleasure, as a necessary part of the production of valued offspring, and/or as a means of acquiring social capital (including prestige, debt, etc.), sex plays multiple roles in personal relationships and in broader social alliances (e.g., through marriage). In addition, for persons with characteristics sexually desirable by others, sex has exchange value, and so can function importantly in individual strategies for personal advancement and/or economic survival (for diverse perspectives see Frayser 1985; Gagnon and Simon 1973; Rubin 1975; Symons 1979; Walkowitz 1983; Weeks 1981).

Much recent attention to economic influences on sexual risk behavior has focused on prostitution, and even more recently on "survival sex," by which is implied the exchange of sex for money, shelter, drugs or other goods under exploitative and/or demeaning conditions by persons who see no alternative means of securing their perceived survival needs (e.g., Cochran 1989; Futterman et al. 1990; Schoepf et al. 1988, 1991; Shedlin 1990; Jochelson, Mothibeli, and Leger 1991; Wallace et al. 1990; Worth 1989; Zwi and Cabral 1990).[1] While the concept represents an advance over many earlier representations of sexual-economic exchange and its consequences for reproductive health (for discussion see, e.g., Carovano 1991; Day 1988; de Zalduondo 1991; Schoepf et al. 1988), this more sympathetic approach is also incomplete, and it often implies an apology for sexual-economic exchange where none is needed. The opposition of "love" and "money" that deauthorizes and stigmatizes overt sexual-economic exchange is a particular cultural construction that is part of Western European cultural heritage (Rubin 1984; Schneider 1969). Like other values, the belief that sex for money is morally wrong is not held by all members of North Atlantic cultures which generally endorse this value, and it certainly should not be assumed to exist in all cultures.[2] The inference that all instances of sexual-economic exchange are inherently demeaning (and thus probably involuntary) seems to underlie an undifferentiated treatment of the topic in the public health literature. Studies have explained very diverse instances of sexual-economic exchange as results of largely the same constellation of underlying conditions, including an asymmetry in gender power, women's differential denial of access to economic opportunities (especially education and employment) and women's consequent dependence on men (or on sex with men) for their own and their children's social and economic welfare or survival (e.g., Cochran 1989; Erhardt et al. 1991; Schoepf et al. 1988; White 1986; Wilson et al. 1990; Worth 1989; Mahmoud et al. 1989; Ulin 1991; Wyatt 1991).[3]

The belated attention to gender inequity in AIDS research is welcome, as is the call for research and interventions that address women's disadvantaged social and economic status through promoting legal protections, education, and jobs for women (e.g., Ankrah 1991; Carovano 1991; de Zalduondo, Msamanga, and Chen 1989; La Guardia 1991; Reid 1992; Schoepf 1988, 1991). But corrective responses to asymmetries in gender power must be grounded on locale-specific knowledge of the cultural context (de

Zalduondo 1991a). This knowledge should include empirical data on the broader domain of gender and sexual meanings and goals, and of related environmental problems, such as racial, ethnic and/or class-based poverty, and political powerlessness, which lead men as well as women to exchange sex for survival needs. Epidemiological and social research in Haiti, for example suggests that the deteriorating national economy has led to increases in both female and male prostitution for survival (e.g., Adrien, Clérismé, and Cayemittes 1990; Beauvoir 1990; Farmer 1992). However, a focus on extremes of risk behavior, such as survival sex, can deflect attention from economic pressures on contexts for sexual behavior which apply to larger portions of the population. Our research in urban Haiti suggests that—over and beyond the need for expanded HIV/STD education and services—preventing or reducing high-risk sexual behavior will require interventions that make normative, conjugal relations more feasible, and which promote review, and perhaps revision, of some sexual and gender role ideals.

The aim of this essay is to illustrate the value of a holistic, ethnographic view of the cultural and economic context of gender relations for understanding sexual behavior, and to depict the interlocking system of internalized (learned) values and beliefs, and environmental opportunities and constraints, which must be altered if changes on sexual risk behavior are to be achieved on a large scale. Our analysis is based upon ethnographic, focus group and in-depth sexual history interview data collected through a three-year collaborative team research effort in a very low income urban zone in Haiti (Désormeaux et al. 1991). We argue that the challenges for sexual risk behavior are amplified in this context, because the sexual culture is in flux in the mobile, high density urban setting, and also because escalating poverty, and socio-political barriers to its reduction, make it difficult both for men and for women to establish mutually supportive, conjugal unions—a goal which (in different ways) is shared by men and women.

While we will focus on the life conditions and sexual histories of very low income individuals in one zone of the capital of the Republic of Haiti, many of the problems raised are shared by large areas of the contemporary world which have plural and unequal cultural traditions due to legacies of colonialism, slavery, and racism (see, e.g., Gilliam 1988; Kanji, Kanji and Manji, 1991; Schoepf 1988; Trouillot 1990 for discussion).

THE RESEARCH SETTING

Once touted to be "the jewel of the Carabees" (Diederich and Burt 1986) by nineteenth century French colonists, Haiti is today the poorest nation in the Western hemisphere. The infant mortality rate is between one hundred and twenty-six and one hundred and eighty per one thousand and some degree of malnutrition is said to affect eighty-seven percent of children age one to five (World Bank 1990). Life expectancy at birth is fifty-four years—the lowest in the region (Delbeau 1990:50); and the per capita gross national product, $300 in 1981, is one of the lowest in the world (Trouillot 1990:182-183). Despite glorious beginnings in 1804 as the second Republic in the Western hemisphere, the Haitian population is today divided by powerful economic, class, and cultural polarities which often are expressed in terms of language and skin color and urban versus rural identification. (e.g., Brodwin 1991:49–64; Leyburn 1966; Mintz 1979; Trouillot 1990). The division between rich and poor is so profound that scholars have referred to these sectors of society as "class-castes" (Leyburn, 1966), or "socio-cultural sections" (Brodwin 1991).

The elite section has monopolized the lucrative government and import-export sectors since the time of independence, employing numerous licit and illicit strategies to control and expropriate the national wealth from the peasantry, with the assistance of foreign governments and investors (e.g., Abbot 1988; Trouillot 1990). This elite stratum, literate and fluent in French (and often English), looks culturally to France (see Hoffman 1984), and more recently to North America. In contrast, the majority of the Haitian population speaks only Haitian Creole (hereafter, "Haitian"), is unschooled and non-literate, and tends to view the Haitian elite—as well as North Americans and other foreigners—with suspicion. This majority (seventy to eighty percent of the population) dwells in dispersed rural settings on land holdings held in common by kin (see, e.g., Herzkovitz 1937; Lowenthal 1987; Lundahl 1979; Murray 1977). Members of the rural majority struggle to subsist through small scale farming and the sale of produce to the swelling urban markets in the capital and regional cities (e.g., Mintz 1979). This majority or popular section has become progressively poorer as soil erosion, population growth, and over-farming have reduced the productivity of the land, while state (elite) control of local commodity prices and lack of investment in rural services and infra-structure lock peasants into a downward spiral of economic marginality and despair.[4] Whether in the countryside or in towns, the culture of the majority or popular section is a distinct system whose values, institutions, and language more explicitly and pervasively reflect and valorize the population's West African roots.

Virtually all of the Haitian and expatriate elite live in the capital city, Port-au-Prince, or one of its luxurious suburbs. Port-au-Prince is home to twenty percent of the nation's population, but consumes eighty percent of state expenditures (Trouillot 1990:184). The wealthy tend to live as high as possible on the mountains surrounding the city. The rest live lower on the slopes where the climate is hotter and more humid, and where insect pests, odors, and other dangers and inconveniences are more abundant. At sea level, directly on the Bay of Gonaves, is our study site, "the Cité"—a district of five kilometers square, built in the 1970s to house thirty to forty thousand on a land-fill reclaimed from the bay itself. The population of the Cité today is approximately 175,000 (C.D.S. 1990), having grown many times faster than the supply of permanent housing, as individuals and families from the impoverished interior come to the capital in the hope of finding a way out of their poverty (see Bernard 1988; Farmer 1989; Locher 1978; Lundahl 1979; Trouillot 1990). Circulation between "the provinces" and the city, a traditional pattern in Haiti (Mintz 1979), leads to high mobility into, within, and out of the Cité. Sanitation facilities are minimal, with only half the population having access to a latrine, and water is brought in by truck and purchased by the gallon by those who do not have access to the three piped water sources in the area.

Several non-governmental service organizations (NGOs) have provided health and social services in the Cité since the 1950s. These include religious organizations such as the Salesian Fathers, and international organizations, such as the International Planned Parenthood Federation. The largest and most diversified of the local service NGOs, the Centres pour le Développement et la Santé (CDS), has also engaged in numerous collaborative epidemiological and clinical research projects with faculty from the Johns Hopkins University School of Hygiene and Public Health (JHU), and with other universities and organizations in the Cité over the past decade (C.D.S. 1990). Data discussed here were gathered by the multi-disciplinary collaborative team of the JHU/CDS project: "Culture, Health and Sexuality: Reducing HIV Risk in Haiti" (CHS project), which has been conducting ethnographic research in the Cité since 1991 (see Désormeaux et al. 1992, for description of the project methodology).

I. PLURAL CULTURAL MODELS OF SEXUAL RELATIONSHIPS IN HAITI

Divisions between the favored urban elite and the disadvantaged rural majority in Haiti are far too many and too complex to discuss here. Reviewing theoretical discussions of the separate and unequal elite and popular or peasant sections of Haitian society, Brodwin summarized the separation as follows: "Articulated through a pervasive ideology of natural-ized racial characteristics, this bi-cultural system shapes language use, religious participation, kinship and conjugal patterns, and even conceptions of illness and therapy." (Brodwin 1991:61). These cultural differences are matched and enforced by the elite's monopoly on power, not to mention their control of economic opportunities and conditions (e.g., Leyburn 1966; Trouillot 1990). Important for present purposes, however, is the fact that members of the Haitian elite, or outsiders from other European-based cultures have framed most of what is written about sexual behavior in Haiti. The bulk of the available data on sexual behavior in Haiti has been collected by and for demographers and family planning service providers. A central theme in studies of family formation and fertility behavior in Haiti (and elsewhere in the Caribbean) has been the low prevalence of "marriage," and the "instability" of conjugal relationships (e.g., Charbit 1980; Durand 1980; Leridon and Charbit 1981). Anthropologists and sociologists working in Haiti (and other Caribbean societies) have been at pains to counter such Eurocentric assumptions about family formation and reproduction, and instead, to build understanding of Haitian conjugality in its own terms (e.g., Allman 1982; Bastien 1961; Herskovitz 1937; Leyburn 1966; Lowenthal 1984a, 1987; Murray 1976; Rubenstein 1983). In so doing, these authors have recognized a spectrum of mating relationships which imply varying degrees of social approval, permanence cohabitation, mutual obligation, and legal protection, and which have different meanings in the majority and elite sections of Haitian society.

While legal and church-sanctioned marriage is recognized by both the majority and the elite sections, the numerically, historically, and culturally primary form of conjugal relationship in Haiti is not marriage, but *"plaçage"* (or *plasaj* in Haitian orthography).[5] Often glossed as "common law union" in the demographic and family planning literature (e.g., Allman 1982, 1985; Boulos, Boulos, and Nichols 1991), *plasaj* is a socially binding form of conjugal union involving enduring mutual economic and sexual rights and obligations, and the establishment of a new household by the man in which he "places" his woman and where he maintains at least partial co-residence with her. In the culture of the majority sections, *plasaj* and marriage are very similar in terms of day to day economic support and spousal interaction. In elite circles, however, marriage in the European tradition, and performed in the official (Roman Catholic) church, is the expected, socially sanctioned form of conjugal union for men and for women.[6]

A. Obligations and Meanings of Conjugal Unions

In the majority Haitian cultural model of sexual relations, all conjugal relationships (marriage, *plasaj*, and "visiting unions" referred to by demographers in Haiti as *"viv avek"*) involve making a "relationship/agreement" (*fè afè*). The type and conditions of a relationship are defined through an explicit discussion between a man and woman (or boy and girl), a process known as to "set the terms" (*fè kondisyon*) for the union. In negotiating a union, economic exchange is fundamental: the man will provide generalized economic support to the best of his ability, and the woman will provide to the man her domestic and marketing labor—especially, cooking his food and washing his clothes, selling produce, and buying the necessities to keep the household functioning. In the majority, popular culture, the defining features of a *plasaj* union are that a man provides a house for his new spouse; he lives in it with his spouse as much as his circumstances permit; he makes a garden, the produce of which he will turn over to her to use for their joint benefit; and she cooks, keeps house, and markets the produce from her spouse's land, and honors him with strict sexual fidelity (Lowenthal 1987).

Girls receive no formal training in these negotiations, much less on sexual practices, or contraception (see Fouchard, Maglore and Manigat 1988). However, in the rural majority setting, girls are closely supervised and are prevented from spending time alone with boys/men once they reach puberty (*fome*).[7] Thus the conditions for intimate talk leading to love (*renmen*) and/or sex are not supposed to occur. Girls are supposed to be modest and discouraging to boys who do pay them suit. Yet, boys are resourceful and persistent, and if the girl likes the boy they may establish a secret relationship, until they are ready to undertake a proper (and public) union. The average age of first union is late relative to many developing country norms, being 19.1 for rural and 18.2 for urban women (Allman 1985). Sex may come before the formal establishment of a conjugal relationship when the couple has fallen in love (*renmen*). If the boy/man really did intend to form a union, pregnancy may be the event that precipitates the public, social negotiations for *plasaj* or marriage. These arrangements involve the families of both the boy/man and the girl/woman. When the protagonists' families know each other (which in rural settings they usually do), and if the families want to maintain good relations, the boy/man's family can and will intervene to require a boy to "assume his responsibilities" (*pran devwa'l*) for a girl whom he has gotten pregnant. Even if he does not establish a union with her, he should take life-long economic responsibility for their child.

Cultural norms require sexually exclusive monogamy for women, and sexual propriety, but not monogamy, from men. If a man has the wealth to support more than one woman and her children, and has the personal charm or appeal to convince additional women to be his partners (instead of holding out for an exclusive arrangement from someone else), he may do so, as long as he does not neglect his present spouse(s), economically or in terms of spending time with her/them. In the majority culture, no social stigma is implied in a polygynous union, unless the man or his family are devout Christians and he has had, or aspires to, a church wedding. As Allman (1985) has stressed, *plasaj* may be either a final conjugal union form, or a stage in a union that the parties later reconstitute through marriage.

Bastien (1961), Métraux (1958), Moral (1961) and Lowenthal (1984a,

1987) have explained the greater prevalence of *plasaj* (versus marriage) unions in terms of the largely non-literate rural peasantry's rejection of state (elite sector) intervention in their affairs, and in terms of the economic cost of the ceremonies surrounding marriage. Marriage is an expensive affair, involving a series of social events whose lavishness provides a visible index of the couple's wealth (see Lowenthal 1987:181). A marriage sanctioned by law and the church is very difficult to dissolve, since divorce is possible under only rare circumstances in the Catholic church. Furthermore, Haitian laws concerning property rights and inheritance discriminate married women and their "legitimate" children, from women in, and children of, other forms of union. A married man is prohibited by law from giving his name, or bequeathing his property, to any children he may have with *other* women after he becomes married.

Producing children is a core value and aspiration of men and of women, and accepting paternity is both an honor and an obligation. Thus responsible men are reluctant to enter a union which will foreclose or impede their ability to enter into *other* responsible unions—for a man who fathers children and who does not provide for them is not behaving responsibly (Lowenthal 1987).[8] Indeed, isolated from the Euro-centered elite who value Roman Catholic observance as an emblem of status, and served by village priests or pastors who discourage polygyny more than they insist on marriage, for the vast majority of the Haitian population, marriage is an alien and unnecessary superstructure for conjugal life, a form of "conspicuous consummation" (Slater 1977, quoted in Lowenthal 1987:181). While recognizing the economic and social prestige associated with marriage, the widespread attitude among both men and women is: "Better a good *plasaj* than a bad marriage."

B. Extra-Union Sexual Relationships

A serious limitation in the data available for depicting and understanding sexual relations in Haiti is the focus of demographic research (the bulk of the available data) upon conjugal unions, to the exclusion of other kinds of sexual relationships and activities. Demographic research in Haiti (and elsewhere) has typically *excluded* individuals who are not involved in a "stable union," defined by their civil status or by other study criteria (e.g., Allman 1982, 1985; Boulos, Boulos and Nichols 1991; Williams, Murtley and Berggren 1975).

Lowenthal's ethnographic study (1987) provides an alternative approach to understanding the spectrum of sexual behavior in the Haitian context, by taking as a point of departure the fact that conjugality and sexuality are distinct, though linked domains. He notes:

> "Conjugality" refers broadly to those behaviors, attitudes and values characteristic of a relationship between "spouses."...What kinds of activities are actually organized and ordered through the conjugal relationship, as well as the extent to which such activities are exclusively appropriate to spouses—as opposed to other pairs of individuals—are *specific* features of *particular* social systems. Child-rearing, co-residence, religious ritual, economic activity, even sexuality—all may be more, or less, important aspects of conjugal relations in any given society." (Lowenthal 1987:3–4)

Conjugal relationships are only one kind of sexual relationship, one that implies a change of the participants' social status from free agents to mutually obligated spouses.[9] In Haitian culture, conjugal unions are contrasted with non-union sexual relationships (e.g., *byen ak, ti zanmi, fè dezod*) in terms of the contingency, durability, and extent of the economic and labor obligations the parties undertake toward one another, over and beyond the greater public legitimacy of conjugal unions. Lowenthal illuminates the links between sexuality and conjugality in rural Haitian culture by explicating their relation to gender, including ideas about the different sexual natures of women and men, on the one hand, and about the fundamental economic interdependence of women and men on the other.

Family life for the rural-based majority culture, he observes, is conditioned by logically prior premises about the profound gender-based division of labor (Lowenthal 1984b, 1987). Agricultural production, the paradigmatic economic activity for the rural majority, is perceived as *men's* work. Marketing excess produce and purchasing goods needed for the household, as well as food preparation, laundry, and other tasks in household maintenance are *women's* work. Child care is equally the right and obligation of men and of women, though the types of care expected vary by gender. The cultural salience of this division of labor is very high, such that men who perform "women's work," and women who perform "men's work" are either pitied or despised. They are *pitied* when their personal endowments or circumstances prevent them from finding a suitable conjugal partner, or when conditions take the partner away for long periods, and they are unable to find or pay someone to substitute. They are likely to be despised when they are believed to do the other sex's work by choice or by personal inclination (Lowenthal 1987; CHS Focus Group data). The terms *gason makomè, masisi,* and *madavinez,* that are glossed locally as "effeminate man," "homosexual man," and "homosexual woman," respectively, are pejorative, according to both male and female informants in our Focus Groups.[10] Affirming Lowenthal's proposition, our informants defined the terms first in terms of gender role behavior, and only second (if at all) in terms of inferences about their sexual behavior (see below).

Lowenthal explains that with no economic alternative to agriculture (in the rural areas where these models of gender relations originate), and with agriculture and domestic labor assigned to the male and female role, respectively, women and men are seen explicitly as *interdependent*. Men depend on women to do the cooking, laundry, and marketing that is essential to a healthy life, just as women depend on men to provide shelter and income for themselves and their children. A woman in union is not seen, by herself or others, as the man's "dependent" but as his partner. That "men make gardens" (men produce) is a fundamental feature of the male gender role. But equally key is the construction that men do not produce for themselves: a man works his garden *for a particular woman*—a woman with whom he has a conjugal relationship and who provides him with the range of essential domestic services just described (Lowenthal 1987:52). A Haitian man who has not formed a union of his own can rely on his female kin, usually his mother, to perform the daily tasks that men "do not do." But adulthood for both men and women involves establishing one's own household and raising children in a conjugal union. Thus it is a valued life goal for women and men.

While economic exchange (male labor for female labor) is the material base of conjugal unions, Lowenthal noted that consensual sexual relations, including conjugal and extra-union relations, are perceived and constructed in the majority Haitian culture as an exchange of male economic inputs for female sexual access. Both men and women recognize the value of women's economic work, yet the female resource that is salient in all sexual negotiations, and that the woman can withhold pending satisfaction of her bargaining terms, is sex. Women's sex is explicitly perceived to have economic exchange value—to be "her assets." Women in the majority section may refer to their genitals as *"té m"* (my land) or *"byen'm"* (my assets), as well as *"natir'm"* (my genitals). A woman whose spouse has not provided adequately for her needs may publicly humiliate him by calling out, while clutching her crotch: "Why did God give me this?" [if not to be properly recompensed!?] If a man is not providing adequately for his spouse, no one will be surprised if she leaves him, or accepts "help" *(èd)* from another man. Thus conjugality confers upon the woman a generalized, long-term "lien on her mate's economic productivity" (Lowenthal 1987:150) in return for "her assets."

Our informants in the Cité share the expectation that a woman is owed economic support from her man, as is illustrated in remarks such as the following (from two CHS Project Focus Groups with women):

[FG01/E20] Moderator:
> What is a woman expecting from a man?

P9   The first thing a woman is expecting from a man is money (*tyotyo*).

P7   The reason why a woman takes a man [as her man] is because she needs
            some money, because women cannot live without money. They send the
            man to work; once he gets back he has to bring the money. And then what
            a woman needs in a man is love; because those two things are why they
            need men most. Men do two things for women: give her money to have a
            small trading business [*ti komès*] every day, and then make love. Those are
            the only things a man does for a woman.

[FG09/E24] *Moderator*:
            What does a woman expect from a man?

P7   The woman expects the money that a man can give to her.

P3   Well, the man has to give me money so I can make the house pretty.

P4   If the man is not working he is not doing anything; he can just walk out [as
            far as I'm concerned].

Elsewhere, in this and all the other focus group discussions, it is apparent
that women and men conceive themselves to be interdependent (*yon antre
nan lot*), and women explicitly look to men for things other than money—
including affection and physical protection (from thieves and other threats).
This does not detract from the salience of sexual-economic exchange as an
organizing metaphor for normative sexual relations.

C. Gendered Sexuality and Non-Conjugal Sexual Relations

While Haitian women's demand for (and men's readiness to provide)
economic compensation for sex is an explicit and salient feature of conjugal
negotiations, it is no more (or no less) a form of commercial sex or prostitution than is the marriage contract in Western industrial societies (see de
Zalduondo 1991b). What is distinctive here is that women's economic
returns for sexual and conjugal relations are legitimated, and thus rendered
"thinkable," by the cultural constructions of female and male sexuality. The
normative view holds that women do not enjoy sex at all (Lowenthal 1987).
Women speak of sex as "*work*," which is only supportable and justifiable
when compensated by tangible prestations. Such prestations are not
commercial payments—which would be impersonal and highly insulting—
but personal, respectful evidence of the man's regard, and gratitude for the
favor the woman does him through her sexual "work." This "work" may or
may not result in her "making a baby *for* him" (*fè pitit pou li*) which, as noted
earlier, is an event of supreme personal and social importance. Any woman
who has sex with a man without requiring or being offered tangible
(economically   valuable)   benefits   in   return,   is   considered
inconsequential/frivolous/disreputable (*pa serye*), stupid (*bèt*), or deviantly
sensual/lascivious (*chanel*). From a good woman's point of view, "Even the

suggestion of an exchange of *"dous pou dous"* ("sweetness for sweetness," or mutual sexual gratification)—sometimes made by a plucky, yet obviously desperate man—is laughable" (Lowenthal 1987:76).

Women are respected for driving a hard bargain for their sexuality, uncompromisingly requiring "their due" support from a man. However, the bargain, in principle, is to be struck with only one man, or more precisely, with only one man at a time. Serial monogamy is acceptable, and more the rule than the exception (e.g., Allman 1985). A woman who is neglected economically by her man is within her rights to leave him and find another man who will better support her and her children. But a woman who accepts prestations from more than one man at a time is disreputable, engaging in "fast living" *(vi lib)* or immoral sexual promiscuity *(jenes)*, and that is bad *(you kritik)* for her and for her family (CSH Project Focus Group data).[11]

Lowenthal asserts that women and men privately acknowledge that women's dislike or disinterest in sex is a "myth," and that women actively perpetuate the myth because it increases their leverage in negotiations for economic support from their men. It is "a codified bargaining position" (Lowenthal 1987: 75). Rather than see this as a false bargaining stance, our data suggest that women's coolness about sex is a cultural ideal that fits some people better than it fits others. Women's felt or feigned position that sex is "work" may vary according to their personal sexual experience. Men use violent terms for describing intercourse (e.g., *koupe* or "cutting", *kluwe* or "nailing"), and these terms aptly describe some men's sexual styles (see Beauvoir 1990). In addition, the public model of proper female sexuality is socially enforced. A woman who expresses interest in sex, or pursues even one man for sex, is *cho* (hot), or overly sensual *(chanel),* and a *cho* woman, is improper at best and dangerous at worst. A woman who expresses "desire" *(anvi)* for sex is suspected of being unfaithful, or of requiring tight control to prevent her being unfaithful (CHS Project Sexual History data). Such a woman may be socially sanctioned *(calmé)* in a number of ways that cause her shame, if not physical abuse:

> A friend of NP's who was in secondary school in St. Marc was pursued by a girl in his class. She approached him constantly and let him know in all sorts of ways that she loved him, and was interested in having sex with him. NP's friend tried to brush her off, to no avail, and finally decided to teach her a lesson. He agreed to a rendezvous in a private place after school, but instead of going alone, he brought along two friends. They had sex with her one after the other, and commented to each other on "how she was" afterwards. The girl was thoroughly shamed, since no man who loved a woman would bring friends along to share her. Fortunately, she did not get pregnant from this "meeting," but she never approached the boy, or any other boy again. [BZN930414]

Indeed, while the CHS Project Sexual History data contain many reports, by women and men, that women *want* affection and caresses (see below), the normative model of female sexuality constrains their sexual expressiveness, and legitimates social sanctions, often violent physical sanctions, against women who do not conform to the myth.

The complementary stereotype of male sexuality is that men have a virtually continual and indiscriminate desire for sex. The Catholic and Protestant churches teach that men must control their desires and have only one lifelong partner, but even those men and women who aspire to adhere to church doctrine say *"moun se moun"*—people are only human (CHS Project Focus Group data). Lowenthal's male and female informants' reported that men "will drop almost anything for sex," that men need frequent sex to be healthy, and that men tend to be indiscriminate in their desires—"men are like dogs" (*"gason se chien"*).[12] Conjugal relationships provide the socially approved context in which men are supposed to satisfy their sexual desires. However, our informants in the Cité maintain that "[most] men can't live with only one woman" (CSH Focus Groups data). Clearly, this construction of male sexuality makes for potential conflict with women, given women's prescribed disinterest in sex. It also suggests that any man who is not rich is likely to be sexually attracted to more women than he can support in a socially approved conjugal union, and that any woman who is improperly supported by her partner may be on the lookout for a better provider.

One low-cost tactic for exploring the potential for a sexual liason is talk. To have success at all, a man must "know how to talk to a woman" (Lowenthal 1987; CHS Project Focus Group and Sexual History data). When men meet with resistance, which they fully expect to do, the rules of the game permit them to flatter and make promises that go beyond what they can, or intend, to proffer. It is up to the woman to determine whether or not a man is serious about her—that is, is willing to establish a conjugal union with her. Women receive no instruction on how to tell if a man is serious, except that, if so, he should show it by being willing to persue her (*swivi'l*) despite repeated rejections, for months, and preferably for years. This gap in sexual socialization implies the presumption that women are in economic circumstances where they can wait (e.g., supported by their parents).

If the man does not love the woman/girl, feels unable to support a spouse, or if she is already in a conjugal relationship, he may have a less permanent arrangement in mind—a fling, or a mutually satisfactory affair (*ti zanmi; yon relasyon deyo*). These are constructed by men as fun *(banboch),* or adventures, (e.g., *ti pat chat*) in which men take it as a point of pride to extract maximal benefits from the woman (domestic service and/or sex) while minimizing the costs to themselves (the time and resources spent on the woman) (Lowenthal

1987). Such sexual "opportunities" *(okasyon)* are constructed quite differently from unions *(zafè),* Indeed, establishing a union transforms sexuality from this kind of *competitive* transaction to a long-term, generalized exchange relationship (Lowenthal 1987). As we noted earlier, this is accomplished through direct negotiations, over a period of time, in which women and men often have different objectives and endpoints in mind.

Contrary to norms for "casual" sex in many other cultures, from both the male and female perspective, the ideal woman for an uncommitted affair is one already *in* a partnership with another man, since such a woman is already the economic responsibility of someone else. She may be willing to accept sexual advances for relatively small amounts of "help" since her long-term social and economic needs are spoken for.

In principal, a "serious" and desirable single woman will withhold her sexuality until she extracts the maximal commitment (a conjugal relationship) from a man. But once in a conjugal relationship, a woman may be dissatisfied with her spouse, and be open to a charming, secret suitor who provides for her emotional and sexual desires, as well as her economic needs:

[FG07/E22] Moderator:

What is a woman expecting from a man, in everyday activities, or in terms of affection?

P10   A woman might be living with a man that will give everything to her that she needs in a house, but if he is not giving her affection, I don't think that she will stay with him. The woman thinks that she should have what she needs, but the reason why she has a man, it is for affection. It is the reason why a woman can be living in a house with a man and she will behave like a prostitute behind his back [*fe bouzin sou li*]; if the man cannot give her affection, she will be looking for other men.

P11   If she does not have any affection for the man you might know that is because the man is not affectionate to her. If she loves the man for the properties that he has, you can know that she has another man that is giving her affection [and, by implication, sex].

Haitian women of the popular class are perceived as entitled to rather than dependent upon men, but they still must tread a delicate balance. They must provide a happy and comfortable atmosphere at home, meet their spouse's domestic needs and satisfy his sexual desires, and "follow his orders," or else they will be accused of pushing him away or into external affairs (CHS Focus Group data). Yet they must not initiate sex or request sexual satisfaction themselves, or they risk bringing suspicion of their fidelity.

[FG09/E23] *Moderator:*

What is a man expecting from a woman in affection and in everyday activities?

P1 When it is time for him to eat you will have to give it to him on time and with ease; you will have to wash his clothes, and iron them. Man is a vicious animal [*bet visyè*] when he lays down next to you. You will have to put your hand over his head; when he needs what you know that he likes when he lays down next to you, you have to give it to him, for him. When you do this you will not have any problem with him.

Since men need have no regard for their spouse's sexual satisfaction (she is not supposed to care), any sexual needs women do feel must be satisfied passively with their spouses, or through relations with outside partners. While only one of sixteen women who recounted their sexual histories to us spoke of having sexual desires, much less affairs, it is interesting that several of our male sexual history informants reported that their first sexual intercourse was with a woman who already had a spouse. Most of these relations, involving young men and older women already in union, *were initiated by the woman*. We believe this is because, for a married woman, a secret affair with an inexperienced youth would be a relatively safe way to express her sexual desires. A man is considered justified in beating or even killing his wife and her lover if he catches them in an extramarital affair, and while an older, more experienced man might see the affair as a conquest, and be tempted to brag, a youth is likely to remain discreet, fearing exposure and the beating that would inevitably ensue.

In sum, far from being idiosyncratic results of male and/or female non-compliance to sexual and conjugal norms, non-conjugal sexual relations are predictable consequences of the interlocked sexual, economic, and moral premises that underlay male and female gender roles and men's and women's expectations regarding conjugality. Both men and women acknowledge the value of a good conjugal relationship: a good *plasaj* or marriage is an important personal goal, as well as a social expectation. However, sex has different meanings and consequences for men and for women prior to union, and once union is established, the stereotypes of male sexual insatiability and female sexual disinterest permit some men and require some women to satisfy their sexual desires in outside relationships.

II. SEXUAL IDEALS AND ECONOMIC REALITIES IN A VERY LOW INCOME URBAN SETTING

At the start of this paper we asserted that economic pressures increase HIV/STD risk behavior for the population of the Cité but that a "survival sex" model does not properly represent the risk situation in this setting. Under both the majority and elite Haitian cultures, men with economic assets have resources that they can and do use to secure sexual favors from women, and women who need or want money can and do look to a man (or several men) to provide it. The CHS project's ethnographic and sexual history data include numerous cases of individuals—male and female—who have met immediate economic needs (such as need for housing, need for money to buy food or pay school fees) in this way. Yet, in the majority culture, the economic dimension of sexual-economic exchange is proper—a woman's proper use of her assets and a man's proper payment for sharing them. It is not an index of women's dependency. Economic conditions in the Cité do indeed impact sexual and family relationships. In this section we show how the interaction of internalized sexual ideals and environmental conditions, including the gender-based division of labor, the local job market and housing conditions, and the economic and social linkages between urban and rural families together create an epidemiologically dangerous, but quite distinctive, sociosexual setting.

As indicated previously, the physical and economic environment of the Cité reflects elite-controlled, national and regional political and economic forces which are beyond the scope of this essay. However, structural economic and power relations at the national level doubly impact residents of the Cité by exacerbating rural poverty—thus increasing the push to the city—and by perpetuating an inadequate and purposefully exploitative urban job market for the majority classes. In this sense, all relations in the Cité, including sexual relations, are a result of the class-stratified, national political-economic system that limits the life chances of the non-elite population.

Once in the Cité, the environmental conditions that prevail make realizing the gender-specific ideals of a stable conjugal relationship very difficult for most, and impossible for many. Recall that these ideals require that the man must build or provide an independent residence for the woman, and that he provide economically for her by turning over the fruits of his labor. In the Cité, all the habitable land and housing is owned or claimed by someone, so a man must have capital to buy, rent or build a dwelling (or must have family willing to provide it), before he can meet this core obligation for establishing a conjugal union. In the crowded context of Port-au-Prince, where the city-wide unemployment rate is at approximately sixty percent (Ministère du Plan/UNPP 1986, cited in Fouchard, Magloire and Manigat, 1988), "producing" requires more than a man's willingness to work, it requires that he find a job or the capital to get a business started. There are some residents of the Cité who are secure economically—some entrepreneurial individuals have built up substantial businesses, own private schools, and own land and housing which they rent out to others. Yet very few individuals come to the Cité with capital to invest or are able to accumulate savings. Indeed, most people who live in the Cité are there because they *cannot* afford to live anywhere else in Port-au-Prince (CHS ethnographic data). Once there, unemployed men and women compete with others in the unemployed half of the population for the few available jobs and income generating activities, and survive through a complex web of borrowing and sharing that often depends on remittances from relatives abroad (see Fass 1988; Locher 1978). Contrary to common belief, the majority of the unskilled or non-professional salaried jobs that are (or were until recently) available in or near the Cité, such as work in clothing assembly plants and domestic service, are offered preferentially to women (e.g., CPFO 1988; Locher 1978:112). The informal sector in the Cité also is dominated by women. The most common and most widely distributed income generating activity is petty commerce (*ti komès*), a form of "self-employment" involving selling water, charcoal, drinks, fruit, cooked foods, or other goods on the street (see Fass, 1988). With a few dollars, a person can buy his or her stock of goods, transport and process the materials, and sell them in smaller units, eking out enough profit to replace the stock and have something left over for subsistence. Many of the items sold on the street are considered unsuitable for trade by men. The culturally constructed division of labor defines the bulk of *ti komes* as women's work, so men simply won't and/or can't do it.[13]

On average then, in the Cité, women's productive capacity exceeds that of men. Unlike in rural agricultural communities, where farming is the basic productive activity and "men make gardens," a woman in the Cité can get along without a man's economic input. Indeed, according to our Focus Group participants, there are women who have abandoned the rural model of conjugality as a personal goal.

[FG11/E16] *Moderator:*

Can a woman live without a man?

P1   There are some women who can live without a man. They say that they do not need any husband.

P2   A woman can live without a husband. I can make a decision to live without a husband. [I'd rather that] than to have a husband and then he will be here and there [having affairs]. I'd rather live without any husband.

Men, on the other hand, cannot get along without a woman:

[FG06/E17] *Moderator:*

"Can a man live without women, and can a woman live without a man?

PX   (Lots of reaction) A woman is a bad thing but necessary. We cannot live without her.

P9   When I am looking at my neighbor, he has a wife to do everything for
              him, laundry, cooking, and so on. Myself, I have these problems [needs]
              also, so I need to have a woman. I need sexual relations also. For all these
              things, I need a woman.[14]

Note that men's "needs" for domestic services—food preparation and
laundry—are more salient and more urgent on a daily basis then their sexual
desires.

Furthermore, in addition to internalized premises about their need for
women's labor, social sanctions are imposed upon men who live without a
woman. Men who do not conform to the prescribed division of labor are
pitied or derided:

[FG06/E18] Moderator:
              If a man does not have a woman what will he do?
P9   This man will have to live his life in two parts [doing both women's and
              men's work]. This means that if he is going to work, before leaving, he will
              have to buy two cents worth of soap to do his laundry before he leaves.
              When he gets back, if he has time, he will have to do his ironing.
Moderator: How do people view such a man?
P9   As a familiar sight!
P11   As a bachelor (selibatè)
P3   As a (koyorèd) [someone too stingy to give money to a woman to do his
              domestic work].
P7   As someone who has [sex with] other men.

Just as a man in the Cité needs a woman (since only an effeminate man
will try to take care of daily domestic tasks himself), women too have instrumental rationales for wanting a conjugal lien on a man's labor, even if they
can survive without it. The return on most women's work is steady, but its
yield is very small—rarely enough to cover emergencies such as the costs of
illness or school fees (see Fass 1988). In contrast, a man who gets a job in
construction will earn ten to a hundred times as much in a month as will a
woman who works as a domestic, or who sells mangoes or soap chips in
low-end ti komès—although he will have nothing after the construction job
is finished. Thus the best, most secure economic arrangement for men and
women in the Cite remains a long-term economic partnership of the type
codified in a conjugal union. In such a partnership the man earns relatively
large sums of cash when he can find the work; he turns his earnings over to
his woman to provide for the family; and she takes whatever is left beyond
survival needs and uses it for her ti komès, which provides continuous,
though small returns. Even if a man is not working today, he has the potential to bring in the lump sums of cash that are needed in emergencies, such as
in the case of illness—which the crowding and lack of sanitary facilities make

an all too frequent cause of economic crisis (see Fass 1988). In addition, women in the Cité spoke of wanting a man in the house to protect them against gossip, against thieves, against unwanted attention from other men, and in case someone needs to be carried to the doctor.

Another influential feature of urban life for residents of the Cité is the separation of families that occurs with chain migration from rural Haiti to the capital and abroad. While population-based studies on the migration history of residents of the Cité are not available, it is clear that the bulk of the population has migrated to the Cité from rural communities. Because of the powerful religious significance of the family land and homestead or *lakou* (see Murray 1977; Laguerre 1976; Locher 1979; Bernard 1988), people retain strong ties with their kin at home, sending remittances and visiting when they can. Migration disrupts social ties, and given men's enduring need for a woman to perform domestic duties, disruption of one conjugal tie implies the need for a new one. Yet any new partner with whom a man takes up in the city is vulnerable to the prior claims of earlier partners—especially if the earlier partner(s) had children "for" him. The farther the parties are from their families of origin, the less women can count on knowing a man's history—as opposed to his courting rhetoric—and the less a woman can count on family members (particularly fathers and brothers) to defend her (and their) interests in the face of competing claims.

In the managing of male-female relationships under the difficult life circumstances of the Cité, our data indicate that instrumental economic justifications are intertwined with personally felt, culturally prescribed ideals. A woman who gives her sexuality (and her domestic labor) "for nothing" is considered foolish, but conjugal ideals hold that a man and woman in a good union will *help each other*. Thus, if a man can convince a woman that he loves her, and that he is doing the best he can to support her when he can find work, then when he is out of work she should "help him" to the best of her ability, including providing their dwelling and their food, in addition to the domestic labor and sexual access that are her proper contributions to the union. As one woman put it during a discussion of what men and women expect of each other:

[FG03/E23]

P7   Well, once there is good affection, good caresses, good love, you have a good life. He will ask you to settle [move into the same house with him]. If he does not have any money and you have a little trading business (*ti komès*) you can help him. Even if he is living with other women and you have [money] you have to help him.

Short-term relationships and extra-conjugal sexual favors can be won with smaller sums than can a stable conjugal partner. Thus low and intermittent male employment and dismal long-term economic prospects are less of a constraint on *extra-conjugal* sexual relations than on conjugal unions. From the women's side, the persistence of the conjugal ideal, women's desires for "affection" which they cannot express to their spouses, the insecurity of the social environment, and the hope of large (if occasional) economic inputs lead women to seek sexual-economic relationships with men, even when they know or suspect them of being unfaithful. In sum, the precarious economic conditions in the Cité interact with the background gender and sexual culture to increase the incentives for, and decrease the costs of, non-conjugal sexual relations. The latter are by definition contingent and transient. In the age of STDs and HIV, this is a dangerous combination.

III. Discussion and Implications for Research and Intervention

In the majority Haitian sexual culture, sex, negotiated as sexual-economic exchange, is supposed to be enjoyed as one part of a comprehensive relationship that involves economic production, domestic labor, child-rearing, security, social respectability and affection. At the same time, the sexual culture explicitly authorizes, and even applauds, non-conjugal sexual relations, as long as these do not interfere with the core responsibilities men and women have to their offspring. In the "traditional," rural environment, girls mature in a family setting where their contact with boys/men is limited, where rules and prohibitions protected them from importuning suitors, making sex education less necessary, and where suitors are able and required to "take on their responsibilities." Thus the conjugal and extra-conjugal sexual goals of individuals can be kept in balance.

In the economically disadvantaged setting of the Cité, few of these conditions presently exist. Since earning money is crucial in the proper fulfillment of a man's conjugal obligations in the Cité, as well as in negotiation of particular sexual encounters, structural conditions that limit men's productive earning power interfere with men's abilities to properly undertake and to discharge the male conjugal role. Men's dependence on women for domestic services other than sex tips the material power balance in favor of women in the Cité (makes men more immediately dependent on women than women are upon men). Not all poor men and women in the Cité are involved with multiple sexual partners. We have talked with men who live with relatives and avoid sexual relations because they aspire to and cannot meet the requirements for a stable partnership. Some of our female informants are still in solid monogamous relationships with their only lifetime sexual partner. And many women say they have sworn off men entirely, or are waiting to find a reliable partner. Yet these individuals, like everyone else, are coping with an extremely difficult environment; one in which sexual-economic exchange is normative and fundamental and where the spectrum of domestic, sexual, and conjugal relationships define each other, and must be analyzed together.

This ethnographic view of the concerns and life conditions of people in the Cité provides insight into the kinds of health programs and services that are more and less likely to be feasible and helpful in this particular setting. While numerous concrete interventions are suggested by the present analysis, here we will outline intervention implications of only two of our themes.

The first theme is the power of the gender-based division of labor, and its role both in constructing men's need for women and in constraining men's options for earning in the trade-focused economy of the Cité. To the extent that there are gender-based health and social services today, these focus heavily on women, particularly on mothers, and on sex workers (see Caravano 1991). Most "Women and AIDS" interventions were designed in social settings where women's low social status and economic dependency impair their ability to negotiate for safer sex practices (e.g., Caravano 1991; Mahmoud et al. 1989; Ulin 1992; Worth 1988). Yet our data show that most women in the Cité who *have* work, and who feel economically independent, still want a man to "help them," and for "affection." Their problem is the difficulty of finding a man who will be faithful and who is earning enough to contribute to the household. To help these women, interventions are also needed *for men*: interventions to provide stable employment for men at a living wage; and interventions to promote discussion and revision of norms regarding the sexual division of labor.

Health education messages could be designed and conveyed through appropriate channels (e.g., popular songs, or discussion groups) to destigmatize men who are living alone or with male friends or kin, men who do their own cooking and laundry, and men who take up whatever small commerce they can find. Depicting such men as responsible and worthy (for example, as doing what is necessary to remain faithful to an absent spouse) rather than as effeminate or homosexual, should help to free men from the gender stereotypes that impel them into transient, contingent, non-conjugal sexual relations. Regarding employment needs, some women in the Cité need a job (or a different and better paying job) for themselves. Other women need a job for their spouses or prospective partner, or for their daughter's boyfriend—so that those men can "take up their responsibilities."

Our second theme concerns features of the majority Haitian sexual culture which offer culture-specific opportunities for more broadly construed sex education. In contrast to the norm in many societies, Haitian men and women are *expected* to discuss their desires and/or requirements and to set conditions for a sexual relationship *(fè kondisyon)*. Through this expectation, urban parents could be sensitized to the need to think about the sexual social-ization of girls and boys, given that it is impossible to simply keep them apart in the urban context. Sex education could be presented as a way to support or assert the traditional *(fè kondisyon)* process. Training to promote a return to long courtships before sexual contact, and to include condom use, STD screening, and an HIV test in traditional pre-conjugal negotiations may be more feasible in Haiti than in cultural settings where male-female negotiation about sex is traditionally taboo (see Lowenthal 1984b).

IV. CONCLUSION

Outsider analyses of sexual behavior in the Cité, and in other disadvantaged settings like it, might summarize the forgoing discussion by saying that "poverty," "the anonymity of urban life," and the "breakdown of the family" are conducive to "unstable mating relationships." Indeed this is a familiar representation, recalling an era of macro-level social theorizing about marginalized, disadvantaged social groups that ultimately "blames the victim" (Ryan 1971). Its very *neatness* and simplicity tends to foreclose further discussion and the search for solutions. In contrast, the "experience near" (Geertz 1973) ethnographic view forces us to penetrate and decon-struct such generalities, and to reject the banalization or despair that macro-level renderings can provoke (e.g., Herdt and Boxer 1991; Farmer 1992; Kane and Mason 1992; Parker 1991). An ethnographic view demon-strates that to alter sexual behavior is to alter a system that includes not only sex, but the division of labor, the family and kinship, the economic system, the class structure, health beliefs, religion and ethics—the interrelated set of conditions upon conditions which prompt and constrain the wishes and actions of individuals as they cope with a particular social and economic environment. Ethnographic data help us to identify many tractable strands in the heavy rope that is tying the hands of the poor in this particular setting.

Having begun this descriptive task, ethnographers (like ourselves) can and must alert the community to our findings and promote discussion of them, and action on those finding with which people agree (see Farmer 1992; Schoepf 1992). Sex/gender systems (Rubin, 1975), like political/economic systems, are complex and overdetermined, but they do change; people change them. The challenge of change often appears too daunting or too vague when cultural and economic constraints are summarized at the national level. Yet change is under way, and by focusing community atten-tion on the new consequences of old norms discussed here, one by one, additional strands of the rope can be loosened.

NOTES

Acknowledgments: This paper is a collective product of the Culture, Health, and Sexuality Project's teams. The "CDS Team" in Haiti includes Jean Maxius Bernard, Reginald Boulos, Calixte Clérismé, Julio Désormeaux (Co-Principal Investigator), Marie Carmen Flambert, Gladys Mayard, and the CHS Project Research Assistants: Rose-Michelle Abelard, Nesley Phelles, Monique Moleon, Esaie St. Louis, and Myriam St. Louis. The "JHU Team" in the USA includes David Celentano, Barbara de Zalduondo (Principal Investigator), Neal Halsey, Elizabeth Holt, and Constance Nathanson. We are thankful for the critical comments and insights contributed by Shelagh O'Rourke, Alexis Gardella, Ira P. Lowenthal, and Jean Paul Poirier on the previous draft of the manuscript. Opinions, conclusions and errors in this paper, however, are our own.

The Culture, Health and Sexuality Project is part of the NIH/USAID/FHI AIDS Behavioral Research Program. Support is provided by Family Health International (FHI) with funds from the US Agency for International Development (USAID). We are grateful for the assistance and support of Carol Jaenson and Paula Hollerbach (FHI) and of Shelagh O'Rourke, David Ekerson and John Burdick (USAID/Haiti) who believed in the importance of health intervention research even (or especially) in Haiti's present, turbulent times. Many people of the Cité have entrusted to us their concerns and their stories, as assistants, informants, and friends. To them we owe, not just a footnote of thanks, but action toward their improved health and welfare.

1. By sexual risk behavior we mean: sexual or sex-related actions which increase the probability of acquiring or transmitting disease, as indicated by available scientific knowledge.

2. For example, a prominent advocacy group for the rights of women's prostitution is named COYOTE, for "Call Off Your Old Tired Ethics" (see Horton 1987 for discussion).

3. This is not to say that such issues are not important or that the analyses are wrong. Our point is that these characterizations may too easily ring true, and thus foreclose further interrogation of the barriers and opportunities for change (e.g., Kline, Kline, and Oken 1992).

4. Ira Lowenthal (Personal Communication, June 10, 1993, Port-au-Prince) argues that "subsistence farming" is a misnomer for the rural Haitian economy today, since many peasants are unable to produce enough on their lands to subsist. Rather, they engage in an intricate conversion system, selling their small yields of high quality foods (e.g., from domestic animals) to city dwellers for larger quantities of lower-grade foods (e.g., rice, wheat flour) in order to stave off hunger.

5. According to data from the national census of 1982, for example, of those persons deemed to be in a conjugal union, 64% were *plase,* as compared to 36% married.

6. An unmarried woman who has or aspires to elite status would be unlikely to enter into a *plasaj* relationship. Such a woman who cannot marry (or cannot marry sufficiently "well") may keep her own family's standing, increase her material welfare, and even increase her own informal prestige by being the (secret) long-term mistress of a wealthy and powerful man. This form of "concubinage" is widely known in the elite sector. It is not widely admitted however, since it contravenes official law and church dogma.

7. In his classic ethnograhy of village life in Mirbalais, Melville Herskovitz wrote: "As early as seven years of age... girls are cautioned not to permit boys to play with them sexually, while a girl who reaches puberty is carefully watched, not being permitted to go for firewood or on other errands, unless accompanied...no explanation for this is given. She is simply forbidden to leave the house alone" (Herskovitz 1937:102).

8. Other factors have been cited to explain the prevalence of *plasaj* unions in rural Haiti, including the fact that, in the colonial past, Catholic marriage was prohibited among slaves, so that a sexual union could be disrupted at any time by a slave-holder who

wished to sell (and thus permanently separate) one or both partners (see e.g., Allman 1985, Bernard 1988, Leyburn 1966).

9. Between free agents and spouses are people in *renmen* and *fyanse* relationships. These represent publicly declared intentions to become *plase* or married at some future time. Couples in these intermediate, "promised" relationships are not supposed to have sexual relationships, though this is often honored in the breach.

10. These glosses are provided by medical professionals and social scientists, as well as by lay people. Few of our colleagues have been exposed to the recent North American and European psychology and sexology literature on the differences between gender identity, sexual preference, and actual sexual behavior.

11. These terms merit further analysis. The association of "freedom" with sexual misconduct on the part of women is common in West and Central Africa, where commercial sex workers are termed "*Femme Libres*" (literally, "free women"). *Jenes,* which in Haitian means "a sexually undisciplined, promiscuous lifestyle," also means youth; indeed, youth is seen as a time of sexual experimentation and intense activity.

12. Three times per week was the rate Lowenthal's rural informants reported; more than five times per week was considered dangerous, as too much sex saps a man's strength.

13. Our informants point out that if a man tried to move into a gender-inappropriate *ti komès,* "no one would buy from him." As with all shared cultural norms they guide both individual behavior and the responses of others (they are socially reproduced).

14. Our male moderator exhibited here his cultural frame, altering the question to ask if a man can live without *women* (plural), or if a woman can live without *a man* (singular).

SOCIAL AND SEXUAL NETWORKS

Part Four

A Sociological Perspective on Sexual Action

10

Edward O. Laumann, John H. Gagnon

THE STUDY OF HUMAN SEXUALITY IN THE SOCIAL AND BEHAVIORAL sciences is now a little more than one hundred years old. Any review of the theoretical, methodological, and substantive development of the field of sex research must come to the conclusion that progress has been remarkably slow, perhaps even halting. In some measure, this rate of development is a consequence of the modest rate of development in other areas of the social and behavioral sciences; but, more importantly, it is the result of the competition between social and behavioral approaches to the understanding of sexual life and other powerful belief systems. Thus religious values and institutions, the legal system, the field of medicine, and, more recently, the mass media, through the transmission of fictional sexual narratives as well as the reformulation of scientific and pseudo-scientific knowledge, are important players in the debate about what role sexuality has and should have in the lives of individuals and in the social order.

During the time in which a tradition of sex research has developed in the United States and Western Europe, there has been a general shift to a more secular orientation toward aspects of sexual life and a somewhat lowered intensity of efforts to control sexual expression by indirect social means (e.g., by legal or other impersonal third party interventions in individuals' private lives). It is not unreasonable to believe that research on sexuality has been the beneficiary of these larger secularizing processes as well as having served to move them along. In the last decades of the nineteenth century, the ideological boundary between approved and disapproved sexuality was marked by such traditional distinctions as those between good and evil, virtue and sin, and the spiritual and the animal. Somewhat more secularized figures used the distinction between the natural and the unnatural to make the same point (see Davidson 1987). In such formulations nearly all forms of sexual conduct fell into the domain of the evil, the sinful, the animal, and the unnatural, which may have accounted for some of its attractiveness to the artistic and intellectual avant gardes of the time.

The declining moral intensity attached to sexual conduct is suggested in the proliferation of new labels for distinguishing approved sex from disapproved sex. The first ideological move was to shift the ground from morality (good and evil) to issues of physical or mental health (thus the contrasts between healthy and perverse, mature and immature and normal and abnormal). As sociologists have attempted to claim sexuality for their own purposes, it has become more fashionable to contrast conformity with deviance and, with even less moral weight, to distinguish between the conventional and unconventional. Not only have the number of available distinctions increased (though none has disappeared), but, in general, more forms of conduct are now found in the approved category than in the past. This secularizing tendency should not obscure the specific fact that there are some forms of sexual conduct which are now the objects of greater efforts at social control (e.g., rape, sexual harassment, and sexual abuse) and the more general fact that each of these distinctions for approved and disapproved sexuality has a number of supporters who may be divided among themselves about which forms of activity to put on which side of the distinction (e.g., the anti-pornography and anti-sex feminists versus the anti-censorship and pro-sex feminists [MacKinnon 1987; Vance 1984, 1993] or the anti-sex conservatives versus the libertarian conservatives [Posner 1992]).

This general trend toward greater social tolerance for a variety of forms of sexual conduct has not ended the struggle for the right to conduct sex research that is secular, non-judgemental and as disinterested as is possible in a post-positivist and post-modern world. Scientific inquiry in the area of sexuality still remains a dubious enterprise to many social collectivities (Laumann, Gagnon, and Michael n.d.). Even within the various social and behavioral science disciplines, research on the sexual has remained at the margin of the enterprise. Indeed, in sociology the word sexual usually appears only as an adjectival modifier to the noun deviance.

INSTINCT, DRIVE, SCRIPT: ALTERNATIVE WAYS OF UNDERSTANDING SEXUALITY

The understanding of human sexuality during the scientific era has often been a history of conflicts between different interpretations of the same sets of facts. Instinct and drive theories have their roots in either pure biological or mixed bio-social explanations while scripting theory is one of a number of pure socio-cultural theories (by pure we mean that there are no necessary biological elements contained in the explanations) of human sexual conduct.

Instinct

A belief in a "sexual instinct" developed in the nineteenth century as important discoveries were made in the biological sciences. By the 1920s there were nearly as many proposed instincts as there were forms of behavior—so there were instincts for survival, for reproduction (the maternal instinct), for aggression, and against incest. These theories fell into disuse because they were not very parsimonious (each behavior had its own unique explanation), and for each instinct there were many situations in which conduct contrary to the instinct was expressed. For example, people were willing to die in war or protecting their loved ones, many people voluntarily did not have children, there were many non-aggressive people, and there was evidence that sex with relatives of various degrees of closeness was normative in some cultures and societies. The study of other cultures contributed to discrediting instinct theories because they found so many examples counter to what was thought to be instinctive in European cultures.

These deviations from the "instincts" were often treated as perversions from the program of proper behavior that had its origins in "nature" or "evolution" or in the survival of the species. Women who did not have children were believed to be violating their own "maternal instinct" or were thought to be lacking it, and people who lived particularly risky lives lacked an instinct for personal survival. It was not thought odd that the "nature" most people talked about agreed with the values of the specific culture in which people lived. There is now an attempt in the field of socio-biology to rescue some of these ideas in which "non-reproductive" behaviors by some people are treated as instinctive attempts to increase the likelihood of the survival of their own genes. For example, some socio-biologists (e.g., Symons 1979, 1987) argue that men who do not marry, but contribute to the welfare of their sibling's children, are actually engaged in helping their own genes to survive.

The existence of counter examples (when what the instinct predicts does not happen) or lack of parsimony (for each behavior another instinct is invented) are not the only grounds on which to doubt the validity of "instinct" theories. Instincts or closed genetic programs seem to appear only in non-mammalian species. A closed genetic program occurs when a complete pattern of behavior appears in an animal either at a given moment in its developmental history as an individual or when a specific stimuli releases a sequence of behavior that is fixed and unvarying. Thus when some species reach a certain age, without any environmental input except for having survived to that age, they begin rituals of conduct that are aimed at reproduction. In some cases there are environment-organism interactions in which automatic responses are produced in one animal in a species as the result of the apperance of another animal in the same species. These behaviors are often complex, but entirely under the control of the genetic program of the organism.

Treating human behavior as instinctive often rests on the view that there is an inevitable negative conflict between the biological nature of human beings and the cultures in which they are reared; that is, that human beings have a nature that either must express itself or that must be curbed or inhibited by social training. Thus some will argue that children are aggressive by nature and that the goal of child rearing is to reduce this aggressiveness. Others share the view of an inevitable conflict between nature and culture, but come to opposite conclusions. They believe that children are naturally sexual (for example), but that our culture distorts this primordial sexuality by its training methods. The opposition between these points of view rests primarily on a difference between the views that human beings when they are born are either naturally evil or naturally good.

There is no evidence for such patterns as closed genetic programs in human beings. Instinct when used with reference to human behavior is a metaphor which usually means that the behavior refered to is both common and highly valued. It is not a description of the actual mechanisms that produce and control conduct.

Drives
Some drive theories overlap with instinct theories and are often substitutable for them. There are people who propose a sex drive, a maternal drive, a drive for success, etc.; such proposals suffer from a lack of parsimony and a failure to specify the mechanisms by which the conduct is expressed. Indeed, these versions of drive theory share all of the problems of instinct theory.

There are other drive theories which are more complicated and which have a more bio-social character. In some of these a primary drive is posited and in the process of development, ancillary or derivative drives split off from the primary and have an autonomous character. Thus a primary drive for survival can be shaped or split during childhood to include other goals (e.g., sex, success, love). Drives in this case become associated with specific social or psychological aims that are shaped in social interaction. The "libido" or "sex energy" that was posited by Freud was "sublimated" or its original "sexual aim" inhibited in early childhood so that the sexual energies (the primary drive) were directed toward other goals (work, cultural creation, love, etc.).

"Drive" can also be used in another way which is closer to the meanings that people give it in their everyday lives (a folk use or understanding). We often say that someone has a strong drive for success, is driven at work, or has a strong sex drive. What we mean by drive in this circumstance is that a person who is labelled that way has a strong interest in or spends a lot of time trying to accomplish that goal. We do not use "drive" in all such cases (no one would say that someone has a strong drive to collect stamps). Explicit in that usage is the belief that there are strong and weak drives and sometimes there is an implicit belief that these are based on biological differences between individuals. People who have a lot of sex or express constant interest in sex have "strong sex drives" while people who have little sex or don't express much interest are thought to have "weak sex drives." Such folk theories usually do not have very carefully thought-out understandings of how the drive works or how it influences behavior. Often such descriptions are simply a form of shorthand by which we distinguish between people with different patterns of conduct.

There is another folk usage which depends on the concept of drive. That is when people say that they are "horny" or "hot" or feeling "sexy" or "turned on." Such self-statements (and similar statements about other people) are often made to indicate a higher than usual state of desire or arousal. These statements are often used as justifications for future sexual activity or explanations of past sexual activity. Often such statements refer either to periods of sexual deprivation or to situations which have provoked particularly strong desires for sex. In both cases individuals are referring to felt states of desire which appear to them to be coming from inside of them, from a felt state of need. Often people attribute this "felt state of need" to biological sources such as a "sex drive."

This folk theory has a counterpart in scientific psychology. In such psychological drive theories there is either a buildup of "sex tension" or "sexual need" during periods of deprivation or during particularly erotic environmental circumstances. This need is something like the pressure that builds up in a steam kettle when it is heated on a stove. The increasing pressure seeks a release; the individual experiences it as sexual tension which seeks an outlet. When sexual activity is experienced, the drive is satisfied or the need reduced. Such cycles of increased drive and resultant satiation are often used to explain hunger and thirst, and, by analogy, sexual conduct. There is a logical similarity between the folk versions of the sex drive and the drive theories held by many psychologists.

Scripts

Scripting theories of sexual conduct rest on quite different assumptions about the ways in which specific sexual patterns are acquired and expressed. First, they assume that patterns of sexual conduct in a culture are locally derived (that is, that what is sexual and what sex means differs in different cultures). Second, they assume that there is no innate sexual instinct or drive and that infants do not possess any information about sex or specific sexual aims when they are born. Infants may vary biologically in activity level and temperament, but there are no direct links between this variation and what they will do sexually as adults. Third, they assume that individuals acquire, through a process of acculturation that lasts from birth to death, patterns of sexual conduct that are appropriate to that culture (including those patterns that are thought to deviate from the norms of the culture). Fourth, they assume that people are not simply mirrors of the sexual scenarios provided by their culture and that as they get older they make individual adaptations to what is originally provided by the culture. In complex and contradictory cultures such individual adaptations will be very diverse.

Given these assumptions, people acquire scripts for sexual conduct (who they should have sex with, when they should have sex with them, where they should have sex with them, what they should do sexually, and why they should do sexual things). These scripts embody what the intersubjective culture treats as sexuality (cultural scenarios) and what the individuals believe to be the domain of sexuality. Individuals improvise around the cultural scenarios and in the process of social action create a changed sexual culture for the society. Individual sexual actors as well as those who create representations of sexual life (e.g., the mass media, religious leaders, educators, researchers) are reproducing and transforming sexual life in a society. For example, introducing condoms into sexual activity as part of an AIDS education and prevention program requires changing scripts for sexual conduct on the part of individuals. If large numbers of individuals use condoms, they will change the health situation around sexuality by reducing AIDS, other sexually transmitted diseases, unwanted pregnancies, and abortions.

How does scripting theory (with its basic assumptions) deal with the ideas of drive and instinct? It dismisses them as potential explanations of sexual conduct at the scientific level. However, it admits their reality both as alternative cultural explanations of why people are sexual (scientists and others say that people have instincts and drives and this influences what people believe and what cultural scenarios are current in the society) and as statements made by individuals to justify and rationalize the sexual activities in which they are involved. From the scripting perspective such explanations, when they are offered by scientists, are part of the intersubjective cultural scenarios about sex that are current in the society, and such explanations when made by individuals are part of the "why" of interpsychic (what we say to ourselves) and interpersonal (what we say to others) sexual scripts.

From a cultural and social-structural point of view, these individual statements which refer to internal states of sexual deprivation or heightened sexual desire are underanalyzed. Few people actually examine with any care the environmental circumstances in which they feel "hot," "carried away," or needing "to have their ashes hauled," or examine the social and cultural history by which they have acquired such explanations of their current feeling states. Some examples:

1. Groups of young men standing around on the corner talk about sex. However, their felt need is not a result of the biological states of the individuals, but of the interactional and cultural situation that requires certain kinds of sex talk.
2. Young women talk to each other about sex and passion in ways that have some similarities and some differences, but which are equally organized by gender and sexual scripts.
3. Gang rape or groups of men going to prostitutes is produced by young men behaving in reference to each other's sexual talk rather than how "hot" they feel biologically.
4. Being "hot" or "horny" is usually not the result of pure deprivation, but deprivation in the context of stimulation, either through the media, the specific circumstances (a disco), or through the presence of what appear to available partners.
5. Becoming a non-virgin for a young woman is rarely a consequence of her "sex drive," but rather a function of affection or even of membership in a group in which other young women are already sexually active.

The appropriate social and cultural analysis of the history of the person and his/her current environmental circumstances suggests that the "feelings of desire" are not outcomes of even temporary drives, but of how people have learned to interpret the presence or absence of sexual activity and the internal feelings that they have learned to label in a sexual way. "Hot" or "horny" and "sex drive" are not biological names, but names that individuals give to states that have been acquired and enacted in socio-cultural circumstances.

THE INDIVIDUAL SEXUAL ACTOR

While there has been a substantial transformation in what forms of sexual conduct can be studied and with what methods, there has been one important constant in the history of sexual research. From Freud and Havelock Ellis at the turn of the century to Kinsey and his associates in the 1940s to contemporary research on sexuality and HIV/AIDS (see, for example, Catania et al. 1990) the focus has been on the *individual* actor.

    While individuals may have acquired their patterns of sexual conduct (preferences for a particular gender, age, physical attribute, race, ethnicity, technique in sexual interaction) through the process of socialization or acculturation, and while the sexual conduct of these same individuals may be influenced by various social category memberships (gender, race, class, religion), the analytical point of interest about these individuals was their performance as individual sexual actors. The volume or type of sexual activity that individuals accumulated in their "sexual life histories" was viewed as (1) a direct function of their intrinsic biological instincts, drive or potentials, and/or (2) the result of social and cultural inhibitions on sexual instincts, drives, or potentials provided either by early learning or by current cultural circumstances. Similar explanations accounted for differences in sexual preferences, techniques, or fantasies. For both Freud and Kinsey, following the great traditions of European individualism, the relation of the individual to culture or social structure was necessarily adversarial. Sexuality remains one of the least "secularized" forms of social conduct; the focus on the individual sexual actor follows from a continued cultural emphasis on sexuality as an exemplary measure of individual morality.

SCRIPTS: COLLECTIVE, INTERPERSONAL, AND INTRAPSYCHIC

Even work in the more sociological or social constructionist tradition has usually placed its primary emphasis on the individual sexual actor, despite directing attention to the importance of social background and social context as shaping sexual conduct. In part, this has been a result of the methodological predisposition to study sexuality through the use of surveys which gathered information only about the survey respondent. Even field research has put the individual actor at the center of attention rather than examining the ways in which actors mutually shape each other's conduct.
    The scripting perspective on sexuality distinguishes between cultural scenarios (the instructions for sexual and other conduct that are embedded in the cultural narratives which are provided as guides or instructions for all conduct), interpersonal scripts (the structured patterns of interaction in which individuals as actors engage in everyday interpersonal conduct), and intrapsychic scripts (the plans and fantasies by which individuals guide and reflect upon their past, current, or future conduct) (Gagnon and Simon 1973; Simon and Gagnon 1984; Gagnon 1990). In this description of social conduct, a reflexive individual participates in concrete social interaction with others, guided in part by a meaningful system of individually interpreted cultural instructions. The strength of this model is that it brings together the two levels of meaning (the intersubjective or cultural and the intrapsychic) and links them to a system of interpersonal action. On the other hand, the

two systems of symbolic meaning (the cultural scenario and the intrapsychic script) have been better specified than the performed interaction itself. Further, while this approach is concerned with sexual dyads and encounters (including issues of dyad formation, maintenance, and dissolution), it has not examined the social features of both actors in the dyad nor has it treated the relevant extended social networks as either influencing the conduct of the individual or the dyadic interaction itself. Simply put, it has not examined sexual conduct as a joint product of multiple actors.

While social interaction has an important place in scripting theory, it has not developed a well-articulated place for considerations of social structure. In part this is the result of the greater interest of scripting theorists in the symbolic environment (culture) and the interpreting individual (mental life) than in the social structuration of sexual interaction, but it also reflects a residual commitment to an individualistic approach to sexuality rather than to a concern for the actual contexts and enactments of interaction that shape sexual conduct as a social performance.

Improving the fit between scripting theory and social structure requires that a conceptual bridge be constructed that will link different effects of social structure on the variety of ways in which individuals enact social scripts. Perhaps the most important components of a script are the social features of the individuals who enact them. These are the publicly accessible features of individuals, which they and the co-participants and audiences for their conduct use to guide and understand their social performances. We have labelled these as the "master statuses" of individuals, and we define them as those features of a person that most significantly shape how they conceive of themselves and their possible courses of action (the scripts they can enact) and how they perceive that others facilitate or retard these self-conceptions and courses of action. In the United States these master statuses are socially interpreted physical attributes such as gender, race and age, or other socially salient characteristics, such as marital status, educational background, political orientation, or religious affiliation. In other societies there will be different master statuses which link relevant scripts to social structure, e.g., prowess in war, ancestry, or magical powers.

Master statuses are about the important dimensions of *who people are* and how these features shape what an individual believes is possible to say and do (and often think) and what other people think is appropriate for an individual who bears such social markings to say and do. We expect that single people will behave differently than the married or the widowed, that people who have gone to college will behave differently than those who have gone to grade school, that old people will behave differently than young people, that persons in different ethnic groups will behave in different ways. Not only do we (as members of the society) believe this, persons who have different master statuses believe that they should behave in ways appropriate to these statuses. Specifically, script theorists define master statuses to be those characteristics that (1) are a major basis for the ways in which social interaction is structured, (2) are a basic component of the self-identity of the individuals who possess them, and (3) organize the cognitive maps or modes of understanding that individuals bring to social circumstances.

With respect to the first element of this definition, master statuses organize and structure social relationships between people. This has frequently been documented, for example, in empirical studies of friendship networks (see Laumann 1973; Hallinan and Williams 1989). These studies found that people are more likely to report having friends with the same or similar status characteristics as their own. Similar patterns have also been shown to obtain among discussion networks (Marsden 1988), work relationships (Baker 1990), collegial ties (Heinz and Laumann 1982), and even sexual relationships. What is important about these findings is that relationships are the conduits through which such processes as persuasion, sanction, discussion, and admiration are directed (see Blau 1964). As a result, we may expect to find differences in normative understandings about what is appropriate sexual conduct that correspond to certain status characteristics.

In addition to structuring social relationships, evidence indicates that although people differ in the way that they describe themselves to others, attributes such as those we have mentioned are often a prominent feature of self-descriptions. This is important from a sociological perspective because it indicates which groups people look to as reference points in evaluating the appropriateness of their own behavior. These reference groups can consist either of specific people, such as a person's priest and/or fellow parishioners, or cultural artifacts, such as one's perception of what "women" are like. In either case, possessing the status characteristic becomes important in determining how that person will conduct himself or herself, although the manner in which and the degree to which this occurs will vary across individuals.

The third element of our definition of master statuses involves the extent to which they structure the ways in which people think about those around them. The ways in which we perceive those around us becomes important in determining what is and is not appropriate behavior in a given situation. Thus, a young person is likely to act differently in interactions with his or her age peers than in interactions with those who are older. Similarly, people are likely to express themselves differently when they are surrounded by people who share their political views than when they are surrounded by people who do not. The significant point here is that, in each case, an individual's particular master status characteristics are used to formulate expectations about his or her attitudes and conduct. Being master identities that have widely ramifying implications for normatively appropriate social action, they are especially likely to be used in inferring a reference person's sexual attitudes and behaviors.

Together, these three features define what we have identified as master statuses. However, before exploring their usefulness for explaining patterns of sexual behavior, it is important to note some of the empirical properties of these statuses that determine how they are implicated in specific social processes. For example, these statuses differ in the extent to which they can be recognized. In the United States, gender is usually an attribute that cannot escape even the most cursory face-to-face encounter, while political orientation is a latent characteristic that is often quite difficult to determine, even for those with whom one has considerable interaction. Another property of these statuses is that people who possess them vary in the degree to which they consider them to be important. Thus, an individual who is a devout Catholic is likely to take the label more seriously than an individual who does not attend church and is a Catholic by default (i.e., his or her parents are Catholic).

Yet another property of master statuses is that they are not implicated in a homogeneous manner throughout the population. Thus, being Catholic in New England means something different than being Catholic in St. Louis. Similarly, being a woman means different things in different places; one might expect that a woman college student has more opportunity to actively pursue a male sexual partner without being labeled deviant than a middle-aged woman living in a small, Southern town. Not only is there variation in the meanings attached to specific statuses, but in most cases a specific status does not operate in isolation. Instead, each individual embodies several statuses simultaneously, and must manage the expectations and requirements associated with each of these statuses at the same time. These later two properties—that specific statuses have different meanings in different segments of the population, and that they do not operate alone but in concert with each other—suggest that we should be less interested with a particular status in isolation and instead focus on the set of social positions consisting of all possible combinations of status characteristics.

A methodological virtue of the concept of master statuses is that it is possible to gather information in surveys about such features of individuals. It is in the interpretation of the meaning of such variables that we differ from many analysts. It appears to us that viewing, for example, marital status as master status means that we understand the conduct reported by an individual as the result of interaction between the self-identity and the modes of understanding of that individual, as well as with the structure of social relations that are attendant upon that master status. Since master statuses are features of who actors are in the scripting sense, this offers a bridge between the narrative order of social action and the structure of social action.

Critical to our framework is the view that sexual relationships are special cases of social relationships, and, as such, should conform to some of the "regularities" that have been observed regarding social relationship more generally. One such regularity is the tendency toward equal status contact. With the exception of gender, we expect that sexual relationships are more likely to form between individuals who share the same or similar status attributes than between individuals with different status attributes. One reason is that since the majority of social interaction occurs within groups of similar status individuals, it is likely that an individual chooses a romantic partner from an already preselected group of similar others (Feingold 1988). Another reason is that in many cases, romantic partners are seen as potential marriage partners (this is clearly a Euro-American example). Since marriages tend to occur among status similars, it is possible that the prospect of marriage acts to discourage sexual relationships between people with different status attributes.

Another important "observed regularity" in explaining the dynamics of social relationships concerns the involvement of interested parties—in this case people who know one or both of the potential partners and have a particular interest in facilitating or preventing that partnership from occurring. These third parties may attempt to influence one or more of the partners, of which may result in increased tendencies toward same status contact. For example, it is likely that many parents want their son or daughter to marry someone with a similar background, so that religious and cultural traditions can be carried on, and so that the spouse will be an appropriate addition to the family. Similarly, groups of friends who share a given set of status characteristics are likely to influence each other to have sexual relationships with partners who have the same set of status characteristics, so that the partner will readily fit into ongoing group activities.

In addition to increasing the tendency toward equal status contact, the involvement of third parties may also directly affect the number of sexual partners that a person can have. An obvious example of this would be attempts by parents to discourage their children from being sexually active. Taken together, these two premises can be used to generate several hypotheses about differences in observed sexual behavior across status groups.

SOCIAL NETWORKS AND SEXUALITY

We shall argue that the study of social and sexual networks provides an important analytic complement to the individualistic model of sexual conduct. Sexual activity is, first and foremost, a social transaction in which pairs of actors (in some cases more) mutually shape each other's conduct (the case of solitary conduct will be taken up below). A network approach to the issues of sexuality provides a sophisticated means to make empirically concrete the relations between the two levels of meaning identified in the scripting perspective. Actors bring with them to potential sexual situations the various instructions provided by their culture (cultural scenarios) as well as their unique individual sexual biographies (the intrapsychic) as these are shaped and defined by their master statuses. These resources allow them to understand the "potential of the situation" and guide their attempts to actualize or prevent it.

But an individual's attempt to coordinate sexual conduct with another involves going public—that is, disclosing one's intentions and expectations for a particular other in a particular setting. In other words, individuals are required to play out a socio-sexual drama for which there are audiences, both those physically present and those closely connected to the participating actors having interests in the outcomes of the drama. The social networks of the several parties thus determine, at least in part, the potential of the situation—indeed, whether a situation exists and how it will resolve. Put another way, the presence or absence of acceptable alters, their social characteristics, and the character of the ties between the actors (and other contextual variables of social locale and time), as well as the characteristics of the audiences, jointly determine whether and what sexual conduct will occur.

In general, across the life course, sexuality is typically enacted in dyads that form, endure for a while, and dissolve. Individuals who participate in these sexually active dyads belong beforehand to pre-existing and, for the most part, non-sexual social networks that themselves influence the formation, maintenance and dissolution of the sexual dyad. In turn, the composition of these non-sexual networks are influenced by the formation, maintenance, and dissolution of the sexual dyad. A young woman and a young man who meet and engage in a relatively conventionalized affectional/sexual relationship will become as individuals and as a dyad the object of comment and management by members of their personal networks. As the dyadic tie stabilizes, there will be changes in the patterns of extra-dyadic social interaction. The longer the dyad exists, the more stable and perhaps irreversible the expectations and interactional patterns of the pair's personal networks will become. In some cases, the personal networks of the two individuals will selectively merge, whereby some of one party's friends become friends of the other and some friends of both parties become mutual friends. Such patterns of sexual pairing take on different forms among adolescents who date or young adults who cohabit or marry. Personal network members, including the focal pair, will make different investments in the dyad and its support at different points in the life courses of the constituent individuals. The general process of pair formation, maintenance, and dissolution proceeds at varying rates across the life course of individuals.

Like all aspects of social life, sexual conduct is divided into phases that are public and those that are private. But the emphasis on the private phases or moments is especially strong in the sexual domain. Actual sexual performances are expected to occur in private and even certain preliminaries are restricted to private or semi-private places and limited to highly selected co-present audiences. Public sex is usually criminalized and displays of nudity or semi-nudity is restricted to specific locations. Audiences to actual sexual performances are usually restricted to the performing individual or the pair (here we treat actors as audience to their own conduct).

Audiences, composed both of commentators and of those who have some stake in the interactions of the individuals, do have occasion to observe and participate in the activities that lead up to a sexual encounter and to those activities that follow upon it. Most of the time the sexual component of these activities will be latent—for exemple, two married couples going out on the town or on a shared vacation are unlikely to comment on the increased likelihood of the sexual activity of the other couple. There are social groups in which potential sexual conduct may be more manifest and may result in open social commentary (e.g., among persons in a bar or at a wedding).

In contemporary Western societies the vast majority of actual sexual activity either by single individuals or sexual pairs (or larger, sexually interacting groups) occurs out of the sight of non-participants. While there are exceptions to this pattern (which have quite interesting social characteristics), the doing of sexual things beyond the point of hugging and kissing, is commonly restricted to relatively private locales. While such locales may be public, the sexual actors usually believe themselves to be alone (as in a field or wood or on the beach).[1]

In general, however, audiences for sexual activity are at least at one remove from the sexual occasion. This has important consequences for the social regulation of sexual encounters since audiences are privy only to the testimony of actors about what went on in the interaction itself. This has positive and negative social consequences—sexual encounters may be entirely trial-and-error and independent of regulation, a situation leading to sexual experimentation (particularly in a bedroom culture), or they may be occasions in which the participants deliberately or ignorantly exploit or violate each other.

The surveillance of the sexual dyad by outsiders is remarkably difficult. Indeed, the formation of most affectional-sexual dyads are marked by what Slater (1963) has called "dyadic withdrawal." In adolescence particularly, but in later life as well, an important phase in affectional/sexual dyad formation is withdrawal from other social responsibilities. Thus young people not only withdraw from parents, but from peers, during intense love relationships which may or may not involve sexual activities. Similar patterns occur later in life when persons "fall in love." When they form couples where one or the other person has children from prior relationships, opportunities for withdrawal are either truncated or problematic for certain bystanders. Such withdrawals are signals to bystanders of the increased sexual potential of the relationship, but at the same time reduce the rates of interaction between dyad participants and members of their personal networks. These reduced rates of interaction reduce the amount of both negative and positive commentary on the choice of partners. There is little research on this point, but there may be more withdrawal among what appear to be "socially unsuited pairs."

The non-surveillabilty/invisibility of sexuality means that the sexual conduct of most other persons is rarely salient in everyday life. In most periods of the life course and in most social interactions, individuals do not think directly and concretely about the sexual behavior of other persons. We may know that a person is married or that another person is a gay man (a social role with "sexual" connotations), but most of the time we do not think specifically about what they do with their sexual partners. While we may gossip about the sexual affairs of others, the language is largely moral rather than explicitly physical; our focus is ethical rather than genital. This does not mean that private speculation about the sexual availability of other persons or private internal commentaries about the sexual attractiveness of other persons is not common. It only means that such speculations or comments are self-directed, the erotic fantasies usually involving the actor and the target of the fantasy, not the target and some other partner.

As a result of the invisibility of sexual conduct and of the self-referential nature of most fantasy, it is impossible to create a public social ranking based solely on sexual performance or prowess. Zetterberg (1966) made this point in an unremarked, but interesting article on "the invisible hierarchy." While there are persons who are "sexually notorious" or targets of collective sexual desire of different publics (particularly persons in the entertainment industries), we do not have any concrete evidence that their "desirability" is based on their sexual competence. Their implied "sexuality" is a function of second-order evidence based on the numbers and attractiveness of the persons who surround them and appear to desire them, or on the parts that they play in mass-entertainments, or on their representation in the trash media. Our untested inferences about their sexual competence are nearly all based on estimates of physical attractiveness. As far as the authors know, no reputational studies of sexual ranking within small interacting groups have been conducted nor do we have "studies of gossip" about the imputed levels of sexual activity/desirability in the same kinds of collectivities.[2]

EXTENDED SOCIAL NETWORKS AND SEXUAL CONDUCT

While sexual activity is, above all, a social transaction in which pairs of actors mutually shape each other's conduct, this pairwise shaping does not exhaust the influence of social structure, since sexual actors are embedded in larger social networks. The social networks in which individuals participate, despite the invisibility of actual sexual performances, have a number of important effects on patterns of sexual conduct. Networks offer both opportunities for and limitations on the formation of ties in which sexual activity can go forward, and they provide audiences for the public behavior of individuals as they form and maintain ties that have a sexual component. While such third parties to the sexual interaction are only sometimes privy to the actual sexual performances of other persons, such network relations are deeply influential in terms of legitimating many of the specific sexual practices of persons in sexual relationships. Thus the legitimacy of oral sex in youthful sexual relationships is dependent on gendered support networks that supply different legitimations for these forms of conduct to both male and female adolescents (see Udry et al. 1985).

STAKEHOLDERS AND AUDIENCES

In Reproduction

Of all the audiences for sexuality, the most visible are those who have a stake in the reproductive activities of a couple. Prior to marriage (or a similar legitimate status), the stake of the audiences is in non-reproduction; after marriage (or some similar passage), the stake of various audiences is in the couple fulfilling their reproductive potential.

This situation is actually rather complex since those who are concerned with preventing untoward reproduction have somewhat different attitudes toward the sexual activity that might produce offspring. There are many including parents who would prefer that young people, in particular, but also older persons who are not in marital pairs, would refrain from vaginal intercourse with the potential for pregnancy. There are, of course, some who would prefer that the young and the old would refrain from *all* sexual expression unless they are married and engaging in sexual activity with the potential for reproduction. There are others who do not necessarily disapprove of sexual activity among the unmarried young or old, but whose sole interest is in preventing the unwanted pregnancy (and hence the unwanted abortion or unwanted child.) Such audiences include those who supply sex and contraceptive information as well as abortion and adoption services to women who (for whatever reason) become pregnant.

Stakeholders in reproduction are probably the best organized of all groups that have an interest in sexuality. They range from individual parents to large scale collectivities like planned parenthood organizations, that supply services, lobby for their points of view, and seek private and governmental resources and support for their programs. Control of reproduction involves a complicated relationship to the control of sexual activity by interested stakeholders. Conservative stakeholders engage in moral instruction, policing the sexual content of the media and of education, limiting information about contraception as well as the availability of contraceptive devices, attempting to limit the access of the potentially sexually active to services for the prevention of sexually transmitted disease (including HIV), and so forth. More liberal stakeholders seek to provide the above-mentioned services, while remaining somewhat indifferent to the sexual expressions of persons over age sixteen or so. These activities are, of course, at some distance from the sexual acts themselves and facilitate or limit only at second hand the actual practices of individuals or pairs.

Stakeholders in reproduction also differ among themselves in dramatic ways. Thus parents may wish to see their children reproduce regardless of their gender preference for sexual partners. Parents can become grandparents no matter if their children are gay or lesbian or straight. On the other hand, there are those who have a stake in preserving the traditional family, and who resist not only the existence of same gender affectional and sexual pairs, but such pairs being allowed to have children or the other benefits of marriage between women and men. Each of these sets of stakeholders in reproduction affect sexual practices in various ways—conservatives make it more dangerous and consequential for "errant" individuals, while liberals make it less dangerous and less consequential.

In Extramarital Sex

Most persons in the United States, when answering questions about the morality of extramarital sex (that is, sex outside marriage by a person who is currently married,) report that they always find it morally wrong; and there is some evidence, as we shall see, that the annual incidence of such intercourse among the married is modest. On the other hand, large numbers of persons in the United States do get divorced, and sexual activity with a person other than a spouse often accompanies the dissolution of marriages. What seems to be the case is that extramarital intercourse is usually irregular for most individuals and, while having a larger prevalence across the life course, is infrequent within any limited period of life.

In general, most individuals who engage in extramarital sex try to conceal what they are doing from their marital partner. This is usually achieved by segregating the audiences for their conduct. Audiences for performances of fidelity are usually composed of both strangers and friends in front of whom the unfaithful spouse engages in "fidelity displays." These represent a variety of enactments that include "not looking at other women," indications of emotional and familial concern, all of which add up to the "good spouse" role. Audiences for the performance of infidelity are normally strangers, people who have no stake in the conduct of the two individuals. However, specialized gender-segregated groups may serve as support networks for infidelity. Thus groups of men at a convention or simply groups of men "out for a good time" may support extraordinary levels of sexual norm violation (including rape and sexual harassment). These audiences for manhood displays of sexuality push the envelope of sexual expression for many men while converting others, who would normally disapprove of such conduct, into silent onlookers. Similar support networks may emerge among women, though they are less remarked upon. Thus the unhappy wife may be encouraged by her friends to have a sexual adventure, or her friends may protect her by providing excuses for her absences. Of particular importance to these relationships are single or post-marital friends who have space and time for enabling someone else's nonmarital sexual adventures.

Perhaps one of the most important structural features that limits extra-marital sex is the very large proportion of individuals in the society who are already in relationships. While a married individual in the United States may have a taste for sexual adventure, it is clear that at any given moment and age the supply of potential partners may be relatively limited. After age 30 the numbers of the the currently uncoupled or married (happily or unhappily) who are also interested in sexual adventure is quite small or, at least, difficult to identify. This structural stricture on the market is not only a function of the proportion of the population that is married, but of the proportion cohabiting. This is particularly important among the young, whose cohabiting is often a precursor to marriage.

The sexually adventurous married person faces a serious problem of identifying the supply of easily available partners. Without substantial resources it will be difficult to attract a partner from the currently uncoupled who have a network that will work against the relationship. The married individual must be willing to be involved in a personal network where he or she appears to be exploiting the uncoupled person. When the potential partner is in an embedded relationship (including perhaps children, parents, and friends who have a stake in the ongoing relationship), the sexually adventurous individual must be the bearer of great personal and/or material resources. The price of defection will be very high for those already in relationships, cohabitational or married; and if the adventurous persons are themselves married, the problems are even more complex.

The problems of accomplishing extramarital sex do not rest on values alone, but on the structures of social relations and on the logistics of managing both personal resources and social networks. The number of easily available partners is limited and the costs of defection are high. Most audiences have a stake in maintaining a current paired relationship because of their connections with the couple (and often their children). When defections are acknowledged and become part of the public discourse of the relationship (and the personal networks of the individuals), different stakeholders take different sides on the outcome of the defection. We know very little about the structural sources of side-taking in these circumstances, though there is extensive anecdotal evidence that side-taking is common, and either restrains or facilitates the end of the relationship.

In Sexual Practices

Partner characteristics also shape what kind of sexual practices are regarded as legitimate. What the social relationship is between an individual and a sexual partner will determine what the sequence and character of the actual sexual performance might be. Thus anal sex and oral sex may be more common in relationships which are transitory or in which the partners are defined as sexually degraded and/or exciting. Relationships in which one has a past or a future may be more carefully scripted because the person is concerned with "what kind of person will I be thought to be in the future." Sex with strangers, pickups, or prostitutes all have the potential for different kinds of sexual activity than those with long-term partners. Prostitutes, on the other hand are far more likely to insist on the use of condoms with customers than they are with those men with whom they have a permanent or quasi-permanent relationship.

Status discrepancy and status similarity between pair members play key roles in mobilizing conforming and non-conforming sexual scripts. "Fast track" sexual conduct is institutionalized on status discrepant social relations: between persons of different religions, ethnic groups, educational levels, levels of celebrity or popularity. Marriage is reserved for same status partners. Here the master statuses of individuals will influence their sexual practices.

In Solitary Sex

Even masturbation is a social transaction between an individual and the intrapsychic narrative which is necessary for its performance ("what kind of person am I to be doing this," what kind of socially derived fantasies are required to produce the physiological response, etc.). While masturbation is in most cases solitary, there are some instances in which self-masturbation is performed in the presence of others. In couples self-stimulation may occur in front of a partner as a way to excite the other person or oneself or to complete a sexual act in which socio-sexual stimulation has not resulted in orgasm. Among boys, "circle jerks" are reported, in which a group will masturbate to orgasm, often in some competitive fashion (to see who will ejaculate the most rapidly, who has the largest penis or how far the ejaculate travels). Gay men may observe other men masturbating in baths or in safe sex clubs.

Perhaps more common is the influence of second order audiences, who influence masturbation either through instructions (in earlier eras masturbation was linked to madness or hairy palms), or through the policing of private contexts in which individual young people might find themselves. As the opportunities for privacy increase beyond the bathroom in many homes, the capacity to police solitary masturbation is weakened. Parents and educators influence the practice of masturbation by providing information about it. Peers influence it by providing gossip, particularly in single gender groups, about its effects.

While masturbation is an activity usually performed in private, it is intensely social in its inception and organization. Difference in the expression of masturbation between young men and young women is a function of the more prevalent "talk" networks among young men rather than of different drive states or of the automatic recognition of the penis as a sexual organ. Work by Udry and his colleagues (1985) suggests that hormonal differences among young men do not generate differences in sexual conduct. These conduct differences seem more likely to be elicited by changes in visible signs of sexual maturation that make such conduct plausible to both actors and audiences.

The individual decision that masturbation should occur in private is a general outgrowth of more generalized modesty rules about exposing or touching the genitalia (there is no instructional system which contains the rule "you will masturbate in private"). Perhaps the most obviously social dimension of masturbation is the content of the fantasies that usually accompany its performance. These fantasies generally evolve in complexity during adolescence, taking their context from the surrounding social environment and from the content of the available media.

The resistance to masturbation by adult audiences rests on the belief that it is in some ways anti-social. To many audiences it appears to be caused by or is a sign of loneliness, social detachment, personal encapsulation, or low network densities. Its heightened significance among the married is probably a consequence of the belief that it involves a withdrawal of sexual energy from the marital pair as well as that it places a negative judgment on the sexual adequacy of the sexual partner.

In Sexual Gossip and Fantasy

The persons who are subjects of a fantasy cannot be properly treated as members of real networks, but their selection by an actor has to fit some legitimating framework. Who is in a fantasy must meet some criteria. There are networks in fantasies, in talk (who do you talk to about sex), or in sexual behavior. These networks, however, are rarely isomorphic, with fantasy partners rarely being coincident with talk partners or with sexual behavior partners.

In Sexual Pleasure

Of all of the aspects of sexual life, perhaps that least attended to by persons outside of a sexual pair is whether or not there is sexual pleasure in the relationship. In part, this is because members of the pair are remarkably reticent about disclosing to third parties whether or not they find pleasure in their sexual life. This appears to be especially problematic for men, who are expected, as a result of certain gender role conventions, to be experts on sexuality and to find pleasure in sex relatively automatically. As a result, sexual ignorance and incompetence cannot be confessed to an audience of other men. Women, in part because they are expected to be sexually ignorant and in need of tutoring, have a greater opportunity to complain about a failure to have sexual pleasure. Other women will understand and often engage in supportive talk and advice; however, the significance of this lack of pleasure is often downplayed, even by other women. Women who complain are often told by others that sexual pleasure is not very important, especially in contrast to children, economic security, and a good husband who does not stray or drink.

Perhaps the most important stakeholders in sexual pleasure in the United States are magazines devoted to women. Across all class levels, ethnic divisions, and age groups, women (except for the very young whose sexual education is largely cosmetic) are told by magazines that sexual pleasure should be theirs. There is considerable advice about getting and keeping men through skilled sexual practice, though in practical terms it is unclear how women will be able to introduce such skills into a relationship in which the man is the socially defined bearer of sexual high technology. Giving the less powerful (women) instructions on how to introduce novel conduct, which will attract the moral suspicions of the more powerful (men), is probably ineffective. While it may be appropriate for men to request (by gesture or word) fellatio in a relationship, women do not have a similar right to request cunnilingus.

The problem is that there are no stakeholders for sexual pleasure in a relationship except the participants, and there are many stakeholders for the continuation of the relationship. Such stakeholders have little concern for the pleasure of the participants. One may only speculate how this denial of interaction with or concern for the sexual pleasure of others is linked to cultural scripts rooted in Puritanical beliefs.

THE NEED FOR STAKEHOLDERS AND AUDIENCES

Since it is not possible for people to observe sexual activity, it is impossible for them to judge the expertise that is displayed. While gourmet cooking can have a larger audience than two (including the self), gourmet sex cannot. The lack of an audience makes sex a very private phenomena. That is one reason why young boys tell certain audiences about their sexual exploits; the story-telling supplies the audience for the conduct that the behavior cannot provide. Girls collect certain kind of finery: rings, sweaters, ankle bracelets ("slave bracelets") that display emotional or sexual ownership.

The need for social support in the maintenance of sexual life (at the individual and collective level) is severely underestimated, largely because sex, in folk wisdom, appears to be so pleasurable that it is self-reinforcing. Nothing could be further from the truth and it might be argued that the extraordinary level of media attention to sex exists because sex has very little intrinsic re-enforcement and requires constant elicitation of support.

What seems to sustain men's sexual activity with women (particularly when young) are networks of other men who offer audience support through sex talk and observation of the activities of others. This recognition raises the question of how sexual activity is sustained for the long term couple after such extrinsic rewards decline. What is needed is an assessment of the ways in which the variety, frequency, and character of sexual events are socially maintained in all sexual relationships.

THE IMPORTANCE OF PAIRS

Since sexual pairings are not random and have a socially structured character (a fact that all students of mating processes have understood), sexual pairings in the society will show areas of high and low density. The low density areas often demark the boundaries between various strata in the society, those social aggregations we call class, ethnicity, and religion. What is striking about gender is that though it is a societal stratum for certain purposes, the vast majority of sexual ties occur across the gender boundary.

Sexual pairings also have another property which is linked to the life course. Much of sexual activity is organized around persons being in and not being in a couple. The pattern of sequential sexual pairing is now the dominant form in the United States, beginning in the early teens and then stretching into later adulthood. This recombinant cycling of persons from pair to pair, with periods of search in between, is a special characteristic of sexual/affectional life in the United States. This particular network phenomenon interacts with other networks in the society. Changing primary partners changes people's secondary and tertiary networks of relatives, friends, children, job opportunities. (It may also increase the likelihood of incest: e.g., stepfather-stepdaughter.) Within differing social strata, rates of turnover in pairs and the patterns of search between pairings may be quite different. There is substantial evidence that in the process of reconstitution of pairs, women (and especially women with children and minority women) are at a particular disadvantage.

Sexual life is in part organized by this pattern of pair turnover. In general, pair formation is a process of affectional and sexual bonding (sometimes associated with cohabitation or marriage or reproduction) in which sexual exclusivity is part of the bargain. Large numbers of these pairs break up (more among adolescents, many among cohabitators, less among those married) which reinstitutes a search for a new sexual/affectional partner. These periods of search may lead to errors in judgment (date rape, sexually transmitted diseases, emotional trauma) and may involve a number of attempts at pair bonding that do not work out.

THE STRUCTURE OF SEXUAL ACTION

In recent work on entirely different substantive issues, Laumann and Knoke (1987) have examined the ways in which actors and events may be understood in sociological research. Using their work to treat the discussion above as a set of examples of the roles that networks of audiences and stakeholders play in the processes of organizing, shaping, constraining, and eliciting sexual conduct, it is possible to create a general approach to the issues of how sexuality is socially constructed, both among sets of interrelated actors and among sets of interrelated events.

Laumann and Knoke (1987: 20) describe a fourfold table which links actors and events with the level of analysis in the following fashion:

Table One: A Typology of Frameworks for Sociological Analysis

	Events Level of Analysis	
	Individual	Relational or Systematic
Actors Level of Analysis — Individual	*a*	*b*
Relational or Systematic	*c*	*d*

The table makes several simple but critical points. It asserts that actors and events may be treated analytically from two distinct points of view, what we shall call levels of analysis. From the "methodologically individualist" point of view—the customary perspective of most survey methodology—a sampled individual actor or event from a population of actors or events is free-standing in the sense that any observations regarding an individual or event are statistically independent of the observations made for any other individual or event in the sample or population. There is, by explicit assumption, no interrelatedness or interdependence among the set of sampled or enumerated objects being studied. If this assumption were untrue, the elaborate machinery of statistical inference in survey analysis would be inappropriate. In contrast, the "relational" level of analysis postulates that the ways in which individual actors or events are related to one another play essential roles in accounting for the behavior of individuals or sets of interrelated individual actors or events. Note further that the table suggests that both actors and events can, in principle, be analyzed at the two levels of analysis and that crossing levels of analysis is also possible.

In cell *a* the intersection of actor and event as independently-defined, individual elements does not raise issues of structure, except for the interpretation of the background variables as proxies for unmeasured structural arrangements. The individual actor's conduct, for example, might be solely determined by "background" or master status variables. In voting studies, for example, the individual's voting behavior is determined by such individually measured variables as class, ethnicity, or gender and the dependent variable is a discrete event, e.g., voting for the Republican or Democratic candidate in the Presidential election. In nearly all studies of sexuality a similar pattern of analysis and understanding predominates: a number of background social or biological variables from a collection (very rarely constituting a proper sample) of unconnected individuals are measured and these are used to predict some singular sexual outcome (e.g., rate of sex activity, number of partners, sex with women or men).

Our first analytic move is to go from *a* to *c* in Table One. We shall use social networks (individuals in specific social relationships) to examine individual sexual outcomes. To do this, we usually treat the individual respondent as an informant describing not only his/her own individual behavior, attributes, resources, and attitudes but also his/her personal networks of significant nonsexual and sexual others. Individuals will be treated as actors who are endowed with particular *interests* or stakes in the activities of themselves and others and with particular *resources* they can deploy to further their interests or to prevent activities that are contrary to those interests (see Coleman 1990). Resources thus include any physical, social or symbolic facility that possesses the capacity to reward or punish individual actors (see Parsons 1951, 1961, 1967; Laumann and Knoke 1987:152–62,343–73). An array of individuals will be analytically identified on the basis of their potential and actual levels of interest (proactive or reactive) in a focal actor's social and sexual activities and their willingness to expend resources in the service of those interests. This array of individual actors is embedded in networks of social relationships of various sorts (e.g., marital, friendship, co-worker, neighbor, casual by-stander). These individuals can be distinguished with respect to their physical co-presence at various points in a focal event (transaction) and with respect to their symbolic linkage to that event.

To illustrate this approach, consider a focal sexual pair (wife-husband), each member of which has particular and usually different stakes in the sexual interaction over time. These interests are likely to change, for example with the arrival and departure of children. Moreover, each brings to the relationship various resources (e.g., physical attractiveness, vigor, competencies, financial prospects, conversational resources, enjoyable friends, social standing or reputation, etc.). In extramarital affairs, if both members of a pair are married to others, their stake in the relation will differ from that of pairs in which only one of the pair is married. This relation will also differ if children are present in one or both of the marriages. As a further example, consider sexual contacts with women prostitutes. The content of such interactions will characteristically differ when the clients are a group of young men on a drinking spree in contrast with a paid encounter with a solitary businessman. In the former case the structure of relations among the young men will increase the likelihood of violence against the woman when compared with the single client.

Using this system, events can be readily organized into larger sets of interrelated elements that must be studied at the appropriate level of analyais. An interesting example of a "cell *b*" type of analysis would be the consideration of the menu of events that took place in the individual's most recent sexual encounter. Here we might have in hand a random sample of individuals who reported the content of their last sexual events. Analysis might focus on characteristic patterns of sexual events (e.g., co-presence of anal intercourse and oral sex and the presence/absence of vaginal and anal intercourse) associated with individuals possessing different constellations of master statuses. An instance of a "cell *d*" type of analysis might be the identification of individuals who have both characteristic patterns of acquiring sex partners and specific patterns of sexual conduct with respect to frequency and content.

To consider Table One more systematically, we need a heuristic device to take account of the structural features of the interrelationships among actors (e.g., their social networks) and among the unit elements that constitute events and sets of interrelated events (according to some criterion of interrelatedness). To start, we define a rectangular matrix in which the rows are a set of actors (*i*) and the columns are a set of events (*j*) in a system of action (see Figure One). Entries in the cells of the matrix indicate the nature of the relationship between each actor and event. For example, a "1" might indicate that the actor participated in some way in the event, and a "0," that he/she did not. Two critical questions arise immediately:

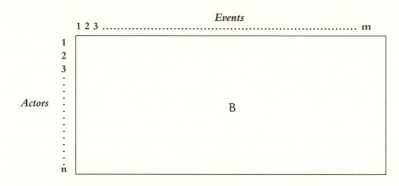

Figure One: A Rectangular Matrix of Actors by Events

(1) what is the boundary-specifying principle that defines the set of actors belonging to the joint space of actors/events?, and (2) what is the boundary-specifying principle that defines the set of events belonging to the joint space of actors/events? (see Laumann et al. 1982, for an extended discussion of the problem of boundary specification in action systems). As we shall see, the matter is much more complicated than the above questions imply. In fact, there are a multitude of "valid" framing rules for any given system of action, each of which treats the set and subsets of rows and columns in fundamentally different ways. Each alternative has profound implications for selecting the methodology appropriate for empirical analysis.

Before developing this argument about multiple framing principles, we find it useful to form a triangular matrix out of the rectangular matrix depicted in Figure One by taking into account the interrelationships among events and among actors. In Figure Two we have added an events-by-events triangular matrix, A, that refers to the interrelationships among events (*m*) and an actor-by-actor triangular matrix, C, that defines the (dyadic) interrelationships among the actors (*n*). The third-dimensional column indicates the absolute properties of events and actors stacked together, which include variables such as the actors' master statuses, subjective preferences, or amounts of resources, plus the events' public visibility or relative cultural

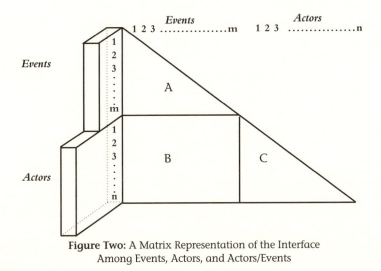

Figure Two: A Matrix Representation of the Interface
Among Events, Actors, and Actors/Events

attractiveness. The entries in the matrix itself represent information about the ways actors and events are related to one another in three modalities: within events, within actors, and between actors and events. This is our specification of the individual versus relational level of analysis for a given system of action.

Matrix C is familiar to social network analysts who study links among actors. It can readily be interpreted as a symmetrized social choice matrix. Of course, the asymmetric choice matrix, n by n, would be the customary starting point for a network analysis, but we do not believe that the generality of our argument is lost if we confine attention to the symmetrized submatrix for the sake of simplicity. What may be new for us to think about is the event-by-event matrix, which raises all-too-often-neglected questions about the organization of events and the resulting impact of that organization on the actor-event interface, B.

Let us first think about the framing perspective assumed in cell a of Table One as it would apply to the data structure depicted in Figure Two. In the radically individualist framing of the problem, an event is regarded as a well-defined given (e.g., a presidential election day or a sexual event involving anal intercourse) and considered merely as a response expressive of the individual actors' predispositions. The event as well as the actors are treated as statistically and sociologically independent units; no information about the relations among the actors in the set (rows) and the events (e.g., the influence of different events over the course of a campaign on a given actor's maturing decision to vote for a particular candidate or the various sexual activities constituting the sexual transaction as a whole) is taken into account. The analysis focuses attention on a single event column vector in Figure Two where the rows refer to individual actors endowed with purposive orientations and other individual-level measures of actor characteristics. Even if the investigator should choose to speak of the impact of the social context of a given actor, as indicated, for example, by the preferences of his circle of intimates (see Laumann 1973; Scheuch 1965), these intimates are, by definition, actors outside the sampling frame constituting the set of actors *n*, which are sampled as free-standing individuals from the population universes of voters or sexual actors in our two examples.

Now let us consider the case that introduces selected structural considerations, combining the individual and relational levels of analysis (e.g., cell *a* plus cell *c* in Table One). Here we assume that relational information about actor ties contained in triangular matrix C of Figure Two can be used, in addition to the individual-level actor information, to explain the behavior of individual actors with respect to a given event (i.e., one of the columns describing an event). Thus, the triangular matrix C in Figure 2 might describe the dyadic relations among actors in a communication network. The diagonal elements of the triangle are, using Lazarsfeld and Menzel's (1969) term, the relational properties of each actor derived from such a matrix: for example, his centrality in the network.[3] Now, the behavior of individual actors with respect to this given event (e.g., their participation in the event) can be analyzed in terms of the absolute properties of actors (note the third dimension sketched in Figure Two), the relational properties in the main diagonal, and the pairwise relational properties in the off-diagonal elements of the triangle. The event is still considered to be externally given and independent from all others. A considerable literature has emerged that addresses the methodological issues posed by treating individual- and contextual-level variables of actors in the same analytic framework (see, for example, Blalock 1984; Erbring and Young 1979).

The literature is less helpful with respect to the structure of events, since most theorists treat the organization of events as extrinsic to their explanatory problem. Even the most methodologically sophisticated discussions of structural or contextual effects have dealt exclusively with the composition of actors and their surroundings, ignoring the sequencing and structuring aspects of events in which actors engage.[4] By contrast, because of our interest in scripts and narratives, we postulate that events themselves possess properties in the absolute sense of individually characterized occasions or as organized contextuality that have consequences for the ways actors behave. The organized contextuality of an event is based both on its horizontal context (i.e., embeddedness in institutional space) and its longitudinal context (i.e., embeddedness in time). We argue, therefore, that the interconnection of events in these contexts has a fundamental methodological implication for our framing of the data analysis and interpretations of the results. Thus, anal intercourse means different things when embedded in a set of sexual activities currently taking place between two Catholic teenagers attempting to preserve virginity before marriage and when embedded in a set of sexual activities occurring for the first and only time between a prostitute and a particular client.

Defining the structural relations between individuals is not as difficult as defining the boundedness of events. In the sexual arena one can examine a scripted sequence of actions for a romantic seduction or honeymoon and break out the sub-units nearly indefinitely. When does the sexual act begin and end? Can one examine the alternative sequences in a sexual transaction that includes hugging, kissing, and anal sex? What specific sub-gestures need to be examined in the sequence of co-present actions?

These "breakouts" of events are often either convenient or conventional. The committee meets tomorrow between six and seven, the assignation begins at 4:30 and ends at 10:00. In the latter there is not only sexual activity, but conversation, going to the toilet, eating, drinking, sex talk and non-sex talk. The encounter can be called "an extramarital sex unit event."

Events can thus be structured with respect to one another in at least three different ways. (1) Events may be arranged in a temporal sequence (at t1, t2, . . . tn) that has *causal order* as one subevent precedes and "causes" the next as a necessary, if not sufficient, condition—as in the series of physiological events that successively moves from arousal to ejaculation in vaginal intercourse. (2) When considering a set of events as ordered from the point of view of *strategic action*, one identifies an end state goal (e.g., having sex with a particular individual) and then identifies a set of intervening contingent events that the actor undertakes in hopes of advancing to this desired end point (e.g., arranging a romantic dinner with soft music under the stars and the opportunity for being alone together). Note that both parties to the action would be pursuing their goals independently of one another—thus creating contingencies to which the other must accommodate if the joint action of the individuals is to be coordinated. (3) A cultural script identifies a generally shared understanding of the parties and relevant audience(s) about a *normatively appropriate* set of interrelated events (e.g., the appropriate elements required to constitute a Polish Catholic as distinct from a Greek Orthodox wedding). Individual actors orient their conduct in unfolding events in terms of their understanding of the details of a particular cultural script. The extent to which it is shared with other observers and participants will determine the script's effectiveness as a coordinating mechanism. Of course, collectively knowing the script does not guarantee that it will be followed in every particular. Here social organization, as conceived above, drives the action: the interests and incentives of the several parties to comply and to secure the compliance of others to the shared understanding of the script's elements will determine the character of the enactment of the script.

CONCLUSION

We have attempted in this chapter to accomplish four tasks. The first was to distinguish between socially driven and biologically driven theories of sexual conduct by distinguishing between drive (or instinct) models and a strong socio-cultural theory of sexual action which is based on the theory of sexual scripts. We have not in this process done justice to those theories which propose bio-social interactions, but would argue that no biological factor finds its way into the behavior of an individual except through socio-cultural mediation. Second, we have discussed the historial significance of the individual sexual actor in traditional research on sexuality, even that which has been social in its orientation, pointing out that even social scripting theory has often not taken systematic account of the role of social structure in shaping sexual conduct. Third, we have indicated the ways in which the interconnections between individuals directly and indirectly influence various types of sexual conduct. These necessarily sketchy descriptions should serve as an introduction to ways in which sexual encounters are shaped by the characteristics of sexual partnerships, stakeholders, and audiences.

Finally, in the last section, we have attempted the fourth task, seeking to take a theoretical leap by creating a framework for moving from the analysis of the behavior of isolated individuals and events (the usual form of sociological analysis) to more complex data structures and analytic schemes. In this section we discuss non-sexual as well as sexual examples of the kinds of data that might be gathered and problems that these kinds of data will produce for traditional forms of statistical analysis. In this scheme we bring back a concern for scripting theory by pointing out that these are examples of narrative sequences of events.

From a sociological perspective, the most appropriate data sets are those that link together socially identified interacting sets of individuals (persons in real or symbolic networks) who are enacting event sequences (scripted narratives). Our best example of this was the wedding in which an identifiable network of actors with specified social relations participate in the ordered sequences of role enactments that constitute the social occasion. In this social drama persons actually change their relationships as the sequence of events unfolds. The analysis of sexual life can have the same complexity— a group of young men go out on the town, they have a hierarchy of relations within the group as well as relations with family and community. In the course of the evening they meet a group of young women who also have a complex set of relationships. Depending on who these young people are socially, and to whom they are connected socially, a variety of likely sequences of sexual action can be enacted. The outcomes can be violence or love, casual sex or marriage, pleasure or disappointment. This is the complexity of social analysis that sexual studies require.

NOTES

1. Sexual conduct often involves a change of consciousness on the part of the participants. This change of consciousness accompanies the felt sense of socially-induced physical arousal and emotional excitement that are often involved in moving from a nonsexual state to a sexual state. The sexual state is "engrossing" and there is a split experienced between the "turned on"/"aroused" state and the "turned off"/"unaroused" state. This "turn-on/turn-off" is probably interactive with the felt state of "aloneness"; being without an audience facilitates arousal while arousal facilitates the sense of aloneness.

2. This is not to say that anecdotal evidence for such explicit social hierarchies based on sex does not exist, expecially in groups composed entirely of men or boys. For instance in March of 1993 there were a number of newspaper stories about a group of young men in a Southern California suburb who keep score of the number of young women with whom the individual members of the "posse" had sex. It is not reported how the members checked on each others allegations, but it is reported that in some circumstances a girl who had sex with one member would be passed on to other members of the group or that group members would have "gang" sex with a girl. The numbers of girls were used to create a social hierarchy among the young men involved. While criminal charges were filed against some of the young men (for rape and for sex with a ten year-old girl), the Los Angeles District Attorney's office decided that this was a matter to be left to schools, churches and parents (Jane Gross, "Where 'Boys Will be Boys', and Adults are Befuddled," *New York Times*, March 29, 1993 A1 and 13).

3. Note that network theorists often call such variables positional variables (see, for example, Burt 1980).

4. For a review of multilevel research, see van den Eeden and Hüttner (1982). See also Erbring and Young (1979).

Networks and Sex 　　　　　　　　　 **11**

The Use of Social Networks as Method and Substance in Researching Gay Men's Response to HIV/AIDS

Anthony P.M. Coxon

THIS CHAPTER IS BASED UPON THE VIEW that much behavioral research on gay men and their reaction to the AIDS pandemic is not so much psychologistic as overly individualistic in approach and that this severely limits its utility and prevents us from tackling the most challenging substantive and methodological (and hence policy-relevant) issues.[1]

This bias in the design of such studies often begins with the words: "Since a random sample of gay men is not possible, we used snowball sampling . . ."

They usually didn't—and the bias continues into the heartland of sexual behavior. Despite the building up of wave upon wave of prevalence figures for this and that sexual act, we still know little more than Kinsey did about the context of relationships.

A critical deficiency is the lack of a network perspective—network concepts, notions and methodologies. Now it may well be that networks are believed by the research community to be too complex to study and that they do not really add value sufficiently to compensate for their undoubted problems. In part this is true: it is often difficult enough to persuade an individual to participate in sexual behavior studies, without having to go on to recruit couples or—more relevantly—casual partners. It may also be that sex researchers shy away from the greater involvement and commitment of such detailed research methods, and prefer to rely upon the tried-and-tested survey.

I want to explore the applicability of network notions in three areas that loom large in our own research and in many other projects on sexual behavior. Network notions impinge most directly in the areas of:

- design,
- in networks of sexual contacts, and
- in identifying (unknown) sexual partners.

In so doing I shall be frank and realistic, so that others may learn from our mistakes and be a little more adventurous than funding authorities might sometimes like us to be!

1. DEFINITIONS AND SAMPLE SELECTION

From the outset, Project SIGMA resisted any attempt to produce a random sample of gay and bisexual men.[2] This was done on both principled and practical grounds. In principle, the tendency for policy-makers and others to think of "homosexuality" as a lasting and recognizable attribute was not to be encouraged, and Kinsey's research (1948:650–657) illustrates well how prevalence estimates of "homosexual men" can be made to range from four percent to almost fifty percent by successively relaxing the criteria of the type of sexual contact and the time-period of sexual involvement with those of the same sex (Coxon 1987).

But practical issues were paramount; no general population survey of sexual behavior was then envisaged in the U.K. and the cost of attempting to sample randomly on a two-stage basis (initially "combing" to produce a population frame, and secondly sampling within it) would be well outside funding agencies' means. In any event, the relevant population is narrower than the notional category of "homosexual men," being concerned with potential or actual HIV transmission rather than sexual identity. By this time, the causative agent of AIDS was known to be viral and the first crucial network-contact study (Auerbach 1984) had been published.

The strategy finally adopted by SIGMA was therefore to structure respondent selection round the two factors known to maximize variation in homosexual behavior:

- Age, and
- Type of Relationship.

Enter the network, via Rapoport (1953, 1957), Rapoport and Horvath (1961), Fararo and Sunshine (1964)—and snowballing.

1.1. Sampling Via a Large Social Network: Theoretical Ideas

The conceptual basis of the sampling strategy was motivated by the question of how to obtain systematic (ultimately unbiased) information about a large, unknown, and connected social network of sexually active gay and bisexual men. I was familiar through earlier sociometric interests with Rapoport's models of diffusion through large networks. His original application in mathematical biophysics had been to the neural net, estimating the "gross statistical properties" (Rapoport 1963: 512) of a huge network of unknown size and structure, and in particular the "close-knittedness" and the "ultimate connectivity" of the neural net.[3] This approach was applied in turn to communication and (by Fararo) to friendships among young and institutionalized offenders.

The aim in these social studies was to explain diffusion within these empirical social networks, the manifest divergence of these processes from diffusion in a purely *random* baseline network, and to do so by identifying and estimating significant *bias parameters* (Rapoport 1957, Fararo and Sunshine 1964, Skvoretz 1985). These parameters, when incorporated into the "reduced axone density" (in effect: the "slowed-down" effective out-degree, referred to as a), explained the (lower) ultimate connectivity and rate of increase in new contacts by means of such modifications of a random Polya model.

In this model the expected fraction contacted at time t is given by the iterative equation (Rapoport 1961:285):

$$p_{t+1} = (1 - X_t)\, (1 - e^{-ap_t})$$

where p_t denotes the expected proportion of new contacts at step t in a random net, and X_t the cumulative proportion contacted at time t. The expected ultimate connectivity X, satisfies the transcendental equation:

$$X_{,} = 1 - (1 - p_O)\, e^{-aX_{,}}$$

where $X_{,}$ _ is the asymptotic value of the cumulative fraction contacted. The epidemiological parallel is of course obvious, and in later work Rapoport actually referred to the model as the (Polya) "contagion process model" (Rapoport 1979).

The method for making the estimates of diffusion or "infection" is the "tracing," which consists of producing a rooted tree giving the new contacts at each ordinal step t. Starting at a small initial fraction of nodes, the tree is "grown" by consulting the sociometric contact matrix at each new contact, until no new contacts occur. A small illustratory example is useful.

1.1.0. The Tracing
Let us suppose that the network structure is known (which is often not the case, but simplifies the exposition), and is given by the adjacency matrix **A**, whose element *aij* is 1 if there is a relational link between points *i* and *j* and is 0 otherwise. An example is given in Figure One(A). Here the number of points, N, is 10 and the outdegree of each point (number of contacts made) is a constant 2. The *starting set* for each tracing is always small compared to N, and in the two examples shown it consists of a single point: point E in Figure One(C)(i) and point E in Figure One(C)(ii).

	A	B	C	D	E	F	G	H	I	J
A	0	0	1	1	0	0	0	0	0	0
B	0	0	1	1	0	0	0	0	0	0
C	0	1	0	0	0	1	0	0	0	0
D	0	0	1	0	1	0	0	0	0	0
E	0	0	0	0	0	1	0	0	0	1
F	0	1	0	0	0	0	0	1	0	0
G	0	0	1	0	0	0	0	0	1	0
H	0	0	1	0	0	1	0	0	0	0
I	0	0	1	0	0	0	1	0	0	0
J	1	0	1	0	0	0	0	0	0	0

Figure One (A)
Network Adjacency Matrix, N = 10, a = 2

Step	0	1	2	3	4	5	6
$p\,(t)$	.1	.2	.24	.16	.06	.05	.03
$X\,(t)$	.1	.3	.54	.70	.76	.81	.84

$p\,(t)$ proportion of new points contactd at step t
$X\,(t)$ Cumulative proprtion of new points contactd by step t

Figure One (B)
Network Tracing Distributions Averaged over 10 Starting Sets
(each point taken in turn)

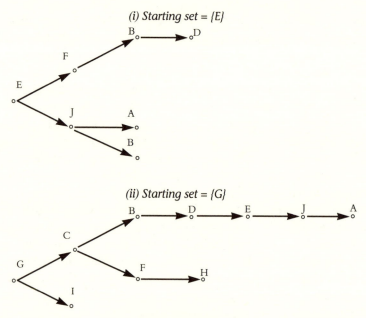

(i) Starting set = {E}

(ii) Starting set = {G}

Figure One (C)
Illustratory Network Tracings

(iii) Redundant Tracing: Starting set = {G}

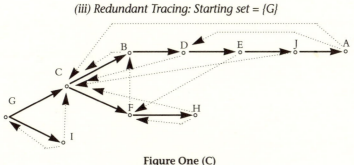

Figure One (C)
Illustratory Network Tracings (cont.)

Each tracing proceeds by defining the starting set (step $t = 0$) and then noting the contacts which this starting set makes. These constitute the set of (two) new points contacted at step $t = 1$, and these are counted into n(1) (the number of new contacts at step t.= 1). The contacts of each of these new contacts in turn are now identified, but only if they have not been contacted previously do they count in n(2). This tracing process continues until there are no new contacts; this stage of "ultimate connectivity" may be complete (contacting the entire set of 10 points as in tracing (ii)) or partial (as in tracing (iii) in Figure One (C)). Notice that the number of points newly contacted at each step and the number of steps taken to reach the end of the tracing differs depending on the starting set.

To emphasize the fact that it is *new* contacts only that are considered at each step, tracing (ii) starting with point E is represented in tracing (iii) by drawing in the redundant (already contacted) links at each step as a dotted arrow. Because they have already been contacted, they of course point backwards.

A given tracing is characterized by the fraction of the population finally contacted (average ultimate connectivity) and by the number of steps taken to reach this stage. In Rapoport's theory, a number of tracings are made, until the *average* tracing distribution (i.e., averaged at each step over all the tracings) stabilizes to within a desired limit. This asymptotic tracing distribution is given in Figure One(B). The *proportion* of new points contacted at each step is (simply $n(t)/N$) is given in $p(t)$, and the *cumulative* proportion of points contacted by step t is given in $X(t)$. The "ultimate connectivity" of the network is given by the last entry. Thus *on average*, eighty-four percent of the points are ultimately contacted by the sixth step when a tracing is made in this network.

The interesting difference between the neurological and the normal social science applications is that tracings are usually produced in the social science case by referring to a *known* sociomatrix (i.e., relating to a population of known size and contacts), and hence what is constructed by the technique is a *synthetic* tracing. By contrast, the original mechanism proposed by Rapoport referred to a network of unknown size, and used the empirical physical process of exciting the initial neurone/s and observing the pattern of firing across neurones. These then produced estimates of the size and connectivity of the population. Paradoxically, the use of Rapoport's techniques in the case of tracing hidden populations thus means reverting to his original conceptualization.

1.1.1. Sociological Implementations

The conceptual analogy with sampling gay men seemed well-nigh complete. Implementing a tracing (or several) provides an excellent methodological specification of what sampling a hidden population should be. If continued to completion (and without error) such tracings would provide an enumeration (of at least connected subsets) of the homosexual population and also information about its local network characteristics. This is, of course, an ideal type and is practically unrealistic as a technique *in toto*. Nonetheless, it tells us what "snowball sampling" should be. A close parallel to the tracing process was known to sociologists from Coleman's study of diffusion (Coleman 1958), where physicians were asked to name those of their colleagues to whom they gave information about a new drug, a method now known as the "chain-referral" method (e.g. Biernacki and Waldorf 1981).

But there are important differences. In the sociological examples, attention has shifted from Rapoport's interest in the inherent properties of the network and the mechanism generating it to the usefulness of a *strategy* for reaching hidden or hard-to-reach populations. To be sure, the underlying assumption is that there exists a network of contacts (for otherwise why would snow-balling work?), but even considerations like the number of stages/steps and the outdegree (constant or average number of contacts) slips out of sight.

Paradoxically, most statistical work on snowball sampling (Goodman 1961, Holland and Leinhardt 1979, van Metter 1990, Snijders 1992) has not generally been directly relevant since it typically refers not to populations of unknown size, but rather to issues of inferring population network properties from samples. Few indeed are the studies claiming snowball status which come in any way near satisfying requirements such as sampling to exhaustion. Perhaps, given the wider meaning nowadays given to snowball sampling—in effect, the cumulative but haphazard acquisition of a quota or convenience sample—it is better to use the term "tracing sample" to refer to tracing procedures which follow contacts-of-contacts to the exhaustion of new contacts.

1.1.2. Sampling Gay Men: SIGMA's Sampling Procedure

The sampling process used in SIGMA was two-stage: first to obtain easily-accessible respondents in each of the nine Project Design typology cells (chiefly from gay pubs, clubs and voluntary organizations);[4] secondly to use these initial contacts as starting samples for producing tracing trees. The imagery sometimes used in SIGMA to refer to this process was "burrowing into the iceberg"; indeed, given the fact that those most "out" are a highly biased group representing only the tip of the iceberg, the idea of obtaining less "out" contacts of the same Age x Relationship-type by snowballing is attractive. But notice the looseness of the relational definition we used; in practice the interviewer asked the initial respondents to name other potential respondents who were of the same (Project) type as themselves, but preferably less "out" as gay. It was left to the interviewer to satisfy him/herself that this definition was understood by the respondent, and we were rarely able to ascertain whether this had actually been done.

The attempt by SIGMA to implement tracing sampling was noble, but ultimately deficient, and for a number of instructive reasons:

- often a given gay man's friends and acquaintances are *not* of the same Age-Relationship type as himself, so that it was frequently quite difficult for a respondent to name someone of the same type, let alone someone that was less "out."

- the *number* of contacts to be named was never specified; more relevantly, there was no criterion provided by which the respondent could decide when the number of his nominees was sufficient.

- as a Project we had bound ourselves to anonymity in the form of not recording or making use of the name of anyone named in the research context. We therefore had to rely upon the respondent to contact his nominee and ask him to participate in the Project. Consequently we might never know that a specific person had been thus nominated, let alone whose nominee he was.[5]

However, in terms of the stated objectives—to "snowball" into the more covert gay population—there was some degree of success. The first "Question Schedule" contained a number of questions asking who knew that the respondent was gay/bisexual. Inter alia this provided a useful indicator of "outness," and (at least in the South Wales site) this index of "outness" decreased as known contacts were interviewed.

But it must be said that the exercise was not overall a resounding success, and that to all intents the initial SIGMA sample was no more (nor indeed any less) a "snowball" than other such studies. The reasons cited above are enough to account for its lack of success, but in principle each could be remedied. In Section Three, I present information about how critical the actual naming (identification) process is. But the main shortcoming was that the criterion/relation for respondent naming was not only too vague, it was also not related directly enough to the sexual transmission method we were studying. This raises the question of whether a genuine (sexual) tracing sampling technique could have been devised and implemented, and whether it would have been more relevant. Without doubt the attempt might bring to light yet more compelling shortcomings (not least those connected with confidentiality and compliance) and would probably be more expensive in terms of time and money. I shall return to this in the next sections; it remains to assess the depth of the burrowing.

The gay scene in Cardiff and area is a good deal more closely-knit (on any significant criterion) than that of the sister site of London.[6] In Rapoport/Fararo terms, this implies higher values of reciprocity ("sibling bias, s") and transitivity ("parent bias", p).[7] This in turn implies longer chains because the clustering leads to more redundant (already contacted) new contacts at any step, and thus "slow down" the growth of X(t) and of the eventual connectivity asymptote.

Where it was possible to track the contacting process in Cardiff, these redundant new nominations occurred with sufficient frequency that a rule was drawn up that new nominations had to be checked by the site office before being allowed as a new sample member; in London this rarely happened.

For sexual contacts (of whatever variety) there turned out to be a goodly number of cross-cutting circles, but with weak links between them, so that an estimate of ultimate connectivity probably depends rather importantly on whether the sample includes the liaison persons (bridges) that mediate such clusters. Not including bridges would lead to a falsely low estimate of ultimate connectivity (and hence of prevalence). It would also lead to missing certain important subsets of respondents who come in and out of the scene on an occasional basis and who would only normally be contacted via one man; occasional (but not hardened) users of "cottages" are an important example, and a relevant important sub-group epidemiologically.[8]

These assessments of the topology of the homosexual network are largely impressionistic, and would need to be investigated directly as hypotheses. In neither site, however, did we normally exceed a chain-length (let alone a tracing step-length) of more than three, and we argued that a length of four would be necessary to achieve even reasonable coverage, and ten or more would be necessary to come anywhere near encompassing a coherent cluster (Davies 1986).

The question of whether engaging in tracing samples of actual sexual contact (and especially of implicated behaviors such as anal intercourse) would materially improve our network-knowledge and assist in estimating prevalence and prediction is a good deal more moot, and brings us nicely to the second section.

2. Networks of Transmission

The main implicated behavior for the sexual transmission of HIV among gay men is, of course, anal intercourse, with the remoter (and contested) possibility of fellatio (but see Koopman et al. 1992). An important framework for interpreting and predicting transmission is therefore the *sexually defined* network. The defining relation can be sexually multiplex (most gay men don't just have anal intercourse) and will normally need to be restricted to a fixed incidence time-period. The sexual relation is also necessarily asymmetric, since the probability of transmission is greater for the passive partner (Darrow et al. 1983, inter alia).[9] This asymmetry means that sexual networks and tracing trees have to rely on directed graphs. Moreover, sexual role, though normally considered as an individual or point property (see Coxon et al. 1993) can more appropriately be viewed as a dyadic property. Thus, although in individual terms a man may engage in only *A*ctive, only *P*assive, *B*oth (or *N*either) modality (the so-called *BAPN* roles), this is often distributed associatively so that a man is (say) only active with one partner and only passive with another (this will still lead to his being classified as "both" in the individual-based role categorization).

It is important to specify why the Rapoport model is being used as a basis. After all, HIV is not generally highly infective, and one contact is rarely sufficient for infection.[10] We also know that epidemiologically it is necessary to take into account the stage of HIV infection in assigning probabilities of infection. What the Rapoport models do is to provide us with a *potential* infection model—a network structure of routes and paths along which infection can travel, and where (as with a block-model) the zeroes are often as significant as the ones.[11]

Many existing epidemiological models are long on necessary conditions for infection but short indeed on the socio-sexual structure which in large part constrains and contains the infection. Equally, these models often make demands for data that normally are not collected, particularly by survey analysts—such as information on mixing (Anderson et al. 1986) and especially on the second-step information on the number of sexual partners of one's sexual partners. These become crucial parameters in the Anderson model.

2.1. Piloting a Study of a Two-Zone Network of Anal Intercourse
At an early stage in the pilot work of SIGMA in 1984 (reported in Coxon

1986) I began investigating the possibility and viability of mounting a network study of anal intercourse within the South Wales SIGMA site. This would be akin to contact-tracing of STD Clinics but more sensitive and sociologically useful. It is relatively straightforward to obtain information about whether or not a gay man engages in anal intercourse, the rates and number of partners in a given incidence period, and the extent to which condoms are used. These are now routine questions in any socio-epidemio-logical enquiry. Only rarely, however, are the pieces put together so that, for instance, we know whether anal intercourse is engaged in with a particular partner, and with what modalities.

In Project SIGMA we have developed the Sexual Diary as a supplemen-tary method for obtaining precisely this information (Coxon 1988; Coxon et al. 1992, 1993; Davies 1990). The main shortcoming is that by the self-deny-ing ordinance mentioned above, we specifically have *not* asked for the names of partners (though we do ask for their descriptive attributes), thereby appar-ently foregoing the possibility of linking the data to obtain sexual networks.[12]

The other strategy was to attempt to construct an anal intercourse network directly, by following a proper tracing procedure, initially with a single root sample. In this example I refer to one such network, but restrict attention to the initial one-step partners of Respondent #One, although the tracing actu-ally continued beyond this point. The tracing procedure was as follows:

Sex Tracing

0   specify the incidence period (and bounds)
1   choose the root node/s
2   establish how many partners he had engaged in anal intercourse, get their name, information about them, details of act/s of anal inter-course, if possible, including modality, ejaculation and condom use
3   for each named partner, repeat step 2.

(The sociogram of the network centered on Respondent One is given in Figure Two.)

Step 0   This is straightforward. In the example it was taken as a six month period, and limited to the South Wales Project area.

Step 1   This starting node is chosen for good (cautionary) reasons. His position is discussed below.

Step 2   It is fairly unusual for a gay man to have thirteen partners with whom he engages in anal intercourse, but by no means rare. It was not difficult to establish information about the initial thirteen linked partners from him, and his account could be checked against his Sexual Diary account. At the level of whether or not he had had

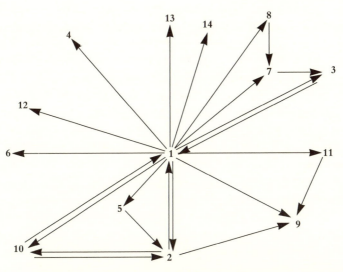

Figure Two: [1] Ego-centric Graph of Anal Intercourse

anal intercourse, and in what modality, the two accounts concurred.

Step 3   Knowing the identity of the partners, it was possible to match ten of the partners with SIGMA respondents (all except Respondents Twelve, Fourteen, and Four), and it would have been possible to find the inter-zone One links from Diaries or Interviews and not have to rely on contacting them directly. Information could *only* be obtained for the three non-SIGMA respondents by direct contact, and in one case at least (Twelve) we knew that he had already refused to be a part of the Project panel, and hence was highly unlikely to give information on his anal intercourse partners. Beyond zone-One (i.e. three-step and beyond) I have only indicated contacts *outside* the initial thirteen.

Several comments are in order:

- The root node (1) is a professional man in his mid-thirties, with two regular partners (two and three); six, eight and ten are more-or-less regular partners—"occasionals" might be a better term. Partner Five is originally an "affair" (regular partner) of Two's. The rest are mostly casual partners, but include a few more-than-once casuals.
- In terms of individual sex-role, almost all of the men are "B" [both active and passive] during this period, but Six is A[ctive only] and Nine is P[assive only].[13]
- In terms of the sociometric structure,[14] the core "clique" (maximally

connected symmetric subgraph) consists of {1,2,10}, with {3} as an important appendage. Partner Nine is a particularly interesting (and at-risk) person, receiving by far the highest number of direct and indirect paths of anal intercourse, whilst Ten by contrast *generates* the maximum number of anal intercourse paths (see Appendix 1).

- In terms of the Rapoport bias parameters, reciprocity is 0.17 (fairly close to the proportion of "Both" in larger studies [Coxon et al. 1993]), and transitivity ("parent bias") is 0.04, which is naturally attenuated in this restricted set, but which is not much less than the value for larger networks—after all, anal intercourse is only likely to be (trivially) transitive among those who are both active and passive (e.g. {1,2,10}), though "genuine" (transitive in one direction) chains do appear, as in {1,7,8}).

- In 1985 (to which the data refer) there is *no instance at all* of a condom being used in this group during the six-month period, but the HIV prevalence rate was also very low in this non-Clinic South Wales subsample (Hunt et al. 1990).

- This small world is by no means self-contained. At the second, and especially at the third step, the contacts begin to leave South Wales, and also include female partners. Partners {10, 3, 13} have a female partner, and {5, 3, 7, 6} have one or more male partners in London, which has always had a higher HIV sero-prevalence rate than South Wales.

It is very dangerous to over-interpret these small and illustrative data; the point of the exercise has been to show that it is a potentially valuable exercise, albeit a difficult one. In particular, it involves considerable data-collection costs and requires extraordinarily sensitive and delicate skills on the part of the interviewer.

With the adoption of the self-denying ordinance in not recording or using names, the attempt to implement anal intercourse tracing was virtually abandoned, not least because the funding agency disallowed it—on financial, not ethical grounds, it should be said.[15] So: was this another resounding non-success? Let us see.

2.2. Inferring Partner Identity

Perhaps the most galling thing about the ordinance about anonymity was that in many instances, respondents *did* give names of partners. The reluctance was not because they did not want to name partners (at least under conditions of confidentiality), so much as their concern that the nominee would find out that he had been named by the respondent. But even when the respondent did not name his partner/s it was sometimes possible to infer his (or her) identity from circumstantial or public knowledge—interviewers themselves were usually involved in the local gay scene—and even from within the interview. The accuracy of such inferences and guesses was much aided by the fact that although *names* were not asked, descriptive information was.

2.2.1. Partner Characteristics: Matching Attributes

From the Wave One "Question Schedule" (1987) onwards, respondents were asked to give a range of attributes for their regular partner/s—Sex, Age, Race, Job, Marital Status and Domicile—and throughout the Project all Sexual Diary keepers are asked to describe each partner during the month in terms of the following characteristics:[16]

Partner Attributes (Sexual Diaries)

0 Partner (sequential number and) Sex
1 Status (Regular, Occasional, Casual/One-off)
2 Age (known or guessed)
3 How long you've been having sex
4 Where met (on this occasion) [Casual partners only]
5 Other information—Job, basis of attraction, payment?
6 HIV status, if known

Members of Professor Roy Anderson's team at [then] Imperial College had expressed interest in using the Sexual Diary data for making estimates of mixing ratios—i.e., of information not only about the number of partners, but also of the number of partners of partners.[17] If partners were identified by name (and, more demandingly, if they were Project diary-keepers themselves), then such a procedure of estimation depends simply on establishing linkage between a respondent's file and those of his partners. But for reasons explained in the last section, the SIGMA Undertaking on Confidentiality meant that this was not possible. Dr. Chris Joyce originally suggested a possible strategy: to use information which a diarist gave about a given partner as a yardstick or template "profile" and then attempt to identify him by searching for (preferably one) respondent whose data matched that information.

One option (not systematically followed out) was simply to use the partner attributes, so that if, for example, Jim had described his Partner Five as:

> *A regular partner / aged 24 / with whom I've been having sex for 2 years / who is a well-endowed teacher from Manchester / and HIV antibody negative*

then a SIGMA diarist, Fred, who was found to have the same characteristics would be identified as putative Partner Five, and the information he gave about the number of his sexual partners would then be derivable from his Diary record. The main difficulties are:

- What counts as "the same characteristics," especially given that the fourth category ("Other information") is open-ended?
- Will a pair describe themselves in the same way? (Thus, Jim's "regular" partner Fred might consider himself an "occasional" partner of Jim.)
- How much "noise" / tolerance for error can be allowed in matching, especially given the fact that reported age is often systematically biased downwards?
- What happens if more than one candidate appears? Suppose Fred1 is *"Regular / 28 / sex for 2 years / student from Stockport / HIV neg."* and Fred2 is *"Occasional / 26 / sex for 2 years / student at Salford University / HIV neg"*; which shall be identified as the "real" Fred?[18]
- In the case of casual or one-off partners, it is quite likely that information will be very deficient and grossly misperceived, making matching virtually impossible. And yet these cases may often be very important epidemiologically.

Matching by attributes (and especially on open-ended and multi-reference ones) can therefore be a very hazardous procedure, and if there are too many mismatches then the subsequent constructed network will become almost misleading and very possibly useless.

But all was not lost; rather than tighten up or extend the partner characteristics, a different tack was employed.

2.2.2 Retrospective Networking
The next ploy was to ignore such individual characteristics (at least initially) and concentrate on much more detailed, relevant and less-easily matchable data. This consisted of "retrospective networking"—namely matching a partner by matching the *sexual session* itself in which they had both participated (after the event, an obvious choice to make!).[19]

The process had three steps: *screening, temporal matching, and behavioral matching.*

2.2.2.1 Screening
First, all solitary sessions (involving only one partner, i.e. the diarist) were removed, which amount to exactly one-third of the sessions: 33.3 percent (Coxon 1990:15) in this set of data.[20]

2.2.2.2 TEMPORAL MATCHING
Obviously, a match should only occur if the sessions involved had taken place at the same date and time. However, some leeway had to be allowed on this, since earlier studies had shown that displacements up to one day between the

partners' accounts were not unusual. The matches produced by this process were then treated as fulfilling a necessary condition for matching.

The results of purely *temporal* matches are presented in Figure Three.

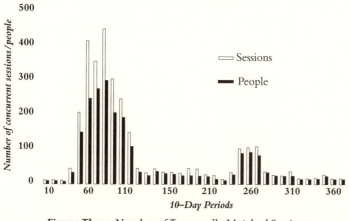

Figure Three: Number of Temporally Matched Sessions and People Over Diaries Epoch

- First, all sexual sessions involving only one person (e.g., solitary masturbation) were excluded, leaving 2783 sessions for 166 diarists.
- These sexual sessions occurred on a total of 359 days, with an average of 7.6 per day (and a maximum of 66).
- The maximum number of diarists reporting one or more session in any one day is forty, with an average of 5.4 diarists/day.
- A possible match consists of any *pair* of sessions which occurred on the same day and which could therefore represent the same session written from each partner's viewpoint. . .
- . . . but this means a large number of potential matches: for these data, either 15,938 matched sessions, or 14,374 potential partners; a truly impressive, but unrealistically large, number.

2.2.2.3. Behavioral Matching

Having established a potential match by temporal matching, the next stage consisted of matching a given session and a potential identically referring (matching) session by comparing the strings (encoded sequence of sex acts) embodying that session.

Before explaining this process, a brief excursus on the encoding of sexual behavior is in order (see Coxon et al. 1992).

2.2.2.3.1 Encoding the Sexual Session as a String

Diaries are initially written in everyday language according to a specified structure (see above). On receipt they are then encoded into a more efficient form as a quasi-linguistic string (Coxon et al. 1992). An example follows:

Diarist's Account:

We'd been drinking in a gay bar in Amsterdam, where we met. He was 30s, from Utrecht, into leather. We went back to my hotel room just after 1 a.m. and after sharing a joint, went to bed. . .

First we kissed, then I sucked him and he then sucked me and after that we moved into a '69' position and he came in my mouth. Then I moved to fuck him and he put a condom on me with KY over it. I entered him (him sitting on me) and he was wanking himself, and we started using poppers and I then came in him and then he came over my chest. After pulling out, we kissed for a while then went to sleep.

Encoding of Account
(PARTNER LIST) C3, 30s, male, Utrecht, into leather
(ANTECEDENTS) Met in gay bar, Amsterdam, drinking; shared marijuana. My hotel room, 13.00 26/8/88.

(encoded string of sex act sequence):
MDK AS PS MS,NM (AF,CN/l&HW,NI)/p MDK

The extended natural language description of the session is thus reduced to the code string (last line), used in all analysis programs.

There are several ways of now performing such a matching; one consists of defining a Levenshtein distance between two sequences (Sankoff and Kruskal 1983:18 et ff), but in this instance a related method was used which was developed in molecular biology for sequence homology searches (Feng et al. 1985).[21] These methods produce a score by which a match could be said to be made if it exceeds a stipulated limit. In brief, the sequence of sexual acts making up a session of the reference subject should be the same as the potential partner's session if it is to match. There are some difficulties and provisos which must be made. First, the respective *modalities* for any act must correspond rather than be identical (e.g., if the reference subject is *active* for a given act, the partner must be *passive* for it). Moreover, allowance had to be made for "chunking": some subjects make finer distinctions than others in describing a sequence. Finally, a "rarity" weighting was applied; some acts (e.g. "fisting," ano-brachial insertion) are very infrequent, and their occurrence therefore has a higher surprisal value.[22] Their occurrence is deemed more important in matching than common acts such as masturbation.

When comparison was also made of the content of the strings, the rate of matching reduced considerably: now only two percent of strings are matched as referring to the "same" session.[23]

Further descriptive information in the diary entries (e.g., the occupation of the partner, or whether drugs were used) can tighten up yet further the likelihood of partner identification, though this has not yet been done to any considerable extent.

2.2.2.4. Evaluating "Anonymous" Identification

At this juncture, little more can be said about the validity of the process: the matching certainly has face validity, but we cannot know that (for this data set) the match is correct, since it is a totally anonymous (unidentified) set of data. The next stage of validation will consist of testing whether the procedure can identify the (known) real partners from their session strings. In the meantime an interesting and potentially very important hypothesis arises concerning the "class of potential partners" in a known sexual session. Quite independently of the question of how to find the "real" partner—but assuming that s/he is in this class—how similar or homogeneous is the subset of candidates for being the partner? Do those engaging in the same (or structurally identical, or similar) sequences of sexual behavior resemble each other in other ways? In particular, is their pattern of other partners similar? If so, this will provide confirmation of the "like-me" characteristics of other social networks, and incidentally provide aggregate estimates of mixing for the Anderson models.[24]

In the meantime there are two ways in which this technique can lead to improved and more extensive matching:

- *"Coverage" should be as high as possible:* even when a match occurs there is a possibility that it is fallacious in the sense that partners *outside* the diary sample were actually involved and the temporal and behavioral matching was therefore purely coincidental. With higher proportions of the sexually active actually involved, this probability is decreased.
- *The date-limits of the diaries, should be as close to identical as possible,* i.e., if most respondents are completing their diaries over the same period, there is again a higher probability of correct matching.

Current research on the reliability and validity of the diary method and its use in this context is also helping to us to understand how and when two scripts or session-strings are to be considered identical.

3. CONCLUSIONS

In Project SIGMA we have tried at all times to keep the atom of social networks—the dyad—as our main unit, rather than the individual. Most obviously this means looking at (non-solitary) sexual behavior as being primarily the outcome of an interaction rather than as an individual propensity, as processes such as negotiation then become central to explaining what is occurring epidemiologically. The recent debate on so-called "relapse" provides a good instance of the difference that this makes in interpretation.

But the larger issues of networks also loom large, and we have to admit mixed success. This chapter has therefore been written in a self-critical mode, so that others can learn from our mistakes and successes. Given the unwillingness of funding agencies to underwrite some of the more ambitious proposals (very possibly with good reason), we have had to take a more pragmatic line than perhaps we would have wished. But the study has also shown us that a surprising amount can be done within the confines of a fairly conventional longitudinal study to examine network characteristics. For example, examination of triads of sexual and other interactions allows direct estimates to be made of transitivity and other "bias" parameters even if we know little about the detailed topology of the entire network. But equally there are some matters which, however difficult and expensive, can only be tackled by a direct, full-blown network methodology. It will be a tragedy if such work has to be abandoned in favor of a purely individual-based mode of enquiry and analysis which cannot represent these crucial aspects of transmission.

NOTES

1. I am grateful to the Department of Health and to the Medical Research Council funding which supports the work reported here; the views expressed are my own and do not necessarily represent those of the funding authorities. I am also especially grateful to Dr. Christopher Joyce (now Research Scientist, AIDS/HIV Division, Communicable Diseases Research Centre, Colindale, London) for his collaboration and work represented in section 2.2 of this paper.

2. The acronym SIGMA represents Socio-sexual Investigations of Gay Men and AIDS. Project SIGMA is a is a longitudinal, non-clinic based, serological and behavioral study of the sexual and social lifestyle of gay and bisexual men in England and Wales. (It is also part of the English study under the auspices of WHO Global Programme on AIDS Homosexual Response Studies).

   SIGMA is one of the largest cohort studies in Europe and the only study in the U.K. to have emerged from the gay community. Initial work began in 1983, and funding followed in 1987. To date, the Project has interviewed over one thousand men, half of whom have been interviewed four times at [median] intervals of ten months. The main aims of the study are to describe the sexual behavior and lifestyles of gay and bisexual men; to monitor changes in sexual behavior in relation to HIV/AIDS; to examine attitudes to different sexual behaviors and relationships; to investigate reactions to safer sex practices; to estimate prevalence of HIV and other viral infections in a non-clinic group of gay and bisexual men.

   Project SIGMA uses several complementary methods of obtaining information, including:

   • The detailed structured interview in which each respondent is asked for detailed information on sexual history and current practices (centered upon the Index of Sexual Behavior [Coxon et al. 1992]), numbers and characteristics (but not names) of sexual partners, health, and attitudes towards HIV and safer sex.

- The sexual diaries (Coxon 1988) are a daily record of sexual activity kept by respondents for a month after each interview. So far we have collected information on about thirty thousand sexual encounters which allows a unique analysis of their structure.

- Blood and/or saliva samples are also collected at the interview by trained staff and tested for HIV-1 antibodies and other viral markers. Results are available to respondents through trained counsellors.

- The postal survey of sexual behaviour is a self-completion questionnaire which appears in the gay press periodically.

3. "Close-knittedness" (although not Rapoport's term) is measured by the average rate of acquisition of new contacts, and the number of steps (links) necessary to reach exhaustion—the latter referred to as the "ultimate connectivity," the fraction of the population finally reached.

4. The two factors of Age and Relationship-type were trichotomized and crossed to produce the nine-fold typology. Age was split at twenty-one (the age of homosexual consent in England and Wales) and thirty-nine (after which men would have grown up when any homosexual behavior was illegal, before the 1967 Sexual Offences Act), and Relationship-type into Closed, Open and No Regular Relationship.

5. At a later stage we decided that the anonymity undertaking might be a case of shooting ourselves in the methodological foot (see the discussion in Coxon et al. 1993), but there were (and are) excellent reasons why gay men need to be persuaded that such information is safe and cannot be used against them.

6. Defined as the old county boundaries of the County of Glamorgan, but perhaps more accurately expressed as "Caerdydd a'r cylch"—Cardiff and the surrounding area.

7.   **"Parent" (p) bias:**   **Pr {xRy | yRx}, and**

   "Sibling" (s) bias: **Pr {xRy | ∃ z, zRx ∧ zRy}.**

   These combine with the actual outdegree ("axone density", **a**) to form the "Reduced axone density", a) by the following expression:

$$a = a - p - (a - 1) s$$

8. A.k.a. "tearooms" (USA) and "beats" (Australia), i.e., public toilets. Sub-projects of SIGMA and of the St. Mary's Paddington group studied this group in various locations—though many aspects were at variance with Humphreys' (1970) conclusions, especially about the considerable preponderance of heterosexually married men frequenting the cottages (though they are a significant fraction.) Although the sex which takes place is by and large safe, there are particular (often more deserted) ones where entirely unsafe sex is the norm.

9. Terminology referring to the modality of sexual behavior is confusing (see Coxon 1988; Coxon et al. 1992). Common medical usage is "inserter" vs. "insertee" (but this is useless for non-penetrative sexual behavior, such as masturbation); and "donor" vs. "recipient" assumes ejaculation. We prefer "active" vs. "passive," which is unambiguous and in common parlance among gay men. Following linguistic usage, the active partner *does X* to the other partner whilst the passive partner *has X done to him* by the other partner. Note that "inserter" is not necessarily equivalent to the "active" partner.

10. Present research suggests that it may well be highly infectious at particular stages, especially after infection and before sero-conversion; more worryingly, the same may be true of fellatio at this stage (see Koopman et al. 1992).

11. I.e. the "never fuck" category (0 link) is often more stable over time than the other individual roles (Coxon et al. 1993).

12. This shortcoming and ways to attempt to overcome it are described in Section Three.

13. Respondent fifteen is P as regards anal intercourse with men, but has active vaginal intercourse with a partner in London.

14. Analysis using UCINET-IV (v1.02) programs (Borgatti, Everett and Freeman 1992).

15. At later waves, this prohibition was relaxed, though not to any considerable extent, and it is still under discussion in the Project.

16. Together with information about the partnership—how long known, sexual in/exclusivity, number and sex of any other partners of the partner, and frequency of seeing.

17. The sexual diary data used were those obtained from the first *Gay Times* cohort, collected in 1986 and documented in Coxon 1990. The total data-set refers to 188 individuals, who performed 7532 sexual acts in an average of 23.4 sessions in the month.

18. The problem is not unusual in any matching context, but five characteristics of this sort are not usually enough fully to disambiguate different candidates.

19. A "sexual session" in the structure of sexual behavior developed by Project SIGMA (Coxon et al. 1992) is the main unit of such behavior: the "sentence" of sexual activity—self-sufficient and intrinsically well-formed. It occurs at a given (specified) time and place, consists of one or more sexual acts, and involves at least one, usually two (and sometimes more) people. It is typically terminated by sleep, a non-sexual intermission, or change of partner. The characteristics of a Sexual Session include four components: the *Setting,* the *Precedents* [e.g., prefatory drink, nitrites], the *Accompaniments* ["toys," leather], and the *Partner Specification* mentioned above, and the main content is the sequential specification of the components' sexual acts.

20. This figure plus or minus five percent holds for all the sexual diary data sets.

21. Which basically estimates the number of insertions and deletions necessary to turn one string into another.

22. A term borrowed from information theory (Luce 1960), where the "surprisal" of an act is inversely proportional to the frequency of its occurrence: $h_i = log_2 p_i.$

23. A total of 344 possible matches involving 298 individuals—i.e., a possible matching of 149 pairs of individuals from a total of 166 diarists.

24. Similar concerns, with a different methodology, have been expressed in the context of research on AIDS in Africa by Orubuloye, Caldwell, and Caldwell 1992.

Appendix One
Volume of Direct and Indirect Paths Between Points in Figure 1

PTS:	1	2	3	4	5	6	7	8	9	10	11	12	13	14
1	0	3	2	1	1	1	1	2	5	3	1	1	1	1
2	2	0	4	2	2	2	2	4	5	2	2	2	2	2
3	1	3	0	1	1	1	1	2	5	3	1	1	1	1
4	0	0	0	0	0	0	0	0	0	0	0	0	0	0
5	2	1	4	2	0	2	2	4	5	2	2	2	2	2
6	1	3	2	1	1	0	1	2	5	3	1	1	1	1
7	1	3	1	1	1	1	0	2	5	3	1	1	1	1
8	0	0	0	0	0	0	0	0	0	0	0	0	0	0
9	0	0	0	0	0	0	0	0	0	0	0	0	0	0
10	2	3	4	2	2	2	2	4	7	0	2	2	2	2
11	0	0	0	0	0	0	0	0	1	0	0	0	0	0
12	0	0	0	0	0	0	0	0	0	0	0	0	0	0
13	0	0	0	0	0	0	0	0	0	0	0	0	0	0
14	0	0	0	0	0	0	0	0	0	0	0	0	0	0

Patterns of Sexual Behavior of High Risk Populations and the Implications for STDs and HIV/AIDS Transmission in Nigeria   12

I.O. Orubuloye

IN 1982, WHEN AIDS WAS FIRST IDENTIFIED IN SUB-SAHARAN AFRICA, there was very little concern about the roads and the large number of people whose daily activities are connected with the transport/commercial industry. Hence, very little research has been done on transport and commercial networks and their relation to sexual activity, STDs and HIV transmission. The studies conducted so far have shown high levels of HIV incidence on the highways, and both the long distance haulage drivers and the women whose daily activities are connected with the transport/commercial system have been linked to high levels of transmission of STDs and AIDS (Tierney 1990).

Most earlier research on this subject concentrated on the eastern segment of the trans-African highways that run through the East and Central African countries, where AIDS was first identified in the continent. These studies reveal high levels of sexual partners and prevalence of HIV among the truck drivers and the women working along the highways when compared to the rest of the population (Nzyuko 1991). In Nigeria, as of June, 1992, about 207,357 blood samples had been taken from blood donors, drug abusers, commercial sex workers, and international travelers. Of the blood samples, 2,240 were reported positive for HIV infection, 379 had developed the disease; with the one percent prevalence, 400,000 adult Nigerians may currently be infected (Ransome-Kuti 1992). It would appear that Nigeria has entered into a major HIV/AIDS epidemic. Although the epidemic is not yet as grave as that in East, Central, and Southern Africa and some of the neighboring West African countries, it is beginning to attract public attention.

The Nigerian component of the sexual networking, STDs and HIV/AIDS transmission project was therefore designed with two ends in view (Orubuloye 1990):

1. If a major epidemic does develop (as would now appear to be the case) the necessary research for government policy in the area of sexual behavior will already have been done.
2. If a major epidemic does not develop, the research will be of basic social scientific value.

At the initial stage of the Nigerian research program, attention was focused on ascertaining the numbers of different sexual partners with whom individuals had relations over specific periods of time, on the identification of the different sexual partners by various characteristics, and on identification of their partners' partners (Orubuloye 1991). The decision to undertake research on the behavior of the truck drivers, the female hawkers and the female commercial sex workers in the clubs, bars and hotels arose from three considerations:

1. By 1991, HIV-positive truck drivers had been detected and there was beginning to be concern in the industry in Nigeria.
2. It was noticed that drivers, passengers, and other men who work in the lorry parks frequently make passes at the itinerant market women (hawkers), who provide services for them.
3. The female commercial sex workers experience high rates of partner change, and twenty percent of those in Lagos were, by 1991, found to be HIV-positive.

In Nigeria, driving and trading are one, and the lorry park or truck and bus stops, the bars and hotels, and the markets are adjacent. It was in this situation that the study of the Nigerian transport/commercial system was planned as part of a joint project of the Faculty of the Social Sciences, Ondo State University, Nigeria and the Health Transition Centre, Australian National University. The project aimed at understanding the transport and commercial networks and their relation to sexual activity, STDs, and HIV transmission. The following studies are reported here:

1. A study of long-distance haulage drivers.
2. A study of itinerant female hawkers in lorry parks and truck and bus stops carried out in June/July, 1991 in Ibadan, Nigeria's third largest city. Ibadan has traditionally been a major administrative, commercial, and transport node, where roads divide and lead to much of the rest of the country.
3. A study of commercial sex workers in two major urban centers in Ondo State.

THE LONG-DISTANCE TRUCK DRIVERS
In Nigeria, road transport has always been important. This importance was

further enhanced during the 1970s and early 1980s, as revenue from oil allowed governments to build many kilometers of modern highway from south to north and west-east, linking a number of towns and villages, thus providing several major commercial and transport nodes.

In June, 1991, we planned to interview all the long-distance haulage drivers who stop on Ibadan's Ring Road, near the junction with the highway North to Ilorin and beyond. At the junction, there is a night stop for long haulage drivers and their vehicles. Here, there are large numbers of huge trucks on both sides of the dual carriage-way for half a kilometer. There is a great deal of noise, movement of people and vehicles, music, dancing, drinking, and eating in the bars. Mechanics are everywere changing oil, tires, and carrying out repairs, while hawkers are selling goods to the drivers and their passengers.

Nine field assistants (three men and six women) were recruited and trained for the study. Three of them spoke Hausa fluently, two spoke Igbo, and all spoke Yoruba and English fluently. By the end of the third day, 258 drivers were successfully interviewed. The refusal rate was low and mainly from drivers who were in a hurry to reach their next destinations.

The characteristics of the drivers are presented in Table One. The average of the drivers is thirty-six years, while the minimum age reported is twenty years, two years higher than the minimum age required for obtaining a professional driving license. The majority are thirty to sixty years old.

The education of the drivers is low. Only one-tenth had more than primary school education, while more than two-fifths had no formal education. This figure is comparable to the one obtained in a study of long-distance haulage drivers a decade earlier (Ogunjemilua 1982). Two factors can explain the low education of the drivers. Until recently, no formal Western educational qualifications were required for obtaining a driver's license. The only requirement for the job was ability to pass a prescribed driving test and the subsequent possession of a valid driving license (Ogunjemilua 1982). The second reason is that nearly two-thirds of the drivers are from the north, where until recently the level of formal schooling was low. This is borne out in the ethnic and religious distribution of the drivers. Nearly four-fifths of the drivers are married, with one-half in polygnous marriages. Because of the high rate of re-marriage and polygyny, a small fraction are separated or divorced from their wives. The married men reported an average number of 5.2 surviving children. This figure does not in any way represent a completed family size, judging from an average of 1.7 wives reported by the men.

Only three-quarters were able to state their income, which ranged from N5.00 (fifty U.S. cents) to N200.00 (twenty U.S. dollars) per day with a mean of N42.00 (four U.S. dollars). The average income per day represents a high level in a country where the per capita income is low and where the minimum wage per month is about thirty U.S. dollars. Certainly the truck drivers are poorly paid, but they supplement their wages by carrying additional passengers and/or goods on their journeys. Such supplements may be small, but they represent a substantial part of the drivers' incomes, and make them financially more stable than their counterparts who work as laborers or as messengers in government establishments. The opportunity which the truck drivers have to supplement their incomes by picking up passengers and by carrying additional goods, plus the ebullient ways of life of the truck drivers, are major attractions to the profession.

Table One

Chracteristics of Long-Distance Haulage Drivers in Nigeria, 1991

Characteristic	Number	Percent
Age:		
20 – 34	87	34
30 – 60	156	61
Not stated	15	9
Education:		
No formal schooling	109	42
Primary only	117	45
Some secondary and above	28	11
Not stated	4	2
Ethnic group:		
Hausa	149	58
Yoruba	81	31
Igbo	21	8
Edo	4	2
Not stated	3	1
Religion:		
Christianity	48	19
Islam	210	81
Marital Status:		
Single	51	20
Now Married	203	79
Divorced/Separated	4	2
Type of Marriage		
Monogamous	104	51
Polygynous	99	49

By Nigerian standards, the truck drivers are well off. The majority of the drivers, eighty-five percent, owned the appropriate E class drivers license required for driving articulated trailers, semi-trailers, and tankers used for hauling goods. The drivers had been driving for between one and forty years with an average of fourteen years. More than one-half drove the articulated trailers and semi-trailers, and one-tenth the tankers. Approximately one-quarter are lorry drivers, while the remainder drove buses and cars. The goods which they carried range from petrol to food, animals, and building materials.

In Nigeria, long-distance haulage driving is a way of life, and the drivers spend much of their lives on the road. A single journey to their destinations takes an average of three nights and four days and a return journey eight nights and nine days. Approximately three-quarters spent less than two weeks away from their families, while the remaining one-quarter spent two weeks or more. At every night stop, the drivers expect a minimum standard of comfort: good food, drink, a place to sleep when night falls. Buildings and shacks which provide these services develop along these night stops. The women who work at these night stops, the commercial sex workers and the young female hawkers who sell their goods to the drivers and their passengers, also provide company and sex to the drivers.

SEXUAL NETWORKING, STD, HIV/AIDS

The main thrust of the drivers study is to investigate whether the transport and commercial system has certain characteristics that make it also an STDs, HIV/AIDS infection system, thus rendering the system dangerous, for those who work on the roads in particular and for the society in general. Therefore, the extent of sexual networking was investigated by asking the drivers to indicate their number of sexual partners, apart from their spouses, over specific periods of time and at each stopping place on route to their destinations. The drivers were also asked whether they know the partners of their partners, how many they are, their age, marital status, occupation, ethnic group, and where they live. Table Two shows the average number of the drivers' sexual partners beyond their wives over specific periods of time and at each stop. They reported an average number of four current sexual partners, and a lifetime average of sixteen partners.

Most drivers make three night stops before they reached their destination, and they reported an average of one partner per stop. This corresponds with the average current number of sexual partners reported, and is slightly higher than the figures reported for a more homogenous and sedentary population (Orubuloye, Caldwell, and Caldwell 1991).

Table Two
Different Sexual Partners Over Specific Periods of Time

Periods	All Respondents		Respondents who report at least one Partner	
	Number	*Mean*	*Number*	*Mean*
Current	232	3.5	220	3.7
Last Month	232	3.3	225	3.5
Last Year	226	6.1	222	6.7
Lifetime	208	15.5	208	15.5
Stopping Place				
1st	165	1.7	165	1.7
2nd	126	1.3	136	1.3
3rd	81	1.3	81	1.3
4th	45	1.3	45	1.3
5th	30	1.0	30	1.0

Only one-third of the drivers reported that they knew the partners of their partners, with three-quarters reporting more than one such partner, the majority of whom are drivers, single, and with an average age of thirty-one years, five years younger than the drivers themselves. Certainly, this is an explosive situation which poses great danger to the more sedentary population the drivers go back to at the end of each trip. Nearly all the drivers have heard of venereal diseases, mostly gonorrhea and syphilis, the two most noticeable and widely reported venereal diseases in Nigeria (Webb, Ladipo, and McNamara 1991). Forty percent of the drivers, and forty-two percent of those who have heard of venereal diseases, reported that they had suffered and had been treated mostly for gonorrhea and syphilis. However, seventy-seven percent of the drivers were certain that their partners had been treated for gonorrhea, syphilis and what they described as itching. One-tenth of the drivers knew at least one person who had been treated for AIDS, of whom the majority are males and close relations or friends of the drivers.

THE ITINERANT FEMALE HAWKERS

Hawking is a feature of most Nigerian cities. In southern Nigeria, the young men hawk along the major highways and where traffic is held-up in the cities, while the young girls hawk in the lorry parks or at the pick-up stops along the road. In the rural areas, hawking is done by both boys and girls and from one door step to another. Their wares consist mainly of food items—particularly cooked food. An increasing number of them now sell goods such as cosmetics, clothes, and plastic bags. In June/July of 1991, we interviewed 467 female itinerant hawkers in the lorry parks and at the roadside stopping places in Ibadan. All female hawkers found in each place were

Table Three
Characteristics of Itinerant Female Hawkers in Nigeria, 1991

Characteristic	Number	Percent
Age:		
10 – 19	249	53
20–40	218	47
Education:		
No formal schooling	63	14
Primary only	190	41
Some secondary and above	190	41
Not stated	24	5
Ethnic group:		
Yoruba	406	87
Igbo	28	6
Others	33	7
Religion:		
Christianity	202	43
Muslim	254	54
Traditional	11	7
Marital Status:		
Never Married	331	71
Now Married	125	27
Separated/Divorced/Widowed	9	2
Not Stated	2	0
Type of Marriage		
Monogamous	68	54
Polygynous	57	46

interviewed by six young female interviewers who had earlier taken part in the drivers survey and who are of the same age range as most of the hawkers. Although the hawkers were mobile, they have specific lorry parks and bus stops where they sell to their customers, who are mainly drivers and passengers. Care was taken to prevent accidental reinterviews by assigning one interviewer to one lorry park or bus stop. The characteristics of the hawkers are shown in Table Three. The hawkers were young, with average age of 19.7 years. The minimum age was ten while the maximum was forty years, with fifty-three percent below the age of twenty years. Even by Nigerian standard, the hawkers were well educated. Only fourteen percent had no formal schooling, while some forty-one percent had proceeded beyond the primary school level.

Certainly they are products of the 1979-83 Free and Universal Secondary Education system introduced in Southwest Nigeria. The program has been abandoned since 1984. The introduction of the Structural Adjustment Program in 1986 brought charges back in the schools. A majority of the hawkers are Yoruba, the major ethnic group in Ibadan, or from a small but significant Igbo community who are traditionally both itinerant and sedentary traders. While seventy-one percent of the traders were single, twenty-nine percent were currently married, of whom forty-six percent were in polygynous unions. Partly because of a high rate of re-marriage and mainly because of old age, a small fraction was separated or divorced or widowed.

The average period of hawking for all respondents is slightly above four years with just three percent who had been hawking for more than ten years. Of the married women, only twenty-seven percent had a common budget with their husbands. This can be interpreted to mean that their husbands actually provided the initial capital for the trade. The articles of trade ranged from cooked food, to cosmetics and plastic bags, to chewing gum and iced water. Most hawkers sold one or two items, but they all together sold a total of 130 different items. They earned very little income from retailing, and most of the younger girls were forced to sell their goods for only a little more than they paid for them. Quite often they supplemented their income by selling sex to the drivers and other men connected with the transport system in the lorry parks and bus stops.

SEXUAL NETWORKING AND KNOWLEDGE OF STDs AND AIDS

One of the reasons why the hawkers study was undertaken was our observation that the drivers, the passengers and other men who work in the lorry parks and bus stops frequently make passes at the young girls. Four-fifths of the hawkers reported that men frequently make passes at them. Of this group, seventy-one percent were single while twenty-nine percent were married. These figures represent eighty and seventy-eight percent of all never-married and ever-married women respectively. The mean age of first sexual experience is sixteen years, about one and a half years earlier than the figure observed for a more sedentary population in an earlier study. Only five percent had never experienced sex, fifteen percent of first sexual experiences were within marriage, and a further fourteen percent with people the hawkers described as either a fiancé or with whom marriage agreements had been concluded. The remaining seventy percent were with friends, mostly drivers, teachers, and male hawkers. Although a majority of the hawkers reported that their first sexual experience occurred in friendly circumstances, it is significant that sixteen percent were forced into sex.

The respondents reported their current average number of sexual partners as 2.3 and lifetime partners as 3.8. Given the average age and marital status of the hawkers, the figures are quite large. On the question of contraception, forty-nine percent employed some form of of it during their first sexual experience but only thirty-one percent of these are efficient methods. Of these, sixty-one percent reported use of condoms and thirty percent, use of the pill. The other methods range from local gins to lemon drinks and local herbs. However nearly two-thirds reported that they were currently practicing contraception. This massive increase was probably propelled by the recent program of contraceptive distribution by market women in Ibadan (Webb, Ladipo, and McNamara 1991). Three-fifths reported that they knew the sexual partners of their male friends. One-fifth of the women reported that they had been treated for venereal diseases, mostly gonorrhea or what they described as itching and discharge. This level corresponds with the figure previously reported from other surveys in Nigeria.

Nearly all the respondents had heard of AIDS, with radio and television being cited as the major sources of information. (The school has played a limited role as a source of information, while newspapers were hardly mentioned.) There has been an increasing spread of electronic media (particularly the radio) in Nigeria since the oil boom of the 1970s. In market places, lorry parks, bars, and bus stops, the radio and record players not only provide music and dancing, but are used by the vendors and drivers to attract buyers and passengers. Life in the lorry parks is tough and sometimes hazardous.

COMMERCIAL SEXUAL RELATIONS

The major towns in Nigeria contain a number of small and medium hotels, bars, and night clubs where young women offer sex for payment. The women, who were mostly migrants, deserted or divorced wives and usually mothers, were unlikely to be recognized by people from their home area and thus would not jeopardize their chances for marriage or for returning to respectable motherhood (Orubuloye, Caldwell, and Caldwell 1992). Quite often, their children were left with their maternal grandmothers, who expected financial contributions for their upkeep.

The hotels, bars, and night clubs are entertainment centers where commercial sex workers mix with the customers, drinking, eating, and dancing with them. The hotels also provide accomodation for men who bring in their own girlfriends for short or long time lodging. The hotels provide an environment for non-institutional commercial sex workers who come to solicit for customers.

Commercial sex workers charge different rates depending on the status of, and their special interest in, the customers. In the lean periods, prices are considerably reduced, while higher prices are charged for the weekend or special occasions including moving out of a hotel. Although these young women in the hotels and bars are often happy about their situation, they would prefer to establish some kind of trade or secure office position and move on to more stable marital relationships. It is in the light of these preliminary observations in Ado Ekiti (Orubuloye, Caldwell, and Caldwell 1992) that a survey of commercial sex workers was undertaken in Ondo town and Okitipupa in 1991 as part of a larger ongoing research program on sexual networking (Orubuloye 1991).

Ondo town is a major commercial center on the direct road south from Ile-Ife, with a population of around two hundred and fifty thousand. Okitipupa, with a population of around one hundred thousand, is the major commercial hinterland that serves the coastal district of Ondo State.

A survey of all hotels, bars, and clubs was undertaken in Ondo town and Okitipupa. This yielded population sizes of institutional commercial sex workers of ninety-eight and forty-seven for Ondo and Okitipupa, respectively. These figures fall short of the probable number of commercial sex workers in the two towns. Most commercial sex workers do not work from any institutional base. The non-institutional sex workers are more likely to be young, single traders, or school-girls and students who need additional income to supplement the income from their parents.

Table Four
Chracteristics of Commercial Sex Workers in Ondo Town and
Okitipupa (Percentage Distribution)

	Ondo Town N = 98	Okitipupa N = 47
Mean Age:	33.0	33.04
Education:		
None	4	6
Primary only	42	44
Secondary and above	54	50
Marital Status:		
Never Married	58	25
Married	42	46
Divorced/Separated	—	29
Ethnic Group		
Igbo	36	25
Edo/Urohbo	18	75
Yoruba	36	—
Hausa and Tiv	10	—

The characteristics of the commercial sex workers are shown in Table Four. As shown in the Table, the commercial sex workers were well experienced and well educated, with about one-half proceeding beyond the primary school level. The majority of the women in Ondo were single, while those of Okitipupa were married, divorced, or separated. In terms of ethnicity, all the women in Okitipupa were migrants, mostly Edo from Edo State, to the east of Ondo State. One-third of the women in Ondo town were Yoruba, probably from other Yoruba towns than Ondo. This is a reflection of the urban and commercial status of the town. Ondo is large and heterogeneous enough to accomodate women from other Yoruba towns and villages, who were unlikely to be recognized by people from their home area.

A battery of questions was asked of the women to elicit the economic component of commercial sex. The results are shown in Table Five. The most striking aspect of the results was the similarity in the average number of customers, charges per customer and daily earnings.

From the information supplied, it would appear that the women in Ondo were better off than their counterparts in Okitipupa. The expenditure incurred by each commercial sex worker is difficult to estimate. However, the hotel where they were lodged charge five naira per day, while each woman made a daily savings of five naira per day. The remaining fifteen naira was spent on food, clothing, and medical care. Drinks were usually supplied by their male partners. Although the average monthly income of each commercial sex worker was about four hundred naira (forty U.S. dollars), it was certainly higher than the minimum wage in the public sector of the economy. The role of commercial sex in the national income should therefore not be underestimated.

Table Five
Average Number of Commercial Sex Worker's Customers and Income

	Ondo Town N = 98	Okitipupa N = 47
Average number of customers per day	7	5
Average number of customers per week	40	35
Average cost per customer	N5	N6
Average income per day	N25	N25
Average income per week	N129	N92

On the question of whether the women knew most of their customers, a majority of them thought that they did. This is probably the case because the hotels and bars tend to be general entertainment centers in which the women mix with the customers and the men often come back repeatedly to their favorite girls (Orubuloye, Caldwell, and Caldwell 1992).

CONCLUSION
This study reveals that the number of sexual partners of the truck drivers, the itinerant female hawkers, and the commercial sex workers is high and probably higher than that of the population around them. This would appear to pose a serious danger not only to them but to the entire society. Sex is hardly

protected by the use of condoms, and many continued to suffer from sexually transmitted diseases because they seek inappropriate and inefficient treatment. The whole transport/commercial/sexual system is best understood within the context of the nature of the society and the economics of sexual relations. Polygyny on the scale still reported in Nigeria has inevitably taught men to believe that relations with one woman are not part of man's nature. The practice of post-partum sexual abstinence makes women unavailable for sex for a considerable length of their reproductive lives. Hence, most men in monogamous marriages continue to look for other sexual partners outside marriage when their spouses are undergoing the prescribed post-partum abstinence period and/or when they are away from home. Some of these relationships are with commercial sex workers, who always have large numbers of different sexual partners and who stand a greater risk of catching STDs and AIDS.

The present economic difficulties facing Nigeria, like most of the countries in Africa, and the consequent Structural Adjustment Program (SAP) have pushed many poor families into sending their young women to the streets, lorry parks/bus stops, and to the bars and hotels looking for money to supplement family income. Because of the poor capital outlay of female hawkers, the rewards do not come quickly, thus putting pressure on the young women to offer sex in return for money. The distinction between the drivers' partners on the highways, the itinerant female hawkers and commercial sex workers is slight. Hence, the risk of being infected with STDs and HIV is high. Although the sexual behavior of the truck drivers, the passengers, the female hawkers, the commercial sex workers, and the other women at the roadside is a way of life special to the highway, it has serious implications for the larger society. Therefore, the ongoing safe sex campaigns on the major highways should be intensified among other high risk populations in Nigeria.

THE SOCIAL CONSTRUCTION OF SEXUAL RISK

Part
Five

The Construction of Risk in AIDS Control Programs

Theoretical Bases and Popular Responses

Carl Kendall

THE PAPERS IN THIS VOLUME DEMONSTRATE the rich historical and social dimensions of the construction of sexuality. Long avoided in scientific literatures, sexuality was an implicit or explicit part of literary, moral, religious, and even architectural writings. In essays here, authors have been able to demonstrate the ways in which these constructions not only attempted to envelope and tame the sexual, but the ways in which sexuality itself was transformed and created by these constructs.

Relatively unexplored in the sciences, sexuality was often treated as a biological conundrum. This confounding of sex and sexuality lent itself to the naturalistic pretensions of science, which could then reject social, artistic, and literary constructions. This attitude is even now found commonly among AIDS basic science researchers, and visible in their rejection of the plasticity of human sexual behavior implicit in the success of condom promotion programs for HIV prevention.

Another important theme has been the challenge to create a study of sexuality in its own right, rather than the studying of sexual behavior as part of STD or HIV control programs. As has often been pointed out (see, for example, Parker 1987, 1989; Parker, Herdt, and Carballo 1991), epidemiologists or other social or natural scientists who have studied sexuality over the course of the HIV epidemic have not appreciably advanced the field of sexuality research.

Although I am sympathetic to arguments made by colleagues in this stigmatized field of research, I am also made uncomfortable with the categorization of knowledge by the commonplace academic divisions of the university: arts and history vs. science; social vs. natural science; and qualitative vs. quantitative methods. To state the obvious, human sexuality has multiple dimensions—biological, psychological, physiological, social, cultural, and economic—and is informed and shaped by popular discourse as well as by science. This interaction or reflexivity between the sciences, particularly the social sciences, and public behavior and discourse has been discussed by Giddens (see Giddens 1984:xvi,xxii–iii) and others. It follows that basic concepts of public health, such as risk, are reflexively considered in popular discourse, shape behavior, and are reflected in new expert system explanations of risk and behavior (see Yates and Stone 1992). "Risk," then, formerly in the domain of epidemiology, can only be defined in a multidisciplinary sense as a socially constructed concept—which must be historically situated, particularly in relation to the study of human sexuality (see, for example, Connors 1992; McCoy and Inciardi 1993; McGrath and Rwabukwale 1993; Parker 1987, 1992).

This essay explores "risk" not from the perspective of epidemiology, but from the perspective of the social sciences, first as it is discussed by two major social theorists, and then as it is used as a popular category. It concludes with a brief list of diverse, socially defined "risk" categories that could be used in categorizing perceived risk beyond the "high" and "low" now found universally in the epidemiological literature on AIDS. At the same time, it demonstrates how understanding these local categories would require substantial investigation that would, in turn, expand our knowledge of sexual risk-taking and sexuality in general.

EPIDEMIOLOGICAL CONSTRUCTION OF RISK

Risk is a key concept crucial to public health and epidemiology. Risk is used to describe the differential morbidity or mortality pattern associated with a given hazard or behavior. Technically, the term risk refers to excess morbidity or mortality associated with exposure to an environment, condition, or pathogen.

But these simple definitions should make obvious a weakness in the expert definition of risk. Clearly a model of the body and environment, of healthy and unhealthy, normal and abnormal, must underlie the design and analysis of these expert studies. How are the myriad elements of behavior or an environment winnowed down for inclusion or exclusion in a study? How is spurious correlation dealt with?

Risk is also a portmanteau category used to describe behaviors commonly associated with illness, whether, in a particular case, they produce illness or not. Risk is also used to rank and prioritize illnesses and health conditions within the health sector, and to promote healthy behaviors to the public. As can be imagined with concepts as central as risk, its meaning is rarely explored directly. This makes some sense in traditional epidemiological literature where a precise calculation can define it, but makes little sense when this same literature talks about people engaged in "risky" behavior or "taking risks." The simple observation that technically defined risk (i.e., risk as a knowledge category produced in epidemiological expert systems) and popularly perceived risks must differ—although recognized in public health—seems to many public health practitioners to be a matter of lack of information or skills, not an actual subject for investigation.

The traditional way that health education is structured is to identify in the expert literature the risks to be avoided, i.e., behaviors or environments associated with transmission. This compilation of risks (such as anal intercourse without a condom), is constructed with the results of both retrospective and prospective studies, and practical knowledge accumulated through medical experience or experiments (as with condoms and the virus). This risk is then communicated to the public.

An example will help clarify this discussion. In one study conducted in San Francisco and Oakland (Eversley et al. 1993) the researchers concretely defined risk as:

- Having an intravenous drug user as a partner.
- Vaginal sex with other than primary partner.
- Five or more partners in past five years.
- History of an STD.
- Primary partner has other partner.

Subjects were also asked if they perceived themselves at risk. The authors comment:

> Perceiving oneself at risk was significantly associated with having sex outside of a primary relationship in the past year, with having five or more sexual partners in the last five years, and with having a primary partner who has other partners. We found no significant relationship between perceiving oneself at risk and adopting risk reduction strategies, such as inquiring about a partner's risks or using condoms. (Eversley et al. 1993:92)

Although the authors conclude that this data represents the need for "risk communications skills" for women, the findings can be interpreted in another way. Certainly some of the participants in the study may have shared the expert system view that some of the behaviors they practiced were "risky," although they may not have understood the epidemiological basis for that concern. On the other hand, the behaviors that were identified as "risky" are also proscribed behaviors in other domains, such as the moral or relational, and relate to the social appropriateness of certain kinds of behaviors and relationships or relationships of power within the relationship. These behaviors would be "risky" in this sense as well.

The second observation of the study—that this popular recognition of risk was not associated with risk reduction behaviors on the part of the partici-pants—is also widely reported in the literature. Information about risky HIV-linked behaviors is very widespread, yet acted on only in certain circum-stances. In this particular case, risk reduction behaviors were defined as:

- Has asked previous partner about number of previous partners.
- Has asked a partner about I.V. drug use.
- Always uses a condom with other partners.

But one can see that there are many conventional, non-disease related reasons why these events may not occur. One can see how these behaviors identified with risk reduction by an epidemiologist may not be perceived as the same by participants in the study, but might even augment social and physical risk. Participants may not be impeded by poor skills in communi-cating (a catchall phrase itself), but rather by social, power, and conventional constraints on behavior within relationships.

SOCIAL SCIENCE DISCUSSIONS OF RISK

Ordinarily papers that discuss HIV risk have little resort to social theory. Even when researchers acknowledge the social construction of illness cate-gories, this literature, which seems too abstract and theoretical, is little cited. This is unfortunate, since social theory embodies and manifests concern for epistimology and ontology that lie at the core of social science disquiet with the biomedical construction of illness categories. Social theory also usefully summarizes decades of debate about major conceptual postures—such as the role and significance of the concept of the individual—that have enormous signficance for the design of HIV prevention programs. I will try to illustrate these points.

Risk has been a touchpoint for arguments that illuminate theoretical postures for both Mary Douglas and Anthony Giddens. Risk is the starting point for discussions that bring social theory to bear on explanations of popular use and understanding of risk. Their positions also frame competing approaches, one focused on the individual and the other, the community, that bracket interventions and behavioral science research on AIDS.

Giddens argues that the construction of risk as a concept is a recent event, a manifestation of modernism which overlays such traditional concepts as fate, fortuna, and destiny (see Giddens 1991). Giddens argues that fate and destiny (the former associated with death and the latter with birth) are associ-ated with ultimate outcomes over which the individual has little control (Giddens 1991:109). Fate, argues Giddens, undergoes transitions, first in the pre-modern era to fortuna, linked to the Christian ideal of divine providence and associated with a notion that individual behavior will affect ultimate outcomes, and finally in the modern secular era to the calculated probabilities embodied in the term *risk* as used by epidemiologists. Although Giddens is willing to see that expert notions of risk are continuously compromised by residual meanings, he implies that expert system concepts, in their scope, explanatory power, and manifestation, are distinctly different from traditional, pre-modern concepts. This disjunction between pre-modern and modern is essential for Giddens, who argues that the pace and scope of change in the world have created a sharp disjunction between present and past, and that this disjunction has created new and modern sensibilities.

Mary Douglas, on the other hand, and looking backward, argues a theme first presented in *Purity and Danger*, where her goal was to "vindicate the so-called primitives from the charge of having a different logic or method of thinking" (Douglas 1992:3). While science argued from effects to material causes, primitives were accused of arguing from spiritual causes. Even when these causes were functionally deciphered by anthropologists as concerns about societal norms and duties they still demonstrated a politicized and moralized "cause," and thus a distinctive mentality that rejected objectivism and materialism. Mary Douglas then argues the obvious point that contemporary science is a politicized and moralized social activity, and that current constructions of risk, even in their scientific manifestations, are profoundly similar to primitive constructions when they are used, perceived, and applied (Douglas 1992).

The issue is not the claim to the objectivity and truth value of science, since neither author would care to argue that point in relation to the concept of risk, but rather the role of psychology and internal, mentalistic, representations. For Giddens the role of the self and the apotheosis of individual consciousness embody the reflexive project of modernity. This, along with the disembedding of local institutions associated with the modern state, leads Giddens to focus on the individual and the self, even if his earlier works discussed structure incessantly. Structuration theory is, after all, a way to link the discussion of macrosociological structure to that active agent, the self (see Giddens 1984). Society itself, Giddens, argues, is nothing but the continuous re-creation of structure by the individual. Giddens discusses these issues with reference to an idiosyncratic psychology that has led him to write several volumes on the self and modernity.

Mary Douglas, on the other hand, archly rejects what she terms "individual cognition" attribution theory, i.e., psychology. Focusing on the structure of society, community, and culture, she draws little distinction between previous and current manifestations of risk—between risk and taboo—and she gives no prominence to an individuated perspective. As she puts it, "all cognition is politicized," and turns to the description of communities of power and suffering. One can substitute "lay persons" for "pre-moderns" or "primitives" to see that the relevance of these two positions can be found represented in the literature on AIDS and behavior.

As shown in the discussion above, AIDS prevention focuses on convincing people to either reduce or avoid situations or behaviors that enhance the risk for transmission of HIV. Although these efforts have met with success in populations of intravenous drug users and gay populations, they are not considered to have been successful in many other populations. Undoubtedly these intervention efforts are as far advanced as smoking cessation or dietary modification for coronary heart disease were after five years of effort. Still, some of the difficulty of assigning success or failure to programs is due to the failure to recognize the committments to social and psychological theory embedded in their evaluations.

As the article by Yates and Stone (1992) cited earlier demonstrates, health education consists of "information" from the expert system transmitted to communities with different contexts for interpretation. From the perspective of the individual, we have little in the way of an adequate theory of sex or intimacy through which to understand the interpretation of these behavioral prescriptions. From the perspective of the community, we have both little in the way of social theory to account for community development and change in the modern era, and little purview in evaluation to explore relationships that extend beyond program participants and inputs to understand the community construction of a response to threats and interventions.

These are among the reasons that the process of communicating risks is not straightforward. Although experts in epidemiology may argue for a message that intends to say "the risk of acquiring HIV is enhanced if anal intercourse is practiced without a condom, or that a condom, if used correctly, and if it doesn't break, appears to provide enhanced protection," the reality is that the message is interpreted to mean something else (i.e., "safe sex") or is not acted upon until a process of community sanctioning has made it acceptable. The understanding often generated by the message in populations is that a contrast needs to be drawn between risky (i.e., "dangerous") sex and "safe" sex, between risky and non-risky individuals, and between high-risk and low-risk or not-at-risk (!) populations.

Secondly, although health education is often couched as if information is what was needed to bring about behavior change, that rarely is the case. The literature on family planning education often discusses a KAP-GAP, or a gap between expressed knowledge and attitudes, on the one hand, and practices on the other. Where the source of this resistance lies is at the heart of continuing debates to shape prevention interventions. Is it in the individual, lodged in personal history and proclivities, or does it lie elsewhere? Theories common to behavior change in psychology, such as the theory of reasoned action, the health belief model, or stages of change, are clinical models and place this locus in the individual constructed as agent. These theories have clear links to Gidden's work. Consequently, what's missing is an effort to reflexively place the discourse of safe sex, and of rapidly changing individual behavior in response to risk profiling, in its social and community context.

Mary Douglas accomplished some of this task in her article, "The Self as Risk-Taker: A Cultural Theory of Contagion in Relation to AIDS" (Douglas 1992). Here, she first attacks "established theories of individualistic psychology" (Douglas 1992:102). Although she acknowledges the empirical research conducted in psychology, she rejects the "intuitive, subjective sources" of these empirical categories (Douglas 1992: 103). Douglas comments:

> If a person is heard to reject advice about safety and to take grave risks in the name of this knowledge of his own self, the evidence about himself is stronger than anything which he puts on record replying to questionnaires and doing tests in the psychological laboratory: stronger because the person is putting his life where his mouth is. When action and talk support each other, you have something to go on. (Douglas 1992:103)

So much for the KAP-GAP.

Douglas goes on to argue that the self and community are reciprocal notions. These community identities which define responses to AIDS are expressed in terms of varying constructions of the body, of contagion, and of the status of professional advice. Her arguments are linked to new approaches to behavior change that focus on community norms and sanctions. The four communities she identifies: the center, the dissenting enclave—in this case the homosexual community—the individualist or entrepreneurial community, and the "community" of isolates, define sharply different patterns of response to the epidemic. She concludes:

> . . .dialogue about infection follows the dialogue about the community's cultural project. The centre community and the homosexual enclaves both develop faith in an immunity conferred by a territorial community envelope. Both are indeed tempted to pay more attention to protecting the community envelope than to protect the vulnerable points of access in the body itself. The centre community uses this confidence combined with a profession of risk-aversion to control its periphery. The enclave uses it to justify a risk-taking attitude towards dealing with fellow members of the community. (Douglas 1992:119)

The history of the course of the epidemic in the United States, particularly in San Francisco, would seem to support these comments. Within this dissenting enclave, the response to the epidemic is political. Within the body politic, there is no unitary risk community, but a fragmented response. Her conclusion that "the conscience of the central community is not essentially compassionate to all the citizenry" (Douglas 1992: 120) is particularly apt.

But can behaviors associated with response to the epidemic be so neatly accounted for by this quadrapartite distinction? First, the argument appears cavalier in its assumptions about "community" and community identities. Implicit in the construction of non-center communities is the personal political priority of community membership. Is a dissenting, well-organized gay community necessary? No, this would be true only in an environment of sexual repression. And "communities" of individualists and isolates look more like portmanteau categories than "communities." The overlay of the four communities and patterns of response does not have a necessary character. Although interesting avenues for research are suggested, such as the link between alternative sexual identities and community, we must still wonder about the utility and efficacy of these community-based interventions in other, more fragmented, population groups.

More importantly, it appears that couples' responses to the epidemic have an individuated and particularistic character. Risk is constructed and considered by individuals, and with partners, as well as by communities. This can be illustrated by exploring popular conceptions of risk, in the epidemiological literature and in the behavioral science literature on AIDS.

POPULAR CATEGORIES OF RISK

Baseline or involuntary risk.[1] Living is a risky endeavor. Risk provides no solace, as do the concepts of fate or destiny, and life is a complicated balancing act of benefit and risk. Pleasure and desire must be balanced against risk, and choices are never unitary. Baseline risk is never zero, although the center community sometimes talks and acts as if risk can be avoided altogether.

Institutionally structured risk environments. We commonly accept a high level of risky behavior in our daily lives. We drive, for example, or expose ourselves to cigarette smoke, or live sedentary lives in offices. These don't often appear as "choices" or options, because they're common. However, these risks are not constant, and human populations do accept high levels of risk as "normal" if they are shared by others. The willingness of populations to have unprotected sex in risky settings is sometimes perceived as normal. In a recent study in Thailand, more than eighty percent of Thai males reported using prostitutes in the past six months (Havanon et al. 1992). Such use is not seen as particularly risky. Many other examples from the AIDS epidemic, such as use of contaminated blood products, builds risk into an institutional setting over which the individual has little control. Medical anthropology has extensively chronicled similar processes in studies of diarrheal diseases, acute respiratory diseases, and many other common infectious diseases.

Additive risks. Risks do not exist in isolation from other risks, but are cumulative. Street-children in Brazil not only need to worry about the risk of transmission of HIV, but also simple survival, either from the predations of each other or authorities, or from the dangers inherent in stealing to eat. Their primary risk is their marginal social position, from which others follow. The same is true for other "high-risk" groups. A hierarchy of risks and the social context of risk are rarely presented in discussions of risk or in responses to health education programs.

Negotiated risks. The issue of relapsing high-risk behavior in the AIDS epidemic is sometimes confused with that of negotiated risk. A couple may decide to accept each other's word that they are seronegative and have no other partners. The couple do not feel that their unprotected sex is risky, and the risk, if felt, is the risk that one or both of the partners are lying. At stake may be the character and quality of their relationship, rather than concerns about health.

Time out behavior: voluntary risk. Much high risk behavior is associated with a strategy of temporary or time-out risk taking. What's the chance of transmission of HIV if you have high-risk sex once? What's the balance of risks for low incidence, high-risk events?

Eroticized risk. Clearly, risk-taking is attractive to many and heightens their appreciation of the behavior.

CONCLUSIONS

This list is far from exhaustive. However, it does demonstrate that risk as a concept is more complicated than most current epidemiological construc-tions, and resonates with both substantive and methodological concerns of the social sciences, including the study of sexuality. The themes preferred by Giddens and Douglas, one focusing on individual as agent, and one focusing on community and norms, are at the core of theoretical debates about behavior change and health communication.

The community of meaning, the creation and changing of norms, the relationships of class and power, the two-dimensionality of self are necessary foci for theories of behavior change and health communication, as well as of sexuality, and, as yet, are little studied. Community (albeit the community of action sets), networks, and the communion created in high-risk locales, recruitment to and formation of groups, the creation of individual and group identity, and the transformation of institutions need to be themes for those who study and intervene in the field of sexual behavior. There is also an active agent, both public and intimate, at the core of all action, especially sexual behavior, and researchers and public health authorities need to recognize the complex interaction of community and personality.

I hope I have laid to rest the concern that applied research would provide little opportunity for exploration of sexuality or social theory. A research program that begins with the tortured and painful construction of sexual risk and blame in the time of AIDS can be the basis of powerful insights into human behavior, and of a growing acceptance of our need to positively shape it.

NOTES

1. I would like to thank Dr. Ron Stall, Center for AIDS Prevention Studies, University of California, San Francisco, for his help with this section.

Women's Lives and Sex   14
Implications for AIDS Prevention

Geeta Rao Gupta and Ellen Weiss

ACCORDING TO THE WORLD HEALTH ORGANIZATION (WHO), over fourteen million people worldwide have been infected with the human immunodeficiency virus (HIV), the etiological agent which causes AIDS (WHO 1993). At present, it is estimated that women constitute forty percent of the global total of adult HIV infections (Mann et al. 1992). In Sub-Saharan Africa, equal numbers of men and women are infected, and in Asia and Latin America, the HIV gender gap is closing as the number of women infected rapidly increases (Mann et al. 1992). By the mid-1990s, therefore, it is believed global adult HIV infections of women will equal that of men (Mann 1993).

To control the spread of the epidemic, current AIDS prevention programs emphasize four behavioral recommendations: condom use, mutual monogamy, partner reduction, and treatment for other sexually transmitted diseases (STDs). In order to promote behavioral change, prevention programs use a variety of communication channels such as mass media, printed material, peer educators, and health professionals. Typically, these communication channels are used to increase awareness of the need to adopt the behavioral options, to teach the skills needed to practice the behaviors (such as negotiating and using a condom), and to create peer support for, or positive public opinion about, the reduction of risk behaviors.

These AIDS prevention efforts, however, are deficient in two critical ways. First, the only women who are being targeted by AIDS prevention programs are commercial sex workers, and to some extent, school-based

The authors would like to thank Daniel Whelan of the International Center for Research on Women for editorial and research support. An earlier version of this chapter was published in the December 1993 issue of *Culture, Medicine and Psychiatry*. It is reprinted here by permission of Kluwer Academic Publishers.

female adolescents. Therefore, programs do not reach the majority of women in the community even though epidemiological data indicate that women of all ages and socioeconomic backgrounds are being infected with HIV through sexual contact with an infected partner. Second, the interventions pay little attention to the broader social and economic determinants of high risk behavior and to the cultural context within which sexual behavior takes place. Yet, it has been known for some time now that for behavior change to occur and to be sustained over time, it is critical that efforts be made to target both the behavior itself and its broader socioeconomic and cultural determinants. One of the reasons for this deficiency in the design and implementation of AIDS prevention programs for women has been a lack of reliable data on women's sexual lives, and the ways in which socioeconomic and cultural factors act as determinants of their sexual experiences.

Table One
Barriers to Women's Adoption of Risk Reduction Behaviors

Condom Use	Partner Reduction/ Mutual Monogamy	Accessing Appropriate STD Treatment
Lack of Knowledge and Skills		
• Do not know that condoms provide protection from infection.	• Do not relate their own sexual behavior nor the behavior of their partners to risk of HIV and STDs.	• Cannot identify abnormal gynecological signs as symptoms of STDs.
• Believe that condoms will get stuck inside or travel to the throat. • Do not know how to use condoms correctly. • Do not know how to negotiate condom use.	• Do not know how to communicate with partner about fidelity.	• Inappropriately self-medicated with anitbiotics as treatment for STD symptoms.
Social Beliefs, Norms, and Realities		
• Condoms signify lack of trust and intimacy.	• Socially acceptable for men to have multiple partners.	• Belief that vaginal discharge and abdominal pain are a woman's lot.
• Condoms are associated with illicit relationships.	• Women cannot question men about their sexual behavior.	• Acknowledging STD symptoms and their association with illicit sexual behavior is shameful for women.
• Condoms reduce sexual pleasure. • Talking about sex, including condom use is taboo and can result in violence.	• Physical violence and abandonment are consequences for women who question male fidelity.	

Recent findings from the Women and AIDS program, a research effort undertaken by the International Center for Research on Women (ICRW) with researchers and program practitioners from around the world, have provided insights into the realities of women's lives—their sexual behavior and experiences and the ways in which sociocultural and economic factors affect their vulnerability to HIV.[1] The program supports seventeen research projects in thirteen countries.[2]

The research findings that appear in Tables One and Two are grouped into two categories of factors that influence women's risk of HIV infection. The first category includes the findings that relate to the most immediate barriers that women face in adopting risk reduction behaviors, such as those that relate to a lack of knowledge or skills, and the specific social norms and beliefs that constrain women's ability to protect themselves from HIV.

The second category of findings refers to the socioeconomic determinants of women's risk of HIV at the individual and household level that in turn result from broader macro-level economic and social conditions.

Table Two
Socioeconomic Determinants of Women's Risk of HIV Infection

Macro	Micro
• Widespread economic recession and poverty.	• Low economic and educational status of women.
• Political and economic instability.	• Threats to women's physical safety and high incidence of domestic violence and nonconsensual sex.
• Unequal power balance in gender relations.	• Women's social status linked to marriage and motherhood.
• Legal discrimination against women.	• Increasing female headship due to migration, abandonment, and divorce.

POLICY AND PROGRAM ACTIONS TO TARGET BARRIERS TO RISK REDUCTION

The research findings listed in Table One suggest a set of policy and program actions to target the most immediate barriers that women face in adopting HIV risk-reduction behaviors which include using condoms, practicing mutual monogamy, reducing the number of sexual partners, and seeking appropriate treatment for other STDs.

Educate women and adolescent girls about their bodies and sexuality as well as about HIV and STDs.
Studies carried out in India (George and Jaswal 1993), Mauritius (Oodit et al.

1993), Guatemala (Lundgren et al. 1992), Brazil (Goldstein 1993), Thailand (Cash and Anasuchatkul 1992), and South Africa (Abdool Karim et al. 1993) found that women and adolescent girls lack basic information about their reproductive anatomy and physiology, as well as STD/HIV prevention, and that this lack of information constrains their ability to adopt risk reduction behaviors. For example, some rural women from South Africa, and urban women from low-income communities in India and Brazil, reported not liking condoms because they feared that if the condom fell off inside the vagina, it could get lost and perhaps travel to the throat, and, if removed, might pull out the reproductive organs with it (Abdool Karim et al. 1993; George and Jaswal 1993; Goldstein 1993). For poor urban women in Bombay, India, lack of information limits their ability to identify abnormal gynecological symptoms that could signify a sexually transmitted infection (George and Jaswal 1993). Even when women were aware of the symptoms of STDs, some took inappropriate measures for their treatment. For example, Jamaican women, working in the free-trade zone of Kingston, generally were aware of the signs of STDs, but when they detected a symptom, some reported self-medicating themselves with antibiotics that they shared with one another (Chambers 1992).

Educating women about their bodies also may help to limit the practice of certain high risk sexual behaviors. For example, some women from the South African study sample reported inserting external agents into the vagina to dry the vaginal passages because of the belief that the increased friction is sexually more satisfying for men (Abdool Karim et al. 1993). The agents used include herbs and roots, as well as scouring powders that can cause vaginal inflammation, lacerations, and abrasions, thereby significantly increasing the efficiency of HIV transmission.

Accurate information on HIV transmission also will help women to determine their level of risk. Data from the study conducted in Mauritius, for example, showed that young unmarried women did not believe themselves to be at risk for pregnancy or STDs because they were engaging in "light sex," which they distinguished from sexual intercourse. In-depth questioning revealed, however, that "light sex" did in fact involve rubbing the penis against the vagina as well as some penetration and therefore was a risky practice (Oodit et al. 1993). Young adolescent girls in Chiang Mai, Thailand, also believed that they were not at risk of getting infected because they were "good girls" and did not engage in sex unless they were in love with the man (Cash and Anasuchatkul 1992). Clearly, women need to be better informed, because an accurate perception of risk is a critical first step in the process of behavior change.

Increase women's condom literacy.
Since condoms are the only AIDS prevention technology currently available, skills training workshops for girls and women on how to use one properly and on how to negotiate with a male partner to use one need to be designed and implemented.

Existing condom promotion and education programs generally target commercial sex workers and have not reached women who have to handle condom negotiation and use in more intimate or long-term relationships. Many women from the slums of Bombay, young women working in garment factories in Chiang Mai, Thailand, and secondary school girls in Khon Kaen, Thailand, had never before handled a condom and did not know how to use one (George and Jaswal 1993; Stoeckel and Thongkrajai 1993; Cash and Anasuchatkul 1992).

Innovative and creative methods have to be developed to help desensitize women to the embarrassment of handling a condom and talking about sex. The research team in Chiang Mai, for example, developed a board game called "anti-AIDS siamsee," which resembles the popular game *Monopoly* in that players are rewarded with play money and free turns if they respond correctly to a set of questions on HIV/AIDS prevention. The team also developed a comic book about an invisible, flying condom which serves as a guardian angel for young women, advising them on how to negotiate condom use.

These materials, used as part of a peer education program for young, female factory workers, have proven to be very popular in the factories and dorms where the girls work and live and have succeeded in helping them to overcome some of their reticence about talking about condoms and sex (Cash and Anasuchatkul 1992).

Continue to support face-to-face education and mass media campaigns that destigmatize the condom and weaken its association with illicit sex.
Among women living in a rural area and a peri-urban squatter community of South Africa, nearly three-fourths of those interviewed indicated that a barrier to condom use for them was that it signified a lack of trust and intimacy (Abdool Karim et al. 1993).

Similar findings were reported from the studies in Brazil, Jamaica, and Guatemala. For the women from these studies, condoms are for having sex with "the other" and not with a stable partner.

For women of Brazil and Guatemala the condom is for women "of the street, not the home;" in Jamaica, for "outside and not inside relationships"; and in South Africa, for "back pocket partners" (Goldstein 1993; Lundgren et al. 1992; Chambers 1992; Abdool Karim et al. 1993)

Provide women with opportunities for individual counseling and group interactions to share personal experiences and model new behaviors.

Such opportunities enable women to discuss their sexual lives and the consequences of adopting or negotiating the risk reduction options, allow women to realize that they are not alone with regard to their fears and worries, and permit them to try out new behaviors in a non-threatening environment.

The young women factory workers in Mauritius, for example, reported feeling very alone with regard to their sexual lives. Because virginity among unmarried women is highly valued, these young women are afraid of asking peers or family members for information for fear that it will be assumed that they are sexually active (Oodit et al. 1993).

The researchers who conducted this study, as well as those doing studies with adolescent girls in Thailand, Brazil, and Zimbabwe, and with adult women in South Africa, Guatemala, and Brazil, reported that the process of data collection opened the floodgates—women were relieved that they could finally talk to someone about their sexual concerns, and once they started talking, they demanded that they be given more information and additional opportunities to talk. They requested, for example, that focus group discussions or workshop sessions be continued past their scheduled hour or day of completion (Oodit et al. 1993; Cash and Anasuchatkul 1992; Goldstein 1993; Bassett 1992; Abdool Karim et al. 1993; Hirschmann 1993; Vasconcelos et al. 1992).

In the case of Chiang Mai, a research assistant on the team who was closer in age to the girls being interviewed began to get visits at home from them, wanting to talk to her about their sexual experiences, fears, and worries (Cash and Anasuchatkul 1992).

Providing opportunities for women to talk is a crucial step in overcoming the social norms that define a "good" woman as one who is ignorant about sex and passive in sexual interactions, and those that label inter-partner communication on sex, particularly when initiated by the woman, as taboo. Such norms and beliefs make negotiating the use of a condom or raising the issue of monogamy a very difficult task. Women from Papua New Guinea, Jamaica, Guatemala, and India cited physical violence as a possible consequence of bringing up condoms or infidelity (Jenkins 1992; Chambers 1992; Lindgren et al. 1992; George and Jaswal 1992).

It is interesting that many women interviewed from Brazil and India reported that they chose sterilization over other methods of contraception because they wanted to avoid discussing sex and contraception with their partners, often an unpleasant experience (Goldstein 1993; George and Jaswal 1992).

Make STD services more accessible and available to women by integrating them with family planning and maternal health services.

Data from the program suggest that one of the reasons that make it unlikely that women will seek treatment for STDs is that they are unaware of their signs and symptoms (Lundgren et al. 1992; George and Jaswal 1993). Moreover, as reported by the study conducted with low-income women in Bombay, India, the vaginal discharge, itching, burning, and abdominal and back pain that are characteristic of an STD is accepted by many women as an inevitable part of their womanhood, or in the words of one woman: "it's a woman's lot" (George and Jaswal 1993).

One way to overcome this reluctance to seek treatment is to integrate STD diagnosis and treatment services with family planning and maternal care services, which by all accounts are services that women are more likely to use regularly. Regular screening procedures during a prenatal or a family planning visit could also help to identify asymptomatic STDs which increase women's risk of HIV infection.

Promote sexual and family responsibility in programs targeted at men and adolescent boys.

The research results clearly indicate that women's ability to negotiate condom use or ensure fidelity in partnerships is largely dependent on men, because socio-cultural norms give priority to male pleasure and control in sexual interactions. In São Paulo, Brazil, for example, some women factory workers reported engaging in anal sex not for their own pleasure but to satisfy their husbands. The women spoke of the pressure that their partners exerted on them to engage in anal sex, and said that their partners often threatened them with finding what they wanted on the street if the women did not consent (Goldstein 1993).

The condoning of multiple-partner relationships for men is another social norm that increases women's vulnerability to HIV. In many cultures both men and women believe that variety in sexual partners is essential to men's nature but is not appropriate for women. Adolescent boys in the Zimbabwean study recognize this double standard. As one young man said: "It feels o.k. about boys having more than one partner. But girls should be faithful to one boy" (Bassett 1992). Though many women expressed concern about the infidelities of their partners, they were resigned to their lack of control over the situation. Women from India, Jamaica, Papua New Guinea, Zimbabwe, and Brazil report that raising the issue of their partner's infidelity can jeopardize their physical safety and family stability (George and Jaswal 1992; Chambers 1992; Jenkins 1992; Bassett 1992; Goldstein 1993).

Concern is rising in many communities with regards to the "sugar daddy" phenomenon, which involves young girls having sex with older men in exchange for money, gifts, or favors. When school girls in Zimbabwe were shown a picture of an apparently affluent man suggestively eyeing a young girl, the students acknowledged the existence of "sugar daddies" in their community and one adolescent girl remarked: "These days there is ESAP (the Zimbabwean structural adjustment program) so maybe this girl is not getting enough money from home, so she will be hoping to get a lot of money from a sugar daddy" (Bassett 1992).

There is a tremendous need, therefore, to design programs for men and boys that go beyond condom literacy by promoting partner communication and family responsibility. Some of the pregnant women sampled in the Guatemalan study felt that men would pay more attention to sexual responsibility if they were clearly told of the fatal consequences for their children. In addition, these women felt more empowered to discuss AIDS/STD prevention with their husbands during pregnancy because they felt their partners would be more likely to listen and less likely to resort to physical violence because "I am carrying his child" (Hirschmann 1993).

Support biomedical research necessary to develop a female-controlled technology to prevent HIV transmission.

The studies found that domestic violence and non-consensual sex is a reality in the lives of many of the women interviewed through this program (Jenkins 1992; Chambers 1992; Lundgren et al. 1992; George and Jaswal 1993). A repeated concern of women all across the globe is the fact that the condom is ultimately a male-controlled device, and discussing its use raises the suspicion of infidelity—of both the woman and the man—which can result in violent interactions. Thus, these women fear bringing up condom use and monogamy for discussion with their partners. Moreover, women in Bombay, Guatemala City, and the highlands of Papua New Guinea pointed out that men often demand sex under the influence of alcohol, making condom-use negotiation an unrealistic option (George and Jaswal 1993; Lundgren et al. 1992; Jenkins 1992). In addition, because the condom is a contraceptive, it interferes with many women's most cherished life goal—to be a mother.

One way to address these difficulties is to develop a technology that does not have contraceptive properties and that women can use without the knowledge or consent of their partners. The female condom, a female-controlled technology that is currently available, is unlikely to meet the needs of many women because it cannot be used surreptitiously nor does it permit conception. The diaphragm with nonoxynol–9, a female-controlled barrier method that can be used without partner consent, may be another alternative, though research on its effectiveness as a preventive technology for HIV remains inconclusive.[3] Moreover, the diaphragm, like the male and female condom, prevents pregnancy. The development of a microbicidal compound without spermicidal properties that can be used vaginally without knowledge of the partner would be an ideal alternative for women who want to become pregnant and yet protect themselves from infection.[4] A microbicidal compound would also increase the range of available preventive technologies against HIV and other STDs for both men and women, and thereby be more likely to result in effective HIV prevention. It is important, however, that the development of a microbicide go hand-in-hand with efforts to change gender power dynamics and women's socioeconomic status, rather than be viewed as a technological fix in lieu of broader structural changes affecting women's lives.

POLICY AND PROGRAM ACTIONS TARGETING THE SOCIOECONOMIC DETERMINANTS OF WOMEN'S HIGH RISK BEHAVIORS

The findings listed in Table Two highlight the need for the following policies and programs to improve women's social and economic status, and thereby reduce their risk of HIV infection.

Provide women with economic opportunities.

Over the past few years, data from many studies have clearly shown that economic impoverishment is the root cause of women entering into multiple or temporary partnerships and for bartering sex for economic gain and survival (Schoepf et al. 1990; Bledsoe 1990; Ngugi 1991). For such women, "Stick to your partner" or "Love Faithfully" messages are inappropriate to motivate behavior change. It is critical, therefore, that AIDS prevention programs provide women for whom bartering sex is a matter of survival with alternative income-generating opportunities. Simultaneously, on a broader policy level, it is essential that efforts be made to improve women's economic status through appropriate measures, including access to credit, skills training, employment, and primary and secondary education.

Direct resources toward strengthening existing community-based women's organizations to improve and expand the provision of services.

In addition to the provision of HIV/STD education, condom distribution, and STD diagnosis and treatment, the studies have highlighted the need for additional services which include support networks, income generation, and shelters for women who are victims of domestic violence in order to facilitate individual behavior change in women. In many countries, community-based women's organizations already provide such services and address the micro- and macro-level socioeconomic determinants of women's risk through collective action in fighting legal, economic, and social discrimination. Typically, however, such groups struggle to survive with inadequate funds and technical resources. Findings from the Women and AIDS program that highlight the extent to which women's health is compromised by lack of information, economic resources, support systems, and domestic violence underscore the urgent need to strengthen existing community-based women's groups so that they are better able to meet women's needs.

Design programs through participatory research that mobilize communities to question the norms that shape the unequal power balance in relationships.
AIDS, more than any other epidemic, has exposed the fatal consequences, for all of society, of women's powerlessness. The fatality of AIDS provides the undeniable moral and economic imperative to make the necessary structural changes to empower women.

Results from the Women and AIDS program indicate that one mechanism to begin a process of community mobilization around AIDS issues is through the conducting of research. However, such a process of questioning and change is more likely to occur if the research is of a particular kind—action research—in which the findings are translated into program interventions and participatory research which involves members of the community in the research process.

For example, while in the process of trying to ensure the participation of adolescent girls in focus group discussions and educational sessions in an environment where young girls are very protected, the research team in Bombay held several consultations with male community leaders and elders and with women who were held in high esteem within the community. The team also organized a street play in the community which raised issues related to women's low status and its implications for the health of families and communities. The play was interactive and required members of the community to participate at several points as actors and discussants. As a result, not only did the community elders permit their girls to attend the discussions and educational sessions, they encouraged them to attend, and in the case of one particular father, who wanted to know why his daughter was not being included in the sessions, even demanded that they attend. Moreover, the team reported that the research process created an awareness about AIDS and a demand for more information and services. More importantly, the research has set in motion a process of introspection on the link between women's status and the health of communities (Bhende 1992).

Participation of the community in the research process was achieved in other ways as well. Research teams working in Recife, Brazil, in Nigeria, and in South Africa involved members of the community in the design of the data collection instruments, discussion of the findings, and planning of the interventions (Vasconcelos et al. 1992; Uwakwe et al. 1993; Abdool Karim et al. 1993). In Papua New Guinea, South Africa, and Recife, Brazil, members of the study populations were used as field investigators (Jenkins 1992; Abdool Karim et al. 1993; Vasconcelos et al. 1992).

As demonstrated through these experiences, participatory research leads to community ownership of research findings and to sustained participation in the resulting actions. It is also an effective way to ensure the cooperation of the study population in responding to questions on sensitive and intimate topics such as gender relations and sexuality.

Promote the collaboration of researchers and program practitioners in the conduct of participatory research.
Experiences gained from the program indicate that linking researchers and program practitioners, such as those from non-governmental organizations, is an effective way to conduct participatory, action research that is useful and relevant for the community. Such partnerships help to ensure the immediate utilization of findings for the design and implementation of interventions. They maximize the skills and strengths of each partner, because each is responsible for what she or he does best. The researchers are responsible for the research design and methodology, and the program practitioners are responsible for ensuring that the goals of the research and the process of data collection meet the needs of the community and that the findings are translated into meaningful program interventions.

The program supported several collaborations of this kind. For example, in Guatemala City, researchers from DataPro worked with the Asociación Guatemalteca para la Prevención y Control del SIDA (Guatemalan Association for the Prevention and Control of AIDS), a local NGO, to conduct an action research program targeting pregnant women. In Brazil, researchers affiliated with the University of Pernambuco worked with Casa de Passagem, an NGO in Recife, to carry out a participatory research study with low-income adolescent girls.

In conclusion, the Women and AIDS research program has generated valuable, substantive data on women's lives and the factors that contribute to their risk of HIV and STDs. In addition, the program has elicited important lessons about the process of conducting applied research on sexuality and AIDS. But perhaps most importantly, by disseminating the findings of their research in-country, each of the research projects is serving as a catalyst for policy discussions at the national level on the critical importance of gender issues in AIDS prevention.

[270]   The Social Construction of Sexual Risk

NOTES

Acknowledgment: The authors would like to thank Daniel Whelan of the International Center for Research on Women for research and editorial support.

1. The Women and AIDS research program of the International Center for Research on Women is supported by the Office of Health and the Office of Women in Development of the U.S. Agency for International Development (AID).

2. The thirteen countries are Malawi, Mauritius, Nigeria, Senegal, South Africa, and Zimbabwe in Africa; India, Papua New Guinea, and Thailand from Asia and the Pacific; and Brazil, Guatemala, Jamaica, and Mexico from Latin America and the Caribbean.

3. Recent data show that the diaphragm used in conjunction with nonoxynol–9 does offer protection against cervical infection, including gonorrhea, trichomonas, and chlamydia (Rosenberg and Gollub 1992; Cates and Stone 1992).

4. The advantages of such a compound and the possibilities to develop it are discussed in a recent paper written by Dr. Christopher Elias and Lori Heise of The Population Council entitled *The Development of Microbicides: A New Method of HIV Prevention for Women.* (The Population Council, Programs Division, Working Papers, No. 6, 1993.).

AFTERWORD

Culture, Structure, and Change 15

Sex Research After Modernity

Shirley Lindenbaum

THE ESSAYS IN THIS VOLUME CHALLENGE US TO REFLECT on what we know about culture, society, and behavior change, both past and present. Changing cultures, social forms, and sexual activities as they relate to the demography and epidemiological status of populations, for example, have been of central concern to policy makers and social analysts in the past few decades. Our perception and understanding of these matters, however, has undergone recent change.

In 1993 we inhabit and conduct research in a world undergoing the loss of old certainties. The postwar decades from about 1945 to 1970 were characterized by U.S. hegemony, of which modernization theory was the most confident expression. American policies, as well as dominant voices in the academy, assumed that societies could be induced to change from a state of "underdevelopment" to one of "development," even if the change occurred at different rates. The past fifteen years, however, have witnessed deepening crisis and restructuring. World systems theory and postmodern thought, which began as critiques of modernization theory, can be seen as intellectual expressions of that crisis (Polier and Roseberry 1989:259).

Although anthropologists may be registering postmodern distress in a particularly florid manner (in that even recently accepted methods of writing and representing ethnographic data have been querulously examined), a sense of epistemological doubt appears to afflict many quarters of contemporary social science. For example, the broad consensus that existed in demographic circles in the early 1980s as to why fertility falls appears to have evaporated. Contrary to expectations, "developing" nations are not experiencing the classical demographic transition that occurred in many industrialized nations over the past century (Robey et al. 1993). Instead of a single demographic transition common to all places and all times, we now see that there are many demographic transitions, each driven by a combination of social and cultural forces that are temporarily specific. It has been said that the closer we get to understanding specific fertility declines, the further we move from a general theory of fertility transition (Greenhalgh 1990:85).

A similar trajectory appears to have occurred in the way we see both the world-wide mortality decline, and what has been called the "epidemiological transition."[1] That is, in contrast to earlier understandings, we now view both the "demographic transition" and the "epidemiological transition" as being far from uniform processes. Recent literature has begun to identify the diverse forces that have contributed to the different timing and causes of both, even within the same historical period and in seemingly similar populations (Schneider and Schneider 1984; Kertzer and Hogan 1989; Kunitz 1990).

What we once viewed as standard units of analysis have also, on closer inspection, broken into fragments. The household, for example, is no longer viewed as a unit of harmonious production, but is seen to be a site of both cooperation and potential conflict. Households are the locus of the reproduction of labor power, in which women are subordinated, and in which individuals may follow strategies that differ by gender, generation, and class, as the essay by Gupta and Weiss in this volume illustrates. Carmen Deere (1990) has even suggested that individuals in peasant households may simultaneously occupy multiple class positions, based on their participation in distinct kinds of class projects. Our current analyses of social processes and social forms thus seem compatible with a postmodern view of life as fragmentary, in a disordered world.

SEX RESEARCH AND SOCIAL CHANGE

The abandonment of a scientistic search for transhistorical laws, as well as our current lack of unanimity concerning associations that earlier seemed to lend themselves to broad generalizations, is not necessarily bad news, however, as many of the essays included in this volume clearly illustrate. The loss of the "authoritative voice" of an earlier period has been replaced by a more cautious but more precise examination of behaviors and ideologies in specific social and historical contexts.

Such analyses go beyond the image of culture and political and economic conditions as "backdrop" or as a set of variables, and take instead a more active view of social processes. Thus, current readings look at the way in which individual selves and communities are culturally differentiated, each formed within processes of uneven development that affect individual actors' understandings of the world, of other people, and of themselves (Roseberry 1989:13–14).

This more complex view of social change as itself the subject of analysis is recommended in different ways and to different degrees by a number of the present authors.[2] In discussing recent approaches to the concept of risk, for example, Carl Kendall identifies two theoretical extremes: one that focuses on the individual and the self (recommended by Giddens) and the other, Mary Douglas's recipe for a risk analysis that rejects psychology and focuses instead on structure, community, and culture. As Kendall notes, these two positions can be readily found represented in the current AIDS literature on risk and behavior change. Judging each approach to be incomplete at best, Kendall proposes a theory of behavior change, and a research program, that take account of the simultaneous creation of both individual and group identity in relationships of class and power. Attention should be given also to the complex interaction of both personality and community in the process of rapid social change.

Gupta and Weiss take a stance that recommends a similar kind of double vision, one that sees economic and political processes as providing both the framework and substance of women's and men's social and economic lives in different communities and households, at the same time contributing to constructions of sexuality that result in the gender inequalities that limit women's ability to negotiate safer sex. Kendall as well as Gupta and Weiss avoids sweeping generalities and directs our attention instead at the way in which the person, the community, and behaviors are mutually produced and culturally constructed in different contexts of power.

Reflecting on the histories of desire, Karin Lützen and Mattias Duyves adopt a somewhat different strategy. A focus on particular historic cases discloses, in each case, the political and intellectual construction of specific notions of "sexuality." Lützen proposes a most productive method of historical investigation that rests on inversion, contrast, and implicit understanding. Her method is highly compatible with an anthropological approach that begins by questioning the assumptions and key terms of any inquiry (a procedure Carl Kendall follows when he juggles different concepts of "risk"). Here, Lützen suggests that things now seen as "sexual" should be regarded with skepticism until we establish the historical meaning of words and behaviors in particular situations.

Our current humility concerning the ability to fully comprehend earlier meanings of sexuality stems surely from the effects of the new reproductive technologies on our understanding of the "facts of life." As Franklin (1991) notes, conception narratives provide an analogue for understanding social and moral arrangements in our own and in other cultures. The achievement of conception in the laboratory by teams of professionals thus constitutes a primal scene with which we are only now beginning to come to terms. Long-held beliefs about procreation, which have long provided the foundation for our definitions of parenthood, kinship, gender, sexual difference, inheritance, and descent have been undermined by the dramatic technological separation of procreation from sexuality. Many boundaries have been breached in a postmodern world that can freeze embryos so that "twins" are born eighteen months apart, in which embryo transfers permit a woman to give birth to her daughter's child, or in which semen storage techniques enable a woman to conceive a child by her husband after he has died (Franklin 1991:25).

In addition to a well-placed skepticism toward ahistorical approaches to the meaning of key terms, Lützen shows that we can also learn much about the sexual understandings and cultural identities of individuals by considering what they fail to say about certain incidents as well as by what they do say about the behavior of others. This theoretical position fits well with the view of culture and society proposed by Kendall, Gupta, and Weiss. As Lützen observes, "the existing gender, class, and regional differences in any society also penetrate the sexual arena" and must be included if we wish to understand and explain sexual behaviors in any particular context.

Mattias Duyves's rich ethnography of Amsterdam as the Gay Capital takes a stance shared by the other authors and follows John Gagnon's imperative that "sexual conduct of all kinds. . .has to be understood as local phenomena"—a view that I indicated earlier was compatible with contemporary social experience in a late capitalist world.

Duyves suggests that we include the notion of "space," in this case urban space, in our theories of desire. The social construction of sexuality is thus extended by considering what he calls the "sexology of spaces" and "geographies of desire."

Taking Amsterdam as a case study, Duyves tracks the use of public space for gay purposes across several centuries, noting the more dramatic changes that have occurred since the 1960s as gay happenings and street theatre changed to the political action of the 70s and 80s. The image of Amsterdam as the "gay capital of Europe," Duyves suggests, is composed of five spatial scripts: the use of public space in street life; the amenities in goods and services of a clientele culture; a significant gay public consisting of residents (mostly immigrants to the city) and tourists; a calendar of public events and gay festivities; and the image-creation that is the product of the media and of tourist advertising directed at an international market, as well as the product of a local, expressive culture of theatre, cabaret, poetry and the dialect of "gayspeak." With this reading of sexual desire, Duyvas gives us a cultural geography that is part culture, part history, part political economy.

SOCIAL THEORY AND SOCIAL LIFE

The several essays I have discussed lead us to ask whether in directing our attention toward more local phenomena, we might now be unable to establish wider connections. Has our ability to grasp social and cultural wholes slipped away, and are we left merely with a postmodern strategy of celebrating the fragmentation of social life?

The authors represented in this volume would, I think, reject this latter approach and assert that we must attempt to place our fragments within the larger structures, systems, or histories that have produced them and placed them in certain kinds of relationships (see Polier and Roseberry 1989). De Zalduondo and Bernard, for example, propose such a view when they speak of the need to analyze the "interrelated set of conditions upon conditions" that increase the incentives for non-conjugal sexual relationships in Haiti.

This can be done in the form of historical or ethnographic case studies (Duyves, Lancaster, Lützen) or by comparison (Gupta and Weiss, Heise, Herdt and Boxer). Using the case study of Amsterdam as an example, it would be interesting to combine the two approaches. A comparative strategy might enlarge our understanding of the nature of social space, gay culture, politics, and behavior if we compared Amsterdam with another world capital such as Bangkok. In Thailand, sex is also vigorously marketed, but Bangkok holds a different place in our imagination as "the brothel of the East"—a place occupied by Shanghai until about 1949 (Manderson 1993). This is a clue to the shift in world capitalism from old to new epicenters, as well as to the constricted sensibilities of some regimes—such as China and perhaps Cuba—toward both sex and capital. (Lützen implies a similar comparative strategy when she observes that Denmark and Sweden have effected a division of labor between sex and danger).

By placing Duyves's Amsterdam case study in a broader landscape, we see that the world we inhabit and attempt to understand is the product of both local and global interrelations. And, in what might appear to be a contradiction, the more global our relations and flows of commerce, money, and people, the more rather than less we cling to place, neighborhood, nation, region, ethnic grouping, or religious belief as specific marks of identity. The increasing importance of multinational corporations and the flow of capital and labor across borders thus tends to create both homogeneity and difference. Multinational capital, which sees the whole world as an open market, and which reduces time as well as spatial barriers, creates a new respect for identity and geography. As David Harvey suggests, small-scale and finely graded differences between the qualities of places (their labor supply, infrastructure, political receptivity, resource mixes, and market niches) become more important. "Places, in turn, become more concerned about their own climates for potential development, and thus the real and fictional qualities of a 'place' increases. Globalization curiously generates its opposite, and the geopolitics of place become more rather than less emphatic" (Harvey n.d.:26).

Thus the same historical forces have contributed to the production of both

Amsterdam and Bangkok as unique sexual landscapes. The competition in Amsterdam between the Chamber of Commerce and the gay profit sector concerning the image of the city, as well as the limited involvement offered to gay organizations in the redevelopment of the urban area stems, in part, from the fact that Amsterdam, unlike Bangkok, is less dependent on the marketability of sex as a product and image. That is, both global and local histories explain the contemporary status of Bangkok and Amsterdam as different kinds of sexually potent cities.

When undertaking research that requires both understanding and intervention, as in AIDS research, for example, we should thus keep in mind the lesson that the groups, communities, and even individuals whose lives we study have a local and global "face." Tourists to Bangkok from Australia and South East Asia have sex with women drawn temporarily from the Hill Tribes of Thailand; Romanian and Russian women in Turkey trade sexual favors for money that they also intend to invest back home in Bucharest or Moscow. Similarly, the lives of truckers on the highways of Nigeria described by Orubuloye, like those of the young women described by Gupta and Weiss, of immigrants and tourists in Amsterdam, are the products of social circumstances and larger histories that give rise to new (and sustain older) social forms and unequal relationships. They also provide the circumstances for, or impediments against, change.

Although we may not often be well placed to intervene at global, national, or perhaps even local levels, we should not abandon a stance that tries to grasp the larger histories that have produced an apparently disconnected world. The theoretical framework we hold allows us to recognize new and old social interests and social forms, to identify the communities and coalitions that produce and are produced by the international traffic in wealth and people, and to understand (if not always to predict) the reasons why some individuals and groups would promote behavior change, and why others might be hostile, inhibited, or resistant. Although our analyses and interventions might focus at times on what appear to be social fragments and local meanings, they are driven by broader assumptions and perceptions about the nature of social process.

NOTES

1. This refers to the transition experienced by most societies during the past two to three centuries from a regime of high, fluctuating mortality and low expectation of life at birth caused largely by infectious diseases, to a regime of low, stable mortality and high life expectancy, resulting from the decline of infectious diseases and the greater importance of noninfectious and "manmade" diseases. In the latter case, infants, children, and women were the main beneficiaries (see Kunitz 1990:647).

2. Although I focus here on a number of essays that are especially concerned with the relationship between culture, structure, and change, all of the essays included in this volume contribute in many ways to the refinement of social theory in sex research.

Contributors

Richard G. Parker is Professor of Medical Anthropology and Human Sexuality in the Institute of Social Medicine at the State University of Rio de Janeiro and Director of the Brazilian Interdisciplinary AIDS Association.

John H. Gagnon is Professor in the Department of Sociology at the State University in New York, Stony Brook, in the United States.

Karin Lützen is in the Women's Studies Center at the University of Copenhagen in Denmark.

Jeffrey Weeks is Professor of Social Relations and Director of the Centre for Social and Economic Research at the University of the West of England, Bristol, in the United Kingdom.

Mattias Duyves teaches in the Department of General Social Sciences and Urban Studies at the University of Utrecht in the Netherlands.

Gilbert Herdt is Professor in the Committee on Human Development at the University of Chicago in the United States.

Andrew Boxer is Assistant Professor in the Departments of Psychiatry and Director of the Evelyn Hooker Center for Gay and Lesbian Mental Health at the University of Chicago in the United States.

Michael L. Tan is a medical anthropologist and Director of the Health Action and Information Network in the Philippines.

Dennis Altman teaches in the Department of Politics at La Trobe University in Australia.

Lori L. Heise directs the Violence, Sexuality, and Health Rights Program of the Pacific Institute for Women's Health, Los Angeles, California, and Washington, D.C., in the United States.

Roger N. Lancaster teachers in the Department of Anthropology at Columbia University in the United States.

Barbara O. de Zalduondo is in the Division of HIV/AIDS, USAID Office of Health and Nutrition, Washington, D.C., in the United States.

Jean Maxius Bernard is Director of the Bureau D'Etnologie and Professor in the Faculte d'Etnology of the State University in Haiti.

Edward O. Laumann is Distinguished Service Professor of Sociology at the University of Chicago in the United States.

Robert T. Michael is Dean at the Harris School of Public Policy Studies at the University of Chicago in the United States.

Anthony P.M. Coxon is Professor in the Department of Sociology at the University of Essex in the United Kingdom.

I.O. Orubuloye is Professor in the Department of Sociology at Ondo State University in Nigeria.

Carl Kendall is Professor in the Department of International Health and Development at Tulane University in the United States.

Geeta Rao Gupta is in the International Center for Research on Women, Washington, D.C. in the United States.

Ellen Weiss is in the International Center for Research on Women, Washington, D.C. in the United States.

Shirley Lindenbaum is Professor of Anthropology at the Graduate School and University Center of the City University of New York in the United States.

Bibliography

Abbot, E.
    1988 *Haiti: The Duvaliers and Their Legacy.* New York: Touchstone Books.
Abdool Karim, Q., E. Preston-Whyte, and N.D. Zuma
    1993 "Prevention of HIV Infection for Women by Women in Natal, South Africa."
    Durban: Research Institute for Diseases in a Tropical Environment. Preliminary
    Findings, ICRW: Women and AIDS Program.
Adam, B.
    1986 "Age, Structure, and Sexuality: Reflections on the Anthropological Evidence on
    Homosexual Relations." *Journal of Homosexuality* 11:19–33.
    1989 "Homosexuality without a Gay World: Pasivos y Activos en Nicaragua."
    Out/Look 1(4):74–82.
    1992 "The State, Public Policy and AIDS Discourse." In J. Miller, ed., *Fluid Exchanges.*
    Toronto: University of Toronto Press.
Adams, R.N.
    1956 "Cultural Components of Central America." *American Anthropologist*
    58:881–907.
    1957 *Cultural Surveys of Panama-Nicaragua-Guatemala-El Salvador-Honduras.* Scientific
    Publications, no. 33. Washington D.C.: Pan American Sanitary Bureau, Regional
    Office of the World Health Organization.
Adrien, A., C. Clérismé, and M. Cayemittes
    1990 "Enquete Qualitative sur les Comportements et Valeurs Reliés au SIDA en
    Haite." Programme National de Lutte Contre le SIDA, Ministère de la Santé Publique
    et de la Population. Port-au-Prince, Haiti. May 1990. (Unpublished).
Advisory Report
    1992 *Een Kijk op je Voorkeur in de Stad van je Voorkeur.* Foundation Album Amsterdam.
Aldrich, R.
    1992 "Not Just a Passing Fad: Gay Studies Comes of Age." In Robert Aldrich and
    Garry Wotherspoon, eds., *Gay Perspectives: Essays in Australian Gay Culture.* Sydney:
    University of Sydney.
Allen, S.M.
    1982 "Adolescent Pregnancy Among 11-15 Year Old Girls in the Parish of
    Manchester." Dissertation for diploma in Community Health. Kingston: University of
    the West Indies as cited in C.P. MacCormack and A. Draper, "Social and cognitive
    aspects of female sexuality in Jamaica." In P. Caplan, ed., *The Cultural Construction of
    Sexuality.* 1987. London: Tavistock Publications.

Allman, J.
1982 "Fertility and Family Planning in Haiti." *Studies in Family Planning* 13(8/9):237–245.
1985 "Conjugal Unions in Rural and Urban Haiti." *Social and Economic Studies* 34(1):27–57.

Almaguer, T.
1991 "Chicano Men: A Cartography of Homosexual Identity and Behavior." *Differences: A Journal of Feminist Cultural Studies* 3(2):75–100.

Altman, D.
1972 *Homosexual: Oppression & Liberation.* New York: Outerbridge & Dienstfrey.
1982 *The Homosexualization of America.* Boston: Beacon Press.
1986 *AIDS In the Mind of America.* New York: Doubleday.

Anderson, R.M., G.F. Medley, R.M. May, and A.M. Johnson
1986 "A Preliminary Study of the Transmission Dynamics of the Human Immunodeficiency Virus (HIV), the Causative Agent of AIDS." *Journal of Mathematics Applied in Medicine and Biology* 3:229–263.

Anderson, T.P.
1971 *Matanza: El Salvador's Communist Revolt of 1932.* Lincoln: University of Nebraska Press.

Ankrah, E.M.
1989 "AIDS: Methodological Problems in Studying its Prevention and Spread." *Social Science and Medicine* 29(3):265–276.

Apt, C., and D. Hurlbert
1993 "The Sexuality of Women in Physically Abusive Marriages: A Comparative Study." *Journal of Family Violence* 8(1):57–69.

Arndt, R.
1872 "Krankheit oder Schamlosigkeit?" *Vierteljahrschrift für gerichtliche Medizin* 17:49–70.

Arnoldussen, P.
1993 "Plattegrond van Bakken in Amsterdam." *Het Parool.* March 6.

Ashworth, G.J., P.E. White, and H.P.M. Winchester
1988 "The Red Light District in the West European City: A Neglected Aspect of the Urban Landscape." *Geoforum* 19(2): 201–212.

Auerbach, D.M., et al.
1984 "Cluster of Cases of the Acquired Immune Deficiency Syndrome." *American Journal of Medicine* 76:487–491.

Austria, L.T.
1993 "Sport Lang." *The Citizen,* January–February 1993, p. 10.

Baker, W.E.
1990 "Market Networks and Corporate Behavior." *American Journal of Sociology* 96:589–625.

Bakhtin, M.
1981 *The Dialogic Imagination: Four Essays.* Austin: University of Texas Press.
1984 *Rabelais and His World.* Bloomington: Indiana University Press.

Banwell, S.S.
1990 "Law, Status of Women and Family Planning in Sub-Saharan Africa: A Suggestion for Action." Nairobi: The Pathfinder Fund.

Barnhoorn, J.A.J., et al.
1941 *Het Vraagstuk der Homosexualiteit.* Roermond-Maaseik.

Bassett, M.
1992 "Female Sexual Behavior and Risk of HIV Infection: An Ethnographic Study." Harare: University of Zimbabwe. Quarterly Report, ICRW: Women and AIDS Program.

Bastien, R.
1961 "Haitian Rural Family Organization." *Social and Economic Studies* 10(4):496–502.
Beattie, V.
1992 "Analysis of the Results of a Survey on Sexual Violence in the UK." Cambridge: Women's Forum (unpublished manuscript).
Beauvoir Dominique, R.
1990 "Rapport sur l'enquette qualitative KAP-SIDA." Port-au-Prince, IHE/CDRH. (Unpublished).
Becker, J.V., L.J. Skinner, G.G. Abel, and E.C. Treacy
1982 "Incidence and Types of Sexual Dysfunctions in Rape and Incest Victims." *Journal of Sex and Marital Therapy* 8:65–74.
Bell, A.P., M.S. Weinberg, and S.K. Hammersmith
1981 *Sexual Preference: Its Development in Men and Women.* Bloomington: Indiana University Press.
Beneria, L., and M. Roldan
1987 *The Crossroads of Class and Gender.* Chicago: University of Chicago Press.
Bergh, R.
1888 *Beretning fra Vestre Hospital.*
1902 "Om Tatoveringer hos Fruentimmer af den offentlige og hemmelige Prostitution." *Hositalstidende* 10:947–955.
Bernard, J.M.
1988 "La Migración de los Campesinos Haitianos y el Surgimiento de los Nuevos Movimientos Religiosos en Puerto Principe." Doctoral Thesis, Department of Anthropology. Mexico City, Universidad Iberoamericana.
Berube, A., and J. Escoffier
1991 "Queer Nation." *Outlook: National Lesbian and Gay Quarterly* 11(Winter 1991):12.
Bhende, A.
1992 "Evolving a Model for AIDS Prevention Education Among Underprivileged Adolescent Girls in Urban India." Bombay: World Vision Relief and Development. Quarterly Report, ICRW: Women and AIDS Program.
Biernacki, P., and Waldorf
1981 "Snowball Sampling: Problems and Techniques of Chain Referral Sampling." *Sociological Methods and Research* 10:141–163.
Blalock, H.
1984 "Contextual-Effects Models: Theoretical and Methodological Issues." *Annual Review of Sociology* 10:353–372.
Blau, P.M.
1964 *Exchange and Power in Social Life.* New York: Wiley & Sons.
Bledsoe, C.
1990 "The Politics of AIDS, Condoms, and Heterosexual Relations in Africa: Recent Evidence from the Local Print Media." In W.P. Handwerker, ed., *Births and Power: Social Change and the Politics of Reproduction*, pp. 197–223. Boulder: Westview Press.
Blume, P.E.
1902 *Magdalenehjemmet i 25 Aar.* Copenhagen.
Borgatti, S., B. Everett, and L. Freeman
1992 *UCINET IV Version 1.0 Reference Manual.* Columbia: Analytic Technologies.
Borge, T.
1985 "Women and the Nicaraguan Revolution." In B. Marcus, ed., *Nicaragua: The Sandinista Revolution; Speeches by Sandinista Leaders*, pp. 46–60. New York: Pathfinder Press.
Boswell, J.
1992 "Concepts, Experience, and Sexuality." In E. Stein, ed., *Forms of Desire: Sexual Orientation and the Social Constructionist Controversy*, pp. 133–176. New York and London: Routledge.

Boulous, R., et al.
1991 "Perceptions and Practices Relating to Condom Use among Urban Men in Haiti." *Studies in Family Planning* 22(5):318–325.

Bourdieu, P.
1977 *Outline of a Theory of Practice*. Cambridge: Cambridge University Press.

Bowker, L.H.
1983 *Beating Wife Beating*. Lexington, MA: Lexington Books.

Boxer, A.M.
1990 "Life Course Transitions of Gay and Lesbian Youth: Sexual Identity Development and Parent-Child Relationships." Ph.D. dissertation. University of Chicago.

Boxer, A.M., et al.
1993 "Gay and Lesbian Youth." In P.H. Tolan and B.J. Cohler, eds., *Handbook of Clinical Research and Practice with Adolescents*, pp. 249–280. New York: John Wiley and Sons.

Brodwin, P.E.
1991 Political Contests and Moral Claims: Religious Pluralism and Healing in a Haitian Village. Doctoral Dissertation. Department of Anthropology. Harvard University.

Brown, N.O.
1990 *Love's Body*. Berkeley and Los Angeles: University of California Press.

Brown, S.E.
1975 "Love Unites Them and Hunger Separates Them: Poor Women in the Dominican Republic." In R.R. Reiter, ed., *Toward an Anthropology of Women*, pp. 322–332. New York: Monthly Review Press.

Browne, A.
1987 *When Battered Women Kill*. New York: The Free Press.

Bullock, L.F. and J. McFarlane
1989 "The Birth/Weight Battering Connection." *American Journal of Nursing*. Pp. 1153–1155.

Burnam, M. A.
1988 "Sexual Assault and Mental Disorders in a Community Population." *Journal of Consulting and Clinical Psychology* 56(6):843–850.

Burr, C.
1993 "Homosexuality and Biology." *The Atlantic* 271(3)(March):47–65.

Burt, R.S.
1980 "Models of Network Structure." *Annual Review of Sociology* 6:79–141.

Butler, J.
1990 *Gender Trouble: Feminism and the Subversion of Identity*. New York and London: Routledge.
1991 "Imitation and Gender Insubordination." In D. Fuss, ed., *Inside/Out: Lesbian Theories, Gay Theories*. New York and London: Routledge.

Cambell, J. and P. Alford
1989 "The Dark Consequences of Marital Rape." *American Journal of Nursing* July, pp. 946–948.

Canadian Government
1984 *Sexual Offenses Against Children, Vol. 1*. Ottawa: Canadian Publishing Centre.

Caplan, P., ed.
1987 *The Cultural Construction of Sexuality*. New York: Routledge.

Carovano, K.
1991 "More Than Mothers and Whores: Redefining the AIDS Prevention Needs of Women." *International Journal of Health Services* 21(1):131–142.

Carrier, J.M.
1976a "Cultural Factors Affecting Urban Mexican Male Homosexual Behavior."

Archives of Sexual Behavior 5(2):103–24.

1976b "Family Attitudes and Mexican Male Homosexuality." *Urban Life* 5(3):359–76.

Cash, K., and B. Anasuchatkul

1992 "Experimental Educational Interventions for the Prevention of AIDS Among Northern Thai Single Female Migratory Adolescents." Chiang Mai: Chiang Mai University. Quarterly Report, ICRW: Women and AIDS Program.

Castiglia, C.

1988 "Rebel without a Closet: Homosexuality and Hollywood." *Critical Texts* 5(1):31–35.

Catania, J.A., D.R. Gibson, D.D. Chitwood, and T.J. Coates

1990 "Methodological Problems in AIDS Behavioral Research: Influences of Measurement Error and Participation Bias in Studies of Sexual Behavior." *Psychological Bulletin* 108(3):339–362.

Cates, Jr., W., and K.M. Stone

1992 "Family Planning: The Responsibility to Prevent both Pregnancy and Reproductive Tract Infections." In A. Germain et al., eds., *Reproductive Tract Infections: Global Impact and Priorities for Women's Reproductive Health*, pp. 93–129. New York: Plenum Press.

Caughey, J.L.

1970 "Cultural Values in Micronesian Society." Unpublished Ph.D. Dissertation, University of Pennsylvania.

C.D.S. (Centres pour le Developpoment et la Santé)

1992 "Annual Report." Port-au-Prince, Haiti.

Centers for Disease Control (CDC)

1989 *Behaviorally Bisexual Men and AIDS*. Washington, D.C.: U.S. Department of Health and Human Services.

(CEPLAES) Barragan Alvarado, L., A.A. Marin, and G.C. Zambrano

1992 "Proyecto Educativo Sobre Violencia de Genero en la Relación Doméstica de Pareja." Centro de Planificación y Estudios Sociales. CEPLAES. Quito, Ecuador.

Chacon, K. et al.

1990 "Caracteristicas de La Mujer Agredida Atendida en el Patronato Nacional de la Infancia (PANI)." San Jose, Costa Rica as cited in Gioconda Batres and Cecilia Claramunt, *La Violencia Contra La Mujer En La Familia Costarricense: Un Problema de Salud Publica*. San Jose, Costa Rica: ILANUD.

Chambers, C.

1992 "Sexual Decision-Making Amongst Jamaicans." Los Angeles and Kingston: University of California-Los Angeles and the University of the West Indies. Focus Group Report, ICRW: Women and AIDS Program.

Charbit, Y.

1980 "Union Patterns and Family Structure in Guadaloupe and Martinique." *International Journal of Sociology of the Family* 10(1):41–66.

Chesebro, J.W., ed.

1981 *Gayspeak: Gay Male and Lesbian Communication*. New York: Pilgrim Press.

Chodorow, N.

1974 "Family Structure and Feminine Personality." In M.Z. Rosaldo and L. Lamphere, eds., *Woman, Culture, and Society*, pp. 43–66. Stanford: Stanford University Press.

1978 *The Reproduction of Mothering: Psychoanalysis and the Psychology of Gender*. Berkeley and Los Angeles: University of California Press.

Cohen, A.

1986 *The Symbolic Construction of Community*. Chichester and London: Ellis Horwood/Tavistock.

Cole, S.
1989 *Pornography and the Sex Crisis*. Toronto, Canada: Amanita Enterprises.
Coleman, J.S.
1958 "Relational Analysis: The Study of Social Organizations with Survey Methods." *Human Organization* 17:28–36.
1990 *Foundations of Social Theory*. Harvard: Belknap Press.
Collinson, H., ed.
1990 *Women and Revolution in Nicaragua*. London: Zed Books.
Cook, R., and D. Maine
1987 "Spousal Veto Over Family Planning Services." *American Journal of Public Health* 77(3):339–344.
Comaroff, J.
1985 *Body of Power, Spirit of Resistance: The Culture and History of a South African People*. Chicago: University of Chicago Press.
Comaroff, J., and J. Comaroff
1991 *Of Revelation and Revolution: Christianity, Colonialism, and Consciousness in South Africa, Vol 1*. Chicago: University of Chicago Press.
Combs-Schilling, M.E.
1989 *Sacred Performances: Islam, Sexuality, and Sacrifice*. New York: Columbia University Press.
Connell, R.W.
1987 *Gender and Power*. Cambridge: Polity.
Connell, R.W., and G.W. Dowsett
1992 "'The Unclean Motion of the Generative Parts': Frameworks in Western Thought in Sexuality." In R.W. Connell and G.W. Dowsett, *Rethinking Sex*, pp. 49–75. Melbourne: Melbourne University Press.
Conners, M.M.
1992 "Risk Perception, Risk Taking and Risk Management among Intravenous Drug Users: Implications for AIDS Prevention." *Social Science and Medicine* 34:591–601.
Conroy, M.E.
1990 "The Political Economy of the 1990 Nicaraguan Elections." *International Journal of Political Economy*, Fall, pp. 5–33.
Counts, D., J. Brown, and J. Campbell
1992 *Sanctions and Sanctuary: Cultural Perspectives on the Beating of Wives*. Boulder: Westview Press.
Coxon, A.P.M.
1986 *Report of Pilot Study: Project on Sexual Lifestyles of Non-Heterosexual Males*. Cardiff: SIGMA Working Paper No. 2.
1987 "The 'Gay Life Style': Epidemiology of AIDS and Social Science." In P. Aggleton and H. Homans, eds., *Social Aspects of AIDS*. London: Tavistock.
1988 "'Something Sensational. . .': The Sexual Diary as a Tool for Mapping Detailed Sexual Behaviour." *Sociological Review* 36(2):353–367.
1990 The Effect of Age and Relationship on Gay Men's Sexual Behaviour. London: Project SIGMA Working Paper No. 13
Coxon, A.P.M., and Carballo, M.
1989 "Research on AIDS: Behavioural Perspectives." *AIDS* 3(4):191–197.
Coxon, A.P.M., P.M. Davies, T.J. McManus, P. Weatherburn, and A.J. Hunt
1992 "The Structure of Sexual Behaviour." *The Journal of Sex Research* 29(1):61–83.
1993 "Sex Role Separation in Sexual Diaries of Homosexual Men." *AIDS* 7(6):877–882.
Coy, F.
1990 Study cited in Delia Castillo et al., 1992, "Violencia Hacia La Mujer en Guatemala." Report prepared for the First Central American Seminar on Violence

Against Women as a Public Health Problem, Managua, Nicaragua, March 11–13, 1992.

C.P.F.O. (Centre pour le Promotion des Femes Ouvrieres)
1988 "Street Food-Venders in the Industrial Area of Port-au-Prince: A Study of Working Women in Haiti." Research Report. (Unpublished).

Daniel, H.
1993 "Above All, Life." In H. Daniel and R. Parker, *Sexuality, Politics and AIDS in Brazil*, pp. 135–143. London: The Falmer Press.

Daniel, H., and R. Parker
1993 *Sexuality, Politics and AIDS in Brazil*. London: The Falmer Press.

Darrow W., H. Jaffe, and J. Curan
1983 "Passive Anal Intercourse as a Risk Factor for AIDS in Homosexual Men." *The Lancet* 2:160.

DataPro SA and the Association Guatemalteca para la Prevención y Control del SIDA
1991 "Guatemala City Women: Empowering a Vulnerable Group for HIV Prevention." Guatemala City: DataPro.

Davidson, A.I.
1987 "Sex and the Emergence of Sexuality." *Critical Inquiry* 14:16–48.

Davies, P.M.
1986 *Some Problems in Defining and Sampling Non-Heterosexual Males*. London: SIGMA Working Paper No. 3.
1990 "Patterns in Homosexual Behaviour: Use of the Diary Method." In M. Hubert, ed., *Sexual Behaviour and Risks of HIV Infection*. Brussels: Facultés Universitaires Saint Louis.

Davis, N.Z.
1978 "Women on Top: Symbolic Sexual Inversion and Political Disorder in Early Modern Europe." In Barbara A. Babcock, ed., *The Reversible World: Symbolic Inversion in Art and Society*, pp. 147–190. Ithaca: Cornell University Press.

Day, S.
1988 "Prostitute Women and AIDS: Anthropology." *AIDS* 2:421–428.

de Certeau, M.
1984 *The Practice of Everyday Life*. Berkeley and Los Angeles: University of California Press.

Deere, C.D.
1990 *Household and Class Relations: Peasants and Landlords in Northern Peru*. Berkeley and Los Angeles: University of California Press.

De Jong, R.
1993 "Stad Voor Een Dagje En Dan Hup, Weer Weg." *Het Parool* April 10.

DeKeseredy, W., and K. Kelly
1992 Private communication. Preliminary data from "First National Study on Dating Violence in Canada." Family Violence Prevention Division, Department of Health and Welfare, Ottawa, Canada.

Delacoste, F., and P. Alexander
1987 *Sex Work: Writings by Women in the Sex Industry*. Pittsburgh: Cleis Press.

de Lauretis, T.
1991 "Queer Theory: Lesbian and Gay Sexualities: An Introduction." *Differences: A Journal of Feminist Cultural Studies*. Vol. 5. Summer 1991.

Delbeau, J.C.
1990 *Société, Culture et Médicine Populaire Traditionnelle*. Port-au-Prince: Henri Deschamps.

D'Emilio, J., and E. Freedman
1988 *Intimate Matters: A History of Sexuality in America*. New York: Harper and Row.

Denich, B.
1974 "Sex and Power in the Balkans." In Michelle Rosaldo and Louise Lamphere, eds., *Women, Culture, and Society*. Palo Alto: Stanford University Press.

Dentan, R.
1979 *The Semai: A Nonviolent People of Malaya.* New York: Holt, Rinehart and Winston.

Désormeaux, J., B.O. de Zalduondo, M.C. Flambert, J.M. Bernard, D.A. Celentano, G. Mayard, C.A. Nathanson, E. Holt, R. Boulos, and N.A. Halsey
1992 "The Importance of Local Concepts of Contagion and Sexual Conduct for AIDS Education: A Case From Urban Haiti." Johns Hopkins University, Population Center Working Paper.

de Zalduondo, B.O.
1991a "AIDS Prevention for Women in African Countries: Pros and Cons of a Relativist Approach." Paper presented at the 119th Annual Meeting of the American Public Health Association, Atlanta, Georgia, November 10–14.
1991b "Prostitution Viewed Cross-Culturally: Toward Recontextualizing Sex Work in AIDS Research." *The Journal of Sex Research* 28(2):223–248.

de Zalduondo, B.O., G.I. Msamanga, and L.C. Chen
1989 "AIDS in Africa: Diversity in the Global Pandemic." *Daedalus* 118(3):165–204.

Diederich, B., and A. Burt
1986 *Papa Doc and the Tonton Macoutes.* Port-au-Prince: Henri Deschamps.

Dirección de Orientación y Protección Familiar
1983 *Informe sobre la familia en Nicaragua.* Instituto Nicaraguense de Seguridad Social y Bienestar, Oficina de la Mujer, Secretaria de la Junta del Gobierno de Reconstrucción Nacional. Managua: Nicaragua.

Dirección Nacional, FSLN
1987 *El FSLN y la mujer.* Managua: Editorial Vanguardia.

Dixon-Mueller, R.
1992 "Sexuality, Gender, and Reproductive Health." Working Paper prepared for International Women's Health Coalition, New York.
1993 *Population Policy and Women's Rights: Transforming Reproductive Choice.* Westport, CT: Praeger Publishers.

Dollimore, J.
1991 *Sexual Dissidence.* Oxford: Oxford University Press.

Douglas, M.
1992 *Risk and Blame: Essays in Cultural Theory.* New York: Routledge.

Durand, Y.
1980 "Familial Structures in Haiti." *Ethnopsychologie* 35(1):47–51.

Duyves, M.
1986 "Bij de Meerderjarigheid van Homostudies: Nederlandse Sociologen over Homoseksualiteir, 1965–1985." *Sociologische Gids* 32:332–351.
1989 "Allemansvriend in Niemandsland: De Dandy." In André Hielkema, ed., *De Dandy of de Overschrijding van het Alledaagse: Facetten van het Dandyisme.* Meppel Amsterdam Boom.
1992 "Keizerskroon met een roze randji." *Het Parool* August 7.
1993 "Geografie van het Amsterdamse Homoleven: De Teloorgang van Meermansbak en Ontmoetingskrul." *Geografie* 2:18–22.

Dworkin, A.
1987 *Intercourse.* New York: Free Press.
1989 *Pornography: Men Possessing Women.* New York: Dutton.

Ehrhardt, A.A.
1991 Speech delivered at the first National Conference on Women and HIV Infection, sponsored by the National Institutes of Health and Centers for Disease Control, Washington D.C.

Ehrhardt, A.A., S. Yingling, R. Zawadzki, M. Martines-Ramirez, Z. Stein
1991 "Barriers to Safer Sex for Women from High HIV Prevalence Communities."

Poster Presented at the Seventh International Conference on AIDS, Florence, Italy, June 16–21.

Elder, G.H.

1980 "Adolescence in Historical Perspective." In J. Adelson, ed., *Handbook of Adolescent Psychology*, pp. 3–46. New York: Wiley.

Elias, C., and L. Heise

1993 "The Development of Microbicides: A New Method of HIV Prevention for Women." *Programs Division Working Paper No. 6.* New York: The Population Council.

Epstein, J., and K. Straub, eds.

1992 *Body Guards: The Cultural Politics of Gender Ambiguity.* New York and London: Routledge.

Epstein, S.

1988 "Nature versus Nurture and the Politics of AIDS Organizing." *Outlook*, Fall.

Erbring, L., and A. Young

1979 "Individual and Social Structure: Contextual Effects as Endogenous Feedback." *Sociological Methods and Research* 7:396–430.

Erikson, E.

1963 *Childhood and Society.* New York: Norton.

1982 *The Life Cycle Completed: A Review.* New York: Norton.

Esche, T.

1920 *Erindringer fra mit Liv og min Gerning.* Copenhagen.

Eversley, R.B., et al.

1993 "Sexual Risk and Perception of Risk for HIV among Multiethnic Family-Planning Clients." *American Journal of Preventive Medicine* 9:92–95.

Fararo, T.J., and M.H. Sunshine

1964 *A Study of a Biased Friendship Net.* Syracuse, NY: Syracuse University Press.

Farmer, P.

1990 "The Exotic and the Mundane: Human Immunodeficiency Virus in Haiti." *Human Nature* 1(4):415–446.

1992 *AIDS and Accusation: Haiti and the Geography of Blame.* Berkeley, CA: University of California Press.

Fass, S.F.

1988 *Political Economy in Haiti: The Drama of Survival.* New Brunswick: Transaction Press.

Fausto-Sterling, A.

1992 *Myths of Gender: Biological Theories about Women and Men*, revised edition. New York: Basic Books.

Feng, D., M.S. Johnson and R.F. Doolitle

1985 "Aligning Amino-Acid Sequences: Comparison of Commonly Used Methods." *Journal of Molecular Evolution* 21:112–125.

Fine, M.

1988 "Sexuality, Schooling, and Adolescent Females: The Missing Discourse on Desire." *Harvard Educational Review* 58: 29–53.

Finklehor, D.

1987 "The Sexual Abuse of Children: Current Research Reviewed." *Psychiatric Annals* 17:233–241.

Firestone, S.

1971 *The Dialectic of Sex.* London: Cape.

Florén, A., and M. Persson

1985 "Mentalitetshistoria och mentalitetsbegreppet." *Lvchnos.*

Folch-Lyon, E., L. Macorra, and S.B. Schearer

1981 "Focus Group and Survey Research on Family Planning in Mexico." *Studies in Family Planning* 12(12):409–432.

Forhøret angaaende Forholdene paa Pigehjemmet "Hebron"
1908 Copenhagen.

Fort, A.L.
1989 "Investigation of the Social Context of Fertility and Family Planning: A Qualitative Study in Peru." *International Family Planning Perspectives* 15(3):88–94.

Foucault, M.
1980 *The History of Sexuality: Vol 1, An Introduction.* New York: Random House, Vintage Books.
1984 "Sex, Power and the Politics of Identity." *The Advocate.* No. 400.
1988 "The Ethic of Care for the Self as a Practice of Freedom." In A. Bernauer and D. Rasmussen, eds., *The Final Foucault.* Cambridge, Mass: MIT Press.

Fouchard, D., N. Magloire, and S. Manigat
1988 "Les Grossesses Précoces en Milieu Défavorisé en Haiti." Report of a UNESCO/UNDP Research Project. Port-au-Prince, Haiti, July.

Fox, R.G.
1991 "For a Nearly New Culture History." In R.G. Fox, ed., *Recapturing Anthropology,* pp. 93–113. Santa Fe, New Mexico: School of American Research.

Franklin, S.
1991 "Postmodern Procreation: A Cultural Account of Assisted Reproduction." Paper in Wenner-Gren Symposium no. 113, The Politics of Reproduction, November 1–9, Brazil.

Frayser, S.G.
1985 *Varieties of Sexual Experience: An Anthropological Perspective on Human Sexuality.* New Haven: HRAF Press.

Freud, S.
1905 *Three Essays on the Theory of Sexuality.* London: Hogarth Press.
1935 *A General Introduction to Psychoanalysis.* New York: Liveright.

Fry, P.
1985 "Male Homosexuality and Spirit Possession in Brazil." *Journal of Homosexuality* 11(3/4):137–153.

Futterman, D., K. Hein, M. Kipke, W. Reulbach, G. Clare, J. Nelson, J., A. Orane, and H. Gayle
1990 "HIV+ Adolescents: HIV Testing Experiences and Changes in Risk Related Sexual and Drug Use Behavior." Sixth International Conference on AIDS. San Francisco. June 20–24. Poster SC 663.

Gagnon, J.H.
1989 "Disease and Desire." *Daedalus* 118:47–77.
1990 "The Implicit and Explicit Use of the Scripting Perspective in Sex Research." *Annual Review of Sex Research* 1:1–43.

Gagnon, J.H., and W. Simon
1973 *Sexual Conduct: The Social Sources of Human Sexuality.* Chicago: Aldine.

Gallen, M.A.
1986 "Men—New Focus for Family Planning Programs." *Population Reports,* Series J, No. 33.

Garber, M.
1992 *Vested Interests: Cross-Dressing and Cultural Anxiety.* New York and London: Routledge.

Garnier, P.
1893 "Un cas de perversion du sens génesique-obsession appétitive et amoureuse du toucher de la soie avec phénomènes d'orgasme génital a ce contact." *Annales d'Hygiène Publique* 29:457–485.
1900 "Le sadi-fétichisme. Rapport médico-légal concernant le sieur Philippe X. . ., 'piqueur de fesses'." *Annales d'Hygiène Publique* 43:112–118; 237–247.

Gavey, N.
1991 "Sexual Victimization Prevalence Among New Zealand University Students."
Journal of Consulting and Clinical Psychology 59:464–466.
Geertz, C.
1973 *The Interpretation of Cultures*. New York: Basic Books.
1983 *Local Knowledge: Further Essays in Interpretative Anthropology*. New York: Basic
Books.
George, A., and S. Jaswal
1993 "Understanding Sexuality: Enthnographic Study of Poor Women from
Bombay." Bombay: Tata Institute of Social Sciences. Preliminary Findings, ICRW:
Women and AIDS Program.
Giddens, A.
1984 *The Constitution of Society*. Berkeley and Los Angeles: University of California Press.
1991 *Modernity and Self Identity*. Cambridge: Polity Press.
Gilliam, A.
1988 "Telltale Language: Race, Class, and Inequality in Two Latin American Towns." In
Jonnetta B. Cole, ed., *Anthropology For The Nineties*, pp. 522–531. New York: The Free
Press.
Gilmore, D.D.
1990 *Manhood in the Making: Cultural Concepts of Masculinity*. New Haven: Yale
University Press.
Ginsburg, F.
1984 "The Body Politic: The Defense of Sexual Restriction by Anti-Abortion
Activists." In C.S. Vance, ed., *Pleasure and Danger: Exploring Female Sexuality*, pp.
173–188. New York and London: Routledge.
1989 *Contested Lives: The Abortion Debate in America*. Berkeley and Los Angeles:
University of California Press.
Goffman, E.
1959 *The Presentation of Self in Everyday Life*. New York: Doubleday.
Goldstein, D.
1993 "The Culture, Class, and Gender Politics of a Modern Disease: Women and
AIDS in Brazil." Rio de Janeiro and São Paulo: Associação Brasileira Interdisciplinar
de AIDS (ABIA) and Coletivo Feminista Sexualidade e Saúde. Final Report, ICRW:
Women and AIDS Program.
Goldstein, R.
1991 "The Implicated and the Immune: Responses to AIDS in the Arts and Popular
Culture." In D. Nelkin, D.P. Willis, and S.V. Parris, eds., *A Disease of Society: Cultural
and Institutional Responses to AIDS*. Cambridge: Cambridge University Press.
Gonzalez, M.
1990 *Nicaragua: What Went Wrong?* London: Bookmarks.
Goodman, L.A.
1961 "Snowball Sampling." *Annals of Mathematical Statistics* 32:148–170.
Grant, R., M. Preda, and J.D. Martin
1991 "Domestic Violence in Texas: A Study of Statewide and Rural Spouse Abuse."
Wichita Falls, Texas: Bureau of Business and Government Research, Midwestern State
University.
Greenberg, D.
1988 *The Construction of Homosexuality*. Chicago: The University of Chicago Press.
Greenhalgh, S.
1990 "Toward a Political Economy of Fertility: Anthropological Contributions."
Population and Development Review 16(1):85–106.
Groot, B. de, and E. van der Veen
1985 "Gay Amsterdam, een Vrolijke Zaak." *Plan* 12:71–74.

Gross, J.
   1993 "Where 'Boys Will Be Boys,'and Adults are Befuddled." *New York Times*. March 29.
Hall, L.A.
   1991 *Hidden Anxieties: Male Sexuality, 1900–1950*. Cambridge: Polity Press.
Halley, J.E.
   1992 "Misreading Sodomy: A Critique of the Classification of "Homosexuals" in Federal Equal Protection Law." In J. Epstein and K. Straub, eds., *Body Guards: The Cultural Politics of Gender Ambiguity*. New York and London: Routledge.
Hallinan, M.T., and R.A. Williams
   1989 "Interracial Friendship Choices in Secondary Schools." *American Sociological Review* 54:67–78.
Halperin, D.M.
   1990 *One Hundred Years of Homosexuality*. New York and London: Routledge.
Handwerker, P.
   1991 "Gender Power Difference May be STD Risk Factors for the Next Generation." Paper presented at the 90th Annual Meeting of the American Anthropological Association, Chicago, Illinois.
   1993 "Power, Gender Violence, and High Risk Sexual Behavior: AIDS/STD Risk Factors Need to be Defined More Broadly." Private Communication, Department of Anthropology, Humboldt State University, Arcata California, February 10.
Harraway, D.
   1989 *Primate Visions: Gender, Race, and Nature in the World of Modern Science*. New York: Routledge.
   1990 "A Manifesto for Cyborgs: Science, Technology, and Socialist Feminism in the 1980s." In Linda J. Nicholson, ed., *Feminism/Postmodernism*, pp. 190–233. New York and London: Routledge.
   1991 *Simians, Cyborgs, and Women: The Reinvention of Nature*. New York: Routledge.
Harvey, D.
   n.d. "Between Space and Time: Reflections on the Geographic Imagination." Oxford: School of Geography.
Havanon, N., A. Bennett, and J. Knodel
   1992 "Sexual Networking in Provincial Thailand." *Studies in Family Planning* 24(1):1–17.
Hegland, M.E.
   n.d. Personal Communication.
Heijer, J.
   1989 "Homo in Twintig Jaar Toneel." In Gert Hekma et al., eds., *Goed Verkeerd*, pp. 97–102. Amsterdam: Meulenhoff.
Heinz, J.P., and E.O. Laumann
   1982 *Chicago Lawyers: The Social Structure of the Bar*. New York: Russell Sage Foundation, American Bar Foundation.
Hekma, G.
   1982 "Profeten op Papier, Pioniers op Pad." *Spiegel Historiel* 17(11):566–571.
   1987 *Homoseksualiteit, een Medische Reputatie*. Amsterdam: SUA Press.
   1992 *De Roze Rand van Donker Amsterdam*. Amsterdam: Van Gennep.
Hekma, G., et al.
   1992 *De Roze Rand van Amsterdam: De Opkomist van een Homoseksuele Kroegcultur, 1930–1970*. Amsterdam: Van Gennep.
Hennessy, R.
   1993 *Materialist Feminism and the Politics of Discourse*. New York and London: Routledge.
Herdt, G.H.
   1981 *Guardians of the Flutes: Idioms of Masculinity*. New York: McGraw-Hill.
   1982 "Fetish and Fantasy in Sambia Initiation." In G.H. Herdt, ed., *Rituals of Manhood:*

Male Initiation in Papua New Guinea, pp. 44–98. Berkeley and Los Angeles: University of California Press.

1984 "A Comment on Cultural Attributes and Fluidity of Bisexuality." *Journal of Homosexuality* 10:53–62.

1990 "Developmental Continuity as a Dimension of Sexual Orientation Across Cultures." In D. McWhirter, J. Reinisch, and S. Sanders, eds., *Homosexuality and Heterosexuality: The Kinsey Scale and Current Research*, pp. 208–238. New York: Oxford University Press.

1991a "Representations of Homosexuality in Traditional Societies: An Essay on Cultural Ontology and Historical Comparison, Part I." *Journal of the History of Sexuality* 2:603–632.

1991b "Representations of Homosexuality in Traditional Societies: An Essay on Cultural Ontology and Historical Comparison, Part II." *Journal of the History of Sexuality* 2:603–632.

1992 "Introduction." In G. Herdt and S. Lindenbaum, eds., *The Time of AIDS*, pp. 3–26. Newbury Park, CA: Sage Publications.

1993 "Introduction." In G. Herdt, ed., *Ritualized Homosexuality in Melanesia* (paperback edition), pp. vii–xliv. Berkeley and Los Angeles: University of California Press.

Herdt, G., and A.M. Boxer

1991 "Ethnographic Issues in the Study of AIDS." *The Journal of Sex Research* 28(2):171–187.

1993 *Children of Horizons*. Boston: Beacon Press.

Herdt, G., and S. Lindenbaum, eds.

1992 *The Time of AIDS*. Newbury Park, CA: Sage Publications.

Herdt, G., and R. Stoller

1990 *Intimate Communications: Erotics and the Study of Culture*. New York: Columbia University Press.

Herrell, R.

1992 "The Symbolic Strategies of Chicago's Gay and Lesbian Pride Day Parade." In Gilbert Herdt, ed., *Gay Culture in America*, pp. 225–252. Boston: Beacon Press.

Herskovitz, M.J.

1937 *Life in a Haitian Village*. New York: Doubleday.

Herzer, M

1985 "Kertbery and the Nameless Love." *Journal of Homosexuality* 12:1–25.

Hirschfeld, M.

1914 *Die Homosexualität des Mannes und des Weibes*. Berlin.

Hirschmann, A.

1993 "Guatemala City Women: Empowering a Vulnerable Group to Prevent HIV Transmission." Guatemala City: Asociación Guatemalteca para la Prevención y Control del SIDA. Preliminary Findings, ICRW: Women and AIDS Program.

Hobson, B.

1987 *Uneasy Virtue: The Politics of Prostitution and the American Reform Tradition*. New York: Basic Books.

Hocquenghem, G.

1978 *Homosexual Desire*. London: Allison & Busby.

Hoffman, L.F.

1984 "Francophilia and Cultural Nationalism in Haiti." In C.R. Foster and A. Valdman, eds., *Haiti-Today and Tomorrow*, pp.57–76. Landham, MD: University Press of America.

Højesteretstidende

1894:292–304 Copenhagen.

Holland, P.W., and S. Leinhardt, eds.

1979 *Perspectives on Social Network Research*. New York: Academic Press.

Humphreys, L.

1970 *Tearoom Trade: Study of Homosexual Encounters in Public Places*. London: Duckworth.

Hunt A.J., G. Christofinis, A.P.M. Coxon, P.M. Davies, T.J. McManus, S. Sutherland, and P. Weatherburn
  1990 "Seroprevalence of HIV-1 Infection in a Cohort of Homosexually Active Men." *Genitourinary Medicine* 66:423–427.
IHCA (Instituto Historico Centroamericano)
  1984 "La familia Nicaraguense en el proceso de cambio." *Envio*, April, pp. 1–12.
  1988 "Sandinistas Surviving in a Percentage Game." *Envio*, December, pp. 10–23.
Isis International
  1988 "Campana sobre la violencia en contra de la mujer," Boletin 16–17, Red de Salud de las Mujeres Latinoamericanas y del Caribe. Santiago Chile: Isis International.
James, J., and J. Meyerding
  1977 "Early Sexual Experience and Prostitution." *American Journal of Psychiatry* 134:1381–1385.
Jameson, F.
  1991 *Postmodernism; or, The Cultural Logic of Late Capitalism.* Durham, N.C.: Duke University Press.
Jansen, A.C.M.
  1989 *Cannabis in Amsterdam.* Muiderberg: Coutinho.
Jenkins, C.
  1992 "Preliminary Report on the National Sex and Reproduction Study of Papua New Guinea." Goroka: Papua New Guinea Institute of Medical Research. Preliminary Findings, ICRW: Women and AIDS Program.
Jochelson, K., M. Mothibeli, and J.P. Lager
  1991 "Human Immunodeficiency Virus and Migrant Labor in South Africa." *International Journal of Health Services* 21(1): 157–173.
Kane, S., and T. Mason
  1992 "IV Drug Users and 'Sex Partners': The Limits of Epidemiological Categories and the Ethnography of Risk." In G. Herdt and S. Lindenbaum, eds., *The Time of AIDS: Social Analysis, Theory, and Method*, pp. 199–222. Newbury Park, CA: Sage Publications.
Kanji, N., N. Kanji, and F. Manji
  1991 "From Development to Sustained Crisis: Structural Adjustment, Equity and Health." *Social Science and Medicine* 33(9):985–993.
Kermode, F.
  1967 *The Sense of an Ending.* Oxford: Oxford University Press.
Kertzer, D.I. and D.P. Hogan
  1989 *Family, Political Economy, and Demographic Change: The Transformation of Life in Casalecchio, Italy 1861–1921.* Madison: University of Wisconsin Press.
Kilpatrick, D.G., C.N. Edmunds, and A.K. Seymour
  1992 *Rape in America: A Report to the Nation.* Arlington, VA.: The National Victims Center.
Kincaid, D.L., et al.
  1991 "Family Planning and the Empowerment of Women in Bangladesh." Paper presented at the 119th Annual Meeting of the American Public Health Association, Atlanta, November 13.
Kinnich, D.
  1992 "The 'Why Not?' City." *Frontiers.* August 14.
Kinsey, Alfred C., Wardell B. Pomeroy, and Clyde E. Martin
  1948 *Sexual Behaviour in the Human Male.* Philadelphia: W. B. Saunders.
Kippax, S., et al.
  1990 "Women Negotiating Heterosex: Implications for AIDS Prevention." *Women's Studies International Forum* 13(6): 533–42.
Kisekka, M., and B. Otesanya
  1988 "Sexually Transmitted Disease as a Gender Issue: Examples from Nigeria and

Uganda." Paper presented at the AFARD/AAWORD Third General Assembly on "The African Crisis and the Women's Vision of the Way Out." Dakar, Senegal. August.

Klein, F., and T.J. Wolf, eds.
1985 *Bisexualities: Theory and Method*. New York: Haworth Press.

Kline, A., E. Kline, and E. Oken
1992 "Minority Women and Sexual Choice in the Age of AIDS." *Social Science and Medicine* 34(4):447–457.

Koenders, P.
1987 *Het Homomonument*. Amsterdam Stichting Homomonument.

Kohut, H.
1971 *The Analysis of the Self: A Systematic Approach to Psycoanalytic Treatment of Narcissistic Personality Disorders*. New York: International Universities Press.

Koopman J.S., C.P. Simon, J.A. Jacquez, M. Haber, and I.M. Longini
1992 "HIV Transmission Probabilities for Oral and Anal Sex by Stage of Infection." Paper presented to the VIII International Conference on AIDS, Amsterdan 1992 (PoC 4101).

Koss, M.P., C.A. Gidycz, and N. Wisniewski
1987 "The Scope of Rape: Incidence and Prevalence of Sexual Aggression and Victimization in a National Sample of Higher Education Students." *Journal of Consulting and Clinical Psychology* 55:162–170.

Koss, M.P., and C.J. Oros
1982 "Sexual Experiences Survey: A Research Instrument Investigating Sexual Aggression and Victimization." *Journal of Consulting and Clinical Psychology* 50:455–457.

Kunitz, S.
1990 "Public Policy and Mortality Among Indigenous Populations of Northern America and Australasia." *Population and Development Review* 16(4):647–672.

Laclau, E.
1990 *New Reflections on the Revolution of Our Times*. London: Verso.

Laclau, E., and C. Mouffe
1985 *Hegemony and Socialist Strategy*. London: Verso.

Lacombe, F.
1989 "Europe: les droits des homos." *Gai Pied* 383:55–63.

Lacquer, T.W.
1990 *Making Sex: Body and Gender from the Greeks to Freud*. Cambridge: Harvard University Press.
1992 "Sexual Desire and the Market Economy During the Industrial Revolution." In D.C. Stanton, ed., *Discourses of Sexuality: From Aristotle to AIDS*, pp. 185–215. Ann Arbor: University of Michigan Press.

LaGuardia, K.D.
1991 "AIDS and Reproductive Health: Women's Perspectives." In L.C. Chen, J.S. Amor, and S.J. Segal, eds., *AIDS and Women's Reproductive Health*, pp. 17–25. New York: Plenum Press.

Laguerre, M.S.
1976 "The Black Ghetto as an Internal Colony: Socio-Economic Adaptation of a Haitian Urban Community." Doctoral Dissertation, University of Illinois at Urbana-Champaign.

Lancaster, R.N.
1988 *Thanks to God and the Revolution: Popular Religion and Class Consciousness in the New Nicaragua*. New York: Columbia University Press.
1991 "Skin Color, Race, and Racism in Nicaragua." *Ethnology* 34(4):339–353.
1992 *Life is Hard: Machismo, Danger, and the Intimacy of Power in Nicaragua*. Berkeley and Los Angeles: University of California Press.

Larrain, S.
1993 "Estudio de Frecuencia de la Violencia Intrafamiliar y la Condición de la Mujer en Chile." Santiago, Chile: Pan American Health Organization.

Laumann, E.O.
1973 *Bonds of Pluralism: The Form and Substance of Urban Social Networks*. New York: Wiley Interscience.

Laumann, E.O., J.H. Gagnon, and R.T. Michael
n.d. "A Political History of the National Sex Survey of Adults." Unpublished manuscript.

Laumann, E.O., and D. Knoke
1987 *The Organizational State: Social Choice in National Policy Domains*. Madison: University of Wisconsin Press.

Laumann, E.O., P.V. Marsden, and D. Prensky
1982 "The Boundary Specification Problem in Network Analysis." In R.S. Burt and M.J. Minor, eds., *Applied Network Analysis*. Beverly Hills: Sage.

Lazerfeld, P.F., and H. Menzel
1969 "On the Relation Between Individual and Collective Properties." In A. Etzioni, ed., *A Sociological Reader on Complex Organizations*, 2nd edition, pp. 499–516. New York: Holt, Reinhart and Winston.

Leacock, E.
1971 *The Culture of Poverty: A Critique*. New York: Simon and Schuster.

Leibbrand, W., and A. Wettley
1972 *Formen des Eros: Kultur-und Geistesgeschichte der Liebe*. Freiburg: Alber.

Leridon, H., and Y. Charbit
1981 "Patterns of Marital Unions and Fertility in Guadeloupe and Martinique." *Population Studies* 35(2):235–245.

Levinson, D.
1989 *Violence in Cross-Cultural Perspective*. Newbury Park, CA: Sage Publishers.

Lévi-Strauss, C.
1969 *The Elementary Structures of Kinship*. Boston: Beacon.

Lewis, O.
1966 "The Culture of Poverty." *Scientific American* 215(4): 3–10.

Leyburn, J.G.
1966 (1941) *The Haitian People*. New Haven: Yale University Press.

Liskin, L.S.
1981 "Periodic Abstinence: How Well Do New Approaches Work?" *Population Reports*. Baltimore, MD: Population Information Program, Johns Hopkins School of Hygiene and Public Health.

Locher, H.C.
1978 "The Fate of Migrants in Urban Haiti: A Survey of Three Port-au-Prince Neighborhoods." Doctoral Dissertation. New Haven, CT: Yale University.

Löfgren, O.
1987 "På jagt efter de borgerliga kulturen." In *Mentalitetsforandringer. Studier i historisk metode*, pp. 106–123. Århus University Press.

Loizos, P., and E. Papataxiarchis
1991 "Gender, Sexuality, and Person in Greek Culture."In P. Loizos and E. Papataxiarchis, eds., *Contested Identities: Gender and Kinship in Modern Greece*, pp. 221–234. Princeton: Princeton University Press.

Lotringer, S., ed.
1989 *Foucault Live (Interviews 1966–84)*. New York: Semiotext(e) Foreign Agents Series.

Lowenthal, I.P.
1984a In C. Foster and A. Valdman, eds., *Haiti-Today and Tomorrow: An Interdisciplinary Study*. Landham, MD: University Press of America.
1984b "Two To Tango: Haitian Men and Family Planning." Paper Submitted to the Public Health Office, USAID/Haiti. May.
1987 "Marriage is 20, Children are 21: The Cultural Construction of Conjugality and

the Family in Rural Haiti." Unpublished Doctoral Dissertation, The Johns Hopkins University. UMI #8807447.

Luce, R.D.
1960 "The Theory of Selective Information and Some of its Behavioral Applications." In R.D. Luce, ed., *Developments in Mathematical Psychology*. Glencoe, III: Free Press.

Lukacs, G.
1971 *History and Class Consciousness: Studies in Marxist Dialectics*. London: Merlin Press.

Lundahl, M.
1979 *Peasants and Poverty: A Study of Haiti*. London: Croom, Helm.

Lundgren, R., B. Bezmalinovic, W. Skidmore, and A. Hirshmann
1992 "Guatemala City Women: Empowering a Hidden Risk Group to Prevent HIV Transmission." Guatemala City: DataPro, S.A. Final Formative Research Technical Report, ICRW: Women and AIDS Program.

Maatman, M., and A. Meijer
1993 *Cruising als Ruimteclaim*. Planologische Verkenningen 67. Universiteit van Amsterdam.

MacFarlane, J., et al.
1992 "Assessing for Abuse During Pregnancy: Severity and Frequency of Injuries and Associated Entry Into Prenatal Care." *Journal of the American Medical Society* 267(23): 3176–3178.

MacIntyre, A.
1984 "The Virtues, the Unity of a Human Life, and the Concept of a Tradition." In Michael Sandel, ed., *Liberalism and its Critics*. Oxford: Basil Blackwell.
1985 *After Virtue: A Study in Moral Theory*. London: Duckworth.

MacKinnon, C.
1987 *Feminism Unmodified*. Cambridge: Harvard University Press.
1989 *Toward a Feminist Theory of the State*. Cambridge: Harvard University Press.
1991 "Does Sexuality Have a History." *Michigan Quarterly Review* 30(1):1–11.

Mahajan, A.
1990 "Instigators of Wife Battering." In Sushma Sood, ed., *Violence Against Women*, pp.1–10. Jaipur, India: Arihant Publishers.

Mahmoud, F., B. de Zalduondo, E. Williams, N. Luo, M. Kabeya, C. Bunura, D. Zewdie, and M.T. Feversteion
1989 "Women and AIDS in Africa: Issues Old and New." Proceedings of the Annual Meeting of the African Studies Association: AIDS in Africa, Atlanta, GA.

Manderson, L.
1993 "Intersections: Western Representations of Thailand and the Commodification of Sex and Race." Paper in Wenner-Gren Symposium no. 116, Theorizing Sexuality: Evolution, Culture and Development, March 19–27, Portugal.

Mann, J.M.
1993 "World Overview of the Heterosexual Transmission of HIV." Speech given to the Royal Society of Medicine, London, UK, March 30.

Mann, J.M., Daniel J.M. Tarantola, and T.W. Neter, eds.
1992 *AIDS in the World*. Cambridge, MA: Harvard University Press.

Marcus, E., and P. Verstraeten
1984 *Amsterdam in je Kontzak: Een Homo-stadsgids*. Amsterdam: JIF.

Marcus, M.
1987 "Horsemen are the Fence of the Land: Honor and History among the Ghiyata of Eastern Morocco." In D.D. Gilmore, ed., *Honor and Shame and the Unity of the Mediterranean*, Washington D.C.: American Anthropological Association, Special Publication No. 22.

Marcuse, H.
1966 *Eros and Civilization: A Philosophical Inquiry into Freud*. Boston: Beacon Press.

Marsden, P.V.
1987 "Core Discussion Networks of Americans." *American Sociological Review* 52:122–131.

Marshall, M.
1979 *Weekend Warriors*. Palo Alto, Calif.: Mayfield.

Marx, K.
1967 *Capital, Vol 1: A Critical Analysis of Capitalist Production*. New York: International Publishers.

Marx, K., and F. Engels
1964 *The German Ideology*. Moscow: Progress Publishers.

McCoy, H.V., and Inciardi, J.A.
1993 "Women and AIDS: Social Determinants of Sex-Related Activities." *Women and Health* 20:69–86.

McGrath, J.W., and Rwabukwali, C.B.
1993 "Anthropology and AIDS: The Cultural Context of Sexual Risk Behavior among Urban Baganda Women in Kampala, Uganda." *Social Science and Medicine* 36:429–439.

Meer, T. van der
1984 *De Wesentlijke Sonde van Sodomie en Andere Vuyligheeden: Sodomieten Vervolgingen, 1730–1811*. Amsterdam: Tabula.
1988 "Zodoms Zaat in de Republick: Stedelijke Homoseksuele Subculturen in de Achttiende Eeuw." In G. Hekma and H. Roodenburd, eds., *Soete Minne en Helsche Boosheit: Seksuele Voorstellingen in Nederland, 1300–1850*. Nijmegen: SUN

Melucci, A.
1989 *Nomads of the Present*. London: Hutchinon Radius.

Metraux, A.
1958 *Le Vaudou Haitien*. Paris: Gallimard.

Mieli, M.
1980 *Homosexuality and Liberation*. London: G.M.P.

Mill, J. S.
1975 *Three Essays*. Oxford: Oxford Universty Press.

Mintz, S.
1979 "Slavery and the Rise of Peasantries." *Historical Reflections* 6(1):213–242.

Mitchell, J.
1971 *Woman's Estate*. London: Penguin Books.

Molyneux, M.
1985 "Mobilization Without Emancipation?: Women's Interests, the State, and Revolution in Nicaragua." In Richard R. Fagen et al., *Transition and Development*, pp. 280–302. New York: Monthly Review Press.

Money, J.
1987 "Sin, Sickness, or Society?" *American Psychologist* 42:384–399.

Moore, K.A., C.W. Nord, and J. Peterson
1989 "Nonvoluntary Sexual Activity Among Adolescents." *Family Planning Perspectives* 21(3):110–114.

Moral, P.
1978 (1961) *Le Paysan Haitien*. Port-au-Prince: Fardin.

Motet, A.
1890 "Etat mental de P. poursuivi pour avoir coupé les nattes de Plusieurs jeunes filles." *Annales d'Hygie Publique* 23:331–340.

Mullen, P.E., et al.
1988 "Impact of Sexual and Physical Abuse on Women's Mental Health." *Lancet* 1:841.

Murray, G.F.
1977 "The Evolution of Haitian Peasant Land Tenure: A Case Study in Agrarian

Adaptation to Population Growth." Doctoral Dissertation. Department of Political Science. Columbia University.

Musterd, S., and B. De Peter
1992 "De Libertijnse Randstedelijke Cultuur." *Randstad Holland: Internationaal, Regionaal, Lokaal*. Assen/Maastricht: Van Gorcum.

National Statistics Office (Manila, Philippines)
1992 *Preliminary Results from the 1991 Family Income and Expenditures Survey*. Typescript.

Ngugi, E.
1991 "Education and Counseling Interventions." Paper presented at the 18th Annual NCIH International Health Conference, Arlington, VA, USA.

Noordam, D.J.
1984 "Homoseksuele relaties in Holland in 1771." *Holland* 16(1):3–34.

Nzyuko, S.
1991 "Teenagers along the Trans-African Highway." *AIDS and Society* July/August 10.

Oetomo, D.
1991 "Patterns of Bisexuality in Indonesia." In R.A.P. Tielman, M. Carballo and A.C. Hendriks, eds., *Bisexuality and HIV/AIDS*, pp. 119–126. Buffalo: Prometheus Books.

Ogunjemilua, S.O.
1982 "Long Distance Heavy Road Haulage Transport in Nigeria: A Case Study of Maiduguri in Bornu State." Unpublished Ph.D Thesis, University of London, London.

Okun, L.E.
1986 *Woman Abuse: Facts Replacing Myths*. Albany: State University of New York Press.

Olsson, H.
1984 "The Woman, The Love, and the Power." In K. Barry, C. Bunch and S. Castley, eds., *International Feminism: Networking Against Female Sexual Slavery*. New York: International Tribune Center.

Oodit, G., S. Ragobar, U. Bhowon, S.L. Schensul, and J.J. Schensul
1993 "Young Women, Work, and AIDS-Related Risk Behaviour in Mauritius." Port Louis: Mauritius Family Planning Association. Quarterly Report, ICRW: Women and AIDS Program.

Ortner, S. and H. Whitehead, eds.
1981 *Sexual Meanings: The Cultural Construction of Gender and Sexuality*. Cambridge: Cambridge University Press.

Orubuloye, I.O.
1990 *Newsletter of the West African Research Group on Sexual Networking*, No. 1. Ondo State University, Ado Ekiti, Nigeria.
1991 *Newsletter of the West African Research Group on Sexual Networking*, No. 2. Ondo State University, Ado Ekiti, Nigeria.

Orubuloye, I.O., J.C. Caldwell and P. Caldwell
1991 "Sexual Networking in the Ekiti District of Nigeria." *Studies in Family Planning* 22(1):61–73.
1992 "The Role of High-risk Occupations in the Spread of AIDS: Truck-Drivers and Itinerant Market Women in Nigeria." *Health Transition Working Paper No. 4*, Australian National University Canberra.
1992 "Diffusion and Focus in Sexual Networking: Identifying Partners and Partners' Partners." *Studies in Family Planning* 23(6):343–351.

Padgug, R., and G. Oppenheimer
1992 "Riding the Tiger: AIDS and the Gay Community." In E. Fee and D. Fox, *AIDS: The Making of a Chronic Disease*, pp. 245–278. Berkeley and Los Angeles: University of California Press.

Paglia, C.
1992 *Sex, Art and American Culture*. New York: Vintage Books.

Parker, R.G.
1985 "Masculinity, Femininity, and Homosexuality: On the Anthropological Intepretation of Sexual Meanings in Brazil. *Journal of Homosexuality* 11(3/4):155–163.
1987 "Acquired Immune Deficiency Syndrome in Urban Brazil." *Medical Anthropology Quarterly*, n.s. 1:155–175.
1989 "Bodies and Pleasures: On the Construction of Erotic Meanings in Contemporary Brazil." *Anthropology and Humanism Quarterly* 14:58–64.
1991 *Bodies, Pleasures and Passions: Sexual Culture in Contemporary Brazil.* Boston: Beacon Press.
1992 "Bisexual Behavior and AIDS in Brazil." Instituto de Medicina Social, Universidade do Estado do Rio de Janeiro: AIDSCOM/AED.
1994 "Sexual Cultures, HIV Transmission, and AIDS Prevention," *AIDS 1994* 8(suppl 1):S309–14.
Parker, R.G., G.H. Herdt, and M. Carballo
1991 "Sexual Culture, HIV Transmission, and AIDS Research." *The Journal of Sex Research* 28(1):77–98.
Parsons, T.
1951 "An Outline of The Social System." In T. Parsons, *The Social System*, pp. 30–79. Glencoe, Ill.: Free Press.
1961 "The General Interpretation of Action." In T. Parsons, E. Shils, K.D. Naegele, and J.R. Pitts, eds., *Theories of Society: Foundation of Modern Sociological Theory*, pp. 85–97. New York: Free Press.
1967 *Sociological Theory and Modern Society.* New York: Free Press.
Peters, S.D., G.E. Wyatt, and D.P. Finkelhor
1986 "Prevalence." In Finkelhor, D., ed., *A Source Book on Child Sexual Abuse*, pp. 15–59. Beverly Hills: Sage Publications.
Peterson, J.L.
1992 "Black Men and Their Same–Sex Desires and Practices." In G. Herdt, ed., *Gay Culture in America*, pp. 147–164. Boston: Beacon Press.
Phillips, H.P.
1966 *Thai Peasant Personality: The Patterning of Interpersonal Behavior in the Village of Bang Chan.* Berkeley: University of California.
Plummer, K.
1992 *Modern Homosexualities: Fragments of Lesbian and Gay Experience:* London and New York: Routledge.
Polier, N., and W. Roseberry
1989 "Tristes Tropes: Post-Modern Anthropololgists Encounter the Other and Discover Themselves." *Economy and Society* 18(2):245-264.
Ponse, B.
1978 *Identities in the Lesbian World: The Social Construction of Self.* Westport, Connecticut: Greenwood Press.
Posner, R.
1992 *Sex and Reason.* Cambridge, Mass.: Harvard University Press.
PROFAMILIA
1992 "Estudio Sobre La Violencia Contra La Mujer en la Familia Basado en La Encuesta Realizada a las Mujeres Maltratadas Que Acudieron Al Servicio Juridico de ProFamilia Entre El 15 de Marzo de 1989 y El 30 de Marzo de 1990." In *La Violencia y Los Derechos Humanos de la Mujer.* Bogata: Profamilia.
Rabinow, P.
1992 "A Modern Tour in Brazil." In Scott Lash and Jonathan Friedman, eds., *Modernity and Identity*, pp. 248–264. Oxford: Blackwell.
Raikes, A.
1990 *Pregnancy, Birthing and Family Planning in Kenya: Changing Patterns of Behavior: A*

Health Utilization Study in Kissi District. Copenhagen: Centre for Development Research.

Ramirez Rodriguez, J.C., and G. Uribe Vazquez
1993 "Mujer y Violencia: Un Hecho Cotidiano." *Salud Publica de Mexico.* Cuernavaca: Instituto Nacional de Salud Publica.

Randall, M.
1992 *Gathering Rage: The Failure of Twentieth Century Revolutions to Develop a Feminist Agenda.* New York: Monthly Review Press.

Ransome-Kuti, O.
1992 Presentation at the meeting of members of the National AIDS Committee. Lagos, Nigeria.

Rapoport, A.
1953 "Spread of Information Through a Population with Socio-Structural Bias." *Bulletin of Mathematical Biophysics* 15: 523–543.
1957 "Contribution to the Theory of Random and Based Nets." *Bulletin of Mathematical Biophysics* 19:257–277.
1963 "Mathematical Models of Social Intection." In R.D. Luce, R.R. Bush and E. Galanter, eds., *Handbook of Mathematical Psychology, Volume II.* New York: Wiley.
1979 "Some Problems Relating to Randomly Constructed Biased Networks." In P.W. Holland and S. Leinhardt, eds., *Perspectives on Social Network Research.* New York: Academic Press.

Rapoport, A., and W.J. Horvath
1961 "A Study of a Large Sociogram." *Behavioral Science* 6: 279–291.

Read, K.
1980 *Other Voices.* Novato: Chandler & Sharpe.

Reid, E.
1992. "Gender, Knowledge and Responsibility." In J. Mann, D.J.M. Tarantola, and T.W. Netter, eds., *AIDS in the World*, pp. 657–667. Cambridge, Mass.: Harvard University Press.

Rigdon, S.M.
1988 *The Culture Facade: Art, Science, and Politics in the Work of Oscar Lewis.* Urbana: University of Illinois Press.

Rist, D.Y.
1992 "Sex on the Brain: Are Homosexuals Born That Way?" *The Nation* 255(12):424–429.

Reed, A.L.
1991 "The Underclass Myth." *The Progressive* 55(August):18–20.

Rhodenbaugh, S.
1991 "Catherine MacKinnon: May I Speak?" *Michigan Quarterly Review* 30(3):415–422.

Robey, B., S.O. Rutstein and L. Morris
1993 "The Fertility Decline in Developing Countries." *Scientific American*, December, pp. 60–68.

Robinson, P.
1976 *The Modernization of Sex.* New York: Harper and Row.

Römer, L.S.A.M. von
1906 "Der Uranismus in den Niederlandwen." *Jahrbuch für Sexuelle Zwischenstufen* 8:365–512.

Rorty, R.
1989 *Contingency, Irony and Solidarity.* Cambridge: Cambridge University Press.

Roseberry, W.
1989 *Anthropologies and Histories.* New Brunswick, N.J.: Rutgers University Press.

Rosenberg, M.J., and E.L. Gollub
1992 "Methods Women Can Use that May Prevent Sexually Transmitted Disease,

Including HIV." *American Journal of Public Health* 82(11):1,473–1,478.
Rosenblum, N.L.
  1982 *Another Liberalism: Romanticism and the Reconstruction of Liberal Thought.*
  Cambridge, Mass.: Harvard University Press.
Ross, M.W.
  1991 "A Taxonomy of Global Behavior." In R.A.P. Tielman, M. Carballo and A.C.
  Hendriks, eds., *Bisexuality and HIV/AIDS*, pp. 21–26. Buffalo: Prometheus Books.
Rubenstein, H.
  1983 "Caribbean Family and Household Organization: Some Conceptual
  Clarification." *Journal of Comparative Family Studies* 14(3):283–298.
Rubin, G.
  1975 "The Traffic in Women: Notes on the Political Economy of Sex." In R.R.
  Reiter, ed., *Toward an Anthropology of Women*, pp. 157–210. New York: Monthly
  Review Press.
  1984 "Thinking Sex: Notes for a Radical Theory of the Politics of Sexuality." In C.S.
  Vance, ed., *Pleasure and Danger: Exploring Female Sexuality*, pp. 267–319. London:
  Routledge & Kegan Paul.
Ruse, M.
  1988 *Homosexuality: A Philosophical Inquiry.* Oxford: Basil Blackwell.
Ryan, W.
  1971 *Blaming the Victim.* New York: Vintage Books.
Sabroe, P.
  1907 *Demokraten.* August 8th.
Sanday, P.R.
  1981 "The Socio-cultural Context of Rape: A Cross Cultural Study." *Journal of Social
  Issues* 37(4):5–27.
  1990 *Fraternity Gang Rape: Sex, Brotherhood, and Privilege on Campus.* New York: New
  York University Press.
Sankoff, D., and J.B. Kruskal
  1983 *Time Warps, String Edits and Macromolecules: The Theory and Practice of Sequence
  Comparison.* Reading, Ma: Addison-Wesley.
Sartre, J.P.
  1963 *Search for a Method.* New York: Knopf.
Schei, B., and L.S. Bakkesteig
  1989 "Gynecological Impact of Sexual and Physical Abuse by Spouse: A Study of a
  random sample of Norwegian Women." *British Journal of Obstetrics and Gynecology*
  96:1379–1383.
Scheper-Hughes, N.
  1979 *Saints, Scholars, and Schizophrenics: Mental Illness in Rural Ireland.* Berkeley and Los
  Angeles: University of California Press.
  1992 *Death Without Weeping: The Violence of Everyday Life in Brazil.* Berkeley and Los
  Angeles: University of California Press.
Scheper-Hughes, N., and M. Lock
  1987 "The Mindful Body: A Prolegomenon to Future Work in Medical
  Anthropology." *Medical Anthropology Quarterly*, n.s., 1(1):6–41.
Scheuch, E.K.
  1965 "Die Sichtbarket politischer Einstellungen in altäglichen Verhalten." *Kölner
  Zeitschrift für Soziologie und Sozialpsychologie* 17:169–224.
Schlörr, J.
  1991 *Nachts in der Großen Stadt: Paris, Berlin, London, 1840–1930.* Zürich: Artemis und
  Winkler.
Schneider, D.M.
  1969 "Kinship, Nationality and Religion in American Culture: Toward a Definition

of Kinship." In Robert F. Spencer, ed., *Forms of Symbolic Action*, pp. 116–125. Seattle: University of Washington Press.

Schneider, J., and P. Schneider
1984 "Demographic Transitions in a Sicilian Rural Town." *Journal of Family History* 9(3):245–273.

Schoepf, B.G.
1988 "Women, AIDS and Economic Crisis in Central Africa." *Canadian Journal of African Studies* 22(3):625–644.
1991 "Ethical, Methodological and Political Issues of AIDS Research in Central Africa." *Social Science and Medicine* 33(7):749–763.
1992 "Women at Risk: Case Studies from Zaire." In Gilbert Herdt and Shirley Lindenbaum, eds., *The Time of AIDS: Social Analysis, Theory, and Method*, pp. 259–286. Newbury Park, CA: Sage Publications Inc.

Schoepf, B.G., R.W. Nkera, C. Schoepf, W. Engundu, and P. Ntsomo
1988 "AIDS and Society in Central Africa: A View from Zaire." In N. Miller and R.C. Rockwell, eds., *AIDS in Africa: The Social and Policy Impact*, pp. 211–235. Lewiston/Queenston: Edwin Mellon Press.

Schoepf, B.G., W. Engundu, R.W. Nkera, P. Ntsomo, and C. Schoepf
1990 "Gender, Power, and Risk of AIDS in Zaire." In M. Turshen, ed., *Women and Health in Africa*, pp. 187–203. Trenton, NJ: Africa World Press.

Sedgwick, E.K.
1985 *Between Men: English Literature and Male Homosocial Desire*. New York: Columbia University Press.
1990 *Epistemology of the Closet*. Berkeley and Los Angeles: University of California Press.

Shedlin, M.G.
1990 "An Ethnographic Approach to Understanding HIV High-Risk Behaviors: Prostitution and Drug Abuse." In C.G. Leukefeld, R.J. Battjes, and Z. Amsel, eds., *AIDS and Intravenous Drug Use: Future Directions for Community Based Research*. NIDA Research Monograph 93.

Shields, R.
1991 *Places on the Margin: Alternative Geographies of Modernity*. London and New York: Routledge.

Shim, Y.H.
1992 "Sexual Violence against Women in Korea: A Victimization Survey of Seoul Women." Paper presented at the conference on "International Perspectives: Crime, Justice and Public Order." St. Petersburg, Russia, June 21–27.

Shusterman, R.
1988 "Postmodernist Aestheticism: A New Moral Philosophy." *Theory, Culture and Society* Vol 5. Nos. 2–3. June.

Simon, W., and J.H. Gagnon
1984 "Sexual Scripts." *Society* 23(1):53–60.

Skvoretz, J.
1985 "Random and Biased Networks: Simulations and Approximations." *Social Networks* 7:225–261.

Slater, P.E.
1963 "On Social Regression." *American Sociological Review* 28:339–364.

Smaablade for Døvstumme
1899 Copenhagen.

Smaatræk fra det daglige Liv
1909 Copenhagen.

Smith-Rosenberg, C.
1975 "The Female World of Love and Ritual." *Signs* 1:1–29.

Smyth, C.
1992 *Lesbians Talk Queer Nations*. London: Scarlet Press.
Snijders, T.A.B.
1992 "Estimation on the Basis of Snowball Sampling: How to Weight?" Paper presented at the Workshop on Generalizability Questions for Snowball Sampling. University of Groningen.
Sogbetun, A. O., K.O. Alausa, and A.O. Osoba
1977 "Sexually Transmitted Disease in Ibadan, Nigeria." *British Journal of Venereal Disease* 53:158.
Sonali, D.
1990 "An Investigation into the Incidence and Causes of Domestic Violence in Sri Lanka." Women in Need (WIN), Colombo, Sri Lanka.
Spartan Warrior (pseudonym)
1993 "An Alternative Lifestyle." *Manila Times*, March 1, 1993, p. 2.
Spiro, M.
1987 *Culture and Human Nature: The Theoretical Papers of Melford Spiro*. Chicago: The University of Chicago Press.
Stacey, Judith
1990 *Brave New Families: Stories of Domestic Upheaval in Late Twentieth Century America*. New York: Basic.
Stark, E., A. Flitcraft, B. Zuckerman, A. Grey, J. Robinson, and W. Frazier
1981 *Wife Abuse in the Medical Setting: An Introduction for Health Personnel*. Monograph #7. Washington, D.C.: Office of Domestic Violence.
Stein, E.
1990 *Forms of Desire: Sexual Orientation and the Social Constructionist Controversy*. London: Garland.
Stewart, S.
1984 *On Longing*. Baltimore: Johns Hopkins University Press.
Stilhoff, H.
1895 "Et Tilfælde af mandlig Hermafroditisme (Kanasagen)." *Bibliotek for Laeger* 6:210–234.
Stoeckel, J., and E. Thongkrajai
1993 "AIDS Prevention Among Adolescents: An Intervention Study in Northeast Thailand." Bangkok: The Population Council. Quarterly Report, ICRW: Women and AIDS Program.
Stoller, R.J.
1975 *The Transexual Experiment, Vol. 2: Sex and Gender*. New York: Jason Aronson.
Stoltenberg, J.
1989 *Refusing to Be a Man: Essays on Sex and Justice*. Portland, OR: Breiten Bush Books
Straus, M.A and R.J. Gelles
1986 "Societal Change and Change in Family Violence from 1975 to 1985 as Revealed by Two National Surveys." *Journal of Marriage and the Family* 48:465–479.
Symons, D.
1979 *The Evolution of Human Sexuality*. New York: Oxford University Press.
1987 "An Evolutionary Approach: Can Darwin's View of Life Shed Light on Human Sexuality." In J. Greer and W.T. O'Donohue, eds., *Theories of Human Sexuality*, pp. 65–90. New York: Plenum Press.
Talbot, D.
1990 "Condom Conundrum." *Mother Jones*, January, pp.39–47.
Tan, M.L.
1990 Synthesis of an AIDS KAP Survey Among Sentinel Groups in Metro Manila. (Unpublished document submitted to the Department of Health and the Academy for Educational Development).

Teske, R. Jr., and M. Parker
   1983 "Spouse Abuse in Texas: A Study of Women's Attitudes and Experiences."
   Austin, Texas Department of Human Resources.
Thompson, S.
   1990 "Putting a Big Thing into a Little Hole: Teenage Girls Accounts of Sexual
   Initiation." *The Journal of Sex Research* 27(3):341–361.
Tieerney, J.
   1990 "AIDS in Africa: Experts Study of Promiscuous Sex in the Epidemic." *New York
   Times*, October 19, P. A10.
Tiefer, L.
   1992 "Feminism Matters in Sexology." In W. Bezemer et al., eds., *Sex Matters*. Elsevier
   Science Publishers.
Tielman, R.A.P.
   1982 "Homoseksualiteit in Nederland: Studie van een Emancipatiebeweging." *Meppel
   Amsterdam Boom*, pp. 186–187.
Tielman, R.A.P., A. Hendriks, and M. Carballo, eds.
   1991 *Bisexuality and HIV/AIDS: A Global Perspective*. Buffalo: Prometheus Books.
Toft, S., ed.
   1987 *Domestic Violence in Papua New Guinea*. Law Reform Commission Occasional
   Paper No. 19, Port Morseby, Papua New Guinea.
Trouillot, M.R.
   1990 *Haiti: State Against Nation*. New York: Monthly Review Press.
True, B.
   1992 "If This Is Queen's Day, This Must Be Amsterdam." In *Metrosource: The Gay
   Guide to the Metropolitan Area*, pp. 55–62. New York: Metrosource.
Turnbull, C.
   1965 "The Mbuti Pygmies: An Ethnographic Survey." *Anthropological Papers of the
   American Museum of Natural History* 50:137–282.
Turner, C.F., H.G. Miller, and L.E. Moses, eds.
   1989 *AIDS, Sexual Behavior, and Intravenous Drug Use*. Washington, D.C.: National
   Academy Press.
Udry, J.R., J.O.G. Billy, N.M. Morris, T.R. Groff, and M.H. Raj
   1985 "Serum Androgenic Hormones Motivate Sexual Behavior in Adolescent Boys."
   Fertility and Sterility 43:90–94.
Ugalde, J.G.
   1988 "Sindrome de la Mujer Agredida." *Mujer*, No. 5., San Jose, Costa Rica:
   Cefemina.
Ulin, P.R.
   1992 "African Women and AIDS: Negotiating Behavioral Change." *Social Science and
   Medicine* 34(1):63–73.
Uwakwe, C.B.U., A. Mansaray, H.O.A. Nwagwu, G.O.M. Onwu, B.O. Sokan
   1993 "A Psycho-Educational Program to Motivate and Foster AIDS Preventive
   Behaviours Among Female Nigerian University Students." Ibadan: Ibadan University
   AIDS Research Consortium. Quarterly Report, ICRW: Women and AIDS Program.
Valdez Santiago, R., and E.S. Cox
   1990 "La Violencia Hacia la Mujer Mexicana como Problema de Salud Publica: La
   Incidencia de la Violencia Domestica en una Microregion de Ciudad
   Nexahualcoyotl." Mexico City: CECOVID.
Valentine, C.A.
   1968 *Culture and Poverty: A Critique and Counter-Proposal*. Chicago: The University of
   Chicago Press.
Valverde, M.
   1987 *Sex, Power, and Pleasure*. Philadelphia: New Society Publishers.

Vance, C.S., ed.
1984 *Pleasure and Danger: Exploring Women's Sexuality*. New York: Routledge and Kegan Paul.
Vance, C.S.
1984 "Pleasure and Danger: Toward a Politics of Sexuality." In C.S. Vance, ed., *Pleasure and Danger: Exploring Female Sexuality*, pp. 1–27. London: Routledge & Kegan Paul.
1991 "Anthropology Rediscovers Sexuality: A Theoretical Comment." *Social Science and Medicine* 33(8):875–884.
1993 "Feminist Fundamentalism—Women Against Images." *Art in America*. September 1993. Pp. 35–39.
van Metter, K.
1990 *Methodological and Design Issues Techniques for Assessing the Representativeness of Snowball Sampling*. Rockville: NIDA.
Vasconcelos, A., A.V. Acioli Neto, C. Braga, M. Pacheco, and S. Dantas
1992 "Research Project on AIDS and Sexuality Among Low Income Adolescent Women in Recife, Brazil." Recife: Casa de Passagem. Quarterly Report, ICRW: Women and AIDS Program.
Venema, A.
1972 *Homoseksualiteit in de Nederlandse Literatuur*. Amsterdam/Brussel: Paris Manteau
Verkerk, C.
1993 "Gelukkig Heerst in Amsterdam Grote Tolerantie." *Het Parool* February 27.
Volosinov, V.N.
1993 *Marxism and the Philosophy of Language*. Cambridge, MA: Harvard University Press.
von den Eeden, P., and H.J.M. Hüttner
1982 "Trend Report: Multi-Level Research." *Current Sociology* 30:1–181.
Vovelle M.
1982 *Idéologies et Mentalités*. Paris: La Découverte.
Walker, T.W., ed.
1987 *Reagan versus the Sandinistas: The Undeclared War on Nicaragua*. Boulder: Westview.
Walkowitz, J.R.
1980 *Prostitution and Victorian Society*. Cambridge: Cambridge University Press.
1983 "Male Vice and Female Virtue: Feminism and the Politics of Prostitution in Nineteenth Century Britain." In A. Snitow, C. Stansell and S. Thompson, eds., *Powers of Desire: The Politics of Sexuality*, pp. 419–438. New York: Monthly Review Press.
WAO (Women's Action Organization)
1992 "Draft Report of the National Study on Domestic Violence." Kuala Lumpur, Malaysia.
Watney, S.
1991 "AIDS: The Second Decade: Risk, Research and Modernity." In P. Aggleton, G. Hart and P. Davies, eds., *AIDS: Responses, Interventions and Care*. London: The Falmer Press.
Webb, G., O. A. Ladipo and R. McNamara
1991 "Qualitative Methods in Operation Research on Contraceptive Distribution Systems: A Case Study from Nigeria." *Social Science and Medicine* 33(3):321–326.
Weeks, J.
1977 *Coming Out: Homosexual Politics in Britain from the Nineteenth Century to the Present*. London: Quartet.
1981 *Sex, Politics, and Society: The Regulation of Sexuality since 1800*. New York: Longman.
1985 *Sexuality and its Discontents: Meanings, Myths, and Modern Sexualities*. London: Routledge and Kegan Paul.
1986 *Sexuality*. Chichester and London: Ellis Horwood and Tavistock.
1991 *Against Nature: Essays on History, Sexuality and Identity*. London: Rivers Oram Press.

Weinberg, M.S., and C.J. Williams
    1974 *Male Homosexuals: Their Problems and Adaptation*. Oxford: Oxford University Press.
White, L.
    1986 "Prostitution, Identity and Class Consciousness in Nairobi During World War II." *Signs* 11(21):255–273.
Williams, S. N. Murthy, and G. Berggren
    1975 "Conjugal Unions among Rural Haitian Women." *Journal of Marriage and the Family* 37(4):1022–1031.
Wilson, D., B. Sibanda, L. Mboyi, and S. Msimanga
    1990 "A Pilot Study for an HIV Prevention Programme Among Commercial Sex Workers in Bulawayo, Zimbabwe." *Social Science and Medicine* 31:609–618.
Wolf, N.
    1992 "Feminist Fatale." *New Republic*. March 16.
World Bank
    1990 *World Development Report 1990*. New York: Oxford University Press.
World Health Organization
    1993 "WHO Estimate of HIV Infection Tops 14 Million." Geneva: World Health Organization, Office of Information. Press Release WHO/38, May 21.
Worth, D.
    1989 "Sexual Decision-Making and AIDS: Why Condom Promotion Among Vulnerable Women is Likely to Fail." *Studies in Family Planning* 20(6):297–307.
    1991 "Sexual Violence Against Women and Substance Abuse." Paper presented to The Domestic Violence Task Force, New York, January.
Wyatt, G.
    1991 Speech presented at the Eighth International Conference on AIDS. Amsterdam. July.
Yates, J.F., and E.R. Stone
    1992 "The Risk Construct." In J.F. Yates, ed., *Risk-Taking Behavior*, pp.1–25. Chichester: John Wiley and Sons.
Young, M.
    1990 *Justice and the Police of Difference*. Princeton: Princeton University Press.
Zapata, C., et al.
    1992 "The Influence of Social and Political Violence on the Risk of Pregnancy Complications." *American Journal of Public Health* 82(5):685–690.
Zetterberg, H.
    1966 "The Secret Ranking." *Journal of Marriage and Family* 28(2):134–142.
Zierler, S., et al.
    1991 "Adult Survivors of Childhood Sexual Abuse and Subsequent Risk of HIV Infection." *American Journal of Public Health* 81(5):572–575.
Zippe, H.
    1878 "Stehsucht eines Onanisten." *Wiener Medizinische Wochenschrift* 23:630–632/24:654–656.
Zwi, A.B., and A.J.R. Cabral
    1990 "Identifying "High Risk Situations" for Preventing AIDS." *British Medical Journal* 303:1527–1529.